Johnson's War/
Johnson's Great Society

Johnson's War/ Johnson's Great Society

The Guns and Butter Trap

Jeffrey W. Helsing

PRAEGER

Westport, Connecticut
London

Library of Congress Cataloging-in-Publication Data

Helsing, Jeffrey W.
    Johnson's war/Johnson's great society : the guns and butter trap / Jeffrey W. Helsing.
      p. cm.
    Includes bibliographical references and index.
    ISBN 0–275–96449–3 (alk. paper)
    1. Vietnamese Conflict, 1961–1975—United States.   2. United States—Politics and
government—1963–1969.   3. Johnson, Lyndon B. (Lyndon Baines), 1908–1973. I. Title.
DS558.H443 2000
959.704′3373—dc21   99–055224

British Library Cataloguing in Publication Data is available.

Library of Congress Catalog Card Number: 99–055224
ISBN: 0–275–96449–3

First published in 2000

Praeger Publishers, 88 Post Road West, Westport, CT 06881
An imprint of Greenwood Publishing Group, Inc.
www.praeger.com

Printed in the United States of America

The paper used in this book complies with the
Permanent Paper Standard issued by the National
Information Standards Organization (Z39.48–1984).

10 9 8 7 6 5 4 3 2

For Alia, Spencer, and, as always, Stephanie

Contents

Preface   ix

1. Introduction: Lyndon Johnson's Guns versus Butter Dilemma   1

2. Great Dreams at Home, Deterioration Abroad   15

3. Poor Policy Planning and an Inadequate Budget Process   47

4. Escalation   71

5. Americanizing the War   99

6. In Pursuit of a "Stalemate"   137

7. The Low-Key Decision for an Asian Ground War   163

8. The Confusion over Military Costs   187

9. The War Overheats the Economy   211

10. Guns or Butter and the Study of the Vietnam War   237

Bibliography   261

Index   269

Preface

This book is essentially an examination of what many analysts and former policymakers in the Johnson administration have acknowledged as a crucial factor in the way in which the United States escalated in Vietnam: Johnson's desire for both guns and butter—that is, his belief that he must stem the advance of communism in Southeast Asia while pursuing a Great Society at home. This is not a new insight, but it has never been explored in depth before.

The book presents two major arguments. The first is that the U.S. government and the president and his key advisers, in particular, engaged in a major pattern of deception in how the United States committed its military force in Vietnam. Some authors have noted how the public was deceived, and many have analyzed Lyndon Johnson's "credibility gap" but there is no detailed analysis of the decision-making process that lays out a pattern of deception.

My second argument incorporates a new dimension to this analysis: that a significant sector of the government was deceived as well. Just as the American public and Congress were deceived, so, too, were the domestic and economic planners in Johnson's administration kept in the dark about the planning for escalation in Vietnam. They were not aware of the contingencies being developed that would command considerable resources from the government's budget and the American economy as a whole. The military and political decisions to escalate in Vietnam influenced (and were influenced by) the economic advice and policies being given the president.

In making this case, I have drawn upon considerable numbers of declassified documents from the Bureau of the Budget, the Council of Economic Advisers, and the Treasury Department in order to show how the domestic and economic advisers were misinformed about Vietnam in the economic advice they gave the president in 1965. Ironically, the resulting economic problems that arose by late 1965 would undermine the economic base of the Great Society, the very thing that Johnson feared if he allowed an open and public debate and an early commitment to fighting a full-scale war in Vietnam.

In particular, I analyze the budgeting process and how the budget officials as well as the Congressional Appropriations Committees were deceived by the White House and Defense Department about Vietnam policy. The congressional budgeting process is important to investigate because in the first half of 1965, those committees (not the Foreign Relations or Armed Services Committees) were about the only congressional venues where questions about Vietnam policy were being asked of key administration personnel (particularly of the military).

As I noted earlier, no one has written anything that has combined the guns-and-butter dilemma into a single, analytical work about the Vietnam escalation. In fact, very little has been written about the effect of the Vietnam War on economic policymaking during that period at all. One of the few accounts I have seen is the Joint Economic Committee of the U.S. Congress' *Economic Effect of Vietnam Spending* (which is 30 years old). A couple of chapters in Robert Warren Stevens' *Vain Hopes, Grim Realities: The Economic Consequences of the Vietnam War* (written in 1976) and the first chapter (entitled "Guns and Butter") of Hobart Rowan's recent analysis of American economic policy for the past 30 years, *Self-Inflicted Wounds: From LBJ's Guns and Butter to Reagan's Voodoo Economics* (1994) try to analyze the dilemmas President Johnson faced as he contemplated military escalation. But most economic analyses look exclusively at how the war affected the economy. What I do is show how the economic policy making and the military policy making affected each other even before the military escalation occurred and the economy began to overheat as a result of the war.

There has been much more written about the decision-making process that led to the U.S. military commitment in Vietnam. A few scholars have superbly built upon the documentary evidence in order to show in-depth how the decisions were arrived at, not just why. The best of these are Larry Berman's *Planning a Tragedy: The Americanization of the War in Vietnam* (1982), George McT. Kahin's *Intervention: How America Became Involved in Vietnam* (1986) and William Conrad Gibbons' four-part series *The U.S. Government and the Vietnam War: Executive and Legislative Roles and Relationships* (particularly appropriate are parts 2 and 3, published in 1985 and 1988, respectively). In addition, one of the best analytical sources of this period is William Bundy's unpublished manuscript, copies of which are in both the Johnson and Kennedy libraries. In many ways, Bundy's manuscript, which I have drawn upon, is a more forthright and honest analysis than Robert McNamara's recent book, *In Retrospect: The Tragedy and Lessons of Vietnam* (1996).

What this book does differently than these other accounts—besides incorporate the economic factors and the guns-versus-butter dilemma, which they either ignore or simply acknowledge but without any significant analysis—is show that there was a pattern of deception in the decision making process. The deception was deliberate, and the military escalation in Vietnam was not the slippery slope that many, most recently, McNamara, have claimed. I trace this pattern of deception in the decision-making process in what I hope is a highly readable account of the escalation period that will appeal to those who are interested in understanding how the United States escalated militarily and why it did so in such a deceptive and secretive manner.

While Robert McNamara's *In Retrospect* is an excellent account of the decision making, I have a fundamental disagreement with him. Essentially, his argument—his mea culpa, as it has been called by some—is that many mistakes were made and that the war in Vietnam was wrong and a grave error. Those mistakes, in his opinion, were honest ones brought about by mistaken assumptions, poor decision making, failure to understand the limitations of modern military technology, and the lack of a full and frank debate over large-scale military involvement. What he ignores is the evidence of duplicity, the pattern of deception and the abuse of the decision making process by the president and many of his top advisers in order to avoid a debate on the course of action in Vietnam and how best to utilize and prioritize America's government resources. McNamara admits that the absence of such a debate was a fundamental error, but he does not really acknowledge the means that were used to avoid such a debate, including the president's and his own culpability.

Ultimately, the political lessons from this are that deception will in the long run backfire and that policy making is an interrelated process—one cannot divorce military policy from domestic policy or economic policy from foreign affairs. They have an impact on each other, and to think of them separately or try to keep them apart is to ignore the interrelationship between them, which is fundamental in American governance. The president and his advisers did it, and most scholars on the Vietnam War separate these as well. I show how this crucial interrelationship helps us understand how the United States escalated in Vietnam.

Finally, I would like to acknowledge the assistance given to me in the research and writing of this book. It evolved out of my Ph.D. thesis at Columbia University, and I remain indebted to my two advisers: Roger Hilsman, who provided both scholarly criticism and the wisdom of one who had been in the middle of U.S. policy making on Vietnam, and Richard Pious, the epitome of an excellent teacher and scholar, who provided valuable encouragement and criticism and made the thesis process both challenging and fun.

This book is based considerably on archival materials. My thanks go to many archivists and staff members. In particular I would like to express my gratitude to David Humphrey and Regina Greenwell of the Lyndon Baines Johnson Library in Austin, Texas. I would also like to acknowledge the helpful assistance of Sue McDonough at the National Archives in Washington as well as the Federal Records Center staff in Suitland, Maryland, and the staff of the Office of Management and Budget Records Division.

I was also the beneficiary of a generous Moody grant from the Lyndon Baines Johnson Foundation to conduct my research at the Johnson Library, for which I am grateful. In addition, I owe a particular debt of gratitude to Ira and Miriam Wallach for their strong support and encouragement during my graduate studies at Columbia University.

It is also important to acknowledge my colleagues at the U.S. Institute of Peace, who have been very encouraging of my completion of this book, particularly those in the Education Program, with whom it is a privilege to work. It must be made clear, however, that the views expressed herein are solely mine and should not be ascribed to the U.S. Institute of Peace.

I would also like to thank James Sabin and Nina Duprey of Praeger for their support in getting this book to publication and making the editing process both enjoyable and efficient.

Ultimately, I must thank my family for putting up with late nights and weekends locked away in the study. One needs their patience as well as their inspiration. Besides my wife and children, I need to thank in particular my in-laws, Cindy and Phil, who during a critical time in the preparation of this book provided a wonderful place to write, and even a computer.

Chapter 1

Introduction: Lyndon Johnson's Guns Versus Butter Dilemma

THE COMMITMENT TO GO TO WAR

At 12:33 PM on July 28, 1965—without going before Congress, without a prime-time address to the nation—President Lyndon Johnson committed the United States to a land war in Southeast Asia. After nearly two months of deliberations among his top foreign policy and military advisers, he announced during his preliminary remarks before a press conference that American forces in Vietnam would expand from 75,000 to 125,000 men. In the week leading up to the escalation announcement those advisers had made it clear to the president that a war would be long and costly. The military situation first required that the American forces prevent the collapse of the South Vietnamese armed forces. Then the American military would go on the offensive to take the initiative away from the communist forces. Finally, the enemy would be forced to the bargaining table when it realized that it could not win and that the United States would uphold its commitment to preventing a communist takeover in South Vietnam. In the week before his decision to escalate, the most common estimate that President Johnson received from his military advisers was that the situation in Vietnam would require 500,000 American soldiers and five years.

Both the manner in which the president informed the American people of his expansion of the war and his choice of words downplayed the ramifications of his decision. This was more than just a "low-key" announcement; Lyndon Johnson clearly did not present the whole picture to the country. The number of troops he mentioned was 125,000; and he added that more would be sent as requested. But many more had already been requested and approved: 100,000 by November for a total of 175,000 and another 100,000 in 1966. He noted that the monthly military draft would be doubled but emphasized that there was no need to call up the reserves. A limited congressional appropriation would be sought until a supplemental appropriations measure could be presented to Congress in January. He did not mention any cost estimates, of which there were many by this point.

President Johnson was unwilling to bite the bullet and let the country understand the seriousness of his actions. He rejected a call by many of his own advisers to proclaim a national emergency. Instead, Johnson emphasized that the conflict in Vietnam would not disrupt the nation's economic prosperity. The American economy was still riding the crest of a record peacetime expansion: 51 months of uninterrupted economic growth. Assistant secretary of state for Far Eastern affairs William Bundy later noted about the July 28 announcement: "In short, the actual decision did not change the substance of the policy decision, but did notably soften the tone of its presentation to the country and the world, avoiding a new congressional mandate and a great debate. Just why the president acted in this way—which history may judge to be almost as important as the policy decision itself—he himself explained only in general terms at his final policy meetings on July 27."[1]

Relief and applause reverberated throughout much of Washington and the rest of the country after the president's announcement. He had apparently committed the country to much less than was expected or feared. The prospect of a limited war fell into line with the wishful thinking of many on Capitol Hill. Lyndon Johnson never mobilized the nation's economic, industrial, and manpower resources to fight the war. He led the nation to believe that the United States could simultaneously fight a limited war in Southeast Asia and create major social programs at home. Sacrifices would not be required. The military commanders would get a significant increase in soldiers, but they would not receive the full wartime backing of American society. There would be no expression of national resolve, so the public was left with a misapprehension about the nature of the commitment the president had made. Lyndon Johnson did not want to have to pay the price for going to war, but neither the president nor his advisers saw any other satisfactory alternative: intervention in Vietnam in 1965 was inevitable and seemed least costly in political terms. Johnson opted for a path by which he believed he could avoid the hard policy choices between the war and his domestic agenda—a path whereby he could minimize the costs by controlling the nature of the escalation.

This book sets out to present one significant part of the answer to the question Bundy posed about "why the president acted in this way." One cannot look just to the military and foreign policy meetings to understand the president's goals and strategies in Vietnam; it is also critical to understand his economic policies and just how they were interrelated with the broader military and foreign policy questions.

For the student of the Vietnam War, it seems that how Johnson chose to resolve the guns or butter dilemma had a major impact on the course of the

Vietnam War and many of the key military decisions made from 1964 through July 1965. I endeavor to show whether, and if so, how, that dilemma shaped the specific Vietnam actions the president initiated and the nature of the decision-making process that has come under strong criticism over the years:

- The incremental manner in which the President chose to escalate and his desire for a cheap solution;
- The fact that he did not give the military everything they requested;
- The undeclared and halfhearted commitment to a major land war (not calling up the reserves and no declaration of war, raising taxes, or going on a war economy footing);
- The desire for secrecy and refusal to acknowledge publicly that the military policy with respect to Vietnam had changed (thus creating a strong credibility problem); and
- The ignoring of the odds against any quick solution.

In order to understand the impact of Lyndon Johnson's desire to avoid paying the price of choosing between guns and butter, it is critical to show the relationship between the escalation in Vietnam and Johnson's domestic policies and objectives—how the military decisions regarding Vietnam and domestic and economic policies such as the Great Society mutually affected each other. This book therefore examines both the critical period of decision making on Vietnam—from the beginning of 1964 through the end of July 1965—and the economic and social decisions and policies that were made at the same time. Analysis of the decision-making process that led to the military escalation shows a clear pattern of deception in how the president and his advisers took the nation into an undeclared war. Lyndon Johnson and many of his top foreign policy officials consistently downplayed the significance of each U.S. military action in order to limit debate on the military costs and policy priorities. The major reason for this deception and its consequences was due, in large part, to the economic and domestic policy making and goals during that same period. Ultimately, the deceptive nature of the escalation of the war (which would, over time, lead to the loss of credibility for the president and his policies as well as erosion of public support for military action in Vietnam) and his desire to keep the costs of Vietnam policy low by doing the minimum necessary would undermine the administration's economic policies. The economic problems would then, in turn, severely weaken the financial base for the domestic programs Johnson worked so hard to create and keep in place.

THE CONFLICT IN VIETNAM

In his recent book, Johnson's secretary of defense Robert McNamara spent considerable time analyzing and admitting to the mistakes of the Johnson administration regarding the Vietnam war. His mea culpa revolved primarily around how poor the policy making was. He wanted, "to show how limited and shallow our analysis and discussion of the alternatives to our existing policy in Vietnam—i.e., neutralization or withdrawal—had been . . . . But we never carefully debated what U.S. force would ultimately be required, what our chances of success would be, or what the political, military, financial, and human costs would be if we provided it. Indeed, these basic questions went unexamined. We were at the beginning of a slide down a tragic and slippery slope."[2] McNamara continued that too little attention was paid to the question of costs and chances for success. This is no doubt true, but the "slippery slope" argument implies that there was a sense of inevitability about the policy. The president and his advisers felt they had no choice but to go forward. But to argue that the lack of good analysis and the poor decision making led down a slippery slope also implies that Washington had little control over events. That was clearly not the case—most particularly, President Johnson and his top officials could and did control the nature of the escalation, the action, the commitment. They had to act; this was not really questioned. But how they had to act and the consequences of the actions could be controlled, and these were manipulated to a significant extent.

Like his predecessors in the Oval Office, Lyndon Johnson was a staunch believer in the foreign policy consensus of containment. The spread of communism was unacceptable. Very few administration officials questioned the premise that Vietnam was strategically important, both in terms of halting the spread of communism and as an example of the firm and inviolable commitment of the U.S. government. Almost no one ruled out the use of force as an ultimate measure to preserve that commitment. President Johnson stated in the summer of 1964 that how the United States reacted to the communist threat in Vietnam would have "profound consequences everywhere." Secretary of state Dean Rusk was more specific: if the United States did not protect Vietnam, "our guarantees with regard to Berlin would lose their credibility."[3] This view was shared by most members of Congress, the bureaucratic elite, private industry, public opinion, and the press.

However, as 1964 began, the conflict in Vietnam was not a particularly high priority with the Johnson Administration and especially the president himself. U.S. policy was to help the South Vietnamese government resist communism, primarily through military and political advice and financial assistance. While the President would not consider letting South Vietnam fall to the communists, at the beginning of the year that possibility was considered remote. But the political and military situation sharply eroded during 1964. The South Vietnamese military was not acquitting itself well against the Viet Cong guerrillas, and the political situation in Saigon was increasingly unstable. Coups, countercoups, and the threats of coups had become a way of political life. There would be seven different governments in Saigon during 1964. The army of South Vietnam was unable to stand on its own without being propped up by the United States.

By the beginning of 1965, most of the president's top advisers—including Robert McNamara, Dean Rusk, national security adviser McGeorge Bundy, ambassador to South Vietnam Maxwell Taylor, and chairman of the Joint Chiefs of Staff General Earle Wheeler—believed that South Vietnam was on the verge of collapse. In order for the United States to preserve its commitment to South Vietnam and deter the Viet Cong and their North Vietnamese sponsors from continued aggression in the south, the administration had no choice but to expand its military activities.

The president's top aides recommended a major bombing campaign on North Vietnam in order to deter the communists and convince them they could not win. After the sustained bombing program, Rolling Thunder, began, American ground forces were quickly deployed to South Vietnam. Unlike the bombing, deploying ground forces was a significant commitment of manpower and matériel; yet it was not analyzed or debated fully in the highest echelons of the administration until thousands of troops were already in place and engaged in combat.

THE NATURE OF THE MILITARY ESCALATION

The documentary evidence that has surfaced in the past few years, in particular, the notes and transcripts from National Security Council meetings in which combat troop deployments were authorized, strongly indicates that prior to July 28, 1965, there were a number of separate escalatory steps. Until July at least, the different deployments of U.S. forces were not the continuation of an already fixed policy of engaging in a land war in Vietnam. Once the initial ground troops had been sent to Vietnam, the question of further military involvement was debated at each point when the military command in Vietnam requested additional combat forces.[4] The nature of the military escalation— how the troops were deployed, how economic resources were committed, and how the conflict was presented to the American public—was a major factor in the lack of understanding of American objectives in Vietnam and in the erosion of public support for the war.

Vietnam was no quagmire or slippery slope. As McNamara has admitted in hindsight, there were many occasions before July 1965 when the United States could have pulled back militarily.[5] For political reasons, the president chose to expand the U.S. involvement. As he commented later, Johnson believed that if he did not deploy more U.S. forces in July, "I'd be the first American President to put my tail between my legs and run out because I didn't have the courage to stand up and support a treaty and support the policy of two other Presidents." In that same vein, he noted that, "if I left that war and let the Communists take over South Vietnam, then I would be seen as a coward and my nation would be seen as an appeaser."[6]

President Johnson was not misled by his advisers about the military goals in Vietnam, the costs of escalation, or how long it would take.[7] The president and his foreign policy advisers did not go into Vietnam blind; they were constantly warned about the odds they were facing. But as McNamara has pointed out with respect to the bombing campaign against North Vietnam: "Data and analysis showed that air attacks would not work, but there was such determination to do something, anything, to stop the Communists that discouraging reports were often ignored."[8] The policy objective was to create a military stalemate that would convince the communists they could not succeed in South Vietnam. McNamara used the term "stalemate" to describe the U.S. military objective to the full cabinet on June 18, 1965.[9] That was never stated publicly, however. There is no evidence that Johnson did not believe his advisers, but it is clear that he downplayed and obfuscated the nature and costs of the military escalation.

While the president and most of his civilian advisers passionately believed that the communists had to be halted, very few were enthusiastic to let loose the full potential of America's industry and resources in order to fight a full-scale war in the jungles of Vietnam. Primarily, they did not feel such a drastic measure was necessary; eventually, the North would see it could not win and would withdraw. But they also did not want to provoke the Chinese. As a result, most of the thinking among Vietnam planners focused on the minimum necessary to convince the communists of the futility of their aggression in the South.

The policy was a deliberate attempt to minimize the nature of the growing American role in the conflict. As more American troops were sent to Vietnam, and their mission evolved from defending airfields to offensive patrols, the President and his advisers (following his lead) continually downplayed the significance of the buildup. For the first half of 1965, Vietnam policy was a series of ad hoc actions and retaliations while the Johnson administration decided on the next step.[10] This became the beginning of a type of incremental thinking that led, as one analyst noted, to an "impression of inevitability . . . because the objective was seldom questioned."[11]

One of the most significant questions for the analyst that emerge after looking over documents and reading memoirs such as those of Robert McNamara is whether or not the mistakes of Vietnam—the "tragedy" of Vietnam, in McNamara's words—were primarily the result of poor policy making and myopic thinking or whether America's Vietnam policy was the result of duplicity. Were Johnson, McNamara, Bundy, Rusk, and the other senior policymakers guilty of making terrible mistakes of policy (based on the seemingly noble goal of containing communism) because, as McNamara argues, the senior officials never examined the alternatives, got the best information or asked the right questions? The essence of McNamara's apology (or defense) is that these officials did the wrong thing for the right reasons. That the poor quality of decision making resulted from the uncritical Cold War thinking seems unquestionable. But that does not fully explain the nature of the Vietnam War. The general outlines of the information that the military provided at the beginning of the decision making process in 1965 were fairly accurate. The military in the spring clearly claimed that a "stalemate" would require 500,000 men over five years. They were essentially correct. The United States did achieve a stalemate—but it could not sustain that, and the American people could not support such an objective. This book argues that there was considerably more knowledge than is admitted and that there was certainly a pattern of deception in order to avoid a debate about priorities and a choice between guns and butter.

As McNamara stated clearly to the cabinet in June 1965, it was important not to let the American people know how they were pursuing the commitment in Vietnam and the containment of communism. American boys would be sent halfway around the world for a "stalemate."

In addition, the extent of the escalation and its probable costs were kept from the domestic and economic planners in 1965. The president tried to escalate the war through supplemental, emergency funding. Consequently, long-term planning was not factored into the budget preparation. This resulted from deliberate deception in 1965 by the Pentagon (in particular, the Office of the secretary of defense) and the president as well as from a bureaucratic process in which the costs of the Vietnam conflict were unaccounted for in the administration's economic forecasting and budget preparation during 1964 and 1965.

But why did Lyndon Johnson choose to fight a limited and undeclared war that he expanded incrementally and even deceptively? A full-blown escalation and a declaration of war that ran the risk of Chinese intervention were one concern. The country had gone down that road in Korea. But there was also domestic pressure on the president not to "lose" Vietnam to the communists. This was rooted in the postwar foreign policy consensus of containment.[12] Thus, the nature of the war—standing firm in Vietnam while avoiding an all-out war—was critical for foreign policy reasons. As national security adviser McGeorge Bundy noted in referring to the decision for sustained bombing of North Vietnam in February 1965, "[E]ven if [bombing] fails, the policy will be worth it."[13] A month later, he and assistant secretary of defense John McNaughton implied that even if the United States lost, it was better to do so after committing 100,000 men. U.S. credibility with respect to its international commitments would be strengthened, and so there was a significant political value to the deployment of U.S. forces in Vietnam. Winning or losing almost seemed secondary to maintaining that credibility.

PRESIDENT JOHNSON'S DOMESTIC AGENDA

To understand truly why the United States escalated incrementally and deceptively in Vietnam, it is critical to analyze the social and economic goals as well as political and bureaucratic pressures and how those factors greatly determined the limited, downplayed nature of the U.S. escalation. There have been studies of the decision-making process that led up to the war and analyses of the economy during the Johnson administration.[14] But no works have looked at the domestic and economic decision-making process in relation to the Vietnam decision-making process. An analysis of economic and domestic policies in 1964 and 1965 helps explain why the president purposely attempted to pursue a military solution without a public declaration of war or even an admission that the role of the American soldiers in Vietnam had changed.

The Johnson administration was harnessing the vast resources of the American economy to create a Great Society at home in 1964 and 1965. Johnson's legislative program included greater medical care, improved education, housing, and transportation; it also embraced equal rights and voting rights for all. He had involved the American people in a War on Poverty, and his administration created a broad-based governmental program to create economic opportunity. The key to funding these new ideas and programs was the continued economic growth and stability in the United States. From November 1963, when Johnson assumed the presidency, through the fall of 1965, the American economy was robust. Prices were stable, productivity and profits were high, and unemployment continued to fall. Another important component in the equation was that during the previous 12 years, the post–Korea War military buildup had placed the country in such a strong military position that through decreased purchases and greater economic efficiency in the Pentagon, defense spending was reduced. The savings from defense would allow for more governmental resources devoted to the Great Society programs. Also, as relations between the United States and the Soviet Union improved, economic planners, encouraged by the Pentagon, felt they could look forward to further reductions in military spending.

The economists in the Johnson administration were much like Robert McNamara and the so-called whiz kids at the Pentagon: Kennedy holdovers who favored bold action and initiative. The activism of the New Frontier was as evident with the economic planners as with the defense planners. They had turned the conservatism of the Eisenhower years on its head. These economists, led by Kennedy's chairman of the Council of Economic Advisers, Walter Heller, were unconcerned about balanced budgets. They promoted fiscal stimulation and growth in order to create more government revenues, which could then help expand the economy and finance needed government programs. There was the risk of an overheated economy, which could result in excessive growth and inflation, but fiscal policy would be able to apply the brakes in plenty of time through deferred tax cuts or even tax increases if necessary. Heller and his colleagues were extremely confident.

One of the critical mistakes that occurred during Johnson's administration was that the economic planners were not informed of the plans for a major jump in the U.S. deployment in Vietnam. So they continued to promote strong fiscal stimulation while military needs were beginning to overheat the economy. The economists also misread or ignored signs that military orders had greatly expanded in 1965, but since they were told that defense spending would increase only modestly, there seemed little reason for concern. The deception of the domestic and economic advisers about the American military commitment to Vietnam affected the advice those experts gave the president about the feasibility of creating the many domestic programs he desired and the long-term prognosis for the economy.[15]

THE GUNS-AND-BUTTER DILEMMA

As the administration pushed forward on its domestic programs, the conflict in Vietnam worsened. So, President Johnson faced a significant dilemma. How could he escalate the U.S. participation in the war in Vietnam while continuing to enact the Great Society agenda and maintain economic prosperity? Could the president fight the war in a way that would ensure both guns and butter? The way in which he chose to escalate the war—low-key, without any wartime measures—was a direct result of his desire to maintain prosperity, contain communism, and create a Great Society. He could not have the latter without ensuring the first two.

Much of the strategy behind Johnson's policy of escalation seemed a result of his strong desire to insulate the American people from the political, economic, and social ramifications of the conflict in Vietnam. Johnson was clearly avoiding trade-offs. He was doing so primarily by denying that any trade-off existed. He felt that he could achieve both: stopping the spread of communism and achieving a Great Society. He consistently advocated both in public. William Bundy later noted that "the question for exploration by the real scholar of as difficult a period as any President of the United States has ever passed through, is how did all of this [the military escalation] relate to what he [the president] was trying to do to get the Great Society enacted on the Hill. That is the contrapuntal theme, and I don't understand how it related; but it's obvious that it cut across."[16]

The significant impact of the guns-versus-butter conflict has been raised by many analysts of the Vietnam War and the Johnson presidency, but too often it has been taken for granted and rarely analyzed in much depth. One observer concluded that "Lyndon Johnson's greatest fault as a political leader was that he chose not to choose between the Great Society and the war in Vietnam."[17] Johnson admitted he wanted both; McGeorge Bundy acknowledged that Johnson's desire to "protect his legislative program" played a key role in shaping his decision to escalate in July 1965.[18]

I would argue that President Johnson did not want to acknowledge the heavy costs in order to avoid a debate in the United States that would force him to choose between guns and butter. Johnson thought he could get Congress to legislate and appropriate money for the Great Society if he played down the costs of the war. Once the U.S. soldiers were in the field, it would be very difficult to vote against military appropriations. The president actually pulled this off—he got the financing and commitment for both the Vietnam War and the Great Society. But he did so at a severe cost: major inflation and the loss of public and congressional trust and confidence in his administration. Had he brought his economic advisers in on his plans for both guns and butter and been honest about the future costs of the war, they most likely would have counseled him against such a tricky and disingenuous strategy, as they began to do by 1966.

Economists have devoted a great deal of study to the impact of the war on the economy, in particular, the inflation that took root in late 1965 and began to have severe political consequences for the president in 1966. But most of the economic analysis has focused on the economic effects, not the Vietnam decisions that led to an overheated economy. In researching the analysis and advice that the president's economic advisers gave the president in 1964 and 1965 as well as the budget decisions, one is struck by the lack of information that the domestic advisers had about the Vietnam policy. In January 1965, while the administration was planning to escalate its military role, the Pentagon submitted cuts in its budget for fiscal year 1966, belying the concern that had strongly emerged by late 1964 among foreign policy and military planners that the United States could become embroiled in a major military commitment in Vietnam. As a result, domestic planning went forward without any hint that Vietnam could assume a substantial commitment of American resources and manpower. There is a great deal of evidence that President Johnson and the Pentagon then deliberately withheld the extent of the military commitment in Vietnam from the domestic and economic planners. These planners did not realize until December 1965 that the conflict would require such a vast commitment of manpower, equipment, resources, and time.

Almost all economic studies have agreed that Vietnam did not begin to have an adverse effect on the American economy and the federal budget until 1966. But the seeds were sown in 1964 and 1965 with the Vietnam escalation. How the war was escalated reflected Johnson's concern for continued economic growth. Economist Murray Weidenbaum stated: "From the viewpoint of demands on the resources of the American economy, the Vietnam war really had its initial impact in fiscal 1966 [July 1965–June 1966]."[19] The Budget Bureau in 1967 estimated that the additional costs of Vietnam had been $100 million or less a year prior to fiscal year 1966, a seemingly insignificant factor. But the war machine had already been geared up in 1965, and when increased military orders occurred in a rapidly expanding economy with virtually no slack, the economy overheated. One of the most significant causes of the overheated economy was the preparation for escalation when the military drastically increased orders in 1965. The economists certainly underestimated how quickly a military buildup affects the economy. But had they been aware of the military plans in 1965, they might well have tried to put the brakes on the fiscal stimulation as they did in December 1965, when the extent of the conflict in Vietnam became clear.

Even though a great deal of domestic legislation was enacted in 1964 and 1965, the Great Society programs did not begin to draw significantly on the budget until 1966, when Vietnam spending also began to absorb billions of dollars. The War on Poverty did not cost very much money in 1964–1965: "Those were the years when goals were being set, when professional staffs were being assembled, enacting legislation passed, and experimental approaches tried out."[20] However, the surge in inflation and competition for resources between Vietnam needs and domestic needs that began in 1966 resulted from the policy process and the decisions of 1964 and 1965, in particular from President Johnson's strong desire to avoid any debate on allocation of government resources and policy priorities. Thus, foreign policy and domestic policy were kept separate—so that the Great Society could move forward with fanfare and congressional and public commitment while decisions on Vietnam moved forward in an ad hoc and surreptitious manner.

As the Vietnam conflict heated up, Johnson hoped that the expanding economy would enable him to prosecute the war without cutting back on social programs. His economic advisers strongly promoted an economy that could afford both guns and butter. Their conception of a strong defense and a Great Society, however, did not envision the escalating U.S. military involvement in Vietnam. No one doubts that the administration economists were slow to recognize the dangers for the economy in the latter half of 1965. They either ignored or did not recognize the warning signs. But did the delay in changing the economic advice they were giving the president make any difference? Clearly, the economists did not know the cost or the extent of the escalation in Vietnam. Would it have made any difference had the economists not been deceived or given the information? What would the president have done differently? He did not accept his economic advisers' recommendations for a tax increase to slow down the overheated economy in December 1965. But, if the economists and domestic policy officials had been informed of the significant plans to escalate in Vietnam, it is much more likely that a debate within the administration and American society itself over policy, resources, and priorities, which Robert McNamara and others later felt was so necessary and so lacking, would have occurred. Such a debate would have served to clarify to the American public and Congress what the policy and priorities in Vietnam were.

By analyzing the domestic, economic, and social priorities during the time the United States escalated its military commitment in the Vietnam conflict, we can better understand how the guns-versus-butter dilemma influenced those decisions to escalate. How did President Johnson's desire to avoid a trade-off between his domestic and economic agenda and his desire to halt the spread of communism in Southeast Asia help shape the decision to send ground forces to Vietnam and the manner in which the conflict escalated? How did that desire contribute to many of the mistakes made by American officials that so many have acknowledged over the years? To find an answer it is important to establish what relationship existed between the military decisions in Vietnam and the president's economic and social goals and how these policy areas affected each other.

As Johnson later stated, on July 27, 1965, when he made the decision to escalate in Vietnam, "two great streams in our national life converged—the dream of a Great Society at home and the inescapable demands of our obligations halfway around the world. They were to run in confluence until the end of my administration." [21] William Bundy cited that sentence as "the most poignant paragraph in his memoirs . . . . [It] may well have been the truly decisive consideration in the President's mind." [22] His desire to have both guns and butter was, in all probability, his downfall and contributed greatly to the limited nature of the Vietnam War and the frustration of the American people at its length and costs and to the economic problems that undermined his Great Society programs.

Lyndon Johnson himself admitted later that he did not want to make the hard choices, nor did he want any debate on policy priorities. Referring to Congress, he remarked, "I knew that the day it exploded into a major debate on the war, that day would be the beginning of the end of the Great Society . . . . I was determined to be a leader of war *and* a leader of peace. I refused to let my critics push me into choosing one or the other. I wanted both, I believed in both, and I believed America had the resources to provide for both."[23]   In contrast, President Kennedy once noted: "To govern, as wise men have said, is to choose. We cannot escape choice," and a President's choice "helps determine the issues of his Presidency, their priority in the national life, and the mode and success of their execution."[24]   In that way, as a leader, Lyndon Johnson failed himself and his country.

NOTES

1. Johnson Library, William Bundy unpublished manuscript, chapter 30, pp. 1–2.

2. Robert S. McNamara, *In Retrospect: The Tragedy and Lessons of Vietnam*, p. 107.

3. As quoted in George C. Herring, *America's Longest War*, p. 115.

4. There is no consensus at all among many of those in decision-making positions at the time as to when the key decision—"the point of no return"—had occurred. Maxwell Taylor, William Bundy, Chester Cooper, George Ball, and Leslie Gelb all cite a different decision or time period. One is struck by the number and variety of opinions as to when the president "crossed the Rubicon." Before July 28 there was no single time, no specific decision that can be pointed to with certainty and declared as the critical choice point when President Johnson committed the United States to a land war in Vietnam.

5. McNamara, *In Retrospect*, p. 321.

6. Johnson Library, Lyndon Johnson Oral History, Augurst 12, 1969; and Lyndon Johnson interview, in Doris Kearns, *Lyndon Johnson and the American Dream*, p. 252.

7. Johnson himself claimed that after a visit to Vietnam in 1961, he commented to President Kennedy that to meet the challenge in Vietnam required "a full realization of the very heavy and continuing costs involved in terms of money, of effort and of United States prestige." (Lyndon Baines Johnson, *The Vantage Point*, p. 54.)

8. McNamara, *In Retrospect*, p. 114.

9. Johnson Library, Cabinet Papers File, Box III, Cabinet minutes, June 18, 1965, pp. 52–53.

10. As Paul Kattenburg, a State Department expert on Vietnam during this period, noted, "The decision to send ground combat forces was probably reached more quickly and with less staffing, planning, and forethought—except by Gen. Westmoreland and the MACV [Military Assistance Command Vietnam] staff in Saigon—than any comparable fateful decision ever made in U.S. history." (Paul Kattenburg, *The Vietnam Trauma*, p. 134.)

11. Gregory Palmer, *The McNamara Strategy and the Vietnam War: Program Budgeting in the Pentagon, 1960–1968*, p. 101.

12. Many works analyze the international context of the Vietnam conflict and American foreign policy goals at this time. One of the best is *The Irony of Vietnam: The System Worked* by Leslie Gelb and Richard Betts. They state that the Vietnam War was a natural response by the military and foreign policy bureaucracies to the theory of containment, an approach that was both outdated and overly relied on, especially with respect to Vietnam.

Others have argued that the seeds for the American intervention were sown during the Kennedy and Eisenhower Administrations and that Johnson should not be solely blamed for what was, after all, the logical extension of past U.S. policy. (See especially George McT. Kahin's *Intervention: How America Became Involved in Vietnam* and Kattenburg's *The Vietnam Trauma*.)

13. "A Policy of Sustained Reprisal," memo from McGeorge Bundy to the president, February 7, 1965, in Johnson Library, National Security File, McGeorge Bundy Memos to the President, Box 2, vol. 8, p. 4.

14. In particular, see the analyses of the decision-making in Kahin, *Intervention*; John P. Burke and Fred I. Greenstein's *How Presidents Test Reality: Decisions on Vietnam, 1954 and 1965*; and Larry Berman's *Planning a Tragedy: The Americanization of the War in Vietnam*. Excellent works that have analyzed the Vietnam War within the domestic political framework of the Pentagon bureaucracy are Robert Komer's *Bureaucracy Does Its Thing*; James Clay Thompson's *Rolling Thunder*; Palmer's *The McNamara Strategy and the Vietnam War*; Robert Gallucci's *Neither Peace nor Honor*, and Townsend Hoopes' *The Limits of Intervention*. Works from the perspective of foreign policy bureaucrats include Kattenburg's *The Vietnam Trauma* (the State Department) and Chester Cooper's *The Lost Crusade* (the National Security Council). Most of these works have taken an overall view of the entire Vietnam conflict and are concerned with the process of decision making within the military and foreign affairs bureaucracies. Military perspectives on the decision-making process include William Westmoreland's *A Soldier Reports* and U.S.G. Sharp's *Strategy for Defeat: Vietnam in Retrospect*.

Economic analyses are Robert Warren Stevens' *Vain Hopes, Grim Realities: The Economic Consequences of the Vietnam War*; The Center for Strategic Studies' *The Economic Impact of the Vietnam War* (text prepared by Murray L. Weidenbaum); Arthur Okun's *The Political Economy of Prosperity*. Analyses of the military budget process, in part, are Arnold Kanter's *Defense Politics*; John Crecine's *Defense Budgeting*; and Alain Enthoven and K. Wayne Smith's *How Much Is Enough?*

15. Most of the evidence is in the Administrative Files of the Bureau of the Budget and the Council of Economic Advisors as well as in memos of key White House aides that are held in the Johnson Library archives, the National Archives, and the Records Division of the Office of Management and Budget. The assertion of deception was first raised by David Halberstam in *The Best and the Brightest* and has also been put forward by Daniel Ellsberg in his *Papers on the War* and Gallucci's *Neither Peace nor Honor*.

16. Johnson Library, William Bundy Oral History, May 29, 1969, pp. 30–31.

17. Berman, *Planning a Tragedy*, p. 150. While Berman raised the "guns versus butter" dilemma, it is not the focus of his book. Another political scientist, Donald Kettl, explored the issue in depth but concentrated his analysis primarily after 1965. See "The Economic Education of Lyndon Johnson: Guns, Butter, and Taxes," in Robert A. Divine (ed.), *The Johnson Years, vol. 2: Vietnam, the Environment, and Science*, pp. 54–78.

18. McGeorge Bundy memo of November 2, 1968 from notes dated July 27, 1965, in Johnson Library, Meeting Notes File, Box 1, July 27, 1965 NSC meeting; Joint Leadership Meeting Folder.

19. Testimony of Murray L. Weidenbaum before Joint Economic Committee, April 26, 1967 in US Congress, Joint Economic Committee, *Economic Effect of Vietnam Spending*, p. 176.

20. Stevens, *Vain Hopes, Grim Realities*, p. 49.

21. Johnson, *The Vantage Point*, p. 324.

22. Bundy manuscript, chapter 30, p. 22.

23. Lyndon Johnson interview, in Kearns, *Lyndon Johnson and the American Dream*, p. 283.

24. See Introduction by John F. Kennedy in Theodore C. Sorensen, *Decision Making in the White House*, p. xii.

Chapter 2 _____

Great Dreams at Home, Deterioration Abroad

VIETNAM: AN IRRITANT AMID THE PUSH FOR U.S. PROSPERITY

When Lyndon Johnson assumed the presidency in late November 1963, Vietnam policy was in a state of flux amid increasing deterioration of the political situation there due to the assassination in October of Ngo Dinh Diem, the South Vietnamese premier. From the end of 1963 through the early summer of 1964, the communist insurgency grew considerably while the government' of Vietnam remained shaky, due primarily to continuous internal struggles for power from within the civilian and military leadership in Saigon. In addition, the South Vietnamese armed forces were rather ineffective in their campaign against the communist guerrillas. Within American government circles, there was a growing consensus about the need to strengthen the resolve of the Saigon government as well as halt the successes of the Viet Cong guerrillas and limit the infiltration of supplies to the Viet Cong from North Vietnam.

Yet, despite the deterioration in South Vietnam, Lyndon Johnson focused most of his time and energy on domestic affairs. As many of his biographers and other analysts of the Johnson presidency have noted, Lyndon Johnson was not interested in foreign affairs nor anxious to involve himself in strategic military questions. The crisis in Vietnam was initially a minor irritant that needed to be handled efficiently so that the communists were kept at bay there and so that failure there did not weaken his presidency in any way that would jeopardize his ambitious domestic plans.

What Johnson hoped would be the legacy of his presidency was taking shape shortly after his ascent to the presidency. President John F. Kennedy had left Johnson with an unfinished blueprint for major domestic programs in the areas of health, education, welfare, and civil rights. The Kennedy administration had already planned much of the domestic and economic agenda that Johnson was to implement. Economic prosperity would be the foundation for building what Johnson was to call the Great Society. The first order of business for the new administration was to ensure the economic growth that would enable the government to expand its domestic programs. At the same time, the president did not want the communist insurgency in Vietnam to distract from his agenda at home or undermine the economic good times. He wanted to ensure that South Vietnam did not fall into communist hands, but only at a minimal cost and with a minimal American commitment.

While the political situation in Vietnam was reaching crisis proportions, it was not yet a political crisis for the president at home. The result of Diem's death had been greater instability in the South and jockeying for power in the aftermath. At the same time, the communists were consolidating their hold on much of the South Vietnamese countryside. Up to this point, the key to American strategy in South Vietnam had been to commit resources, military advisers, and support for the South Vietnamese government in the international community in order both to deter North Vietnam from subverting the government of South Vietnam and to increase the self-reliance and effectiveness of the South Vietnamese armed forces.

There was, at that point, no consideration of greater American military involvement, simply a desire to provide the necessary political support and resources to help South Vietnam establish a stable and effective government that could stem the increasing communist inroads in the Vietnamese countryside. After a mission to Saigon in September 1963, secretary of defense Robert McNamara and chairman of the Joint Chiefs of Staff Maxwell Taylor predicted that the major part of the U.S. military task would be completed by the end of 1965.

Two key policy objectives, continued economic growth as well as reduced military spending, were to provide the economic foundation for greater domestic spending. Strong management of the American economy through an active fiscal policy was viewed by Kennedy's and, later, Johnson's economic advisers as the most effective way to ensure continued economic growth and move toward a full employment goal (accepted as a target of 4 percent unemployment).[1] In November 1963 the top economic officials in the administration were Walter Heller, chairman of the Council of Economic Advisers, Kermit Gordon, director of the Bureau of the Budget, and C. Douglas Dillon, secretary of the Treasury. Together, they were known in government parlance as the Troika.

Walter Heller immediately impressed upon Lyndon Johnson when he assumed the presidency that continued economic growth was the key to achieving domestic prosperity. As Heller later explained, "[P]rosperity and rapid growth put at [the president's] disposal, as nothing else can, the resources needed to achieve great societies at home and grand designs abroad. They enable him to meet their economic costs out of the real output and fiscal dividends generated by dynamic growth—and thus to press ahead with minimum social tension and economic dislocation."[2] Heller had emphasized the same point to Kennedy and worked closely with Kennedy in preparing domestic programs. But with a new president thrust suddenly into the office, he could push harder to move forward on a "War on Poverty," especially as Johnson was a master at dealing with Congress, an area in which Kennedy had been less adept.

THE UNDERLYING ECONOMIC PREMISES IN 1964 AND 1965

In January 1963 President Kennedy had proposed in his State of the Union address a $10 billion tax cut. The economic theory behind the tax cut was that lower taxation would stimulate growth and expansion. The resulting economic prosperity and increasing tax revenues would, in turn, create the base for expanded social programs. Throughout 1963 the tax cut proposal came under attack from both conservatives and liberals. The former argued that it would lead to inflation or deficits, while the latter claimed that tax cuts benefited the rich and would not create growth. At the end of November 1963, as the necessary legislation remained tied up in the Senate, Johnson immediately embraced the tax cut proposal when he became president.

Walter Heller later noted that Johnson's strategy was very different from Kennedy's, particularly as Kennedy believed the new expenditure programs could come only during a second term: "[Kennedy] felt that you had to persuade the public or at least the major movers and shakers, policymakers . . . [h]e felt that he was building this base of understanding in his first term and that he was going to capitalize on it in the second. Johnson's idea was to bring the key policymakers, the key power center, into the room and strike a bargain with them . . . . His idea was that the success of the measure would itself be the education device. Kennedy was quite different. He felt the people had to be persuaded that this was the right way to go and then you could move."[3] Johnson was anxious to act quickly; get the tax cut and then move on to the specific domestic programs.

In 1960 most economists had become very wary of the recurrent pattern of recession every two to three years during the previous decade. Although the tax cut of 1964 was not intended as an antirecession measure, it was designed to achieve the full potential of the economy, and moving toward that was a way to ensure against a recession. From 1956 to 1961 there had been a period of slow growth, high unemployment, and idle or less-than-full industrial capacity. As a result, under President Kennedy, economic growth became an overriding goal. His economists were convinced that a tax cut would help expand the economy, reduce unemployment, and still keep prices stable. There was a growing perception that great benefits could finally be reaped from the considerable post–World War II restraint on the growth of aggregate demand, even to the extent that high employment could be attained without inflation.[4]

In addition to spurring economic growth, another aim of the tax cut was to reduce any fiscal drag that would have kept the economy from reaching its full potential, as had happened during the Eisenhower years. Walter Heller noted that in 1963 and 1964 he used to speak a great deal to key business and financial groups in order to get them to support the idea of the tax cut. He stated that his message went something like this: "Look, this tax cut will speed expansion and provide a substantial revenue feedback. As a result, it won't be long before you have smaller deficits than if you let the economy limp along without a tax cut. So in a sense you can have your cake and eat it, too."[5] The economists were telling President Johnson the same thing: he could have it all. Johnson aide Jack Valenti stated that "[the president] was convinced that if he could really get the economy in terrific shape he could do all the things he wanted to do. As a result he spent a lot of time on budgetary matters, fiscal matters and made sure that the budget was as lean as possible."[6]

A source of additional revenues would come from cuts in the government budget, in particular from defense spending. While the key to the fiscal policy was lowering taxes, savings on defense combined with increased domestic spending by the government would also promote economic growth. Therefore, strong and rapid growth was the grand economic strategy that the economists consistently drilled into Kennedy and Johnson.

Lyndon Johnson opted to deal first with the political obstacles to the tax cut. The size of the budget quickly became an important factor and political symbol for Johnson. In November 1963 preparations for the new fiscal year 1965 (July 1, 1964–June 30, 1965) budget were well under way. The president immediately made it clear that he would take a very hard line in trying to bring the 1965 expenditure estimates under the figure of $100 billion. Notes from Johnson's first meeting on the budget, when his economic advisers urged the consideration of a major tax cut in 1964, revealed that "the President made it clear that he was convinced the Administration would not receive approval of the tax legislation . . . unless the President could convince the Congress that he would come in with a budget of $100 billion or less."[7]

Johnson's political intuition about the reaction of Congress to any administration decision would be a critical theme throughout his presidency. In an election year, a weak economy would certainly jeopardize his campaign. For the most part, Johnson was seldom willing to risk a fight with Congress. He clearly preferred to work behind the scenes and engage less in public campaigns or public debates. Therefore, he wanted everything lined up beforehand so there was little debate or political struggle over any administration proposal. When there was a chance of a real battle over any economic issue, Johnson rarely pushed for it.

The budget numbers were important insofar as they had enormous symbolic and political value for the president's agenda. That is one reason Johnson was adamant about keeping both the fiscal year (FY) 1965 and 1966 budgets below the $100 billion mark, not an important economic figure but something that Johnson could point to in pressing Congress for the approval of legislative measures needed to enact his social programs. With respect to the FY 1965 budget, the $100 billion figure was critical politically in order to gain support for the tax cut of the powerful chairman of the Senate Finance Committee, Senator Harry Byrd of Virginia. As Walter Heller noted later, Johnson was determined to give Harry Byrd what he wanted, namely, a budget under $100 billion, in order to gain Byrd's support for the tax cut. Without Byrd's support, the tax cut would almost certainly not have gotten through Congress. As Heller said, "[T]his totally artificial administrative budget figure was just a will-o-the-wisp, but [Johnson] was convinced that if he gave this assurance on the budget side that he'd get the tax cut. And he did."[8]

The president wanted to convince Byrd that he was committed to a conservative budget in order to get the tax bill passed out of the Finance Committee. According to Jack Valenti, "[The president] had to announce the budget sometime in February or March and he also knew that he had to get that tax cut out. It was his general feeling, after discussing with Walter Heller and Kermit Gordon...that all that President Johnson wanted to do would be hinged to the tax cut. Unless he got the tax cut they weren't sure they could keep the economy moving upward in this ascending spiral."[9] So, the president went to work immediately on Senator Byrd. Valenti noted that the two men engaged in a bit of horse trading over lunch at the White House in December. The original budget figure was to be $107–109 billion. Johnson asked Byrd whether the senator would help with the tax cut if he could bring the budget in under $100 billion. Byrd replied that if Johnson could do that, he might be able to get the tax cut out of the Finance Committee and onto the Senate floor. With Byrd's commitment, the president set about reducing the budget dramatically.

In early January the budget still remained above the $100 billion line. But Johnson actively cajoled the Budget Bureau to find more room to cut. Valenti later noted:

So having now gotten Harry Byrd to make the commitment that if the budget came in under $100 billion the tax cut would be sprung from the committee and brought to the floor, then the President redoubled his efforts with Kermit Gordon. They really rode over every item of that budget and they were hacking away with machetes . . . . Gordon was spending practically every night down at the White House in the President's office going over this budget. Then they would call in department heads, one at a time, and work on them so that the President got the budget down to, I think it was $99.4 billion . . . . I remember that he had a press meeting in his office, called the press in and announced the budget. It was really surprising to the press, caught them off guard, no one really thought the budget was going to be that low. And the President kept that a well-guarded secret; literally only he and Kermit Gordon knew, and I knew by looking at some of the documents . . . . So it came as a total surprise to the press. As a matter of fact, that might have begun the so-called credibility gap. The press thought that they were being misled . . . . I just think that it meant really squeezing everything out, particularly on defense, not putting a lot of new things in defense and going back and cutting everything that could possibly be cut. If something was $100 million, they'd cut it to $80 million; if something was $25 million, they'd cut it to 22 million. By going over every nook and cranny of the budget they were able then to bring it into line.[10]

As one analyst noted, "President Johnson's personal impact on the 1965 budget was staggering. After final figure juggling, total expenditures were reduced from 101.5 billion to 97.9 billion."[11] Another remarked that in working to obtain passage of the tax cut and reduce government spending, "the president was in his element, reveling in the opportunity to count noses, manipulate the minds and emotions of the legislators, and struggle in tandem with overworked staff to achieve goals that were not too far away."[12]

Johnson's domestic strategy was quite clear. Once the interrelated goals of bringing the FY 1965 budget in under $100 billion and a tax cut were achieved, the economic strategy was in place. Then the president could tackle key domestic legislation that was stalled in Congress: the civil rights bill and several education bills. The planning and implementation of other new domestic programs were to follow, in particular, a major antipoverty campaign. The foundation for this comprehensive domestic agenda was to be the economic prosperity triggered by the tax cut. In addition, budget priorities were to be reoriented. Defense spending would be reduced, partly to keep the budget below the $100 billion mark but also to redirect resources toward the domestic arena. Defense secretary McNamara led the way in the push to reduce defense spending, through greater efficiency and with cuts in unnecessary and wasteful programs. He had initiated this early during the Kennedy administration by authorizing an overhaul of the programming and budgeting process in the Pentagon.

During his first State of the Union message on January 8, 1964, Johnson declared his "War on Poverty." The details were still being worked out, but the economic foundation—the reduced budget and the tax cut legislation—was now before Congress. Three weeks later, a request was sent to Congress for stronger housing programs and a major urban renewal effort. The tax cut was enacted in February as the Internal Revenue Act of 1964. Individual taxes were cut by almost one-fifth and corporate taxes, by one-tenth. Johnson's domestic agenda was now in high gear.

THE TAX CUT AND FISCAL STIMULATION

Arthur Okun, a member of the Council of Economic Advisers, noted: "[The tax cut] was the largest stimulative fiscal action ever undertaken by the federal government in peacetime."[13] The result was a major stimulus to the economy. Consumer spending on goods and services increased; investment also grew. As a result, unemployment would fall from around 6 percent to 4.7 percent within the next year.[14] The economists felt vindicated when they could point to declining unemployment with no apparent sign of inflation. The economy's expansion from 1964 through the first half of 1965 was unprecedented. This expansion coincided with the beginning of the president's War on Poverty and the passage of much of the Great Society legislation. Greater revenue was brought into the federal treasury and the federal budget had a surplus in the first half of 1965.

The economic outlook was very rosy, and no obstacles, domestic or foreign, seemed in sight. Kermit Gordon gave Robert McNamara the following economic assumptions, in anticipation of preliminary FY1966 (July 1, 1965–June 30, 1966) budget preparations, in April 1964: "For the purpose of preparing program statements and budget projections, we suggest using the following assumptions: 1) that the current economic recovery will continue without interruption, but relatively full employment (4 percent unemployed) may not be reached until early in the calendar year 1966; 2) that domestic prices—on the average—will remain generally at their present levels; 3) that present classified salary scales will continue; and 4) that international tensions and our international objectives will not change substantially."[15] Gordon made it clear to the defense secretary that budget preparations for FY 1966 reflected assumptions of both continued growth and no major military change.

In 1964 the country was in the midst of an economic expansion that would break the previous peacetime record of 50 months by May 1965. Johnson's economic planners believed that the expansion would continue, but in a controlled manner with just a little restrained growth to prevent the economy from overheating. Most of the Administration economists in 1964 fully believed that the economy would level off in 1965, and some even predicted a recession after so many months of growth. What did not concern them was too much growth, although they were aware that a sudden rise in military spending would seriously threaten the pace of economic growth by greatly overheating the economy. But in 1964 they had no reason to believe that such a change in the U.S. military posture was imminent. In fact, it would not be until the end of 1965 that they would be given any reason to believe any major military changes were imminent. This was critical because if expectations grew that the American military role in Vietnam might expand significantly, the business and industry communities would continue to increase orders to meet the perceived military needs, thus contributing to the strong possibility of an overheated economy. The consequences of an overheated economy, which would be borne out by the end of 1965, are usually inflationary prices and a rise in interest rates. Under such circumstances, even as the economy expanded, a great many Americans would experience an actual reduction in their real net worth.[16] In spite of the strong economic growth and prosperity of 1964 and 1965, by 1968 prices would be their worst in 18 years, and the net worth of Americans would decline.

One major reason that the unforeseen war in Vietnam had such a negative impact on the economy, even though only 2 to 3 percent of the gross national product (GNP) was devoted to the war, lay in the fact that the United States escalated just as the country had gotten about as close to full employment as possible. The almost perfect economic conditions prescribed and achieved by the administration economists were also fragile conditions. So, in 1965, even a 3 percent increase in total demand was too much for the economy without leading to inflation.[17]

Because the concern of the economic policymakers was that the rate of expansion might begin to slow down, not overheat, in August 1964 the Council of Economic Advisers recommended to the president that consideration be given in the 1966 budget to further fiscal stimuli through increased government expenditures, further tax cuts, or some combination of the two.[18] The November 1964 Troika review again urged the president to consider excise tax cuts and other fiscal stimuli in FY 1966.

· The economy overheated after mid-1965 because of increased military demands on the economy's resources overlaid on the already strong growth and prosperity continually pushed by the administration. From 1961 through the beginning of 1965, the economy grew steadily while prices remained stable. In 1965 the economy was growing at a healthy rate of $10 billion per quarter. GNP soared from $500 billion in 1961 to over $650 billion in 1965, and the consumer-price index rose by less than 2 percent each of the preceding three years.[19] Actually, the 1965 rise in GNP far exceeded the January forecast. This was due to much stronger business investment. During the first half of the year, more revenues than had been anticipated from higher individual and corporate incomes came into the federal treasury. This brought the federal budget into surplus (on a national accounts basis).[20] Then, the unexpected rise in military needs greatly stimulated the economy, especially in the second half of 1965. In 1964 and the first half of 1965, this possibility was simply not foreseen because the economists were unaware of the changing U.S. military policy in Vietnam. So they continually pushed for fiscal stimulation.

It is important to understand that in the first two years of his presidency, Johnson listened carefully to his economic advisers. Many analysts have argued that the CEA in particular carried great influence with the president during that time. As a result of Johnson's faith in the CEA, it maintained a highly visible role and worked hard to build support for the new economic policies. The success of the tax cut and the resulting economic prosperity, which were the keys to convincing Congress that the Great Society was feasible and affordable, gave the CEA and, to a lesser extent, the Bureau of the Budget and the Treasury Department tremendous credibility with the president. Arthur Okun claimed that the CEA in this period was "riding about as high a crest of esteem and respect for the success of the tax cut as has ever been achieved."[21]

THE ISSUE OF VIETNAM

Therefore, in mid-December 1963, when the president dispatched McNamara to head a fact-finding mission to Saigon, Johnson was gearing up to launch his domestic initiatives and was putting most of his energies in laying the economic base for this. McNamara reported to Johnson that "the situation is very disturbing" and that unless current trends were reversed in the next few months, a communist takeover of South Vietnam was likely.[22] In the midst of his domestic planning, the president could afford neither the collapse of South Vietnam nor the diversion of many resources to saving it.

South Vietnam had become an increasingly frustrating policy problem for U.S. foreign policy makers in the Kennedy administration. The changes in the Saigon government with the death of Diem created further domestic instability in the South. Greater U.S. assistance was given in the belief that it could reverse such deterioration. Yet the increased American presence did not improve the political situation in the South, and the continued communist insurgency became bolder and more directly tied to North Vietnam. By the beginning of 1964, it was all the United States could do to keep the South Vietnamese government propped up and the communists at bay. There was no thought given at this time to a substantial increase in the American presence or U.S. military assistance, but military planners and foreign policy advisers were seeking low-cost actions that could improve the situation in South Vietnam. While McNamara's memo stated that "U.S. resources and personnel cannot usefully be substantially increased," he wrote that plans for covert action into North Vietnam, including "a wide variety of sabotage and psychological operations," had been prepared. Known as Operation Plan 34A, these clandestine military operations against North Vietnam were directed and prepared by the United States and carried out by South Vietnamese forces. The first raids began in February 1964 and were to play a significant role during the summer.

Yet even as events deteriorated in South Vietnam, there was hope in January and February 1964 that the U.S. presence would be reduced. Robert McNamara noted in congressional testimony on February 4 that 1,000 U.S. military advisers had been withdrawn from South Vietnam, and he was optimistic that more could be withdrawn "later this year and certainly next year."[23] McNamara emphasized that "this is a war that the Vietnamese must fight . . . I don't believe we can take on that combat task for them. I do believe we can carry out training. We can provide advice and logistical assistance." He noted that expanded training of the South Vietnamese armed forces began in 1961 and should be completed by the end of 1965. After that, "we should bring our men back." President Johnson also made a similar pronouncement. Optimism within the administration had been heightened at the end of January, when General Nguyen Khanh seized power in a bloodless coup against the post-Diem military junta. U.S. Ambassador Henry Cabot Lodge noted in a memo to secretary of state Dean Rusk how impressed he was with Khanh and claimed that the general was clearly "more able" than his predecessors and was particularly better than Diem.[24]

The prospects for a stronger and more stable government in Saigon were short-lived. The Central Intelligence Agency (CIA), suspicious of the upbeat information sent to the White House, dispatched a special group of experts to Saigon in mid-February under Deputy Director Lyman Kirkpatrick. They concluded that the situation had rapidly worsened.[25] The Viet Cong were making substantial gains in the countryside and were significantly increasing the quantity and quality of their arms. As a result of the CIA report and the growing consensus within the military and foreign policy bureaucracies that the state of affairs in South Vietnam was quite grave, Secretary McNamara returned to Vietnam in March. After his visit, he concluded that the situation was "unquestionably" worse than it had been in the fall of 1963.[26]

SEEKING WAYS TO STOP THE DETERIORATION IN VIETNAM

President Johnson and his foreign policy advisers began to discuss the possibility and desirability of an expanded U.S. role in Vietnam by the time McNamara went to South Vietnam in March. This was a shift away from simply providing advice and resources in helping the South defend against the Viet Cong guerrillas. The primary change was a new policy emphasis on stopping North Vietnam from aiding the Viet Cong directly and a growing consensus that punishing Hanoi was critical. As a result, Johnson directed that "contingency planning for pressures against North Vietnam should be speeded up," particularly those that could "produce the maximum credible deterrent effect on Hanoi."[27] The president and most of his advisers believed that a modest increase in American resources would turn the tide of the deteriorating situation in South Vietnam, either by strengthening the Saigon government or by deterring the communists. This line of thinking was the basis for a decision-making process that would consistently emphasize maximum deterrence at minimum cost. As Vietnam War scholar George Herring has noted, "Johnson and his top advisers shared the major tenets of limited war theory."[28]

The president established an interdepartmental Vietnam Coordinating Committee in February, which explored potential uses of force: (1) covert actions; (2) overt U.S. deployment and actions not directed against North Vietnam; and (3) overt U.S. actions against North Vietnam. Also included in these plans was the draft text of a congressional resolution authorizing military force. One analyst has called this memorandum, which laid out the contingencies and priorities, "the first comprehensive plan for expanding the Vietnam war, and for using overt military force against North Vietnam."[29]

While such planning went forward, President Johnson remained publicly unenthusiastic about any kind of escalation: "The only thing I know to do is more of the same and do it more efficiently and effectively."[30] He did not want to embark on a major change of policy, a theme that would become increasingly prevalent in the next year and a half. Johnson was also quite conscious in early 1964 that he had succeeded a martyred president. He did not want to be seen as out of step with Kennedy's policies, nor did he wish to be perceived as a warmonger, since 1964 was a presidential election year. Vietnam was not yet firmly planted in the public consciousness, so little would be gained by trumpeting the potential escalation in an area of the world few cared about. So he talked tough in order to appear determined to stand firm against communist aggression and prevent the fall of South Vietnam, yet he was reluctant to make any significant policy changes.

When McNamara returned from Vietnam, he recommended that plans be drawn up for both retaliatory bombing strikes and a sustained bombing program. For the first time, the United States put together a program that called for considerable enlargement of the military effort. The basis for this was stated in NSAM (National Security Action Memorandum) 288: "[T]he official recognition that the situation in Vietnam was considerably worse than had been realized . . . involved an assumption by the United States of a greater part of the task, and an increased involvement by the United States in the internal affairs of South Vietnam, and for these reasons it carried with it an enlarged commitment of U.S. prestige to the success of our effort in that area."[31] The possibility of using American soldiers was then explored in the White House and in the Department of Defense. However, the emphasis remained on using American airpower if there was a need for increased military pressure.

It should be emphasized that too much can be made of the government's exploration of military contingencies. Bureaucracies commonly create options, but that in no way implies policy. Policy is made at the top, and while the president was certainly aware of many of the plans, he had made no decision about the long-term U.S. military role. Chester Cooper of the National Security Council (NSC) staff noted that the exploration by the Vietnam Coordinating Committee and other review committees was:

basically to examine all options to see if we could get out of the apparent rut. These options included, among other things, bombing attacks on North Vietnam. We also examined possible contingencies, the "what if" kind of thing. And as a consequence of that there were a lot of plans, some of them quite wild, and some quite moderate, involving a much larger American military commitment in Vietnam . . . including land troops; including naval blockade; and everything. But like many prepared papers in Washington, these were not recommended policies, these were just an exploration of possible military contingencies that might have to be met.[32]

Increased military pressure and American air power was discussed by Secretary McNamara in an informal session before the Senate Foreign Relations Committee on March 26. He stated that new military pressures would not require more U.S. forces in Vietnam because the United States would attack by air.[33] While the use of American soldiers was discussed publicly in Washington, there was a presumption by most policymakers and observers that the United States should avoid becoming embroiled in an Asian land war.

In addition, the United States increased its economic assistance to South Vietnam in the belief that more American resources would help stabilize the government in South Vietnam. During an April 22 NSC meeting, McNamara emphasized that "we should pour in resources now even if some of them were wasted because of the terrific cost that would be involved if we had to use U.S. forces."[34] Such economic assistance was granted, even though U.S. officials were highly critical of the lax approach of the Khanh government toward controlling its budget and the late and inefficient disbursal of American aid in the past.[35] The Americans continued to pursue different approaches to the Vietnamese conflict, from covert operations to aid, in the hope that something would take hold and arrest the serious decline of the American client in South Vietnam.

While increased U.S. involvement did little good, plans for military and political options moved forward, and the United States continued to pass new military action thresholds. On May 21 the U.S. military began reconnaissance flights over communist-held territory in Laos, and American personnel flew combat missions in planes of the Laotian air force. The Seventh Fleet and U.S. troops based on Okinawa were put on alert. At the same time, President Johnson ordered that a military plan and a political plan be drawn up for his consideration. Four working groups were established to do so. One group drafted, according to McGeorge Bundy, alternative congressional resolutions: "[S]uch a resolution is essential before we act against North Vietnam, but that it should be sufficiently general in form not to commit you to any particular action ahead of time."[36]

Based on the conclusions of these working groups, Johnson's key advisers recommended military action as other avenues continued to fail. McGeorge Bundy, in a May 25 memo on behalf of the president's top foreign policy advisers, talked of air attacks and possible troop deployments: "[A] decision to use force if necessary, backed by resolute and extensive deployment, and conveyed by every possible means to our adversaries, gives the best present chance of avoiding the actual use of such force."[37] He added that if such an option was required, "it is our recommendation that these deployments be on a very large scale, from the beginning, so as to maximize their deterrent impact and their menace."

The implication of this course of action was that the threat of bringing the considerable might of the U.S. military to bear on the conflict should have a substantial impact on the calculations of the North Vietnamese. Hanoi had to be convinced that the United States would use its military might to prevent the further erosion of South Vietnam by the communist insurgency. No numbers were mentioned in Bundy's memorandum, and its purpose seems to have been to convince the President that the situation in Vietnam was desperate, and that, in order to preserve the American commitment, serious military actions needed to be considered and prepared. Embodied in these policy papers was the collective judgment of the president's foreign policy experts that to back away from the commitment to South Vietnam would be a major defeat for American prestige and interests.

McGeorge Bundy strongly cautioned that if the United States engaged in "selective and carefully prepared military action against North Vietnam," then the United States must accept "the risk of escalation toward major land war or the use of nuclear weapons . . . or the risk of a reply in South Vietnam itself which would lose that country to neutralism and so eventually to communism." The recommendations in both the Bundy and the May 22 working group memos had not been combined with any of the existing contingency plans of the military. But it was clear, even in the late spring of 1964, that if the communists were not deterred, a major land war was a serious possibility.

A month later, General Paul Harkins, head of Military Assistance Command Vietnam (MACV), was replaced by General William Westmoreland. Harkin had resisted an expansion of military advisers in Vietnam and believed a larger U.S. presence was a disadvantage.[38] At the end of June, Westmoreland requested 900 additional U.S. military advisers and, a few weeks later, 4,200 military personnel for administrative and logistical support. The President approved this buildup, but no new forces were actually sent until after the November election. When the military informed McNamara in early August that they could not complete the buildup by September 30, he canceled it. Apparently not wanting a buildup to proceed in October, he did not bring it up again until after the election.[39]

SOCIAL SUCCESS

Throughout the spring of 1964, as the military and foreign policy advisers came to the conclusion that the United States had to escalate its military commitment in Vietnam, the president was creating major changes in American domestic politics. A week before the 1964 tax cut was signed into law, the Senate began to consider the Civil Rights bill. Jack Valenti noted that civil rights legislation was Johnson's second priority after the tax cut.[40] The White House worked very closely with the pro-civil rights Senate leadership in the development of strategy to ensure passage of the measure. The key was to get the bill (which was, in fact, a House resolution) to the Senate floor without going through the Judiciary Committee, chaired by Senator James Eastland of Mississippi, a staunch opponent of civil rights. Through a month of parliamentary maneuvers, the bill made it to the floor, and then Senator Richard Russell of Georgia led a 57-day filibuster. But the supporters of the bill, in close consultation with the White House and one of the foremost practitioners of parliamentary procedure—the president himself—eventually wore down the opponents.

Johnson's role in the eventual passage of the Civil Rights bill cannot be overemphasized. Joseph Califano claimed that in 1964 the president "devoted a staggering amount of his time, energy, and political capital to breaking the Senate filibuster and passing the act."[41] He would not compromise on any part of the bill, thus not allowing amendments that could weaken it. Also, "[Johnson] was prepared to sacrifice all other legislative action in the Senate and keep the debate on civil rights going . . . . if need be, he would summon Congress back in special session after the nominating conventions and hold it in Washington until the opposition let the measure come to a vote."[42] Johnson personally took the case for the Civil Rights Act around the country to rally the people behind it. Finally, on July 2, after the opposition gave in, the Civil Rights Act was signed.

The president and his domestic advisers were also very busy with the proposed legislation for the new programs of the Great Society. Johnson had announced the goal of transforming America into the Great Society on May 22, 1964, at the commencement address at the University of Michigan. At the heart of the administration's goals were urban renewal, increased housing, and improved education and better educational opportunities. In addition, as part of the War on Poverty, the White House sent legislation up to Congress for increased job training and opportunities.

Within the first six months of 1964, President Johnson had created an incredible national agenda for change in American society. The president's popularity was tremendous; his approval rating was consistently higher than 70 percent from March through June.[43] As one analyst later noted, "Here was a political leader in a position of apparently impregnable strength. He had to decide how to spend national resources that were growing at the rate of 5 percent a year. His economic advisers were telling him they had discovered the secret of perpetual growth."[44] The president and his administration felt that a Great Society could truly be created, and there was no time to lose. All attention and available resources should be devoted to the domestic agenda. Hopefully, the deteriorating situation in Vietnam would prove only an inconvenience.

The momentum leading up to the Democratic Nominating Convention that summer was staggering. The Great Society seemed possible. Vietnam was a distant conflict, a minor irritant at worst, and the Civil Rights filibuster had been broken. The media were generally laudatory in their treatment of Johnson, while usually critical, even contemptuous of the likely Republican nominee, Barry Goldwater. Johnson was hailed for the successes of the first half of 1964 and the possibilities for the future, yet he also avoided being tarred with the failures of the Kennedy administration (such as the Bay of Pigs fiasco and stalled or unsuccessful legislation packages). Economic and domestic success was key to the president's reelection. Any significant policy changes regarding Vietnam could only hurt the re-election effort. Therefore, decisions on Vietnam were usually taken when they would do the least damage to the domestic agenda. For example, the plans for a congressional resolution on Vietnam initially drafted by the Vietnam Coordinating Committee were deferred until after the Republican convention and the passage of the Civil Rights bill.

MIXED SIGNALS

Determined that South Vietnam must not fall to communism, while at the same time, the conflict in Vietnam should in no way divert attention or resources from the domestic agenda meant for President Johnson that the ability to influence congressional and public opinion was very important. Vietnam had begun to seep into the political and public consciousness. During the spring and early summer of 1964, congressional debate about the U.S. role and especially the potential use of American force greatly increased. Some conservatives argued that the administration was not doing enough to prevent communist gains in the South, while liberals cautioned against increased military involvement and argued that President Johnson was pushing the United States toward war. Even as early as 1964, congressmen and senators from both perspectives agreed that the president was not, in the words of Republican congressman Melvin Laird, "completely forthright" about the planning his administration was undertaking.[45]

The standard administration line was, in the words of Secretary McNamara, that this was a "South Vietnamese war." McNamara had been asked by

Congressman Samuel Stratton of the House Armed Services Committee in late January about why the administration contemplated the planned withdrawal of U.S. forces by the end of 1965 when the situation had worsened since the fall of 1963.[46] McNamara replied that the primary responsibility for winning the war lay with the South Vietnamese and that the United States was there only to give advice and assistance. The public optimism of McNamara and other key advisers masked their uncertainty about the situation in Vietnam and what U.S. policy should be. While Congress wanted a clearer picture of where the policy was going, its members did little to challenge the administration. A majority in Congress strongly supported the overall administration policy of not losing South Vietnam to communism, but there was no consensus on how the United States should achieve that. As with the Administration, there was a reluctance to act but a fear of giving up.

More and more, Vietnam had become the dominant foreign policy issue. Senator Wayne Morse, Democrat of Oregon, clamored that the United States was being dragged unwittingly into a war in Southeast Asia. Congressman Laird accused President Johnson of misleading the people about the extent of his plans to escalate U.S. military involvement, implying that Johnson was doing so to appear moderate while, in fact, he was planning to do many of the very things the Republican presidential candidate Barry Goldwater was urging. Other congressmen and senators of both parties strongly urged the White House to pursue a political settlement so that the United States would not get sucked further into the conflict. There is no evidence to suggest that President Johnson had made any decision about what his ultimate policy toward Vietnam would be or any indication that he felt he had to make any decision soon. He encouraged the continued exploration of different military and political options without any foregone conclusions about which way he was leaning.

A CONGRESSIONAL RESOLUTION

Just as military contingency plans were being drawn up, legal and constitutional rationales were also generated to cover any military actions. On June 29, at the president's request, the State Department legal staff prepared a brief on the presidential authority to use armed force. In essence, the legal position was that congressional authority was not needed to deploy American troops in South Vietnam. However, it was then believed by most of the president's top advisers that congressional support would be critical for any direct military action on the part of the United States. Secretary of state Rusk also prepared a memo for the president in which he outlined how to justify sending American fighting forces into Vietnam under international law.[47] Although no decision to go to war was imminent, memos to the president, in particular from McNamara, and notes of NSC meetings show that Johnson was certainly aware of the plans for greater U.S. military involvement that were being prepared by the defense and foreign affairs bureaucracies.[48] For the time being, none of Johnson's senior advisers, except Marine Corps Commandant

General Wallace Greene and air force chief of staff General Curtis LeMay, recommended any increase in U.S. military action.

William Bundy had written in March 1964 that the proposed military actions "would normally require a declaration of war under the Constitution. But this seems a blunt instrument carrying heavy domestic overtones and above all not suited to the picture of punitive and selective action only."[49] The key issue surrounding any congressional resolution was not what type of resolution the president would need from Congress but rather its timing and context. Timing was critical because emotional debate and critical votes on domestic legislation had the full attention of Congress during the spring and summer of 1964. The key was to be in a position to have, in the words of McGeorge Bundy, "a free choice on the timing of such a resolution."[50] It was important, therefore, that Congress keep its attention focused on Johnson's legislative program.

McGeorge Bundy, informing the president of the consensus of his top advisers, noted in June: "The immediate watershed decision is whether or not the Administration should seek a congressional resolution giving general authority for action which the President may judge necessary to defend the peace and security of the area. It is agreed that if such a resolution is sought, it should be general in tone. It is also agreed that the best available time for such a move is immediately after the Civil Rights bill clears the Senate floor. Finally, it is agreed that no such resolution soundings indicate rapid passage by a very substantial majority."[51] There was also concern that if the White House sought a resolution prior to the July Republican convention it would appear to be responding to the hard line of Senator Goldwater. Finally, the president had no compelling reason to go before Congress at that point (i.e., no specific or articulated need to escalate militarily), nor was there a coherent, long-term policy toward Vietnam that would require congressional authority to use American military force. As McGeorge Bundy indicated, a resolution debate might not be quick, and the votes might not be easy to sway. A protracted debate could divert attention from the domestic agenda and damage the president's Vietnam policies, his prestige, and perhaps even his reelection prospects. President Johnson and his advisers wanted to control public and congressional opinion so that, even as they had no clear idea at all of what policy to pursue in Vietnam, they would not be forced to take any action as a result of a groundswell of support for any one particular policy option. In fact, Johnson wanted to avoid any debate altogether so that the focus remained on domestic affairs.

Thus, in the summer of 1964, it was to the president's advantage that the issue of Vietnam remain in the background, unless some event or change occurred that was dramatic enough to coalesce the Congress around one particular course of action. Congress would either be on board or out of the way, depending on how one looked at it. But until such an event arose, Johnson desired to play down the issue of Vietnam, in large measure because he was unsure what to do and felt trapped by the continued deterioration in

South Vietnam, which necessitated some U.S. action in order to maintain U.S. credibility by standing against communist expansion. Again, the administration and the President clearly appeared to be thinking in terms of if the United States had to escalate, military plans notwithstanding. William Bundy later noted that a congressional resolution was rejected in mid-June because "the need for a resolution was impossible to explain adequately to the Congress and the public."[52]

While the president deferred any definitive action, military preparations and buildup continued. This was intended to convince Hanoi and to reassure South Vietnam of the seriousness and durability of the U.S. commitment, without, according to *The Pentagon Papers* authors, "arousing undue anxieties domestically in the United States in a Presidential election year."[53] These activities included pre-positioning of stockpiles in Thailand and the Philippines and the forward deployment of a carrier task force and land-based tactical aircraft within close striking distance of Vietnam. These were not considered of much consequence by most in the United States. At the same time, increasing numbers of coastal raids under OPLAN 34A were carried out. The covert raids were executed by South Vietnamese commandos under the leadership of American military advisers and CIA operatives. Most members of Congress and the press were unaware of these clandestine activities.

THE TONKIN GULF INCIDENT

The Tonkin Gulf Resolution has been held up by many as evidence of the president's secret intention to go to war in Vietnam without congressional approval or a declaration of war.[54] However, there is little evidence for any conspiratorial theory, and it truly appears that the great commitment, in terms of manpower and matériel, was not yet envisioned by President Johnson. There is no evidence that in the summer of 1964 he had any intention of getting involved in a land war in Southeast Asia. While the military prepared to escalate if necessary, Johnson's greatest desire appeared to be securing congressional support and consensus for his policies in Vietnam without a great debate over priorities. Robert McNamara has written that without the action in the Tonkin Gulf, a congressional resolution on Vietnam "would have faced far more extensive debate, and there would have been attempts to limit the president's authority."[55]

On July 15 the NSC apparently decided to resume De Soto patrols in two weeks. These were intelligence-gathering forays off the North Vietnamese coast, last carried out in March. An additional purpose for the De Soto operations was to send occasional destroyer patrols deep into the Tonkin Gulf to show the flag and, in particular, to assert the right of free passage in international waters—which the North Vietnamese claimed to be 12 miles offshore and the United States 3 miles. On July 31 the destroyer *Maddox*, equipped with sophisticated electronic equipment, was dispatched to gather military intelligence, especially information on North Vietnam's radar systems.[56]

For the first time, a De Soto patrol was run concurrently with the 34A raids on the North Vietnamese coast. A series of 34A raids was carried out on the North Vietnamese islands of Hon Me and Hon Niem on the night of July 30. The next day, the *Maddox* came into the Tonkin Gulf. On August 2 it was fired upon by three North Vietnamese torpedo boats. There is no doubt about this attack and the fact that the *Maddox* sank one of the torpedo boats and damaged the other two. The U.S. response was to provide additional support to the *Maddox* by sending the destroyer *Turner Joy* into the Tonkin Gulf on August 3. In Washington the president ordered no retaliation but firmly stated that the United States would not back down.

However, unbeknownst to the public or to Congress, another 34A operation was scheduled for the night of August 3. In fact, top U.S. foreign policy advisers agreed that there was a direct correlation between the previous 34A raids and the attack on the *Maddox*. Secretary Rusk, in a cable to Ambassador Taylor in Saigon, noted: "We believe that present OPLAN 34A activities are beginning to rattle Hanoi, and MADDOX incident is directly related to their efforts to resist these activities . . . . We have no intention of yielding to pressure."[57] The White House told Congress that the *Maddox* had gone inside the 12-mile limit claimed by Hanoi, and the issue was one of preserving the right of free passage in international waters. No mention of intelligence operations was made, and the administration claimed the attack was completely unprovoked.

Behind the scenes, the story was very different. During an NSC meeting on August 4, after reports of a second attack, CIA director John McCone emphasized that the North Vietnamese had not tried to provoke the United States but simply reacted defensively to the 34A raids.[58] In addition, the commander of the *Maddox*, John Herrick, had been monitoring North Vietnamese communications and cabled the commander of the Pacific fleet (CINCPAC) that the North considered the U.S. ships a part of the 34A raids.[59]

On August 4, the *Maddox* reported another attack on it as well as on the *Turner Joy*. However, Herrick quickly amended the reports, stating that the torpedo firings may have been erroneous, due to both human and electronic error. As a result, there are serious doubts as to whether the August 4 attacks ever occurred.[60] But there is no doubt that administration officials misled Congress and the public. Secretary of defense McNamara failed to mention anything of the 34A raids in testimony before the Senate Foreign Relations Committee: "The *Maddox* was operating in international waters, was carrying out a routine patrol of the type we carry out all over the world at all times."[61] He later claimed to have learned of the August 3 34A raids only after his August 6 testimony before Congress. That seems very implausible since Westmoreland sent him a cable on August 4 reporting on those raids.[62]

The administration was so anxious to retaliate that it did not wait for clear confirmation of the August 4 attacks. Three hours after the first report came in, the president ordered that preparations be made for an air strike. Shortly thereafter, the Defense Department received Commander Herrick's message of doubt that the attack actually took place. Most of the afternoon of August 4 was spent simultaneously preparing for the retaliatory strike and trying to pin down what actually happened in the Tonkin Gulf. By this time, the president and his key advisers were all aware that the military lacked confirmation of the attacks. When the president met with the National Security Council at the end of the day, McNamara told him that the Pentagon would know definitely what happened in the morning. A few minutes later, with the concurrence of all present, Johnson ordered the air strike. Shortly thereafter, the U.S. Air Force began a series of reprisal air bombings on the North, the first such American actions in the conflict.

THE TONKIN GULF RESOLUTION

Upon ordering the air strikes, the president met with a delegation of 16 congressional leaders and briefed them on the attack (which, again, had not been confirmed) and on the order to retaliate. With the exception of Senator Mike Mansfield, all present voiced their support for the president's actions. Johnson asked for their help in getting quick passage of the resolution in order to present a united front to the world and to demonstrate to Hanoi and Peking the determined U.S. resolve. He added: "I think it would be very damaging to ask for [congressional concurrence] and not get it . . . . I don't think any resolution is necessary, but I think it is a lot better to have it in the light of what we did in Korea."[63] Congress was boxed in politically, since the incident had been portrayed publicly only as an unprovoked attack on American ships.

It is interesting to note that the president did not feel the resolution was "necessary," at least not from a constitutional standpoint, as his legal advisers had suggested. But it was politically necessary, and the opportunity for overwhelming passage without significant debate was of particular importance. McGeorge Bundy noted later that Johnson "knew in his own mind that he had a problem of a resolution, and he seized that episode to get the resolution."[64] The president could have retaliated without any resolution, and he could have gotten a congressional resolution on Vietnam without the Tonkin Gulf incident. But either way, hard questions on costs and political priorities would have been asked on Capitol Hill, and a debate would have ensued. Such a debate was preempted by the Tonkin Gulf incident because of the apparent urgency of the situation and the need to demonstrate to the world a united resolve in Washington. Not only was there little discussion about whether the president should be granted the authority to retaliate as he deemed fit, but almost nothing was raised about what U.S. policy was or should be with respect to the Vietnam conflict.

The resolution went to Congress on August 5. The key phrase was the following: "The Congress approves and supports the determination of the President, as Commander in Chief, to take all necessary measures to repel any armed attack against the forces of the United States and to prevent further aggression."[65] Much of the subsequent escalation was to be carried out in the name of preventing further aggression by the communists. Johnson now had congressional authorization to "take all necessary steps, including the use of armed force, to assist any member . . . of the Southeast Asia Collective Defense Treaty." The president stated that he would be in constant consultation with Congress any time he planned to draw on this authority and reassured them that he would not abuse his authority and send American young men overseas to fight. Most senators and congressmen believed that Johnson's intentions were limited.

When asked by Senator Daniel Brewster whether the language of the resolution "would authorize or recommend or approve the landing of large American armies in Vietnam or in China," Senator J. William Fulbright, chairman of the Foreign Relations Committee and the manager of the bill on the Senate floor, remarked: "There is nothing in the resolution, as I read it, that contemplates it . . . . However, the language of the resolution would not prevent it. It would authorize whatever the Commander in Chief feels is necessary."[66] Once he had such a grant of power, the president never came back to Congress for anything other than military appropriations for the personnel and operations in Vietnam. Thereafter, regarding Vietnam, the president would deal only unofficially with congressmen and senators, either individually or in small groups.

For members of Congress, the key to their understanding of the Tonkin Gulf Resolution was that they trusted the president to use retaliation sparingly and continue to consult with Congress. Most of the leadership on Capitol Hill, particularly in the Senate, had been colleagues of the president, and many were personal friends. They trusted him. One senator remarked: "All Lyndon wants is a piece of paper telling him we did right out there, and we support him, and he's the kind of president who follows the rules and won't get the country into war without coming back to Congress."[67] In addition, Johnson had public opinion on his side, as polls showed strong support for the president's modest actions in light of what was believed to have happened in the Tonkin Gulf.[68] Both Democrats and Republicans had compelling reasons to support the president. The Democrats were being asked to support a seemingly moderate president right before the Democratic Party Convention and right after the Republican Party Convention, which nominated a candidate who urged greater military action in Vietnam. Democrats were wary of falling prey to conservatives who could use rejection of the resolution to declare them soft on communism. On the other hand, Republicans could hardly oppose a decision to retaliate militarily in light of the hard line many of them had been urging for some time.

For the present, the U.S. government had served notice that it was determined to respond to aggression. Sixty-four sorties were flown against torpedo boat bases, support facilities, and an oil supply depot.[69] But that was it. There was no rush by the administration to escalate under the guise of retaliation.

After the resolution passed with a near-unanimous majority, Johnson did not escalate further. He was much more cautious in the fall, although this can be attributed, in part, to the election campaign. When the De Soto patrols resumed in September, and there were unconfirmed reports of a third attack in the Tonkin Gulf, the administration suspended the patrols, rather than retaliate, demonstrating that at least at that point there was no desire to escalate.[70]

The evidence is fairly clear, however, that the administration misled Congress and the American public about what actually occurred in the Tonkin Gulf and what the American boats were doing there in the first place. One major reason for the deceit was that the administration was too quick to seize the opportunity for a possible congressional resolution before all the facts were in. The timing that the White House had been waiting for all summer seemed perfect: an unprovoked attack on American ships in international waters. But if there was an admission that the ships were actually engaged in a covert operation, the issue of an "unprovoked" attack might have been less clear-cut and resulted in a demand for debate, which the administration clearly wanted to avoid. There are those who argue that the United States provoked the attack just to get the resolution. The evidence for this is the timing of the resumption of the De Soto patrols and the fact that they ran in conjunction with the 34-A raids. The De Soto patrols were authorized by the National Security Council; thus, it was a White House decision, not a military one.

In addition, the Civil Rights bill had been signed into law on July 2 and the Republicans had just concluded their nominating convention, two events that the White House had already made clear needed to be out of the way before tackling a congressional resolution. At the same time, the Economic Opportunity Act (EOA), drafted in the White House and the cornerstone of Johnson's War on Poverty, was in its final stages on Capitol Hill.[71] It was passed by the Senate on July 23 and faced a stiff battle in the House. On July 31 special assistant to the president for legislative affairs Larry O'Brien informed Johnson that the bill was deadlocked, with 30 southern congressmen still undecided. That same night the CIA carried out the De Soto covert intelligence patrols in the Tonkin Gulf. Given the concern he had for the EOA, it would seem unlikely that Johnson wanted an incident in Vietnam just when the vote was due. One of Johnson's great fears was that conservative Democrats would push for stronger U.S. action in Vietnam. This would give them an excuse to pull their support for the Great Society, arguing that the country could not afford both. More than anything, the president wanted Congress to unite around his retaliatory actions and then return their attention to domestic needs. So it is possible that a seemingly unprovoked attack on U.S. forces might have been just what the president needed to rally conservative Democrats—on both the domestic and international fronts. On August 8, the day after the Tonkin Gulf Resolution was passed, the Economic Opportunity Act passed the House, 226 to 185. Almost all the undecided southern democrats voted with the president. Within two months, on October 3,

Congress would appropriate $800 million for the initial War on Poverty programs.

One question that continues to challenge analysts of this period is whether or not the executive branch and the Congress had fundamentally different interpretations of the Tonkin Gulf Resolution when it passed. In August 1964 neither the White House nor Congress felt the resolution was tantamount to a declaration of war or even a prelude to unilateral executive action to pursue a war. Most of the recommendations for a resolution that had come to Johnson from his advisers stressed the need for congressional support to give weight to the president's actions in Vietnam. Johnson most likely wanted a free hand, even a blank check, so that he could pursue actions in Vietnam without a debate over policy priorities and resource allocations. While the evidence shows that the United States might have been provocative, it does not appear that the administration created the Tonkin Gulf incident in order to escalate to an undeclared war later. That President Johnson later used the Tonkin Gulf Resolution as a rationale for military escalation in 1965 and beyond should not be interpreted as evidence that he contemplated major military escalation in the summer of 1964 and that this resolution was the beginning of such a blueprint.

The president's advisers had not warned him that a military solution would require a major commitment of combat forces over a number of years. Most, including the military officials, were thinking in terms of escalating through air power with a minimal commitment of ground forces. George Ball, the undersecretary of state, agreed that the presence of the U.S. destroyers in the gulf was a deliberate provocation, but he doubted "whether you could call it a conspiracy. I find that rather too strong a word. I think it was a tactical opportunity that they were looking for."[72] The issue of international waters was an important one, something the United States has not left unchallenged in other parts of the world. In addition, the covert operations had been intermittently carried out since March.

McGeorge Bundy later noted that "Congress surely did not believe, in 1964, that it was voting for the war that happened."[73] While the language of the resolution could probably be interpreted as a functional equivalent of war, that was not the understanding at the time by Congress or by most in the administration. They saw only limited, retaliatory military action. Many officials in the executive branch fully expected Congress to be consulted prior to any substantial changes in the U.S. military posture in Vietnam. That Congress was not honestly and openly consulted in early 1965 was due more to the incremental and misleading nature of the military escalation at that time than a desire beginning in August 1964 or earlier for a secret war. Much more so than his advisers, President Johnson felt no need to involve Congress in foreign policy. In fact, consultations with key congressmen and senators in 1965 were primarily window dressing.

While the president's Vietnam advisers continued to search for the best option to arrest the continuing decline in South Vietnam, Johnson continued to concentrate on domestic politics and emphasized moderation in his public speeches and appearances. During his campaign in September 1964, he vowed that "we are not about to send American boys nine or ten thousand miles away from home to do what Asian boys ought to be doing for themselves. We don't want to get . . . tied down to a land war in Asia."[74] Most people believed him, and in light of what the country believed occurred in the Tonkin Gulf, most applauded his moderate stance following the communist attacks.

During the presidential campaign, the Vietnam issues were downplayed, and the hard decisions were put on hold. Johnson and his advisers consistently positioned him in the campaign as the man of peace. The president claimed that he would be patient and not escalate the conflict, while painting Barry Goldwater as a man who was itching for war. The image of Goldwater was increasingly one of a reckless adventurer who would risk a war with China and a nuclear war over Vietnam. He made it easy, though, because his rhetoric was peppered with warlike remarks. During a late September speech by Goldwater in Indiana, Charles Mohr of the *New York Times* counted at least 30 references to "holocaust," "push the button," and "atomic weapons."[75] Most importantly, throughout the campaign there was no hint by Johnson or his advisers that any expansion of the U.S. military role in Vietnam was being considered. Johnson greatly downplayed any possibility of escalation. Overall, the war was not the focal point of the campaign, because the administration kept its military posture low-key. Yet, on October 1, McGeorge Bundy hinted to the president that the public rhetoric did not match the ongoing planning: "It is a better than even chance that we will be undertaking some air and land action in the Laotian corridor and even in North Vietnam within the next two months and we do not want the record to suggest even remotely that we campaigned on peace in order to start a war in November."[76]

For his part, the Tonkin Gulf incident notwithstanding, the president never focused much in 1964 on overall (and future) Vietnam policy. The domestic agenda remained his priority then, not Vietnam. During the fall, Johnson's attention was primarily occupied with the election campaign and his domestic programs. According to Jack Valenti, Johnson was busy "laying the groundwork for this overwhelming avalanche of constructive legislation that poured on the 89th Congress beginning with January 2, 1965."[77] Overall, Vietnam still remained a remote problem for President Johnson.

THINKING LONG-TERM

By the end of the summer of 1964, it had become increasingly clear within the Johnson administration that the "Asian boys," as represented by the South Vietnamese armed forces, were not getting the job done. The United States was unable to strengthen the South, either psychologically or militarily, so that the government could mount a sufficient defense against the Viet Cong aggression that was supported and supplemented by the North Vietnamese. At the end of August, General Khanh, against the strong advice of the U.S. Embassy, declared a state of emergency, which paved the way for a series of protests by students and Buddhists over the next few days. Six demonstrators were killed by soldiers, and Khanh was at first forced to resign. He then joined two other generals to form a ruling triumvirate until a permanent government could be installed.

With the growing frustration within the administration over the instability in South Vietnam, a number of contradictory proposals were advanced in the fall of 1964. A memo that circulated in mid-August by Walt Rostow, head of policy planning at the State Department, argued for "limited, graduated military actions reinforced by political and economic pressures" on North Vietnam. The objective "is not necessarily to attack his ability to provide support . . . . Rather, the objective is to affect his calculation of interests. Therefore, the threat that is implicit in initial U.S. actions would be more important than the military effect of the actions themselves."[78] The implication of such a position was that whatever action was taken was not nearly as important as the mere fact that some action, any action, took place. Such thinking was to become a common rationale for military decisions over the next year.

A critique of Rostow's memo was circulated by the Office of the Secretary of Defense and the Office of International Security Affairs. It argued that if the enemy was not persuaded to recalculate its interests "the approach might well fail to be effective short of a larger U.S. military involvement."[79] The critique also noted that accepting the Rostow strategy of limited, graduated military action would require making it public before applying it. This would lead to a public and congressional debate and the possible "public expression of domestic and allied opposition and denunciation."[80] The core argument of the Pentagon memo was that such a policy would be difficult to sell if it became part of U.S. declaratory policy. A major policy debate would most likely ensue. Although much of Rostow's approach of graduated, limited escalation became the military policy in Vietnam in 1965, the Johnson administration never declared it as such and worked hard to avoid making such a strategy public.

THE POSSIBILITY OF DEPLOYING GROUND FORCES

At this time, serious discussion of combat forces slowly crept into the Vietnam debate. On August 31, McGeorge Bundy had written to the president: "A still more drastic possibility which no one is discussing is the use of substantial U.S. armed forces in operations against the Viet Cong. I myself believe that before we let this country go we should have a hard look at the grim alternative, and I do not at all think that it is a repetition of Korea. It seems to me at least possible that a couple of brigade-size units put in to do specific jobs about six weeks from now might be good medicine everywhere."[81] Assistant secretary of defense John McNaughton, in a September 3 memo entitled "Plan of Action for South Vietnam," wrote that new initiatives might include the establishment of a U.S. naval base, possibly at Danang, and a proposal for "large numbers of US special forces, divisions of regular combat troops, US air, etc., to 'interlard' with or to take over functions or geographical areas from the South Vietnamese armed forces."[82]

As political instability continued in South Vietnam, the military situation worsened. The communists had not been deterred, and the possibility that South Vietnam might collapse was increasingly real. As many analysts have explained, Johnson and his advisers greatly underestimated the resolve of the Vietnamese communists. They also did not seem to realize how divided and demoralized the population of the South had become, in particular because of the incredibly corrupt, incompetent government and military leaders (who were becoming more and more interchangeable).

But there was no agreement within the administration about what should be done. George Ball remarked, "There wasn't any consensus. There were a lot of people thinking . . . 'This situation is not good. Let's think of all the contingencies.' And everybody who was working on South Vietnam was writing papers about this or that type of program."[83] But there was a growing sense of inevitability that the United States would have to escalate its military involvement.[84]

Most of the president's advisers favored limited measures, including the resumption of U.S. naval patrols in the Tonkin Gulf and 34A raids and preparations for tit-for-tat responses against North Vietnam for any attack on U.S. units or special actions (not specified) against South Vietnam.[85] Although most of those who attended the September 9 NSC meeting were frustrated by the increasing communist gains, only air force chief John McConnell and marine commandant Wallace Greene favored immediate military escalation. According to the meeting notes, Johnson was quoted as saying, "'[T]he reason for waiting, then, must be simply that with a weak and wobbly situation it would be unwise to attack until we could stabilize our base.' . . . [Johnson] did not wish to enter the patient in a 10-round bout, when he was in no shape to hold out for one round. We should get him ready to face 3 or 4 rounds at least."[86] There was also a growing expectation by the administration's advisers that the president would act once his anticipated reelection occurred.

George Ball, in early October, challenged the assumption that military action was necessary and inevitable. He wrote a memo to Rusk, McNamara, and McGeorge Bundy in which he strongly criticized the presumption "that America cannot afford to promote a settlement in South Viet-Nam without first demonstrating the superiority of its own military power."[87] He concluded that a review of the administration's Vietnam policy and a challenge to its underlying assumptions were necessary "before we commit military forces to a line of action that could put events in the saddle and destroy our freedom to choose the policies that are at once the most effective and the most prudent." One of Ball's primary concerns was the possibility that the United States would "take over the war by the injection of substantial U.S. ground forces . . . the worst of both worlds."[88]

But Ball had almost no allies within the top levels of government bureaucracy who agreed with his warnings. By the fall of 1964, most of the "doves" whose views had considerable weight in the Kennedy administration— men such as Averell Harriman, Roger Hilsman, and Paul Kattenburg of State and Michael Forrestal of the NSC—were either gone or had diminished power. Those who might have dissented from the growing coalition for escalation had been pushed aside.

Therefore, as the situation in Vietnam worsened, almost all of the key advisers from State, Defense, and the NSC—such as William Bundy, who took over for Hilsman as assistant secretary of state for Far Eastern affairs; McNaughton, who succeeded Bundy at the Pentagon; and Rostow, who took over policy planning in the State Department—were more willing to consider military escalation. Most emphasized bombing, but some pushed for combat troops. Only a few voices urged caution and questioned the need for escalation: midlevel staffers in the State Department such as William Trueheart, former deputy chief of mission in Saigon; Allen Whiting, deputy director of East Asian research in the State Department; Robert Johnson of the Policy Planning Council; and Carl Salans of the Legal Advisor's Office.[89]

But only George Ball, whose dissent from administration policy first emerged at the time of the Tonkin Gulf incident, had a voice at the highest levels of the government. Ball was against any deeper U.S. military involvement and warned: "It is in the nature of escalation that each move passes the option to the other side, while at the same time the party which seems to be losing will be tempted to keep raising the ante."[90] This was in contrast to Walt Rostow, who argued that massive U.S. air and naval forces should be deployed in the Pacific to strike at North Vietnam and that American troops should be sent to Vietnam promptly to show that "we are prepared to face down any form of escalation." Rostow also felt that once combat forces were on the ground, "the withdrawal of those ground forces could be a critically important part of our diplomatic bargaining position."[91]

Neither the retaliation for the Tonkin Gulf incident nor the increased pressure of U.S. covert operations seemed to have any effect on the Viet Cong as they increased guerrilla activities and began to engage in full-scale military engagements in the fall of 1964. It was becoming clearer that the North Vietnamese support of the Viet Cong did not diminish either. Four days before the U.S. presidential election, 4 American servicemen were killed and 72 wounded in a guerrilla attack on the Bien Hoa Airfield. The Bien Hoa attack served as a sobering reminder that Americans had become increasingly at risk. The Joint Chiefs of Staff (JCS) and Ambassador Taylor strongly urged the president to retaliate with air strikes on the North. But, since the attack was so close to the American election, the United States made no response.[92] It should be noted that on November 1, in considering the recommended airstrikes, Johnson asked about the advisability of deploying American ground forces in order to protect the air bases and U.S. dependents from guerrilla attacks. Johnson appeared to believe that ground troops would be a key component of any type of escalation.[93]

As the authors of *The Pentagon Papers* noted: "In their Southeast Asia policy discussions of August–October 1964, Administration officials had accepted the view that overt military pressures against North Vietnam probably would be required. Barring some critical developments, however, it was generally conceded that these should not begin until after the new year."[94] While the sustained use of force against North Vietnam became a primary policy consideration, there was no agreement on a specific program of action nor any presidential authorization to develop one. Johnson held military action in abeyance for the rest of the year due to a number of tactical considerations: the election campaign, the shakiness of the Saigon government, the uncertainty of a Chinese response, a need to design actions that would have public and congressional support, and a desire to avoid pressure for premature negotiations.

THE POST ELECTION POLICY REVIEW

Flush with victory at the polls on November 3, President Johnson felt he had received a great mandate and wanted to utilize the goodwill and confidence of the people in his leadership on all fronts, including a reinvigorated Vietnam policy. In addition to his own landslide, so many new Democratic congressmen were elected that the Democrats now had a two-thirds majority in both the Senate and the House. Johnson believed he had more political capital than ever and should soon take advantage of it with Vietnam as well as with his domestic initiatives. His advisers were increasingly urging him to turn his full attention to Vietnam. McGeorge Bundy had warned the president that immediately after the election, decisions on Vietnam that had been deliberately deferred needed full study.[95]

For most of November and early December, however, the president's focus remained almost exclusively on the domestic front, and so the foreign policy planners had to compete for his attention. Johnson acted with political force and determination with his domestic agenda. With respect to Vietnam, he knew only what he wanted to prevent: the communist takeover of the South. At the same time, he wanted the most effective and cheapest means to put pressure on Hanoi. Johnson did not give the conflict much immediate personal attention but put the bureaucracy in motion to come up with possible solutions to avoid collapse and turn the tide in Vietnam.

On the day of his reelection, Johnson established an 8-member interagency working group from the State Department, Defense Department, and the CIA to review the current situation in Vietnam and to make a series of recommendations of the needed actions to preserve U.S. interests there. The working group, chaired by William Bundy, was to report to a panel of senior officials, including Rusk, McNamara, McGeorge Bundy, and Taylor. It was not charged with questioning the basic premises of the U.S. presence in Vietnam or with determining how vital an interest South Vietnam was for the United States. The problem was not whether to do anything in Vietnam but what and when.

At the same time, President Johnson remained very intimately involved in the planning of domestic programs. While the foreign policy experts were busy with the Vietnam working group review in November and December 1964,

Johnson was huddled at his ranch in Texas with his domestic staff working on the budget. The administration's domestic team was busily determining resource allocations for the FY 1966 budget. Legislative and public relations strategies as well as economic priorities were mapped out. It seemed as if the president wanted the Great Society preparations in place before turning to the problem of Vietnam. William Bundy remarked about the work going on in Washington and Texas simultaneously: "The toughest choice of his presidency was being foreshadowed unmistakably in that beautiful Texas fall—guns versus butter, lasting peace in Asia versus making America more humane, or trying to achieve both."[96]

NOTES

1. Unemployment stood at nearly 7 percent when Kennedy took office. From February 1964 to July 1965, unemployment dropped from 5.4 percent to 4.4 percent. By December 1965, unemployment was reduced to 4.0 percent. Anything above 4 percent unemployment was considered "excess unemployment." To get below 4 percent was viewed as very difficult because of the nature of structural unemployment, which would include individuals who were in between jobs, seasonal employment, and so on. It was also considered undesirable because a figure below 4 percent would be accompanied by unstable prices. Johnson Library: BDM Corporation, *The Strategic Lessons Learned in Vietnam,* vol. 4: U.S. *Domestic Factors Influencing Vietnam War Policy Making,* p. 14.

2. Walter W. Heller, *New Dimensions of Political Economy,* p. 11.

3. Walter Heller interview, in Erwin C. Hargrove and Samuel A. Morley, *The President and the Council of Economic Advisers: Interviews with CEA Chairmen,* p. 181.

4. The Committee for Economic Development, *The National Economy and the Vietnam War,* p. 23.

5. Heller interview in Hargrove and Morley, *The President and the Council of Economic Advisers,* p. 206.
According to Arthur Okun, a member of the Council of Economic Advisers (CEA): "The tax cut added to demand by leaving more purchasing power in the hands of consumers and businesses. Consumers responded by spending most of that extra income for added goods and services. For businessmen investment became both more profitable and easier to finance out of internal funds. The direct stimulus of the tax cut was multiplied over time. The extra spending it generated meant more jobs and hence more incomes for many families; it strengthened markets and thus encouraged greater investment to expand capacity." (Arthur M. Okun, *The Political Economy of Prosperity,* p. 47.)

6. Johnson Library: Jack Valenti Oral History, Interview 5, July 12, 1972, p. 8.

7. November 25, 1963, meeting notes of William Carey, executive assistant director, Bureau of the Budget, National Archives: RG51, Series 52.3, Box 166—"Budget 1965—Critique of" folder.

8. Heller interview in Hargrove and Morley, *The President and the Council of Economic Advisers,* p. 210. See also Lyndon Baines Johnson, *The Vantage Point,* p. 36.

9. Valenti Oral History, Interview 2, p. 30.

10. Ibid. pp. 32–33.

11. Larry Berman. *The Office of Management and Budget and the Presidency,*

1921–1979, p. 73.

12. Vaughn Bornet. *The Presidency of Lyndon B. Johnson*, p. 100.

13. Okun, *Political Economy*, p. 47. The size of the tax cut was somewhat higher than the Eisenhower tax cut of 1954 and was about $11.5 billion.

14. Ibid. p. 47.

15. See April 7, 1964, memo from Gordon to McNamara in the Office of Management and Budget: National Security Division documents, Series 51-79-121, Box 75, Budget for 1966 folder 3.

16. See Okun, *Political Economy*, p. 97.

17. Robert Warren Stevens. *Vain Hopes, Grim Realities: The Economic Consequences of the Vietnam War*, p. 11.

18. Johnson Library: Council of Economic Advisers Administrative History, Chapter 2, pp. 10–11.

19. BDM Corporation, *Strategic Lessons*, vol. 4, p. 14.

20. Okun, *Political Economy*, p. 48.

21. Johnson Library: Arthur Okun Oral History, Interview 1, March 20, 1969, p. 14.

22. December 21, 1963, memo to the president from Robert McNamara, in *The Pentagon Papers*, Gravel edition, vol. 3, pp. 494–96.

23. *The Pentagon Papers*, Gravel edition, vol. 2, p. 194.

24. Lodge memo to Rusk, February 27, 1964, as cited in George McT. Kahin. *Intervention: How America Became Involved in Vietnam*, p. 204.

25. See *The Pentagon Papers*, vol. 3, pp. 41–42.

26. March 16, 1964, memo to the president from McNamara, in ibid. p. 501.

27. *The Pentagon Papers*, Gravel edition, vol. III, p. 154.

28. George C. Herring, *LBJ and Vietnam: A Different Kind of War*, p. 5.

29. William Conrad Gibbons, *The U.S. Government and the Vietnam War: Executive and Legislative Roles and Relationships*, Part II: 1961–1964, pp. 235–236. Most of the memo remains classified.

30. March 2, 1964, discussion with Senator J. William Fulbright, as quoted in Doris Kearns, *Lyndon Johnson and the American Dream*, p. 196.

31. *The Pentagon Papers*, Gravel edition, vol. 3, p. 50. McNamara's report on his trip to Vietnam became NSAM 288. Out of NSAM 288, the administration developed a three-phase plan, OPLAN 37, which served as the blueprint for the American bombing campaigns beginning in December 1964. It remains classified. (See ibid. p. 287.)

32. Johnson Library: Chester Cooper Oral History, Interview 1, p. 7.

33. See Gibbons, *The U.S. Government and the Vietnam War*, Part II, pp. 241-242.

34. Johnson Library: NSC files in ibid. p. 246.

35. See *The Pentagon Papers*, Gravel edition, vol. 2, p. 318.

36. May 22, 1964, McGeorge Bundy memo to the president, quoted in Gibbons, *The U.S. Government and the Vietnam War*, Part II, p. 254.

37. Memo to the president, "Basic Recommendation and Projected Course of Action on Southeast Asia," May 25, 1964, in Johnson Library: National Security File, Boxes 18/19, "Luncheons with the President," vol. 1, part 1.

38. *The Pentagon Papers*, Gravel edition, vol. 2, p. 468.

39. For details, see ibid. pp. 470–471.

40. Valenti Oral History, Tape 2, p. 35.

41. Joseph Califano, *A Presidential Nation*, p. 215.

42. Eric F. Goldman, *The Tragedy of Lyndon Johnson*, p. 68.

43. Ibid. p. 96.

44. Godfrey Hodgson, *America in Our Time*, p. 225.

45. *The Congressional Record*, vol. 110, June 2, 1964, p. 12460, as quoted in Gibbons, *The U.S. Government and the Vietnam War*, Part II, p. 265.

46. See *The Pentagon Papers*, Gravel edition, vol. 3, pp. 35–36.

47. Johnson Library: June 29, 1964, memo from Rusk to Johnson (File unknown, this memo was on loan at a special July 1987 exhibition entitled *The American Experiment: Living with the Constitution* at the National Archives).

48. See March 16, 1964 memo on "South Vietnam" from McNamara to the president in *The Pentagon Papers*, vol. 3, pp. 503–504.

49. March 1, 1964, draft memo for the president from William Bundy (who was about to move over to the State Department as assistant secretary for Far Eastern affairs), in Larry Berman, *Planning a Tragedy: The Americanization of the War in Vietnam*, p. 32.

50. May 25, 1964, memo from McGeorge Bundy to the president.

51. Johnson Library: Tab B in June 10, 1964, "Memorandum for Discussion" from McGeorge Bundy to the president, in McNaughton Papers, Book I, Box 7.

52. Johnson Library: William Bundy unpublished manuscript, chapter 13, p. 22.

53. *The Pentagon Papers*, Gravel edition, vol. 3, p. 291.

54. See Peter Dale Scott, *The War Conspiracy*; Paul Joseph, *Cracks in the Empire*, pp. 92–93.

55. Robert S. McNamara, *In Retrospect: The Tragedy and Lessons of Vietnam*, pp. 128–129.

56. De Soto patrols were first authorized by President Kennedy in 1962. The equipment was manned by personnel from the National Security Agency.

57. Washington to Saigon cable #336, National Security Files, Country File: Vietnam, in Johnson Library, as quoted in Gibbons, *The U.S. Government and the Vietnam War*, Part II, p. 287.

58. Ibid. p. 287.

59. Senate Committee on Foreign Relations, *The Gulf of Tonkin, the 1964 Incidents*, February 20, 1968, hearings, p. 40.

60. See Joseph C. Goulden, *Truth Is the First Casualty: The Gulf of Tonkin Affair—Illusion and Reality*; Eugene G. Windchy, *Tonkin Gulf*. The night had been foggy, and eyewitness accounts were inconclusive and contradictory. Sonar readings were unreliable.

61. See Goulden, *Truth Is the First Casualty*, p. 59. McNamara and Rusk briefed members of the Senate Foreign Relations and Armed Services Committees in a closed session. McNamara stated that they informed the senators about both the 34A operations and the De Soto patrol. (McNamara, *In Retrospect*, p. 131.) There were no notes of the meeting, and none of this was admitted by the administration until years later.

62. August 4, 1964, cable from Westmoreland, #040955Z, a copy of which went to McNamara, in Johnson Library: NSF Country File, Vietnam as quoted in Gibbons, *The U.S. Government and the Vietnam War*, Part II, p. 288.

63. Quoted in ibid. p. 295.

64. Congressional Research Service interview with McGeorge Bundy on January 8, 1979, quoted in Gibbons, *The U.S. Government and the Vietnam War*, Part II, p. 301.

65. *The Pentagon Papers*, New York Times edition, pp. 264–65

66. Gibbons, *The U.S. Government and the Vietnam War*, Part II, p. 322. Fulbright went on to say that the resolution did not restrain the president from sending in ground forces. He admitted that "the last thing we want to do is to become involved in a land

war in Asia; that our power is sea and air, and that this is what we hope will deter the Chinese Communists and the North Vietnamese from spreading the war" (ibid. p. 323). There appeared to be a belief that the use of American power and the potential for escalation would be limited to air power and sea power, that ground forces were beyond contemplation. That lesson had been learned in Korea.

67. Senator Wayne Morse relayed this quote to Joseph Goulden, but the unnamed senator confirmed it a few years later. (Goulden, *Truth Is the First Casualty*, p. 49.)

68. In July 58 percent of the American public criticized the president's handling of Vietnam; after the Tonkin Gulf retaliation, 72 percent supported Johnson's policies. (August 10, 1964, *Washington Post*/Louis Harris Poll, in ibid. p. 77.)

69. Stanley Karnow, *Vietnam: A History*, p. 372.

70. See Leslie Gelb, with Richard Betts, *The Irony of Vietnam: The System Worked*, p. 105.

71. The Economic Opportunity Act was a program to increase opportunities for the poor via education and training. New job opportunities were to be created so that the poor could take advantage of new economic growth being created.

72. George Ball interview, in Michael Charlton and Anthony Moncrief, *Many Reasons Why: The American Involvement in Vietnam*, p. 108.

73. Bundy testimony before Senate Committee on Foreign Relations, April 26, 1971, during Hearings on *War Powers Legislation*, p. 421.

74. Lyndon Johnson speech, September 25, 1964, *New York Times*, September 26, 1964, p. A1.

75. See Theodore H. White, *The Making of the President 1964*, p. 325.

76. October 1, 1964, memo in Johnson Library: NSF Aides Files, McGeorge Bundy Memos to the President, quoted in Gibbons, *The U.S. Government and the Vietnam War*, Part III: January 1965–July 1965, p. 16.

77. Valenti Oral History, Tape 4, p. 20.

78. Department of Defense, *United States–Vietnam Relations, 1945–1967* (IV.c.2.—Evolution of the War: Military Pressures against Vietnam, July–October 1964), in Book 4, p. 21.

79. *The Pentagon Papers*, Gravel edition, vol. 3, p. 201.

80. Ibid. p. 202.

81. Johnson Library: National Security Files, McGeorge Bundy Memos, August 31, 1964.

The idea of introducing American ground forces into Vietnam and escalating the conflict did not originate within the Johnson administration. As early as October 1961 the question of using combat troops was raised in the Kennedy administration. One of the goals of a mission to South Vietnam then by Walt Rostow and Maxwell Taylor was to assess the desirability of using U.S. forces. They noted that a military task force of up to 10,000 U.S. ground forces would be the best way to demonstrate American resolve and commitment, although it was publicly reported that they recommended against dispatching combat forces. (See Daniel Ellsberg, *Papers on the War*, p. 56; Arthur Schlesinger, *The Bitter Heritage: Vietnam and American Democracy*, p. 39.) President Kennedy ultimately decided against combat forces, but the idea had been planted in the highest echelons of the bureaucracy.

82. *The Pentagon Papers*, Gravel edition, vol. 3, p. 557. Ironically, this memo is reported to have been drafted by Daniel Ellsberg.

83. Ball Oral History, Interview I, p. 26. See *The Pentagon Papers*, Gravel edition, vol. 3, pp. 202–6 for an excellent summary of the different agency views within the administration.

84. NSAM 314, September 10, 1964, in *The Pentagon Papers*, Gravel edition, vol. 3, pp. 565–66.

85. See the series of early September memos reproduced in ibid. pp. 560–66.

86. Johnson Library: Meeting Notes File, Box 1, September 14, 1964. McNamara, who a few weeks earlier had urged the military to deploy 900 military advisers and 4,200 support personnel to Vietnam by September 30, now added that the price of waiting was low, and the promise of gain substantial.

87. October 5, 1964 memo, "How Valid Are the Assumptions Underlying Our Vietnam Policies?," as reprinted in *The Atlantic*, 230(1) (July 1972): p. 49. The president never saw the memo until February 1965. Ball did not persuade Rusk, McNamara, and Bundy of his argument. McNamara was also very concerned that no one else in the government see the memo.

88. Ibid. p. 36.

89. Paul Kattenburg, *The Vietnam Trauma*, p. 129.

There were a few others whose views became more "dovish" as the escalation increased in 1965, for example, Bill Moyers of the president's staff and Chester Cooper of the NSC. Even McNaughton and McGeorge Bundy began to have serious doubts about U.S. military policy by the end of 1965.

90. Ball October 5, 1964, memo, p. 41.

91. November 16, 1964, memo to McNamara, in *The Pentagon Papers*, Gravel edition, vol. 3, pp. 632–33.

92. William Bundy quoted Johnson as saying, "Well, this is just not a time we can act. There are exceptions to everything, and this is an exception." (Bundy Oral History, vol. 2, p. 3.)

93. Maxwell Taylor, *Swords and Plowshares*, pp. 324–25. Taylor stated that Johnson showed "a surprising willingness to entertain the use of American forces to guard these airfields," revealing "an attitude which was to reappear later." (Johnson Library: Maxwell Taylor Oral History, November 14, 1981, pp. 4–5.)

94. *The Pentagon Papers*, Gravel edition, vol. 3, pp. 206–7.

95. November 2, 1964, memo to the president, "Some Comment on Post-Election Problems," in Johnson Library: National Security File "Papers of McGeorge Bundy," Box 16—File on Management, November 2, 1964.

96. Bundy manuscript, chapter 18, p. 10.

Poor Policy Planning and an Inadequate Budget Process

A SHORTSIGHTED VIETNAM POLICY REVIEW

William Bundy, who coordinated the Vietnam policy review initiated by the president shortly after his re-election, later observed that there was a built-in assumption at work: "Vietnam was worth a great deal, and failure there would be an extremely serious blow to American policy in the world and in Asia." The United States could not let the communists succeed. While the administration was unsure how to accomplish that, the bottom line was a fear of failure. Unfortunately, such an analysis produced a very shortsighted policy review, as William Bundy later affirmed:

[I]n the balance of argument, totally inadequate weight was given to the potential costs of trying stronger action. In this critical month, these costs did not seem to include any possibility that large U.S. ground forces would be needed, and the scope of the bombing programs—even the toughest considered—seemed limited in both cost and damage. Although the best military forecasts were used and the general sense was that things could get tough, the picture in everyone's mind was infinitely short of the later reality. The rejection of withdrawal, when the costs of carrying on seemed moderate, undoubtedly carried its own immense weight of inertia when the costs became visibly greater.[1]

As the review proceeded, the short-term policy choices were narrowed primarily to the scope and degree of a bombing campaign.

The Bundy working group developed three options. Option A was to "continue present policies" and continue limited operations; option B was clear-cut escalation with heavy and systematic pressures on the North; and option C was a more modest and slower-paced escalation against North

Vietnam. The Joint Chiefs favored option B, the "fast full squeeze," although they disagreed among themselves on the timing and intensity of the pressures. This option was envisioned as a "systematic program of military pressures against the north, meshing at some point with negotiation, but with pressure actions to be continued at a fairly rapid pace and without interruption."[2] The State Department and Office of the Secretary of Defense were in favor of option C, the "progressive squeeze-and-talk." Presumably, this carrot-and-stick option of both escalating and opening up communication with Hanoi would offer the greatest flexibility.

The debate by the senior military and foreign policy officials over the working group options led to a recommendation to expand the war in two phases: Phase I would intensify air strikes in Laos and covert action against North Vietnam, and Phase II would incorporate a sustained, escalating air campaign against the North. As defined, Phase II "would consist principally of progressively more serious air strikes, of a weight and tempo adjusted to the situation as it develops (possibly running from two to six months) and of appropriate US deployments to handle any contingency."[3] On December 1, the president approved Phase I: essentially option A for the next 30 days together with the lowest order of option C actions in a manner, as *The Pentagon Papers* authors noted, that "would represent the least possible additional commitment."[4] This was not a major policy commitment but rather a delaying tactic. The president approved the overall text of Bundy's working group recommendations but did not authorize any action. Johnson found the working group's recommendation "generally satisfactory," and the plans were "all right."[5] This was not the strong policy decision the working group preferred. The president's decision, in fact, "represented a substantial deviation from the findings of the Working Group," especially as it believed that option A had little chance of strengthening the Saigon government. It would have no greater impact on South Vietnamese morale than the Tonkin Gulf reprisals.[6] Phase II, the bombing policy, was approved only in principle. Johnson made its implementation contingent upon reform and improvement by the South Vietnam government.[7] The thrust of the policy appeared to be to stall for time so the Saigon government could get its house in order and wait for the right opportunity to move forward with strong U.S. action.

The president had backed away from making a public case or taking any major policy decision. In fact, the working group's draft was downgraded from a national security action memorandum to a position paper. There was no public presentation to the American people or Congress. The working group had envisaged "a whole series of actions to inform the public and Congress on key points." But little was done, and, "in effect, the publicity for the new program boiled down to a White House statement on December 1st, and to quiet consultation with key congressional leaders."[8] As *The Pentagon Papers* noted, "Several changes apparently were made in order not to ask the President to commit himself unnecessarily . . . . Also removed was reference to a major Presidential speech, apparently on the advice of McGeorge Bundy."[9] Johnson rejected his advisers' recommendations to keep the public informed. In a direct memo to the heads of the State Department, Defense Department, and CIA, he stated: "I consider it a matter of the highest importance that the substance of this position [his approval for Phase I] should not become public except as I specifically direct."[10] Johnson clearly wanted to avoid public discussion, much less debate on American policy in Vietnam.

The policy review was essentially a failure because there was really no comprehensive analysis. There was little focus on long-term policy and even less focus on the long-term consequences and costs if the options were not successful. Chester Cooper of the NSC staff later noted that in December 1964, "the time was ripe for a serious reappraisal. Never again in [Johnson's] term of office would he have more political elbowroom to pick and choose among options."[11] The question of ground force deployments was ignored, for the most part. There was no serious analysis of the ramification of combat troop deployments, even though any sustained air campaign would require some ground forces to defend the air bases.[12] Robert Johnson of the Policy Planning Council asked William Bundy why "no significant U.S. ground force element has been included in the [working group's] three alternatives. Should such introduction of U.S. ground forces be excluded from consideration? Should these options be examined?"[13] The administration never conducted another such review until the summer of 1965—after ground forces had already been introduced and were engaged in combat—nor was there another point at which the functions and goals of using combat troops were put forth. What is therefore remarkable is that American ground forces would be introduced into Vietnam with no public or congressional debate and with almost no internal policy debate.

An important reason that the president scaled down the working group's recommendations for a major air campaign was his concern for U.S. dependents in Vietnam. He consistently raised this issue, much more so than any of his advisers. In essence, he wanted to clear the decks before escalating.[14] Unlike many of his advisers, Johnson was not going to push for a bombing campaign simply as a last-gasp effort to turn the tide. The circumstances and timing also had to be right. The withdrawal of dependents was one caveat; the stability of the leadership in Saigon was another. An additional factor was that Johnson had no faith in an air war. Finally, he also had to present the proposed 1966 fiscal year budget to Congress in January and was relying on significant defense cuts to pay for the Great Society programs. Ultimately, the decision did not satisfy anyone, and there remained disagreement as to the pace and scope of any bombing campaign. Since the president did not want to bomb the North until a more stable government arose in Saigon, a waiting game began—one that the United States would lose patience with in February, even though things in Saigon continued to worsen. Initiated in December, Phase I became "Barrel Roll," a program of armed reconnaissance and bombing in Laos as well as a few new 34A raids. A State Department official involved with Laotian affairs claimed Johnson "was privately relieved that he could take such a momentous first step somewhere other than in Vietnam. We had decided it would take some bullets and bombs. Since they had to be fired, Johnson thought it best that it be off in the woods where it would escape notice."[15]

ESCALATION, RELUCTANTLY

By the end of December 1964, U.S. policy toward Vietnam was not that of a superpower rallying around the flag and rushing headlong into war. The key to the American military decisions was a belief that Hanoi would recalculate its interests after suffering enough from superior American firepower. The success of such an approach rested squarely on a firm understanding of what was necessary to deter the enemy and the ability to assess accurately what the opposition was willing to do and capable of doing in order to achieve its objective. On that score, the policymakers in Washington and Saigon fell far short of the mark. In late 1964 most of the key decision makers failed to realize the commitment of time and resources (financial, industrial, and manpower) necessary to convince the communists they could not win and to give up their designs on the South. While Johnson deferred any significant military action, the policy options had increasingly narrowed. Given the stated policy goals, the United States would have to take action sooner or later as South Vietnam continued to deteriorate. It was, as Leslie Gelb and Richard Betts noted, "an undeferable decision."[16]

During most of 1964, diplomacy was viewed as a dead end. While there were a few third-party efforts to bridge the gap and help begin a dialogue between the governments of North Vietnam and the United States, neither side demonstrated much interest in talking, much less negotiating. Clearly, part of the U.S. strategy was to improve the situation in the South to the point where the Americans and their South Vietnamese allies could deal with the North from a position of strength. This approach was twofold: deter the North from further support of the Vietcong insurgents and strengthen the South, in terms of morale, stability, and military strength. There was also a certain arrogance in the U.S. view of negotiations: superior American military might and know-how would force the North Vietnamese to submit to peace negotiations on American terms. Diplomacy was not seen as a means to achieve peace but rather an end goal to be dictated to the enemy.

From late 1964 to early 1965, however, a subtle change occurred in the American perspective. Not only was there a need to preserve and strengthen the South Vietnamese government, but the administration no longer thought in terms of providing advisers and support but felt a responsibility for "protecting" South Vietnam, its government, and people. That responsibility was slowly taken over from the South Vietnam military, which over time became little more than an adjunct to the U.S. military forces.

American thinking was not restricted just to sending in a few soldiers and planes. Dean Rusk brought up the possibility of nuclear weapons, especially if there were a major conflict: "It seems to me of vital importance that we turn our attention to the consideration of the utility and limitation of the potential utilization of tactical nuclear weaponry in other areas of the globe. I particularly have in mind the Far East where we maintain the second largest overseas nuclear arsenal and where, insofar as Southeast Asia is concerned, the prospect for a major US military involvement cannot be overlooked."[17] When one reads of the secretary of state discussing the possible use of tactical nuclear weapons if the conflict in Vietnam grew (he might have been thinking of an expanded war that involved China), it is difficult to reconcile such talk with the lengths to which the military and civilian planners went to play down the conflict to the public and their own domestic planners.

This letter of Rusk's might also explain why he was more reluctant than most other advisers at this time to escalate and bomb the North. He could have seen such action as a trigger that would bring the Chinese into the conflict (a prospect he had witnessed as assistant secretary of state for Far Eastern affairs during the Korean War). However, despite the Johnson administration's attempt to expand American involvement incrementally in order to reach a point where Hanoi would recalculate its interests, the prospect of going down a path to a nuclear conflict remained a possibility, at least in Rusk's mind. The use of nuclear weapons had actually been broached at a June conference on Vietnam in Honolulu. According to *The Pentagon Papers*, Robert McNamara stated "that the possibility of major ground action also led to a serious question of having to use nuclear weapons at some point."[18]

THE PRESIDENT DISCUSSES GROUND FORCES

There was no specific decision or time period when the transition to an Americanization of the war took place. One cannot state that the President decided at a particular time that the United States would escalate its military role in Vietnam. Some analysts argue that although Johnson did not plan in advance to escalate the war, "there is also no doubt that he was determined not to lose it even if winning it required escalation."[19] In late December Johnson was not satisfied that the circumstances in South Vietnam were right for any escalation. When two Americans and 13 Vietnamese were killed and 38 Americans injured in a communist bombing of the officers' billet, Taylor and Westmoreland, backed up by the JCS, urged retaliation against North Vietnam. This was firmly rejected by the president.

On December 30 he cabled Ambassador Taylor to "share my own thinking with you" and clearly hinted that he wanted to escalate but was waiting for the right occasion. In this cable, Johnson showed how he was willing to do whatever was necessary, including the deployment of combat troops. Not only was he much more inclined to use ground forces, but there seemed to be no ceiling:

Every time I get a military recommendation it seems to me that it calls for large-scale bombing. I have never felt that this war will be won from the air, and it seems to me that what is much more needed and would be more effective is a larger and stronger use of rangers and special forces and marines, or other appropriate military strength on the ground and on the scene. I am ready to look with great favor on that kind of increased American effort, directed at the guerrillas and aimed to stiffen the aggressiveness of Vietnamese military units up and down the line. Any recommendation that you or General Westmoreland make in this sense will have immediate attention from me, although I know that it may involve the acceptance of larger American sacrifices. We have been building our strength to fight this kind of war ever since 1961, and I myself am ready to substantially increase the number of Americans in Vietnam if it is necessary to provide this kind of fighting force against the Viet Cong.[20]

The president also showed concern that security arrangements for American personnel were somewhat lax and thus should be strengthened. Therefore, he wanted "an intensified U.S. stiffening on-the-ground by rangers and special forces and other appropriate elements."[21] If he was going to send American soldiers in, he wanted to reduce the risk of incidents that could hurt America's image (and, as a consequence, his own image). The president's message on December 30 was that once such obstacles, including the removal of dependents, were disposed of, the United States could begin to escalate and do whatever was necessary to halt the military deterioration.

There are two important points to be seen from this cable. First, even though Johnson had approved only minimal action with Phase I, the cable appears to show that he was prepared for a very significant deployment, including combat troops. Second, he appeared to be holding back on escalation because he had reservations about the efficacy of bombing and was worried about the timing and the preparations on the ground. By this time, giving in to the inevitability that the United States must intervene militarily, Johnson turned to the question of how—and he had more faith in ground forces. If he had to escalate as his advisers recommended—and he could see no viable alternative politically—then he wanted to control how the United States would fight communism in Southeast Asia. Even if Lyndon Johnson was reluctant to escalate, he was certainly more prepared to deploy ground forces than many of his civilian advisers at this point. Maxwell Taylor later commented: "It had been like pulling teeth to get the President to agree to the use of air power, but strangely enough, he was more inclined to use forces on the ground. The former seemed to me a much less difficult decision to make, although both were hard."[22]

There was some discussion in early January among the senior advisers of limited ground force deployment, but no policy review was conducted. Combat troops were usually an issue only insofar as forces might be needed to protect airfields used for Phase II. There was no consensus within the Pentagon. Westmoreland and the JCS proposed a logistic command and increased logistic support troops. Assistant secretary of defense McNaughton argued against the deployment of ground forces: "[D]o not increase the number of U.S. men in South Vietnam. (Additional U.S. soldiers are as likely to be counterproductive as productive.)"[23]

Ambassador Taylor, responding on January 6 to the cable of December 30, argued that using American troops would be a major political liability. Taylor felt the South Vietnamese should still be able to fight and carry the war.[24] He also emphasized the following: "Since receiving your [cable], Gen. Westmoreland and his staff have made a comprehensive study of the requirements for giving maximum security to U.S. personnel and facilities by utilizing U.S. guard and units. He arrives at the startling requirement of 34 battalion equivalents of army or marine infantry, together with the necessary logistic support. He considers that the total manpower requirement would approximate 75,000 U.S. personnel."[25] Continued American involvement in Vietnam, according to the military, would entail a major commitment of troops. In the words of Taylor, the "U.S. would be directly involved in ground combat." He then made quite plain to the president the negative consequences of a U.S. combat role and expressed strong doubts as to what ground forces could accomplish.[26]

In addition, as another cable from Westmoreland and Taylor noted, it was "inevitable that casualties would occur among Vietnamese non-combatants, thus creating adverse reaction by Vietnamese against U.S. which VC [Viet Cong] would strongly exploit . . . . The Vietnamese Army (ARVN) might tend to leave the tougher problems to U.S. troops and thus gradually abdicate its responsibilities. *U.S. casualties would be high.*"[27] There is no evidence, however, that Taylor's warnings were ever aired in White House policy meetings during this period. By the time a true debate on combat troop deployment was enjoined (in July 1965), the question was not if ground forces should be employed but how many.

However, for the moment, the president backed off in his push for ground forces when he responded to Taylor on January 7 (cable drafted by McGeorge Bundy): "We are inclined to adopt a policy of prompt and clear reprisal, together with a readiness to start joint planning and execution on future military operations both within South Vietnam and against the North, but without present commitment as to the timing and scale of Phase II . . . . it is better to remove dependents before reprisals begin, and we believe that by adoption and public indication of reprisal policy we can provide the necessary demonstration that this act represents firmness, not weakness."[28] While he had not authorized any action, Johnson did approve reprisals in principle, leaving open when and how to initiate such escalation. He had concluded a January 6 meeting on Vietnam by saying that, "now, we are going to have reprisals," even though he did not believe reprisals would stabilize the Saigon government or that they were sufficient to bring the communists to the negotiating table.[29]

One interesting note about the president's January 7 cable is what he deleted from McGeorge Bundy's draft: "We concur in your judgment that large new American forces are not now desirable for security or for direct combat roles." Also deleted was the sentence: "We are not certain that any course of action now open to us can produce necessary turn-around in South Vietnam in coming months, but we are convinced that it is of high importance to try."[30] Like most of his advisers, Johnson believed the most important consideration was that the United States had to try something; but he remained unwilling to commit himself at this point.

THE BUDGET AND THE VIETNAM CONFLICT

Unlike with the hesitancy in taking a policy decision on Vietnam and the desire to keep the process from view, in the first year of his presidency, Lyndon Johnson had put forth a most ambitious blueprint for a Great Society. He had taken bold initiatives with the economy and civil rights, which seemed all the more remarkable in an election year. On domestic matters, the president proved to be a man of action who pushed and cajoled the Congress to enact his programs. Johnson was also concerned that he had to push his programs through the legislature while he had strong support and could capitalize on his popularity. Since he could not back down in the face of communist aggression, he had to prevent his policies in Vietnam from encroaching on, or interfering with, the Great Society push. This was particularly true in the budget process. It is critical to analyze the budgeting process at the time to see how the planning for the military escalation fell through the cracks. Until the end of 1965, the budget experts and financial advisers were unaware of the major military commitment that was made. This was due to the nature of the budget process as well as deliberate deception on the part of the president and his top Vietnam advisers, who were able to exploit weaknesses in that process.

In creating economic policies and preparing budgets, government officials establish priorities and make choices. Vietnam decisions, however, were kept separate from the priorities the domestic and economic planners were formulating. The potential costs of Vietnam, dependent on projections of the number of soldiers and the amount of equipment ultimately deployed there, were kept from the administration economists during the period when American policy in Vietnam escalated from an advisory role to that of a full-scale combatant.

The lack of consensus on long-term Vietnam policy making helped fuel this. The Vietnam policymakers consistently played things close to the vest throughout the escalation period. A critical point to emphasize is that Vietnam planning was almost completely outside the budget process. The Defense Department made its own budgets and then simply let the Bureau of the Budget know what its plans were. This process gave a great deal of autonomy to secretary of defense.

As the president and his foreign policy advisers planned for the possibility of escalation, the domestic planners remained in the dark. Even as American involvement in the Vietnam conflict grew, there was little economic accountability for the consequences of the evolving planning and policy decisions. None of the declassified documents from the economic staffs stored in the Johnson Library, the National Archives, or the Office of Management and Budget contain any mention of Vietnam until July 1965. There is also no evidence that the Defense or State Department alerted the Bureau of the Budget that significant military escalation might occur down the road and could have an effect on budgetary planning.

A month after the Tonkin Gulf Resolution was passed, Johnson and his key advisers agreed during a September 9 NSC meeting that no financial restraints should be placed on the pursuit of U.S. goals in Vietnam. McGeorge Bundy recorded the following exchange: "Secretary McNamara asked if it were clear that money was no object . . . . Secretary Rusk said he very much hoped money would not be regarded as the ceiling, and felt that it would be worth any amount to win . . . . Ambassador Taylor replied that the country team [in Saigon] would ask for any money it needed. The president emphasized his own continuing conviction that it was necessary not to spare the horses. He pointed out that this had been his constant view . . . . [and] reemphasized that money was no object."[31] Most of the men present at that meeting did not envision the massive escalation of the following year, but they also set no limitations, in terms of either military commitments or financial resources, and as with almost every Vietnam-related meeting in 1964 and 1965, there were no economic advisers in attendance.

At a November 19, 1964, meeting between Bureau of the Budget and Pentagon officials to discuss the FY 1966 defense budget, the military needs and costs for Vietnam were not even on the agenda.[32] On December 3, two days after the president ok'd the Phase I bombing program, Joe Califano, then working in the Pentagon, drafted a 10-page outline of a proposed presidential message on defense. Nowhere was Vietnam mentioned. Califano did say: "Now, we can expect the budget to stay approximately constant unless there are unforeseen changes in international conditions."[33] On December 5 the Defense Department circulated a draft memo on the FY 1966 budget from Secretary McNamara along with recommendations by the Joint Chiefs. Once again, Vietnam was not mentioned. The Pentagon budget remained untouched in spite of the fact that a major air campaign awaited the president's approval.

THE PENTAGON AND THE BUDGET PROCESS

The Defense Department had a unique role in the budget-making process prior to 1972, when the system was overhauled and the Office of Budget and Management was established. With the exception of the Pentagon, the Budget Bureau gave each department or agency a rough, but fixed, budget target. With the Defense Department, the procedure was reversed: defense spending targets were provided to the Budget Bureau. So, as one analyst noted, McNamara would "announce" the amount of money needed for defense spending to the director of the Bureau of the Budget and the rest of the government.[34] After incorporating the Pentagon's estimations, the budget director would then issue appropriations targets for non-defense agencies. The Defense Department got first priority in the overall budget, and then all other departments and agencies had to adjust to the Pentagon figures. In addition, military policy was never really coordinated with overall economic policy. During the budget preview sessions each department and agency had with the Budget Bureau, there was a predetermined agenda to go over the programs and the budget objectives, with two exceptions: the CIA and the Defense Department.[35]

A highly placed official of the Budget Bureau stated that both Kennedy and Johnson gave McNamara a free hand: "Ceilings don't exist. The President has given Mr. McNamara more or less a blank check for defense."[36] The Budget Bureau had no policy role in the preparation of the defense budgets, but, as John Crecine noted, several Budget Bureau staff members participated in the Defense Department budget review sessions. They were even "considered by all involved to be members of the Pentagon staff in spirit, if not in fact. They physically move 'across the river (to the Pentagon)' during the 'budget crunch.'"[37] But they were involved in the review of the budget, not the planning of it. While the Budget Bureau had exclusive responsibility for reviewing and cutting requests from non-defense departments and agencies, the Office of the Assistant Secretary of Defense (Comptroller), had the primary responsibility for reviewing service budget requests.

In terms of the relationship between the Defense Department and the Bureau of the Budget (BOB), BOB was more like an accounting firm that oversaw existing expenditures and appropriations, not an agency that worked with the Pentagon in determining the necessary resources for the long-term military projections. Former budget director (under Eisenhower) Percival Brundage described the Budget Bureau's role with respect to the military budget, noting that "Budget Bureau recommendations are primarily related to comparisons of expenditure programs: first with programs already authorized, second with obligational authority, third with expenditures of earlier years, and fourth with future programs."[38] While there was a military division in the Bureau of the Budget, there is no evidence of any consultation on Vietnam spending or on the relationship between the budget numbers and the defense priorities. Budget Bureau documents show that in 1964 and the first half of 1965, the Vietnam conflict was not a budget or economic issue. There is also no evidence that Pentagon officials ever informed the Budget Bureau of military contingencies that were in preparation, nor did they pass on any of the specific cost estimates that they would discuss with the president in July 1965. Finally, as will be seen, because the military escalation in Vietnam was financed by emergency, supplemental appropriation bills in Congress and drawing down on other, already funded Pentagon programs, the Vietnam War was far along (1966) before it was even a part of the budget review process.

Comptroller Charles Hitch stated that "at some point the Secretary of Defense and the President and the Director of the Bureau of the Budget have to decide what the limit is for the Department of Defense as a whole."[39] But former budget director Charles Schultze implied in later congressional testimony that the review by the Budget Bureau and the White House of the military's budget recommendations lacked the independent judgment and healthy skepticism necessary to attain a "balanced view of national priorities."[40] When the secretary of defense claimed he could cut back on the military budget

without damaging national security at all, it was hard to turn him down.
    According to Schultze:

In all other cases, agency budget requests are submitted to the Bureau, which reviews
the budgets and then makes its own recommendations to the President subject to appeal
by the agency head to the President. In the case of the Defense budget, the staff of the
Budget Bureau and the staff of the Secretary of Defense jointly review the budget
requests of the individual armed services. The staff make recommendations to their
respective superiors. The Secretary of Defense and the Budget Director then meet to
iron out differences of view. The Secretary of Defense then submits his budget request
to the President, and the Budget Director has the right of carrying to the President any
remaining areas of disagreement he thinks warrant Presidential review.[41]

Schultze felt that the key player was the president: "The Budget Bureau can
effectively dig into and review what the President wants it to review under this
procedure or many others. It can raise questions of budgetary priorities—
questioning, for example, the work of building forces against a particular set of
contingencies on grounds of higher priority domestic needs—when and only
when the President feels that *he* can effectively question military judgments on
those grounds."[42] But Johnson showed no inclination for debating priorities in
1964 or 1965. The inability to maintain a proper balance between foreign
policy objectives and domestic policy is where Charles Schultze particularly
criticized the budget process as falling short. As it was, disagreements between
the Budget Bureau and the Pentagon comptroller's office were relatively minor;
in the few that did occur between the two staffs that entailed the director of
BOB and the secretary of defense taking their respective cases to the president,
the Pentagon was never over-ruled.[43]
    McNamara would usually take his recommendations for the defense budget
directly to the president, bypassing the Budget Bureau. However, this would
change as McNamara's support for the war waned. Former budget director
Brundage noted that as the war escalated, the military services were able to
gain greater access to the president and as a result budget priorities "seemed to
have been determined without much regard to the views of the Secretary [of
Defense] or the Director [of the Budget Bureau]."[44] But in 1964 and 1965
McNamara was the key figure regarding the military budget.
    In addition, the Bureau of the Budget was not given enough cost data on the
various contingencies and relevant components of forces and weapons systems
that make up the American force posture. Schultze cited a number of
examples, including "the annual cost of the forces we maintain in peacetime
against the contingency of a Chinese attack in South East Asia."[45] Such cost
data in the defense posture statement "are precisely the kinds of information
needed to make possible a rational and responsible debate about the military
budget in the context of national priorities." This was not just a problem
related to the Vietnam escalation; it would be hard for anyone outside the
Pentagon to make an economic assessment of the overall military goals.
Because of the program structure of the military budget, what the Budget

Bureau reviewed with the Pentagon was the cost accounting of the budgeted line-item programs, not the force posture or the policy commitments. Thus, when the Vietnam War hit, the budget process was ill equipped.

APPROPRIATIONS AND BUDGETING

The appropriations and budget processes are critical for governance and policy making. Budget decisions reflect priorities and political choices; in fact, the budget cycle forces decisions. This was particularly true with the Defense Department, which under McNamara had gone to a five-year planning mode and based most of its budgeting on long-range strategic and programmatic needs. Thus, the annual budget was part of a long-range plan. Two new components of military planning were introduced to implement this: the Planning-Programming-Budgeting System (PPBS), which would regulate the military budget preparation, and the Office of Systems Analysis (OSA), which was to enhance cost-effectiveness in military spending. Under this new system, each of the services had to justify its budget requests, and they were all coordinated into one long-range plan with specific budgetary needs and appropriations on an annual basis. The key was to translate the program budget into an annual budget for which appropriations could be authorized in Congress.

There have been many studies of the budgeting program under McNamara, especially as it related to military policy formulation, strategic planning, and management and economic decisions. However, there have been very few analyses of the impact of the budget process on the Vietnam conflict.[46] Even those who have looked at the war began their analysis after the initial escalation. As Arnold Kanter noted in his study of policy making in the Pentagon, "For the purposes of the budgetary analysis, the Vietnam war begins in FY 1967 when the incremental costs of the conflict were first acknowledged."[47]

It is hard to determine exactly the impact the expansion of the war in 1965 had on the budget process because for FY 1966 the Pentagon did not plan for the subsequent military escalation and the deployment of ground forces. The eventual need for emergency, supplemental appropriation requests in May and August 1965 would be important clues to that. But, more importantly, a conflict or war such as the one in Vietnam did not fit into the policy process. Vietnam was not a budget item or a program.[48] It was a crisis, an emergency. However, since war was never declared, no national emergency was acknowledged. As a result, Vietnam had to fall within a process of planning and budgeting that was long-range and cyclical. So in order to continue to finance the escalation of the conflict, supplemental and ad hoc appropriations would be necessary. In addition, the first major escalatory action in Vietnam (the February 1965 bombing) would occur just after the budget review period (October–January). The budget was prepared and reviewed while Vietnam policy remained unclear. The administration could have re-calculated the budget while it was before Congress, but that may not have made much difference. It would have been difficult to fit the gradual escalation of the Vietnam War into a budget process that was ill equipped to deal with cost estimates of a conflict. But the administration did not try to do so.

Robert Anthony (Pentagon comptroller 1965–1968) noted that even at the height of the Vietnam conflict in 1967, "we do not have a cost accounting system for the Vietnam conflict . . . one does not set up a cost accounting system for a war."[49] So there was no set of books called Southeast Asia that programmed all the costs of Vietnam. But the Pentagon analysts and economic planners should have at least been able to estimate and budget for the incremental costs, that is, those costs that would not have been incurred were there no conflict in Vietnam. Those costs were severely underestimated, in great part due to the rapid and undeclared nature of the major military buildup.

This was compounded by the fact that neither the Pentagon nor the White House actually had a firm idea as to how much would be required to meet the military goals. When the first marines went ashore in early March, the economic impact was not a problem, because they were just drawn from existing force and operations budgets. Additionally, McNamara noted that the increase in the cost of the war was being financed by unexpected savings in FY 1965. This actually hid the economic impact of the military escalation for a few months. But by early May, with 35,000 troops in South Vietnam and 40,000 more authorized, the costs had gone beyond the budget—especially in the support area for these soldiers: housing construction, ammunition, supplies, fuel, and so on. McNamara admitted that in preparing the FY 1966 budget the Pentagon "took account of the rates of expenditure at the time the budget was prepared but we have not planned for a rate of expenditure which might be greater than that."[50] What he did not say was that expenditures at the time the budget was prepared included only advisers and military aid to South Vietnam; they did not take into account the introduction of combat troops and support personnel or the sustained bombing.

It seems apparent that those responsible for American policy in Vietnam, from the president on down, did not allow the contingency of war in Vietnam to be incorporated into the budgeting process, and thus in 1964 and 1965 economic and domestic planners had a very distorted view of what the priorities of the government would be for the next few years. Nor did they get a true idea of the military demands on American resources and finances, thus leading to a very inaccurate financial picture by mid-1965. The budget process, which is a significant means for governments to determine priorities, make choices, and map the future, did not work as it was intended. The officials responsible for the entire government budget must see to the big picture; however, if they are not given information about the contingencies of a major component of the government, namely, defense, the big picture could be quite distorted. For this, the Vietnam planners were primarily culpable.

However, the Budget Bureau admittedly did not challenge the Pentagon to account for the impact—short- and long-term—of its military commitments, such as preventing the collapse of South Vietnam. Former secretary of the interior under Johnson Stewart Udall argued that "the military was essentially not being scrutinized [by the Budget Bureau] in nearly the same way as the domestic side was."[51] The Budget Bureau exerted much greater pressure on the domestic agencies and departments than on the military. This was due to the fact that the burden of proof with military matters fell to the Budget Bureau. In the mid-1960s, the military remained sacrosanct, both within the executive branch and on Capitol Hill.

The budget process failed in another way because it was not able to compel the Pentagon to plan ahead. McNamara and the Department of Defense seemed not to have the slightest idea in mid-1965 as to how to plan for the cost of the war. Although Vietnam became a factor in economic planning in late 1965, it was not until 1967 that the Department of Defense and Budget Bureau began to come close in their Vietnam cost estimates. Thus, they worked outside the budget process and, for the first year of the war, simply went to Congress with a hand out for emergency appropriations. The Pentagon could discuss the costs in terms of equipment; that is, for x amount of dollars the Pentagon could buy y number of naval vessels. But how many naval vessels, how much ammunition, how many men would it take to convince the communists that they could not win in South Vietnam? The office in the Pentagon where such long-range and contingency questions could have been most effectively addressed, the Office of Systems Analysis, was ignored. The OSA lacked influence within the Pentagon regarding the Vietnam War. As late as mid-1966, there was no formal discussion in OSA about the war, and according to former OSA staff members, when they did become involved, "they were not a central part in any way of policy-making in the war."[52]

The question for the analyst is, What difference would it have made? If the costs of the war had been known, would President Johnson then not have involved the United States in the war? Or would Congress and the economic advisers have insisted that the United States go on a war footing, which would probably have included many economic sacrifices? What would that have done to the domestic priorities? McNamara asked that of Tom Wicker of the *New York Times*: "Do you really think that if I had estimated the cost of the war correctly, Congress would have given any more for schools and housing?"[53] But it was not a question of whether cost estimations could not be made; it was that they would not be made. As McNamara later noted, "President Johnson believed higher defense appropriations would kill his proposals for the greatest social advance since the New Deal. Today, we see his actions as subterfuge— what is commonly called deceit—but in the process we often overlook his deep desire to address our society's ills."[54] McNamara does not deny the deceit, but as he implied in his response to Tom Wicker, the goal of a Great Society seemed to justify the dissembling on budget estimates for the military escalation in Vietnam.

INITIAL PLANNING FOR THE FY 1966 BUDGET

During the fall of 1964, Secretary McNamara was engaged in cutting the Pentagon's budget and working toward a much greater efficiency in spending and resource and manpower allocation. In fact, total defense expenditures on a fiscal year basis declined from $54.2 billion in FY 1964 to $50.2 billion in FY 1965.[55] In January 1965 the military budget that was presented to Congress was less for FY 1966 than for the previous year, down from $54 billion to $51.6 billion. At first, this is somewhat hard to understand, because defense obligations began to increase beginning January 1, 1965. But this would not last and could not hold, as Robert McNamara surely knew. But Vietnam spending was not a budget item so was, in fact, ignored in the budget planning. As it turned out, the escalation in Vietnam did lead to higher defense spending in the last two quarters of FY 1965 (January–June 1965) than the same period in FY 1964. When the Joint Economic Committee held hearings on the Economic Effect of Vietnam Spending in April 1967, many in Congress were surprised to learn that the increase in defense spending and the impact of Vietnam spending had already occurred at the beginning of 1965, not after the July decision to deploy major ground forces.

The immediate military options presented to the president in early December 1964 were not reflected in the military budget. Only two Vietnam-related areas in the Defense Department budgets from FY 1964 through FY 1966 were presented to, and debated within, Congress: airlift and sealift forces and the Military Assistance Program (MAP). The FY 1965 budget asked for a $100 million increase in airlift and sealift forces. But there was a catch. This figure was for a contingency that seemed arbitrary and greatly inadequate: "stated in terms of tons involved in the airlift of assumed ground and air units to South-east Asia in a 30-day period, which is considered the limiting case."[56] In the FY 1966 budget, airlift and sealift forces were not accounted for programmatically but were folded into other budget areas, so Vietnam was even less of a distinct contingency than before in the budget. Given the escalation plans that were discussed in the fall of 1964, the budget for airlift and sealift forces should have increased, not been eliminated.

The Defense Department did not fight to get more military spending in the budget to deal with Vietnam—as stated before, McNamara was convinced he could cut the budget. The only Vietnam area where there was pressure for more money in the budget was the Military Assistance Program, although not from McNamara. Robert Komer, then on McGeorge Bundy's National Security Council staff, urged Bundy during budget and economic priority discussions with President Johnson in November to push for more assistance money: "I hope you'll put in a good word for a $1.2 billion FY '66 MAP level. McNamara's rough $1 billion MAP ceiling would make more sense if it weren't for distortion created by *Laos/Vietnam*. For FY '65 and '66 they are likely to run us $280-300 million out of MAP alone, which means that the other key programs (Turkey, Greece, GRC [Taiwan], ROK [South Korea]), where most of the money goes, get badly slashed. Logically, of course,

VN/Laos ought to be funded as a special charge (though I see the domestic problem)."[57]   Komer was fighting for a budget increase because he was cognizant of the negative effect Vietnam spending was having on other areas of MAP. As he intimated, McNamara was holding the budgetary line, but also Vietnam kept pulling more and more money away from key strategic areas. What Komer wanted was an acknowledgment that the current situation in Vietnam demanded that it be treated separately from the regular MAP program. American policy in Vietnam should be supplemented rather than other key areas gutted. Otherwise, the emergency needs of Vietnam would continue to hurt other areas of American foreign policy. But Komer's concerns were not taken up then, even though the administration was engaged in policy reviews and strategies across the board on Vietnam issues.[58]

If the Vietnam planners, in both the military and foreign policy establishment, had sincerely believed that any American military involvement in Vietnam would be very swift and cost little, then one could understand the lack of warning to economic planners. But, as the documentary evidence shows, the pattern of decision making in 1964 and 1965 showed a growing realization that there was no simple or short-term solution. A major commitment of men and matériel would be required over a long period. The lack of public and intragovernmental candor, in light of the growing belief that the Vietnam conflict would be long and difficult for the United States, greatly distorted the situation for the Johnson administration's economic planners. They can hardly be blamed for their misplaced optimism about the economy when they were never informed of the potential drain on resources the Vietnam War would have. Although U.S. defense expenditures in South Vietnam had increased from $227 million in FY 1963 to $381 million for FY 1964, that was not a significant amount.[59]

As the economic advisers saw it, even if the trend toward greater American assistance in Vietnam continued, the resulting costs within the parameters of past increases would have had a minor effect on the American economy. There was no reason for the economists and domestic planners to worry: more American planes, advisers, and financial assistance could be planned for. But they had no inkling of what would become a $14.4 billion increase within a year. While Pentagon officials and the key Vietnam policymakers did not know in December 1964 that a specific increase of $14.4 billion would be needed within the year, they were aware of the potential for a major increase in spending needs for Vietnam at that point.

Neither the Pentagon nor the White House even began to caution publicly that the struggle in Vietnam would be a long haul until the spring of 1966. Privately, however, many key advisers admitted that this would be a long commitment and cautioned the president to be up-front with the public. McGeorge Bundy warned the president on December 16, 1964: "No matter what course is taken, it seems likely to us that we face years of involvement in South Vietnam . . . . The Administration has regularly insisted that this problem is not one which will be solved tomorrow, but it may well be important to make this point still more clear to the American public."[60] But too often the public statements and the budgets and policies that were made public did not reflect what concerned the military planners behind the scenes.

THE 1965 DOMESTIC AGENDA

In January 1965, while the White House delayed action in Vietnam, it continued to move full force on the domestic and legislative agenda. As ambitious plans for Great Society programs were drawn up, the FY1966 budget became an important policy focal point. Johnson was spending most of his time finalizing his domestic program and legislative strategy. There was something of a competition for his attention on all these pressing issues, foreign and domestic: "Those who had written the domestic scenario were at his elbow constantly, reviewing programs and bringing messages that were to go to the Hill in sequence all through late January and February."[61]

The desire to create a Great Society led to a sense of urgency in the president and his domestic advisers. He was inheriting the largest Democratic majority in Congress since 1936 and wanted to strike while his mandate was at its peak. Wilbur Cohen, the assistant secretary of health, education, and welfare for legislative affairs and a key point man on the Great Society agenda, discussed one of the critical strategy meetings soon after the inauguration and noted how the president prodded his troops: "I want you to get all my legislative proposals during this session, now! . . . Every day that I am in office, I lose part of my power. Every day that I use power, I have less power left. You must get this legislation through immediately. I want you to talk to those congressmen. I want you to sleep with those congressmen if you have to. I want you to get this legislation through now—while I still have the power."[62]

Most of the ideas were in place. The economy remained quite robust. But the administrative bureaucracy still had to develop the final blueprints for the various programs as well as consult Congress and push hard for the legislation the president would soon send to Capitol Hill. Public opinion also needed to be harnessed and momentum created for a big domestic push. In his 1966 budget message, presented on January 1, 1965, Lyndon Johnson proposed (1) reduced excise taxes; (2) a major increase in Social Security benefits made retroactive to January 1, 1965; (3) an increase in Social Security taxes (to pay for benefits) delayed to January 1, 1966; and (4) a comprehensive Medicare plan introduced under the Social Security proposal. Cuts in defense spending were key to keeping the overall budget down. Johnson had declared in the budget message that, with the "gains already scheduled," U.S. military forces "will be adequate to their tasks for years to come."[63] So, any sign of major military action in Vietnam would dampen the enthusiasm and raise serious questions among members of Congress, the American public and even his own domestic advisers. In addition, Johnson clearly believed that using any of his "power" on Vietnam would lessen the power he needed for the domestic agenda.

White House aide Bill Moyers would later note that President Johnson wanted to take advantage of the unique political position he inherited as well as the strong and expanding economy: "This was, thought LBJ, *the fullness of time economically.* Our resources were growing at the rate of 5 percent a year, and his economic advisers assured (in the words of Walter Heller) that 'in our time, the engine of our economy would be the mightiest engine of human progress the world has ever seen.' Just by shifting a small portion of the additional resources created by growth, it was thought, we could abolish poverty without raising taxes." Moyers also added: "He [LBJ] thought this *the fullness of time politically, as well.*"[64]

President Johnson felt that time was a precious commodity, and it was critical to utilize it carefully and properly. He later noted: "A measure must be sent to the Hill at exactly the right moment and that moment depends on three things: first, on momentum; second, on the availability of sponsors in the right place at the right time; and third, on the opportunities for neutralizing the opposition. Timing is essential. Momentum is not a mysterious mistress. It is a controllable fact of political life that depends on nothing more exotic than preparation."[65] Nor was it enough just to get Congress to allocate the resources and pass the programs. Moyers said about the president: "[H]e thought the government should be adventuresome. He was willing to experiment. He thought there would be time to find out what worked and what didn't."[66] Moving slowly in Vietnam might then give him and the country time to explore what worked before the focus and debate fully turned to Vietnam.

Once the 89th Congress convened, the president moved quickly. During his State of the Union address on January 4, 1965, he locked in on the Great Society and devoted most of the emphasis to his domestic agenda. Less than a fifth of the speech concerned foreign affairs, and only 131 words were about Vietnam, and none about the military situation there.[67] Over the next two weeks the White House inundated Capitol Hill with new programs and ideas. Johnson proposed creating a new cabinet department on housing and urban development as well as a national foundation on the arts and a massive beautification plan. On January 7 Johnson went to Capitol Hill and delivered a Special Message on Health. A $6 billion package was soon presented to Congress, which revolved primarily around Medicare and what form it would take.[68] On January 12 he outlined his educational program for the year to Congress. Johnson quickly sent his proposed Elementary and Secondary Education Act (ESEA) to Capitol Hill. Because the proposals were sent to Congress so quickly, and since there were many new ideas (Medicare being a notable exception), the success of the overall domestic and social program was greatly dependent on President Johnson's prestige and legislative and political skills. In a sense, the White House strategy was to let the Medicare and education bills run interference for the rest of the president's agenda. Those two bills were cornerstones for the Great Society, and "their passage would give momentum to the whole program. If difficulties came, it was better to face and settle them rather than permit them to entangle the rest of the White House legislation."[69]

Lyndon Johnson proved to be an excellent politician—he got Congress to authorize the Great Society, on his terms, and he fought a war in Southeast Asia, again on his terms, without congressional meddling. The legislative agenda he was able to get through Congress in 1965 was remarkable in its scope and ambition. Much of this was due to a combination of his superb political skills, honed while majority leader, and timing. Economic prosperity created the necessary resources as well as courage in Congress, and after January 1965 the political numbers in Washington were all in his favor.

NOTES

1. Johnson Library: William Bundy unpublished manuscript, chapter 18, p. 20.

2. Leslie H. Gelb, with Richard K. Betts, *The Irony of Vietnam: The System Worked*, p. 109.

3. December 2, 1964, "Position Paper on Southeast Asia," Tab 1 to December 7, 1964, memo from the president to the secretary of state, secretary of defense, and director of the CIA, in Johnson Library: National Security File, Box 2, vol. 7.

4. *The Pentagon Papers*, Gravel edition, Vol. 3, p. 246.

5. McNaughton handwritten notes, December 1, 1964, meeting, pp. 8–9, in Johnson Library: Meeting Notes File, Box 1.

6. *The Pentagon Papers*, Gravel edition, vol. 3, p. 246.

7. McNaughton December 1, 1964, notes, p. 8.

8. Bundy manuscript, chapter 19, p. 11.

9. *The Pentagon Papers*, Gravel edition, vol. 3, p. 246.

10. December 7, 1964, memo from the president to the secretary of state, secretary of defense, and director of the CIA, in Johnson Library: National Security File, Box 2, vol. 7.

11. Chester Cooper, *The Lost Crusade*, p. 225.

12. William Bundy claimed that the immediate introduction of a substantial ground force into the northern part of South Vietnam was discussed and rejected. He did not detail how much it was discussed, why it was dismissed, and whether there was any analysis of the long-term ramifications. (Bundy manuscript, chapter 18, p. 32.)
There was also a working paper within the State Department dated November 3, 1964, entitled "Moving US Ground Forces into the Mekong Valley," attached to the memo of the Bundy/McNaughton working group, "Scenario for Action in Southeast Asia" of November 21, 1964. Its contents remain classified, and most likely it was a contingency plan that floated up through the bureaucracy and was circulated to the Bundy working group. (See November 16, 1964, Document 233, *The Pentagon Papers*, Gravel edition, vol. 3, pp. 633–39.)

13. Memo from Robert H. Johnson to William Bundy, November 6, 1964, in Johnson Library: McNaughton Files, Book II, Box 8.

14. At the December 1 meeting on Vietnam, Johnson pointedly stated the "dependents should be out" before there was any U.S. military action. (McNaughton's December 1, 1964, notes, p. 6.)

15. As quoted in Joseph C. Goulden., *Truth Is the First Casualty: The Gulf of Tonkin Affair*, p. 99.

16. Gelb, with Betts, *The Irony of Vietnam*, p. 117.

17. Letter from Rusk to McNamara, November 28, 1964, in Johnson Library: National Security File, Agency File: Department of Defense, Defense Budget FY 1966 Folder.

18. *The Pentagon Papers*, Gravel edition, vol. III, p. 175.

Admiral [Harry] Felt [then U.S. commander in the Pacific] responded emphatically that there was no possible way to hold off the communists on the ground without the use of tactical nuclear weapons, and that it was essential that the commanders be given the freedom to use these as had been assumed under the various plans. He said that without nuclear weapons the ground force requirement was and had always been completely out of reach."

19. Roger Hilsman, *To Move a Nation*, p. 89.

20. December 30, 1964, White House Cable 4375, in Johnson Library: National Security File, National Security Council History, Box 40, Tabs 1–10, pp. 5–6, No. 6. In the cable, Johnson changed the draft wording (the original appears to have been drafted by McGeorge Bundy) from "I myself am ready to double the number of American forces in Vietnam" to "I myself am ready to substantially increase the number of American forces in Vietnam." He may have wanted to avoid any specific commitment, or he may have viewed the ultimate escalation as open-ended. (The original draft with the president's changes are in National Security File, Country File: Vietnam, Box 195, Folder: "President/ Taylor NODIS CLORES and Code Word Messages to and from Taylor.")

21. Ibid. p. 3.

22. Johnson Library: Taylor Oral History, Interview 3, September 14, 1981, pp. 4–5.

23. See McNaughton's Draft Memorandum, "Observations Re South Vietnam," January 4, 1965, in ibid., p. 683.

24. Johnson Library: NSC History: National Security File, vol. 1, Box 40, Tab 3.

25. Johnson Library: National Security File, National Security Council History, vol. 1, Box 40, Tab 3: Taylor in Saigon Embassy to Washington Cable 3 (No. 2056) of January 5, 1965.

26. Johnson Library: National Security File, NSC History, vol. 1, Box 40, Tab 3: Cable #2058.

27. Johnson Library: National Security File, NSC History, vol. 1, Box 40, Tab 3: Cable 2052; emphasis added.

28. Johnson Library: National Security File, NSC History, vol. 1, Box 40, Tab 4—January 7, 1965, cable from Johnson to Taylor.

29. See McGeorge Bundy's handwritten notes from January 6, 1964, meeting on Vietnam in Johnson Library: Papers of McGeorge Bundy.

30. Larry Berman in *Planning a Tragedy*, p. 37, quotes a passage from the first draft of this cable as illustrating "Washington's thinking during this crucial period." Berman gives the impression that President Johnson concurred with Bundy's draft, which Berman cited, when, in fact, Johnson crossed out a few key passages from the cable before it was sent. This includes both sentences referred to in the text, the second of which Berman italicized and gave great weight to. The full text of the exact cable that was sent can be found in the Johnson Library: National Security File, NSC History, vol. 1, Box 40, Tab 4—January 7, 1965, cable from Johnson to Taylor.

The reference Berman uses for the first draft he cites was in the NSC History, Troop Deployment File. At the Johnson Library, final texts and drafts can end up in different files, apparently depending on who retained which copies in the Johnson White House.

31. September 9, 1964, NSC Meeting, in September 14, 1964, memo from McGeorge Bundy to President Johnson, in Johnson Library: National Security File, Bundy Memos to the President, Box 2, vol. 6, pp. 5–6.

32. "Bureau In-House Discussion—FY 1966 Defense Budget", November 19, 1964, Johnson Library: Agency File: Department of Defense, Boxes 14–16, File: DOD Budget

Review.

33. Johnson Library: Agency File, Department of Defense, Box 11, vol. 1, File 1, p. 6.

34. John P. Crecine. *Defense Budgeting: Constraints and Organizational Adaptation*, p. 21.

35. May 1, 1964, policy letter and calendar in the National Archives: RG51, series 52.3, 1966 Budget folder. In November 1964, the Budget Director and the Pentagon analysts, in their one-day budget review, did not discuss Vietnam at all within the context of the budgetary needs. (November 20, 1964, budget review in Calendar of "Director's Review of the 1966 Budget" in National Archives: RG51, series 52.3, Director's Review folder.) This was the last high-level review of the FY 1966 military budget.

36. As quoted in Crecine, *Defense Budgeting*, p. 17. In his study, Crecine interviewed many top and middle-level officials in the mid to late 1960s from the Budget Bureau and the Pentagon.

The Pentagon used the following testimony in many public and internal Defense Department documents issued by Secretary McNamara concerning defense budgets under both Presidents Kennedy and Johnson,

Mr. McNamara: "When I took office in January, 1961, President Kennedy instructed me to—

1. Develop the force structure necessary to meet our military requirements without regard to arbitrary budget ceilings.

2. Procure and operate this force at the lowest possible cost." (McNamara testimony before the U.S. Senate Appropriations Subcommittee, *Hearings on Department of Defense Appropriations*, FY 1963, p. 5. as quoted in ibid., p. 17)

37. Ibid. p. 27.

38. Percival Flack Brundage, *The Bureau of the Budget*, p. 134.

39. Charles Hitch testimony before the Senate Committee on Government Operations, *Organizing for National Security. Hearings before the Subcommittee on National Policy Machinery*, 1961, p. 1033, as quoted in Arnold Kanter, *Defense Politics*, p. 75.

40. Testimony of Charles L. Schultze before the Subcommittee on Economy in Government of the Joint Economic Committee, "The Military Budget and National Economic Priorities," June 3, 1969, p. 68.

41. Ibid. p. 68.

42. Ibid.

43. Crecine, *Defense Budgeting*, p. 27.

44. Brundage, *The Bureau of the Budget*, p. 145.

45. Testimony of Charles L. Schulze, p. 69.

46. One of the only such works is Gregory Palmer, *The McNamara Strategy and the Vietnam War: Program Budgeting in the Pentagon, 1960—1968*.

47. Kanter, *Defense Politics*, p. 7.

48. There were nine mission-oriented categories. The $51.4 billion FY 1965 budget broke down this way:

1. Strategic retaliatory forces ($5.3 billion);
2. Air/missile defense forces ($1.7 billion);
3. General-purpose forces ($18.8 billion);
4. Airlift/sealift forces ($1.5 billion);

    5. Reserve and guard forces ($2.0 billion);
    6. Research and development ($5.0 billion);
    7. General support ($14.4 billion);
    8. Retired pay ($1.4 billion);
    9. Military assistance ($1.3 billion).

Each program area was, in turn, broken down into coded budget categories such as offensive and defensive strategic forces. Many of the specific figures and nature of programs in the Defense Department's budgets remain classified. But the programming was never geographically specific or conflict-specific. In terms of general-purpose forces, the programmatic breakdown was geared to the function of the troop units and weapons, not where they were deployed. (National Archives: RG51, series 52.3, "Defense Program Structure," in Department of Defense Budgeting folder and "Policy Letter," in 1966 Budget folder.)

    49. Testimony of assistant secretary of defense Robert Anthony before the Joint Economic Committee on "Economic Effect of Vietnam Spending," April 24, 1967, p. 17.

    50. See Robert McNamara's testimony in Hearings before the Senate Armed Services and Appropriations Committees on "Supplemental Appropriations for Department of Defense, 1965, Emergency Fund, Southeast Asia," May 5, 1965, p. 12.

    51. Testimony of Stewart Udall before Subcommittee on Economy in Government of the Joint Economic Committee, "The Military Budget and National Economic Priorities," June 6, 1969, p. 264.

One of the later outcomes of Congress' dissatisfaction with the budget process was the establishment of the Congressional Budget Office, which would provide Congress with independent research and analysis of the government's budgetary needs and requests as well as economic forecasting. At the same time, the military came under much greater scrutiny, and with respect to the budget the burden of proof shifted to the Pentagon just as it did for every other department. The secretary of defense would then have to go to the president to question anything the budget director did.

    52. Interviews of former OSA staff members, in Clark A. Murdock, *Defense Policy Formation: A Comparative Analysis of the McNamara Era*, pp. 94–95. The OSA activities on Vietnam were mostly data collection, procurement planning for aircraft and helicopters, and analyses of things like kill estimates and small versus large unit action.

The first major OSA analysis on Vietnam was a report on the impact of the Tet Offensive done for new secretary of defense Clark Clifford in 1968. OSA felt that any additional deployments would only serve to make the war more costly for the United States, not necessarily the communists; and OSA ripped the American policy since 1965 of trying to convince the communists they could not win by gradual escalation. (See *The Pentagon Papers*, Gravel edition, vol. 4, p. 557.) Shortly after this review of the Tet Offensive, Clifford recommended that President Johnson turn down Westmoreland's request for 206,000 more men in early March 1968 and that the United States should de-escalate.

    53. See David Halberstam, *The Best and the Brightest*, p. 740.

    54. Robert S. McNamara, *In Retrospect: The Tragedy and Lessons of Vietnam*, p. 198.

    55. U.S. Department of Defense and Department of Commerce figures, cited in testimony by Murray L. Weidenbaum before Hearings of Joint Economic Committee. *Economic Effect of Vietnam Spending*, vol. 1, April 26, 1967, p. 204.

    56. Johnson Library: National Security File, Agency File: Department of Defense,

Boxes 14–16, Defense Budget 1965 File, Section 1.

57.   Johnson Library: National Security Files, Agency File: Defense Department, Defense Budget, FY 1966 Folder, November 9, 1964. Bundy wrote back, "It didn't come up then."

58.   Memo for secretary of defense from the assistant secretary of defense (comptroller). Subject: FY 66 MAP Budget Request and MAP Dollar Guidelines FY 67–71, undated, in ibid.

59.   Murray Weidenbaum, *Economic Impact of the Vietnam War*, p. 21.

60.   Johnson Library, National Security File, Memos from McGeorge Bundy to the President, Box 2, vol. 7, December 16, 1964.

61.   Bundy manuscript, chapter 22, p. 6.

62.   Wilbur Cohen quoted in William S. Livingston, Lawrence Dodd, and Richard Schott, *The Presidency and the Congress*, pp. 300–301.

63.   January 25, 1965, budget message, *Public Papers of the President, Lyndon Baines Johnson, 1965*, p. 90.

64.   Bill Moyers, "Epilogue: Second Thoughts," in Bernard J. Firestone and Robert C. Vogt (eds.), *Lyndon Baines Johnson and the Uses of Power*, p. 351.

65.   Lyndon Johnson, quoted in Doris Kearns, *Lyndon Johnson and the American Dream*, p. 226.

66.   Moyers, "Epilogue," p. 356.

67.   *Public Papers of the President*, p. 3.

68.   For a more detailed discussion see David I Sheri., "Medicare: Hallmark of the Great Society," in Firestone and Vogt, *Lyndon Baines Johnson and the Uses of Power*, pp. 41–49, and Chapter 5 in *The Great Society: A Twenty Year Critique*, edited by Barbara C. Jordan and Elspeth D. Rostow.

69.   Eric Goldman, *The Tragedy of Lyndon Johnson*, p. 284.

Chapter 4 _____

Escalation

DETERIORATION IN SOUTH VIETNAM

January 1965 was a critical decision-making juncture. There were only 3,000 more American military personnel in Vietnam at the beginning of 1965 than a year earlier. Much had changed in the minds of the American decision-makers through 1964, but nothing had been done in Vietnam that was irrevocable. However, as the military situation worsened, and the Saigon government remained politically unstable, the imminent collapse of South Vietnam was very real. A SEACORD conference (the coordinating mechanism of the U.S. ambassadors and military commanders in Southeast Asia) on January 7 concluded that Phase I results—air attacks in Laos and greater covert activity— were militarily negligible and strongly recommended initiation of retaliatory and Phase II operations of sustained reprisal against North Vietnam, which could no longer wait for a strong Saigon government to emerge.[1] Coupled with the American concern that no improvement was evident in Saigon was the growing evidence that the communists were making major inroads into the South. The Viet Cong had become more aggressive and increasingly selected American targets for guerrilla or terrorist attacks. The Viet Cong continued to step up the pressure and had regained many areas considered free of Viet Cong control only a year earlier. In the first division-size battle of the conflict, the South Vietnamese army, despite substantial American assistance, was soundly defeated at Binh Gia, 40 miles southeast of Saigon, from December 26 to January 2.

After a new government in Saigon was established under Nguyen Oanh, there was a fear in Washington that the head of the military council, General

Khanh, would establish a new government that might go behind Washington's back and negotiate with the communists. Therefore, an additional incentive for greater American military involvement was to prevent any Saigon government from bargaining out of weakness, which most administration officials believed would be the first step toward ultimate communist control over South Vietnam.

THE PRESIDENT IS URGED TO ACT

President Johnson was very aware of the deteriorating military and political situation in Vietnam. He later recalled that "pessimistic reports continued to come to me from my advisers and from the field."[2] Ambassador Taylor warned from Saigon, "To take no positive action now is to accept defeat in the fairly near future."[3] According to Johnson, "That was the view of every responsible military adviser in Vietnam and in Washington. Painfully and reluctantly, my civilian advisers were driven to the same conclusion by the hard facts." Most of his advisers, including Taylor and General Westmoreland in Saigon, believed that the United States was compelled to act militarily. They urged him to initiate Phase II, which was, in the words of McGeorge Bundy, "a policy in which air and naval action against the North is justified by and related to the whole Viet Cong campaign of violence and terror in the South."[4]

Although he had approved reprisals in principle, Johnson did not authorize any specific military action. He was unconvinced that bombing was the answer, but the important factor in his hesitation remained his requirement that the proper groundwork be laid, so that any decision would appear justified and proper. The president's attention still remained divided. He was very involved with the plans for his domestic agenda, and preparations for his inauguration were under way. McGeorge Bundy assured him that "we would try to keep Vietnam quiet until after next Wednesday [inauguration day]."[5]

Two divergent positions (discounting the dissent of George Ball) had emerged among the president's senior advisers. The first, favored by McGeorge Bundy, McNamara, and Taylor, held that limited action was needed soon in order to stem the tide of Viet Cong infiltration and North Vietnamese support. The emphasis was on "limited" action. The second, put forth by the Joint Chiefs and senior military advisers, held that any American commitment to force must be substantial. In their view, the situation in Vietnam did not lend itself to a quick solution. Both favored quick action, but the difference was over how much. The second group contemplated a long-term program. Neither Johnson nor his senior advisers seemed to consider the possibility and implications of much greater U.S. military involvement. There was no discussion of the long-term implications if Phase II did not succeed, if the bombing did not get Hanoi to change its calculations.

During a meeting with congressional leaders and his top foreign policy advisers on January 15, the president downplayed the prospects of escalation. McNamara remarked at the meeting: "We need currently more South Vietnamese troops but not more U.S. forces." Then he remarked: "The President said we have decided that more U.S. forces are not needed in South

Vietnam short of a decision to go to full-scale war . . . . The war must be fought by the South Vietnamese. We cannot control everything that they do and we have to count on their fighting their war."[6]

McNamara's statement demonstrated both a disingenuousness by the president and senior officials and the shortsightedness of administration thinking. McNamara and Johnson told Congress that South Vietnam had to fight its own war at a time when a final authorization to escalate was awaiting the president's approval. That decision was forced on Johnson precisely because the Army of the Republic of Vietnam was incapable of carrying on the war. In addition, McNamara implied that any "decision" for full-scale war would be a specific policy choice. In other words, combat troops would be deployed to Vietnam only after a decision to go to war had been taken. Either no one had thought through the need for ground forces when the hoped-for bombing campaign began, or these congressional leaders were misled. Intentionally or unintentionally, the White House gave the impression that the U.S. role was limited, with little risk.

At the beginning of 1965, there was an increase in the public debate over Vietnam. The press and some members of Congress began to question U.S. policy. Like Senator Richard Russell of Georgia, many felt that "up until now we have been losing ground instead of gaining it."[7] He urged the administration to reevaluate its position in South Vietnam and cautioned that unless a more stable and effective government came to power, there would be a prolonged stalemate at best. A State Department survey of congressional opinion in January found "a generalized frustration with the situation in Vietnam and our involvement there. The great majority of Congressmen are neither satisfied nor dissatisfied; their thoughts are fragmented and they are genuinely perplexed. In this state, they are willing to go along with the people who have the direct responsibility, the experts, in the Executive Branch."[8] Most in the Senate and House did not necessarily agree with the policy, but, as with most foreign policy issues, they usually had to rely on the administration for information. If the White House either suppressed or manipulated the facts about Vietnam and specific military decisions, then Congress would be at a great disadvantage in its attempts to influence policy.

JOHNSON'S INDECISION

The president's advisers began to worry about his continuing deferral of Phase II. McGeorge Bundy remarked later that Johnson "really didn't want to have to decide . . . . [but] no decision was a decision, a decision to lose . . . . As we saw it, the policy wasn't working."[9] Bundy and McNamara wrote in a memo to President Johnson on January 27 that "no one has much hope that there is going to be a stable government while we sit still."[10] They strongly argued that the United States could no longer afford to wait since "our current policy can lead only to disastrous defeat" and implied that Johnson's indecision was exacerbating the problem: "Bob and I believe that the worst course of action is to continue in this essentially passive role which can only lead to

eventual defeat and an invitation to get out in humiliating circumstances."
They urged the president "to use our military power in the Far East and to force
a change of Communist policy." Particularly striking in the Bundy/McNamara
approach was the absence of any estimation of just what it might take to "force
a change of Communist policy." How American military power was to be
employed and tailored to the American goals was not discussed. According to
NSC staff member Chester Cooper, "It was high time, now that the President
had been inaugurated, now that he had the budget message and the state of the
union message out of the way, he could really concentrate on where we were
going in Vietnam."[11]

Since early January, Johnson had agreed in principle to escalate. But his
doubts about airpower and the timing of escalation remained. Maxwell Taylor
had already urged in his January 6 cable to the president that the United States
"look for an occasion to begin air operations."[12] On January 14 Taylor received
a cable from Rusk (the original cable had been drafted under the president's
name) that asked for his recommendation of the desired "reprisal action" once
the enemy attacked again so that Phase II bombing could begin.[13]

Therefore, upon the recommendation of the civilian and military advisers, a
De Soto patrol in the Tonkin Gulf was planned for February 3.[14] The president
had not yet responded to the January 27 McNamara/Bundy memo or authorized
any retaliation, but the commander in chief of the Pacific forces (CINCPAC)
was ordered on January 28 to place U.S. forces on alert while the patrol was
under way and be ready to retaliate immediately after any communist attack.[15]
The Joint Chiefs of Staff called the retaliatory air strike Flaming Dart. It had
been planned for many months: "Military authorities began to work up a pre-
packaged set of reprisal targets that might be politically acceptable, with pre-
assigned forces that would be in a high state of readiness to strike these targets,
and with a detailed strike plan that would provide a range of retaliatory
options."[16]

After Ambassador Taylor learned of the De Soto resumptions for February
3, he cabled Washington that "a DRV [Democratic Republic of Vietnam] attack
on a De Soto patrol followed by immediate strong and effective U.S. retaliation
would offer a priceless advantage to our cause here."[17] However, the De Soto
patrols were postponed from February 3 to February 7 because of the Tet (New
Year) holiday and then were canceled on February 4 because Soviet premier
Alexei Kosygin was to visit Hanoi then. Before they could be rescheduled, the
communists played into Washington's hands and carried out a major attack on
the U.S. barracks at Pleiku.

THE PLEIKU ATTACK

One immediate consequence of the McNamara/Bundy memo was that
President Johnson decided to send McGeorge Bundy to South Vietnam at the
beginning of February. Chester Cooper stated later that when the president
sent Bundy (accompanied by assistant secretary of defense John McNaughton
and Cooper) to Saigon for a firsthand look, Johnson had already made up his

mind: "For all practical purposes he had dismissed the option of de-escalating and getting out, but he didn't want to say that he had, and so the rationale for this trip was that this was going to be decisive . . . . On the basis of this, he would then decide what he was going to do on Vietnam. But, in point of fact, he damn well had decided already what he was going to do."[18] Johnson probably wanted a fresh perspective, which Bundy could provide because he had never been to Vietnam. He may also have desired to depict his administration as carefully considering all options.

There was some disagreement among the top advisers as to the domestic situation in South Vietnam. Taylor felt that General Khanh was a particularly poor choice for American support and urged the administration to reduce its support for his government.[19] The White House felt that for better or worse it must stick with Khanh, primarily because there seemed no other South Vietnamese political or military personality worthy of support. Soon after Bundy arrived in Saigon, he cabled the president: "We [i.e., Bundy and those who accompanied him] tend to differ with the mission . . . we believe that General Khanh, with all his faults, is by long odds the outstanding military man currently in sight—and the most impressive personality generally."[20] Before Bundy left South Vietnam, the Viet Cong attacked the military barracks at Pleiku on February 7. Nine Americans were killed, and 107 were wounded. The national security adviser, along with many others, immediately urged Johnson to retaliate. The president ordered an air strike later that evening. Chester Cooper later remarked, "You just couldn't start bombing North Vietnam, de novo. In order to launch such a major new step, the communists had to do something so atrocious that there would be justification for an attack on North Vietnam. The thought was that we would take our lumps until something dramatic and very obscene occurred. And then we would be able to justify this new, admittedly risky, possibly very unpopular policy."[21] It was hoped that sustained reprisals would be an effective way to punish North Vietnam and make the leaders in Hanoi think twice about the cost they would have to pay to continue their policy of supporting Viet Cong attacks in the South. In addition, in a cable to the president from Saigon on February 7, Bundy stated his belief that "there is one grave weakness in our posture in Vietnam . . . a widespread belief that we do not have the will and force and patience and determination to take the necessary action and stay the course."[22] It was the act of bombing itself that was important, not the extent of the bombing or the specific targets.

THE QUESTION OF ESCALATION

According to assistant secretary of state William Bundy, "The decision the President was making was understood by all to be more than a decision to hit back for one night's attack in a guerrilla war where incidents were legion."[23] One clue to the scope of the decision was that Johnson authorized the bombing raids at the same time as he ordered all U.S. dependents out of Saigon. The stage was set for the Phase II sustained bombing. Pleiku provided Johnson with the opportunity to clear the decks. He could remove dependents without demoralizing Saigon and appear moderate because he was responding to aggression. In addition, he could start escalation in motion.

The president had three separate meetings with top congressional leaders on February 6, 7, and 8 to discuss the situation in Vietnam. At the first meeting, the prospect of retaliation was discussed. All the congressional leaders except Senate majority leader Mike Mansfield approved of retaliatory strikes. After the meeting ended, Johnson ordered the Flaming Dart reprisals. On the eighth, Johnson notified the leaders that he would shortly authorize the sustained bombing program. He explained why the United States could not withdraw and then discussed, and had his advisers discuss, why it was necessary to escalate. Most of the leadership agreed with that policy but were not privy to military and intelligence assessments that concluded little would come of the bombing campaign and that the prospect of a long conflict was likely.[24] Johnson's message seemed contradictory. At first, he stated: "We are now ready to return to our program of pushing forward in an effort to defeat North Vietnamese aggression without escalating the war."[25] A few minutes later he remarked: "We did not intend to limit our actions to retaliating against Viet Cong attacks."

While Johnson's language was fairly ambiguous for his congressional audience, his advisers clearly thought he was escalating, although not everyone was in accord as to what that implied. William Bundy later summed up some of the resulting confusion: "In the three weeks after Pleiku, all sorts of difficulties and uncertainties continued to present themselves. A few at the top of the Administration thought that the immediate objective was to right the balance and permit negotiations, that beyond that effort, nothing had been decided. Others viewed the decision as much more final and irrevocable, right [the] imbalance in negotiations if that could be achieved, but in any event sticking to the job unless the South Vietnamese themselves made it impossible."[26]

When McGeorge Bundy recommended escalation on February 7, to his credit, he did not paint an overly optimistic picture. Rather, he concluded that even with a major show of U.S. military force such an effort would not be easy: "At its very best, the struggle in Vietnam will be long. It seems to us important that this fundamental fact be made clear to our people and to the people of Vietnam. Too often we have conveyed the impression that we expect an early solution when those who live with this war know that no early solution is possible. It is our own belief that the people of the United States have the necessary will to accept and to execute a policy that rests upon the reality that there is no short cut to success in South Vietnam."[27]

Bundy had put forth a realistic picture of how to describe the conflict to the American public. Escalation would demand a broad base of support and investment, politically and financially, from the American people. Yet, in the next four months, Johnson and his advisers did very little to paint a clear picture of American policy in Vietnam. When asked on February 8 by House minority leader Gerald Ford whether the new bombing program required additional military personnel and financial assistance, the president replied that there were enough money and men to meet present needs. Meeting notes show that President Johnson then added, "If the response to our action is larger than we expect, we will then of course make a request for a larger amount of U.S. military assistance and will need additional personnel."[28] But he gave no indication that such a possibility was planned for or even considered.

The impression that Johnson gave was that the United States was retaliating for communist aggression. Yet, he was considering the prospect of major escalation. During the February 8 meeting, a proposal for sustained bombing was on the President's desk along with a request for combat troops to be deployed at Danang in order to protect the air base there. Johnson had also been told by the JCS that the bombing raids would not have quick results. In the recommendation for the initial eight-week reprisal program, the Joint Chiefs clearly stated that "the mere initiation of the new US policy almost certainly would not lead Hanoi to restrain the Viet Cong; Hanoi would probably elect to maintain the very intense levels of activity of the past few days. However, if the United States persevered in the face of threats and international pressures, and as the degree of damage inflicted on North Vietnam increased, the chances of a reduction in Viet Cong activity would rise."[29] This advice reflected the Pentagon thinking that there was a threshold of death and destruction above which North Vietnam would give in and reduce or call off the insurgency in the South. At this point, there was no estimate as to when that might occur.

The question of ground forces was raised very briefly at the February 8 meeting with congressional leaders when JCS chairman General Earle Wheeler noted the difficulty of ensuring the security of the Pleiku base. He said the only real security for an airfield was full combat control of the perimeter two miles out from the field. The president then stated that there was no way to ensure against attacks such as those at Pleiku short of sending a very large number of U.S. troops to Vietnam.[30] At the end of that day, Johnson sent a cable to Maxwell Taylor that he intended to begin the Phase II program of sustained reprisals. In the words of McGeorge Bundy: "While we believe that the risks of such a policy are acceptable, we emphasize that its costs are real. It implies significant U.S. air losses even if no full air war is joined, and it seems likely that it would eventually require an extensive and costly effort against the whole air defense system of North Vietnam. U.S. casualties would be higher—and more visible to American feelings—than those sustained in the struggle in South Vietnam. Yet measured against the costs of defeat in Vietnam, this program seems cheap. And even if it fails to turn the tide—as it may—the value of the effort seems to us to exceed its cost." [31] Bundy later argued in the same memo:

We cannot assert that a policy of sustained reprisal will succeed in changing the course of the contest in Vietnam. It may fail and we cannot estimate the odds of success with any accuracy—they may be somewhere between 25% and 75%. What we can say is that even if it fails, the policy will be worth it. At a minimum, it will damp down the charge that we did not do all that we could have done, and this charge will be important in many countries including our own. Beyond that, a reprisal policy—to the extent that it demonstrates U.S. willingness to employ this new norm in counter-insurgency—will set a higher price for the future upon all adventures of guerrilla warfare, and it should therefore somewhat increase our ability to deter such adventures. We must recognize, however, that ability will be gravely weakened if there is failure for any reason in Vietnam.[32]

This was a thoroughly political analysis. Few military men would agree that even a failed military program is worth whatever losses have been taken. Johnson's civilian advisers viewed the crux of the policy as making a strong stand, not its ultimate success or failure. One of the keys to the equation in Bundy's mind was that the cost would be "cheap"—militarily, financially, and politically. But the costs he discussed were short-term. Such an argument does not jibe with the expectation of a long conflict. While there may have been a long-term goal for the bombing—that is, affecting the North Vietnamese calculation of interests—there was no long-term strategy at all, only short-term actions that would hopefully change the equation.

CONGRESSIONAL "CONSULTATION"

During this period, as the administration took major escalatory steps, key congressmen and senators were briefed, but they were not involved in the formation of Vietnam policy. Johnson usually tried to explain to them decisions and policies already under way. While the president did solicit the opinions of many congressmen and senators (he consistently listened to Senator Mansfield voice his increasing objections to his policies), he rarely consulted them before taking a decision. Congressional expert William Conrad Gibbons queried: "Did the President and his associates, as well as congressional leaders who were present at the meeting [on February 8], consider it to be a decision to go to war, or did they view it as a decision to undertake military action short of 'war'? . . . The paucity of the evidence precludes a definitive answer . . . but it would appear that the decision was viewed by all of the participants as being one involving the limited use of force short of war and of such magnitude as not to require further action by Congress at that time."[33] At that meeting, Johnson referred to the Tonkin Gulf Resolution but emphasized that his legal powers as president enabled him to escalate militarily.[34] He was asking Congress to place their faith in him as a man of moderation; he would retaliate for aggression but escalate sparingly. This was reminiscent of the Tonkin Gulf atmosphere.

Republican congressman Melvin Laird of Wisconsin felt that congressional "consultation" with the president was clearly a misnomer. He later reminded Secretary McNamara of the day after the president's inauguration: "Others on Capitol Hill were content to leave Vietnam policy in the President's hands. During a January 15 meeting with congressional leaders, "The President intervened to say that he had called the leaders together today not to discuss all the details of our programs but to inform them in general and to work out procedures under which such meetings could take place every few weeks . . . . Senator [Russell] Long replied that perhaps he should not be told all of the details. He did not want to hear things that he should not know about."[35]

In early 1965, despite the significant escalation of the American military role in Vietnam, there was virtually no official congressional activity on American policy in Vietnam. No public or executive hearings were held in February or March by either the House Foreign Affairs Committee or the Senate Foreign Relations Committee except for an executive session of the Senate Far East Subcommittee on February 9.[36] One of the few occasions when Vietnam was discussed on Capitol Hill in this period was during the appropriations hearings on the FY 1966 budget in late February and early March.

Dean Rusk later claimed: "President Johnson briefed the Congress on Vietnam more extensively than any President has briefed Congress on anything. When he first became President he used to have briefing sessions at the White House for Senators and Congressmen."[37] While Johnson may have spent a great deal of time with senior members of Congress, records of the meetings demonstrate that he did not give them an accurate impression of his policy. He often stage-managed a big show to make them feel seriously consulted in the hopes of maintaining good congressional relations. He needed Congress to help sell his policies to the public, especially during highly visible decision periods (after the Tonkin Gulf incident, after the Pleiku attacks, after the July escalation announcement, etc.).

"ROLLING THUNDER"

On February 10 an attack by the Viet Cong in Qui Nhon (causing the greatest number of American deaths to date, 23) prompted a U.S. response that widened a single reprisal to a more general retaliation (Flaming Dart II) for "continued acts of aggression." Three days after the Qui Nhon attack, Johnson officially approved the Phase II program of "measured and limited" air action against selected military targets in North Vietnam. The Pentagon called it "Rolling Thunder." Initially, the JCS developed an eight-week bombing program at the rate of four fixed targets per week below the 19th parallel. While many in the military felt the program to be inadequate (the JCS had recommended a much heavier operation in late 1964), they approved of this first step that went beyond mere retaliation.[38] General Wheeler and army chief of staff General Harold K. Johnson also argued that three U.S. ground divisions were needed in South Vietnam in order to protect the airfields from which Rolling Thunder raids would be launched.[39] The first air strikes were carried out on March 2, rather than the week of February 20 as intended. The delay, recommended by Taylor and Westmoreland, was a result of bad weather and the ouster of General Khanh on February 24. But the United States could no longer hold off on bombing until the Saigon government stabilized.

After only two weeks, as General Harold Johnson noted, the scope and frequency of the air strikes were insufficient to "convey a clear sense of U.S. purpose to the DRV (Democratic Republic of Vietnam)."[40] The president then agreed to increase the pace and scope of Rolling Thunder because Pentagon planners felt that there was a point at which Hanoi would calculate that its policy was not cost-effective.[41] This reflected an attitude that had become prevalent throughout much of the administration, in particular, the Defense Department: through cost-benefit analysis the United States could eventually determine the necessary level of military pressure to deter North Vietnam.[42]

Deputy secretary of defense Cyrus Vance later discussed this policy of "graduated escalation": "It was believed that it *should* work . . . . That this would result in a desire and willingness on the part of the North Vietnamese and the NLF [National Liberation Front] to sit down and negotiate a political settlement to the problem."[43] There was overconfidence on the part of many American officials who believed that the United States really could achieve what it wanted when it wanted against a Third World country. There was a belief that the United States, by graduated escalation, could force Hanoi to the negotiating table on American terms. McGeorge Bundy, even though he had argued that the struggle would be long, confidently wrote to the president: "My own opinion on the general diplomatic front is that we can always get to the conference table when we need to, and that there is no great hurry about it right now."[44]

Even those who were not at all confident of bombing success could support the escalation simply for its symbolism. U. Alexis Johnson, deputy ambassador in Saigon, stated that the two primary goals of the bombing were the improvement of morale in the South, by convincing Saigon that the United States would not pull out militarily, and making the movement of supplies more difficult. However, "in the event we did lose in the South and the thing did collapse on us—it looked like it might collapse at that point—we would demonstrate that the other side just doesn't get off free in these situations." [45]

Over the course of the next few months the bombing campaign grew in intensity, in geographic coverage, and in the assortment of targets. Initially, the number of strikes ran from 1 to 2 per week. By mid-1965 they had risen to 10 to 12 per week, and the number of sorties to about 900 per week—four or five times what they had been in early March.

William Conrad Gibbons asked, "What was Rolling Thunder intended to accomplish?" Citing a lack of evidence, he argued: "There was very little discussion of objectives at the meetings which preceded the decision to begin bombing, and few notes were kept at key meetings, such as the one on February 13, 1965 at which final approval was given to continuing action against North Vietnam."[46] Rolling Thunder was an excellent example of using force simply for the sake of taking any action. It was little more than a stopgap measure. The president later remarked about his decision to go ahead with the bombing: "I realized that doing nothing was more dangerous than doing something."[47] That was why relatively minor military actions, an eight-week bombing program and the deployment of marines for defensive purposes, were taken. But that was also why such short-term measures did not succeed and why greater escalation was inevitable; they were inconsistent with the stated goals of deterring the communists. There seemed no coherence to the policy and an inconsistency between the military and political viewpoints.

QUESTIONS OF CREDIBILITY

At the same time, the president and some of his advisers acted in ways that began to create what would later become a serious problem of credibility. During February President Johnson consistently emphasized in public that the escalatory steps he authorized were not "a change in policy." Yet, behind closed doors, the words were very different. According to the notes of a February 10 NSC meeting, Johnson stressed the importance of preventing any leaks to newspapers. "There followed a discussion of how much news should be made public following the air attack. The consensus was that we should not spell out in detail exactly what we had undertaken to do."[48] McGeorge Bundy then argued against discussing publicly the change from Phase I to Phase II: "At an appropriate time we could publicly announce that we had turned a corner and changed our policy but that no mention should be made now of such a decision." Only three days before, he had urged the president to level with the American people that the conflict would be long and there could be no shortcuts.

Johnson "indicated his reluctance to state again what he had said many times previously." He had made a television address on February 8 to justify the first U.S. retaliation raid in response to Pleiku, and so he "said it had been proper and necessary for us to go into great detail publicly about our first raid in order to reassure the press but he did not think it is necessary following the proposed strike."[49] There were no further policy statements or briefings. This began a pattern in which either no public comment was made or the president or White House reiterated the same message that there was no change in policy. The White House let stand the president's speech of February 8, even though the policy was now sustained bombing, not simply retaliation. As Robert McNamara has noted, President Johnson knew very well in February that he was completely ignoring "the magnitude of the change in U.S. military operations" that the bombing program entailed. Johnson, according to McNamara, "chose to stilt his comments and, hopefully, the comments of others." He added that Johnson's refusal to announce decisions or policy changes publicly "eventually cost him dearly . . . . Johnson's continued lack of candor steadily diminished popular faith in his credibility and leadership."[50]

The Pleiku attacks and the American reprisals also led to more press coverage and greater scrutiny of the conflict in Vietnam. Some in the press began to question the policies and their implications. James Reston of the *New York Times* wrote on February 14: "The time has come to call a spade a bloody shovel. This country is in an undeclared and unexplained war in Vietnam. Our masters have a lot of long and fancy names for it, like escalation and

retaliation, but it is war just the same."[51]   Language became particularly
important at this time. The Flaming Dart raids were first couched in terms of
"retaliation" or "reprisal." On February 11 the White House then described
U.S. bombing as a "response" to the continued acts of aggression. According to
The Pentagon Papers authors, this was "clearly deliberate." As a result, "the
new terminology reflected a conscious U.S. decision to broaden the reprisal
concept as gradually and as imperceptibly as possible to accommodate a much
wider policy of sustained, steadily intensifying air attacks against North
Vietnam, at a rate and on a scale to be determined by the U.S."[52]

THE LACK OF CRITICAL THINKING

The decision to use military power against North Vietnam seemed to have
resulted as much from a lack of alternative proposals as from any compelling
logic advanced in its favor.[53] George Ball later explained that since the United
States must preserve its international reputation, "dropping bombs was a
pain-killing exercise that saved my colleagues from having to face the hard
decision to withdraw."[54]   Whenever Ball argued with McNamara about
escalation, the defense secretary "had a set answer, which was 'all right,
George, what do you propose to do?' I had a set answer too. I proposed that
we cut our losses and get the hell out. But that was no [acceptable] answer."[55]

One question that was never analyzed or debated fully was, What would
happen if the communists were willing, as McGeorge Bundy put it on February
7, to pay "a higher price"? Therefore, what risks were then created for the
United States? Two weeks after Bundy's memo, Dean Rusk emphasized "the
importance of conveying a signal to Hanoi and Peiping that they themselves
cannot hope to succeed without a substantial escalation on their part, with all of
the risks which they would have to face."[56] But if the American escalation was
met with further aggression, was the United States prepared to continue up the
escalation ladder? In terms of policy, the question remained unanswered. Only
a few, such as George Ball, Vice President Hubert Humphrey, and Senator
Mansfield tried to get the president and his advisers to answer it.

Vice President Humphrey warned against escalating in Vietnam in a
February 17 letter to the president. He argued that "American wars have to be
politically understandable by the American public. There has to be a cogent,
convincing case if we are to enjoy sustained public support."[57]   After
concluding that there was not a sufficient case for U.S. escalation in Vietnam,
Humphrey then urged the president to get out: "It is always hard to cut losses.
But the Johnson Administration is in a stronger position to do so now than any
Administration in this century. 1965 is the year of minimum political risk for
the Johnson Administration. Indeed it is the first year when we can face the
Vietnam problem without being preoccupied with the political repercussions
from the Republican right."[58]

Ball has stated that he was alone against escalatory bombing in February
1965 in the top councils. However, "some lower-level Department of State
types agreed but were not in a position to be heard."[59] NSC staff member

James Thomson strongly argued against the bombing in a biting memo: "Thus, even though I have seen no intelligence estimates (including that of February 18th) which conclude that Hanoi would 'call off its dogs' in response to a sustained reprisal track, I assume that the track has nonetheless commended itself to the Administration as a means to achieve stability through sustained euphoria in Saigon."[60] He punctuated his criticism with the observation that the previous night Saigon had witnessed another coup attempt. While the Viet Cong attack on Pleiku was just a catalyst for military action that was inevitable, it greatly undercut the arguments of those who disagreed with a greater U.S. military role.

George Ball again urged the president to stop and look at the long-term consequences. Bill Moyers took Ball's October 5 memo, "How Valid Are the Assumptions Underlying Our Vietnam Policies?" to Johnson. While Ball's advice remained very relevant, Moyers' action led only to a meeting with the president on February 26 in which Ball had to defend his position in front of those who were in favor of escalation; they did not have to justify their stance, even though no one could adequately deflect Ball's argument that greater military involvement in Vietnam would suck the United States into a long-term and unwinnable war. Anyone who favored a wholesale rethinking of U.S. policy in Vietnam had the burden of proof. Although Ball continued to play an active role in many meetings on Vietnam, those who disagreed with the policy of escalation had little chance of changing policy because at bottom, they were arguing that Vietnam was not worth the risk of a major military conflict.

The lack of critical thinking seems even more astonishing when one considers that there was little reason to believe that a policy of sustained bombing would succeed. Dean Rusk later remarked that "anyone who ever expected the bombing to end the war ought to have his head examined, because bombing just doesn't do that. It makes it more difficult, but it doesn't prove to be a decisive military factor."[61] Chester Cooper remarked that "retaliation against the Viet Cong was pretty difficult, in part because nobody knew where in the hell they were and they didn't own anything to retaliate against. However, it was becoming increasingly clear that behind the Viet Cong was Hanoi and if we could somehow get Hanoi to turn the thing off, or at least simmer it down, the situation would be manageable in South Vietnam."[62] That the decision to bomb came only after the Viet Cong attack on Pleiku demonstrated that the communists were dictating the course of action and setting the agenda. In the first seven months of 1965, when a specific action failed or was not deemed sufficient, the United States slowly turned the pressure up a notch. Thus, a limited and retaliatory bombing campaign in late February would become a major sustained program by mid-July. Once Rolling Thunder was perceived as ineffective, it was natural and logical that the United States would have to up the ante, escalate in some way, to re-demonstrate its commitment.

In many ways, this can be viewed as a quagmire, but the quagmire theory is premised on the belief that the president and his advisers did not understand the consequences of these short-term measures. The evidence shows that was not the case. For example, the administration stated publicly that the air operations would be an eight-week campaign, designed simply to halt the North's pattern of aggression. But, as McGeorge Bundy remarked a few months later in a memo to the president, "The bombing did not reverse the situation and we did not expect it would."[63]

DOWNPLAYING THE DECISIONS

One of the interesting patterns that emerge in reading the memoirs of many of the president's key foreign policy advisers during this period is the sense most of them had that the deployment of ground forces was implied in the discussions and debates of January and February. Cyrus Vance later remarked that indications in January and February were that ground forces might have to be deployed to stop the communists.[64] On February 14 the press reported that such a move was being considered strictly in the context of providing protection for the air bases. The *New York Times* noted, "At this point, the Administration is not considering any sizable increase in American military missions . . . . if South Vietnam goes through with plans to increase the size of its forces, additional Americans are likely to be sent as advisors, officials say."[65] But in none of the records of White House meetings or papers on Vietnam was the deployment of combat troops a major topic of discussion. Most officials, like Dean Rusk, when talking publicly about the war at all, simply reiterated the president's statement that "we seek no wider war."[66]

After the beginning of the Flaming Dart operation the Chinese promised to send troops into North Vietnam in the event of an American invasion. The Soviet Union offered "all-out aid" if the United States invaded.[67] The U.S. public and the press in particular were aware that the combination of the Pleiku attacks and the American bombing had raised the ante. The international community began to sense that the Vietnam conflict lay on the brink of a potentially major escalation that might engage one or more great powers. In spite of such concerns, the prospect of Chinese or Soviet intervention was not raised as a major factor by Johnson (or by most of his advisers) in the deliberations on escalation or in downplaying U.S. actions. At no point did the president argue that small, incremental military steps were necessary to avoid provoking either Chinese or Soviet involvement in the conflict. Rather, it seems that Johnson intervened and escalated incrementally, not to lessen the reaction of either the Soviets or Chinese (or the international community as a whole) but to avoid provoking the different domestic constituencies and the American public.

The president made a speech on economic policy to a group of business leaders on February 17 in which he briefly discussed Vietnam in his conclusion. Although not intended at the time, this speech served as the administration's major policy statement on Vietnam. While Johnson left the specifics of Vietnam policy for McNamara and Rusk to articulate, this set the tone. Both Rusk and McNamara would refer back over the next five months to the president's words in this speech. He emphasized that the U.S. objective in

Vietnam was a continuation of the policies of his predecessors. The United States sought no wider war, and "our continuing actions will be those which are justified and those which are made necessary by the continuing aggression of others. These actions will be measured and fitting and adequate."[68]

The phrase "measured and fitting and adequate" was to be the cornerstone of almost all public statements on Vietnam policy from February to July. But nowhere did Johnson mention the actual military decisions he had made and why bombing was important. The administration's strategy was put forth in a February 16 cable to Ambassador Maxwell Taylor in Saigon and Ambassador David Bruce in London, in which McGeorge Bundy stated on behalf of the president: "Careful public statements of USG [United States Government], combined with fact of continuing air action, are expected to make it clear that military action will continue while aggression continues . . . . the focus of public attention will be kept as far as possible on aggression, not on military operations . . . . There will be no comment of any sort on future actions except that all such actions will be adequate and measured and fitting to aggression."[69] Deflecting attention away from U.S. military action was also echoed in a February 18 State Department policy directive regarding a refinement of the president's decision on Rolling Thunder: "Focus of public attention will be kept as far as possible on DRV aggression; not on joint GVN [Government of Vietnam]/US military operations. There will be no comment of any sort on future actions except that all such actions will be adequate and measured and fitting to aggression."[70] At a February 25 press conference, Dean Rusk, when asked whether the United States was expanding its military role in Vietnam, simply referred the reporter back to his opening statement, which was a summation of the president's recent remarks, a reiteration of the importance of standing up to communist aggression in South Vietnam and a recitation of the Tonkin Gulf Resolution. Three times he stated, "That is the policy," without at all answering the question. The only allusion to the U.S. military position was the statement from the Tonkin Gulf Resolution that noted that the United States was prepared to use armed force if necessary.[71]

The manner in which American military involvement in Vietnam was portrayed became an important issue within administration circles. Some top advisers parted with the president on this: not about what should be done in Vietnam but how the policy should be presented to the American public and the world. Assistant secretary of state James Greenfield argued that in order to gain the public's support, it was critical to be as open as possible with the press and make the public aware of what the country was in for. Greenfield believed that the administration must be more specific and forthcoming about military policy in Vietnam. In a February 16, 1965, memo to Rusk entitled "Vietnam and the Public," Greenfield stated: "Within the government the tendency so far is to brush aside the general public statement on the excuse that it cannot include all the details demanded by the press. This argument is not valid."[72]

Horace Busby, special assistant to the president, was concerned about the "public silence on Vietnam" and wrote a memo to Johnson in which he recommended a public speech on American policy in Vietnam.[73] Shortly after the first bombing retaliation, McGeorge Bundy and Bill Moyers had urged "a Presidential speech." But Bundy was quickly persuaded by the president that "there is real gain in keeping [the president] out of the immediate military aspect of the matter at this stage."[74] Even Dean Rusk briefly urged Johnson to consider greater public disclosure. At the February 18 NSC meeting Dean Rusk "felt that, in the course of the next week, it may be necessary to make another strong statement of our aims and objectives."[75] This advice was turned aside by the president.

William Bundy noted that the president, in February and March,

> got into a very firm set of mind that this was *not* to be depicted as a change of policy. That we were doing what was necessary, that was the policy; that this was just a couple of new things we were doing, but it wasn't a change of policy. He wanted, in effect, to mute the whole thing. I don't know the reasoning that brought him into that. Its results were some rather sharp stops and starts in the executive branch . . . . I remember Mac [Bundy] telling me, "Look, get this straight. The President does not want this depicted as a change of policy.". . . But I record, I think, the honest feeling of those of us who had been working closely in the whole series of events . . . . that we thought it would in effect *have* to come out as clearly stated upgrading of our resolve and our whole scale of action, and be depicted in that light. And the President did not wish to do that.[76]

It is important to note that not only were the public and Congress given the wrong impression of the steps the United States was taking, but Johnson's domestic and economic advisers were hearing those same words and phrases that were crafted in order to downplay American military policy. The administration's public relations strategy was to keep public attention on communist "aggression," not on U.S. military actions. The key was to consistently talk about why the U.S. commitment to South Vietnam was justified, while downplaying the actual military escalation. Each escalatory step was presented as a small, but necessary, consequence of the communist aggression, while no mention was made of overall policy or future military operations.

The Tonkin Gulf affair had shown Lyndon Johnson that forceful American action was viewed by the public as legitimate in the face of perceived communist aggression. Thus, the rhetoric of Johnson's Vietnam policy was couched in terms of "preserving our commitment" and "protecting our boys." These were both noble and identifiable in the minds of most Americans, and as a result, Johnson's stated Vietnam policy gained very favorable public support in 1965. Bill Moyers sent a memo to the president informing him of a Lou Harris poll done for the White House. After Pleiku, the president's approval rating went from 66 percent (on February 1), to 69 percent.[77]

One of the most telling memos that represented the type of thinking and decision making in the White House at the time was written on February 16 to the president from McGeorge Bundy:

1. I think that some of us—perhaps mostly me—have been confusing two questions. One is the firmness of your own decision to order continuing action; the other is the wisdom of a public declaration of that policy by you . . . .

2. Rightly or wrongly, those of us who favor continuing military action against the North do see it as a major watershed decision . . . .

3. Precisely because this program represents a major operational change and because we have waited many months to put it into effect, there is a deep-seated need for assurance that the decision has in fact been taken . . . .

4. Thus it seems essential to McNamara—and to me too—that there be an absolutely firm and clear internal decision of the U.S. Government and that this decision be known and understood by enough people to permit its orderly execution. This is one side of the problem.

5. The other side of the problem, as I understand it, is that you do not want to give a loud public signal of a major change in policy right now. This is a position which makes a lot of sense on a lot of grounds.[78]

So this "watershed decision" and "major change in policy" were to be greatly downplayed. Only those required to execute the escalation needed to know that continuing sustained and escalatory action was the policy. Everyone else, from the public to government officials not concerned with military affairs or Southeast Asia, was to be kept in the dark. This was to have very significant consequences for the American people and the president's own domestic and economic advisers as the war escalated.

The tone of the memo was clearly different from McGeorge Bundy's professed desire in his February 7 Pleiku memo to be honest and up-front with the nation. For his part, either President Johnson did not believe Bundy's assessment that the conflict in Vietnam would be a long struggle, or he deceived Congress and the American public by keeping the extent of the U.S. commitment from them. In another memo to the president, regarding a newspaper interview Johnson was to give on February 19, McGeorge Bundy gave the following synopsis of current Vietnam policy: "So we are planning to act quietly and firmly and to stick to a policy: that we are helping these people to help themselves and that we are acting appropriately against a sustained and dangerous aggression of a very complex and difficult sort. At the same time, when the appropriate occasion comes, we will be more than ready to state our position, and our cases, and our purposes and our objectives. There is no secret and will be no secret about our policy."[79] But the "appropriate occasion" never arose in the next five months, and the decisions were increasingly clouded with secrecy and deception.

Even after U.S. marines were deployed to Vietnam in early March, as the press began to speculate about the military mission of the American troops, the Johnson administration continued to insist that there was no change in policy. Statements to that effect became stock answers for any press inquiry. Secretary of State Rusk cabled Ambassador Taylor to remind him that the president's February 17 statement, which declared that U.S. actions "will be measured and fitting and adequate," remained "basic," and no one should "go beyond it."[80]

He had cabled Taylor because he was politely critical of a statement by Taylor to the Italian newspaper *La Stampa*, which had quoted the ambassador as saying there was "no limit to our escalation." Rusk added: "Our whole feeling here is that our actions should speak for themselves and we should not be seeking to change our signal in any way through verbal statements or speculation."

An unsigned briefing memo for the president, written prior to his March 13 press conference, included a list of potential press queries and the answers for the president to use. Among the test questions were the following:

Q: What is the explanation of the change in U.S. policy toward Vietnam in the last month?

A: Our policy today is just as it was last month and just as it has been for months, and even years, before.

Q: Doesn't the bombing of North Vietnam and the landing of the marines mean a change of policy?

A: No. The particular actions we take are "those which are justified and those which are made necessary by the continuing aggression of others."

Q: Is the U.S. planning further bombings or further landings of troops?

A: It would be wrong for me to announce our military plans to the enemy before they are carried out and I do not think it is useful to circulate rumors and speculations.[81]

During the March 13 press conference President Johnson referred to the "basic commitment to Vietnam" and made it a point to emphasize strongly that "our policy there is the policy that was established by President Eisenhower, as I have stated, since I have been President, 46 different times, the policy carried on by President Kennedy, and the policy that we are now carrying on."[82] But Johnson would not discuss any specific strategies to carry out that general policy and would for most of his tenure as president use such logic as a means of avoiding any debate about U.S. military policy in Vietnam.

In his press conference, he vaguely hinted at the military changes on March 13: "Although the incidents have changed, in some instances the equipment has changed, in some instances the tactics and perhaps the strategy in a decision or two has changed."[83] But he went no further in talking about any changes at all with respect to American involvement in Vietnam. The problem with such modest statements was that he kept repeating them, claiming that "changes in tactics, in strategy, in equipment, in personnel" did not imply any change in policy.[84] Johnson's use of the term "policy" was probably different from what the press or the public took it to mean, and that helped undermine his credibility. The press could also see that major changes were occurring on the ground in Vietnam and that the situation was decidedly not the same as it was a year ago or 10 years ago, when Eisenhower was president.

SENDING IN THE MARINES

There was now a clear departure from the previous U.S. position that the problem lay in the South, despite Hanoi's assistance to the Viet Cong. An ill-conceived State Department "white paper" was put forth to justify the shift in focus to the North by claiming considerable evidence that communist forces had infiltrated into the South from North Vietnam. Even the authors, including William Bundy, admitted it was poorly done, with flimsy evidence and an unconvincing case.[85] Nevertheless, North Vietnam would be held accountable for the guerrilla activities in South Vietnam. This helped pave the way for the beginning of Rolling Thunder a few days later. The new focus on North Vietnam turned attention away from changes on the ground in the South, thus helping mask what the United States was about to do next: introduce ground forces. The *New York Times* concluded: "The Johnson administration seems to be conditioning the American people for a drastic expansion of our involvement in Vietnam."[86] But the expansion was expected to be in the air, so the focus of the press in March and April remained on the bombing, not the subtle increases in ground forces.

The decision to send combat troops to Vietnam was made quickly and with little fanfare. General Westmoreland had continually pressed for more manpower in February. After he officially requested ground forces on February 22, according to William Bundy, "the JCS must have acted rapidly on the recommendation, for on the 26th, with no work by any staffs outside the Pentagon, the matter was presented to the President at the luncheon meeting, and approved by him."[87]

Unlike the question of bombing, there was little debate over ground forces. There are two possible explanations. First, the bombing decision implied that ground forces would have to be sent to Vietnam, so the February decisions were tantamount to approval of a land war. But that possibility was never discussed in detail. Second, the president's advisers may have expected him to follow the same deliberate and slow decision process he had before he finally OK'd the Phase II bombing. But Johnson had taken his time about bombing because he was not convinced it would do any good and was concerned about the timing. In deploying ground forces he did not have similar doubts and could subsume the initial deployments into the bombing decisions. Also, after Pleiku, the president began to take much more of an active part in the military decision process. It is important to emphasize that Johnson himself pushed for downplaying the Vietnam decisions and creating the impression that policy had not changed.

The rationale for the marine deployment was to provide security for the airfields used in the Rolling Thunder campaign (although some of the bombing missions came off aircraft carriers). In addition, the U.S. Marines could take up the slack for an ineffective and disintegrating South Vietnamese military. Deputy ambassador U. Alexis Johnson explained the military logic: "When we started the bombing of the North, we had the problem of protecting the airfield at Danang against retaliatory raids . . . and we needed to put in a Hawk battalion [of missiles] there to protect Danang. And then it turned out that, for these Hawks to be effective, they had to be on the hills around Danang; and to protect the Hawks, you had to bring in Marines to protect the Hawks."[88] This began a cyclical pattern whereby every decision to escalate created the need to escalate further in order to protect the investment made by the first decision.

The deployment of ground forces was not without its detractors. Maxwell Taylor, in a cable to the State Department on February 22, opposed Westmoreland's request for the two marine battalions: "Such action would be step in reversing long standing policy of avoiding commitment of ground combat forces in SVN. Once this policy is breached, it will be very difficult to hold line."[89] Taylor's primary concern was that if the United States demonstrated a willingness to assume responsibilities on the ground, Saigon would soon unload other combat roles onto the American military. Assistant secretary of defense McNaughton urged the deployment of the 173d Airborne Brigade rather than the marines. According to *The Pentagon Papers*, he apparently wanted to "emphasize the limited, temporary nature of the U.S. troop deployment and to reduce the conspicuousness of the U.S. presence." The military significance was that "airborne troops carry less equipment and look less formidable than the Marines plus they have no history of peace-keeping intervention in foreign wars."[90] While McNaughton may have had good political reasons for his suggestion, for military reasons CINCPAC was adamant that existing military contingencies, first drawn up in 1959, required the marines.[91]

The deployment was announced on March 6. The mission was "to occupy and defend critical terrain features in order to secure the airfield and, as directed, communications facilities, U.S. supporting installations, port facilities, landing beaches and other U.S. installations against attack. The U.S. Marine Force will not, repeat will not, engage in day to day actions against the Viet Cong."[92] The decision was portrayed as purely defensive and a logical extension of the American bombing program. There was no congressional debate about the landing of the marines and little public debate. A few journalists expressed concern, but most of the dissent to American policy in Vietnam focused on bombing, and scant attention was paid to the marine deployment because it was not viewed as a move to engage in ground combat. It appeared to be only a component of the bombing campaign. William Bundy commented that during this period, "bombing the North and all that went with it had been almost the total focus in Washington and of public opinion in America and the world."[93]

On March 8, less than two weeks after Rolling Thunder was authorized (and six days after the first bombing runs), two combat-ready marine battalions went ashore near Danang to protect the airfields there. The administration line was consistent from the White House to the Pentagon: the marines were at Danang for "defensive purposes only," and their mission was "limited."

General Karch, who headed the new ground force, stated at a March 8 press conference in Danang that the marines "will be operating strictly in a defensive role" and "will be patrolling within the zone we are assigned as defensive sector . . . . Base security is the primary mission."[94] Robert McNamara stated the next day that although "the Marines will shoot if they are shot at," the troops would "serve as a security force only."[95] However, on March 3, in Senate testimony, U.S. Army chief of staff General Harold Johnson had already noted that these forces would not be restricted only to "static security."[96] Apparently, since Johnson was not there to testify on Vietnam but on the FY 1966 military budget, there was little follow-up on his Vietnam comments. No one in Congress challenged the general's statement, nor were any questions raised as to whether the deployment might lead to offensive combat operations.

"GET THINGS BUBBLING, GENERAL"

As American military operations in Vietnam grew, President Johnson devoted more time and energy to the war. Increasingly disappointed in the American military progress to date, he was determined to do whatever was necessary not to lose South Vietnam. When General Harold Johnson was dispatched to Vietnam on March 5 to survey the military situation and explore further military options, the president not-so-subtly hinted that a request for more men would be looked upon favorably.[97] The president emphasized that he wanted the general to "get things bubbling."[98]

When Robert McNamara informed Ambassador Taylor of General Johnson's Saigon visit, he sent word in the name of the president that they should develop a list of additional actions the U.S. military should pursue in South Vietnam. Taylor was instructed: "In developing list, you may, of course, assume no limitation on funds, equipment or personnel. We will be prepared to act immediately and favorably on any recommendations you and General Johnson may make."[99] This opened up much greater possibilities for the use of American military power. General Johnson clearly took the president's desire for no limitations seriously. He stated during a meeting of the military in Vietnam, "I am here as a representative of the President of the United States. Mr. Johnson asked me to come and tell you that I came with a blank check. What do you need to win the war?"[100]

General Johnson returned to Washington with a series of recommendations for more American forces, in particular, the deployment of one combat division to protect U.S. bases in South Vietnam. President Johnson did not approve the recommendation for a ground force division in mid-March. But he then urged the Joint Chiefs of Staff on March 15 to devise new measures to "kill more VC."[101] The president was certainly sending mixed signals. He turned down significant increases in the deployment yet encouraged measures and thinking that led to requests for greater military force. Only three days after the president turned down General Johnson's recommendation, General Westmoreland requested, with the full support of the JCS, three divisions (two U.S. and one South Korean—a division was about 15,000 troops, not including support personnel), as well as the immediate landing of a marine battalion at Phu Bai near Hue. Ambassador Taylor opposed the three-division request, while McNamara, although inclined to favor it, wanted more information on the ramifications of such a large number of troops and the likely South Vietnamese reaction. Taylor believed that U.S. forces should be deployed in enclaves in the coastal region of South Vietnam and wanted to try this out first at Danang before bringing in any more soldiers.

Westmoreland would later defend himself against the charge that at this time he was utilizing "a foot in the door ploy to the deployment of U.S. ground troops which I truly hoped to avoid."[102] But he clearly wanted troops and an offensive mission for them and later remarked that "intrinsic in my proposal was that American troops would be used in offensive operations."[103] Westmoreland need not have been so defensive; President Johnson clearly wanted to escalate also. The president was certainly not tricked by the military into sending U.S. forces to Vietnam. He had urged the military to give him proposals to deploy more forces. He believed in a military solution, and his enthusiasm for escalation was apparent. McGeorge Bundy quoted the president as stating in a meeting on March 23, "I don't wanna run out of targets and I don't wanna go to Hanoi. I was a hell of a long time gettin into this. But I like it."[104]

The President was made aware of where the path he was taking—the emphasis on ground forces—was headed. General Johnson emphasized to him that to win the war, 500,000 U.S. troops could be required over five years.[105] There is no documentary evidence to determine whether President Johnson actually believed such a prospect was possible or that he had decided on a major ground war. In the spring of 1965 he did not focus much on long-range consequences.

In March the CIA submitted a proposal to the White House that argued that the problem in Vietnam was a political one.[106] But the CIA was not a major player in the administration, and less weight was given its analysis than that of the Pentagon and State Department. Robert McNamara seemed to acknowledge the CIA thesis when he stated that "the Pentagon and the military have been going at this thing the wrong way round from the very beginning: they have been concentrating on military results against guerrillas in the field, when they should have been concentrating on intense police control from the individual villager on up."[107] Yet, while the defense secretary may have recognized a flaw in administration thinking, too often it was easier to rely on simple military solutions.

Disagreements within the military about the most effective utilization of combat troops also began to emerge in March. Much of the skepticism and opposition to the use of large-scale ground forces was among General Johnson's staff, especially among military men who had previously served as advisers in Vietnam.[108] There was considerable debate about what to do, but it was tempered by the feeling that the United States had little choice in how to prevent the collapse of South Vietnam. Political constraints to major escalation remained, so that slow escalation was, in the words of General Johnson, "the maximum action which is politically feasible within the US at this time."[109]

One later rationale by some of the president's advisers for poor policy decisions was that President Johnson was not provided with any alternatives to slow and incremental escalation. On the political level that is true but only because he had rejected the alternative of not escalating. What he did not get was a variety of military options at this point. By encouraging aggressive planning and looking for measures to "kill more VC" while cutting back on the actual military requests, President Johnson himself bears much of the responsibility for the slow, but steady, escalation.

NOTES

1. *The Pentagon Papers*, Gravel edition, vol. 3, p. 297.

2. Lyndon Baines Johnson, *The Vantage Point*, p. 122.

3. Ibid. p. 122.

4. "A Policy of Sustained Reprisal," memo from McGeorge Bundy to the president, February 7, 1965: Annex A [Document 250] in Johnson Library: National Security File: McGeorge Bundy Memos to the President, Box 2, vol. 8. p. 1.

5. January 14, 1965, Memo to the president from McGeorge Bundy in Johnson Library: National Security File, Bundy Memos to the President File.

6. Johnson Library: "President's Meeting with Congressional Leaders," January 22, 1965—as recorded by Bromley Smith (National Security Council Staff). National Security File, Boxes 18/19: Miscellaneous Meetings File, vol. 1, p. 8.

7. Russell's remarks were made January 11, after a briefing by CIA director McCone. *The Pentagon Papers*, Gravel edition, vol. 3, p. 263.

8. Memo from Jonathan Moore to William Bundy, "Congressional Attitudes on SVN [South Vietnam]," undated but written in January 1965, in Kennedy Library: Thomson Papers, January–February 1965 folder. Quoted in William Conrad Gibbons, *The U.S. Government and the Vietnam War*, Part II: 1961–1964, p. 397.

9. Congressional Research Service interview with McGeorge Bundy, January 8, 1979, as quoted in Gibbons, *The U.S. Government and the Vietnam War*, Part III: January–July 1965, p. 47.

10. January 27, 1965, memo for the president, "Basic Policy in Vietnam," in Johnson Library: National Security File, NSC History—Troop Deployment, p. 1.

11. Johnson Library: Chester Cooper Oral History, July 9, 1969, pp. 9–10. Cooper, who was one of McGeorge Bundy's top aides, later remarked: "He [Bundy] felt that here it was, January 1965, and American policy was really kind of stuck. There was an awful lot of contingency plans...there were now some honest doubts as to where we were going and whether we would get there in terms of the policy we had in mind, there were some very serious doubts about the stability of the Vietnam government. South Vietnamese troops weren't doing well and the situation looked very unpromising indeed."

12. Johnson Library: National Security File, NSC History, vol. 1, Box 40, Tab 3.

13. January 14, 1965, cable from Rusk to Taylor. Johnson Library: National Security File, NSC History, vol. 1, Box 40, Cable 1477.

14. There had been no De Soto patrols since September 1964. The plans called for the patrol to stay 30 miles off the North Vietnamese coast, and 34-A raids were

prohibited for the two days before and after the patrol, apparently to avoid looking as if they were obviously provoking the North Vietnamese.

15. See *The Pentagon Papers*, Gravel edition, vol. 3, pp. 298–300.

16. Ibid. p. 298.

17. U.S. Department of State, Central File, Pol 27, Cable 2359, January 31, 1965, quoted in Gibbons, *The U.S. Government and the Vietnam War*, Part III, p. 52.

18. Congressional Research Service interview with Chester Cooper, April 10, 1979, quoted in ibid. p. 51.

19. Taylor first suggested a visit by Bundy: "In order to assure yourself that we are missing no real bets in this political field, would you consider sending someone like Mac Bundy here for a few weeks to look at this particular field?" (January 5, 1965, cable from Taylor to the president, No. 2057, in Johnson Library: National Security File, National Security Council History, vol. 1, Box 40, Tab 3, p. 3.)

20. February 7, 1965, McGeorge Bundy memo to the president, "The Situation in Vietnam," in Johnson Library: National Security File: McGeorge Bundy Memos to the President, Box 2, vol. 8, p. 3.

21. Cooper Oral History, Interview I, p. 12. McGeorge Bundy's oft-quoted reference to Pleiku being a streetcar (wait long enough, and one will come sooner or later) is supported by the fact that the plans for retaliation were ready. The Americans were waiting only for the communists to carry out some provocative act.

22. February 7, 1965, McGeorge Bundy memo to the president, p. 4.

23. Johnson Library: William Bundy unpublished manuscript, chapter 22B, p. 7.

24. See *The Pentagon Papers*, New York Times edition, pp. 330–32 for an assessment of the pessimism of the JCS and intelligence community.

25. NSC Meeting notes, February 8, 1965, Johnson Library: NSC Meetings File—Situation in Vietnam, vol. 3, Tab 29, Box 1, February 8, 1965, p. 3.

26. Bundy manuscript, chapter 22B, p. 39.

27. February 7, 1965, Bundy memo to the president, p. 4.

28. Johnson Library: NSC Meetings File—Situation in Vietnam, vol. 3, Tab 29, Box 1, February 8, 1965, p. 3.

29. *The Pentagon Papers*, Gravel edition, vol. 3, p. 320.

30. Johnson Library: NSC Meetings File—Situation in Vietnam, vol. 3, Tab 29, Box 1, February 8, 1965, p. 3.

31. "A Policy of Sustained Reprisal," memo from McGeorge Bundy to the president, February 7, 1965: Annex A [Document 250], Johnson Library, National Security File: McGeorge Bundy Memos to the President, Box 2, vol. 8, p. 1. President Johnson claimed in his memoirs that this Annex was prepared by John McNaughton. (See Lyndon Baines Johnson, *The Vantage Point*, p. 127.)

32. McGeorge Bundy, February 7, 1965 memo, p. 4.

33. Gibbons, *The U.S. Government and the Vietnam War*, Part III, pp. 68–69.

34. NSC Meetings File—Situation in Vietnam, February 8, 1965, vol. 3, Tab 29, Box 1, p. 4.

35. Johnson Library: "President's Meeting with Congressional Leaders," January 22, 1965—as recorded by Bromley Smith (National Security Council Staff). National Security File, Boxes 18/19: Miscellaneous Meetings File, vol. 1, p. 82.

36. See Gibbons, *The U.S. Government and the Vietnam War*, Part III, p. 140. Neither committee took up the issue of Vietnam again until the Senate Foreign Relations Committee held hearings on April 2.

37. Johnson Library: Dean Rusk Oral History, September 26, 1969, p. 13.

38. *The Pentagon Papers*, Gravel edition, vol. 3, p. 320.

39. February 17, 1965 memo from the JCS to CINCPAC, in Johnson Library: National Security File, NSC History, vol. 1, Tab 43.

40. General Harold K. Johnson, as quoted in Herbert Schandler, *The Unmaking of a President*, p. 17.

41. See Gregory Palmer, *The McNamara Strategy and the Vietnam War*, p. 79.

42. Planning and budgeting in the Pentagon had been made over under the Planning Programming Budgeting System (PPBS), in which systems analysis and cost-effectiveness calculations were essential for planning. This type of rational calculation and analysis became a major part of the war planning.

43. Johnson Library: Cyrus Vance Oral History, Interview 3, March 9, 1970, p. 12.

44. Johnson Library: National Security File, McGeorge Bundy Memos, Box 3, vol. 9—March 6, 1965, p. 3.

45. Johnson Library: U. Alexis Johnson Oral History, June 14, 1969, p. 14.

46. Gibbons, *The U.S. Government and the Vietnam War*, Part III, p. 115. As Gibbons noted, no public statements or even internal policy papers explained what Rolling Thunder was supposed to accomplish.

47. Lyndon Johnson, as quoted in Doris Kearns, *Lyndon Johnson and the American Dream*, p. 263.

48. Notes of February 10, 1965, NSC meeting, in Johnson Library: NSC Meetings File, vol. 3, Tab 30.

49. Ibid.

50. Robert S. McNamara, *In Retrospect: The Tragedy and Lessons of Vietnam*, pp. 172–73.

51. James Reston, February 14, 1965, *New York Times*, Part IV, p. 8.

52. *The Pentagon Papers*, Gravel edition, vol. 3, p. 306.

53. See Schandler, The Unmaking of a President, p. 10.

54. George Ball manuscript, quoted in Larry Berman, *Planning a Tragedy*, p. 45.

55. Johnson Library: George Ball Oral History, Interview 1, July 8, 1971, pp. 28–29. Ball also noted regarding the bombing in February: "The impetus toward escalation never came from Lyndon Johnson, I can assure you of that." (Ball Oral History, p. 26.) In reviewing the notes of the February meetings, one can see Ball's point that the president was reluctant to bomb, but most of the documentary evidence points to a lack of confidence in the effectiveness of bombing, not a reluctance to escalate in general.

56. Johnson Library: National Security File, NSC History, vol. 2, Tab 82—Dean Rusk paper entitled "Vietnam," February 23, 1965, p. 1.

57. Hubert H. Humphrey, *The Education of a Public Man*, p. 322. As a result of his dissent, Humphrey was frozen out of the decisionmaking process by Johnson.

58. Ibid. p. 323. In fact, the political repercussions that Johnson feared the most were from conservative Democrats.

59. Johnson Library: George Ball Oral History, Interview 1, July 8, 1971, pp. 28–29.

60. Memo from James Thomson to McGeorge Bundy, "The Vietnam Crisis—One Dove's Lament," February 19, 1965. Johnson Library: National Security History, Troop Deployment File—Vietnam.

61. Johnson Library: Dean Rusk Oral History, February 26, 1969, p. 23.

62. Johnson Library: Chester Cooper Oral History, Interview 1, July 9, 1969, p. 11.

63. July 24, 1965, memo from McGeorge Bundy to the president: "The History of Recommendations for Increased US Forces in Vietnam," in Johnson Library: National Security File, Vietnam Chronology, Box 11, Troop Decision File, Tab 3a.

64. Johnson Library: Cyrus Vance Oral History, Interview 3, March 9, 1070, p. 2.

65. *New York Times*, February 14, 1965, p. A1.

66. See, for example, Rusk February 25, 1965, press conference *The Department of State Bulletin*, 52 (1304).

67. See Marvin Kalb and Elie Abel, *Roots of Involvement: The United States in Asia, 1784–1971*, p. 182. See also George McT. Kahin, *Intervention: How America Became Involved in Vietnam*, p. 280. Much of the Chinese rhetoric came from newspaper editorials. Intelligence reports from the CIA and the Bureau of Intelligence in the State Department concluded that the Chinese would come in only if the United States invaded North Vietnam.

68. Remarks to the National Industrial Conference Board, in *Public Papers of the Presidents of the United States: Lyndon B. Johnson, 1965*, p. 205.

69. February 16, 1965, cable from the president to Ambassadors Taylor and Bruce, in Johnson Library: National Security File, McGeorge Bundy Memos to the President, Box 2, vol. 8.

70. *The Pentagon Papers*, Gravel edition, vol. 3, p. 324.

71. See Rusk February 25, 1965, press conference.

72. Johnson Library: National Security File, NSC History, Tab 59: memo to the secretary of state from James L. Greenfield—Subject: Vietnam and the Public, February 16, 1965.

73. See Bundy Memos to the President file, cited in Gibbons, *The U. S. Government and the Vietnam War*, Part III, p. 113.

74. Johnson Library: National Security File, NSC History: February 16, 1965, memo from McGeorge Bundy to the president, "Vietnam Decisions," p. 2.

75. Johnson Library: NSC Meetings File, vol. 3, Tab 31: February 18, 1965, Chester Cooper notes.

76. Johnson Library: William Bundy Oral History, May 29, 1969, pp. 14–15.

77. Johnson Library, February 16, 1965, memo to the president from Bill Moyers, in Confidential File, Box 71, Vietnam, ND19/CO312.

78. February 16, 1965, memo from McGeorge Bundy to the president, "Vietnam Decisions," in Johnson Library: National Security File, NSC History.

79. February 19, 1965, memo from McGeorge Bundy to President Johnson, "Comments on Vietnam for Your Newspaper Visitor." Johnson Library: National Security File, NSC History, vol. 2, Tab 66. (The name of the visitor was not mentioned in the memo.)

80. March 23, 1965 cable from Rusk to Taylor, in Johnson Library: National Security Council History, vol. 2, Tabs 117, 119.

81. The memo was written specifically for the March 13, 1965, press conference, but it was unsigned, and it is unclear whose office it came from. (See Johnson Library: National Security File, NSC History, Tab 107, vol. 2.)

82. March 13, 1965 press conference, in *Johnson Presidential Press Conferences*, vol. 1, p. 276.

83. Ibid. p. 276.

84. March 20, 1965, press conference, ibid. p. 280.

85. See Bundy Manuscript, chapter 22B, p. 38. See also I. F. Stone's March 8, 1965, column, "A Reply to the White Paper," reprinted in I. F. Stone, *In a Time of Torment, 1961–1967*, p. 212, and Roger Hilsman, *To Move a Nation*, p. 531.

86. *New York Times*, February 28, 1965, p. 1.

87. Bundy manuscript, chapter 22B, p. 31.

88. U. Alexis Johnson Oral History, June 14, 1969, p. 21.

89. February 22, 1965, cable from Taylor to Department of State, in *The Pentagon Papers*, Gravel edition, vol. 3, p. 418.

90. Ibid. p. 402.

91. March 3, 1965, CINCPAC memo to JCS, in ibid. p. 402.

92. Ibid. p. 417.

93. Bundy manuscript, chapter 22B, p. 29.

94. Quoted in an undated memo from Joseph Califano in Johnson Library: NSC History, vol. 4, Folder/ Tab 275.

95. Ibid.

96. See Joint Hearings of Senate Armed Services Committee and Appropriations Subcommittee on Department of Defense, *Military Procurements Authorization, Fiscal Year 1966*, p. 605.

97. See William Westmoreland, *A Soldier Reports*, p. 125; David Halberstam, *The Best and the Brightest*, pp. 683–84.

98. Department of the Army Interview with General Harold K. Johnson, November 20, 1970, as quoted in Gibbons, *The U.S. Government and the Vietnam War*, Part III, p. 149. General Johnson was accompanied by McNaughton and General Andrew Goodpaster, assistant to the chairman of the JCS.

99. March 2, 1965, cable from McNamara to Taylor, in *The Pentagon Papers*, Gravel edition, vol. 3, p. 337.

100. General Johnson, quoted by Major General Delk Oden of the MACV staff, in Andrew Krepinevich, *The Army and Vietnam*, p. 140.

101. *The Pentagon Papers*, Gravel edition, vol. 3, p. 406.

102. Letter from General William Westmoreland to Larry Berman, as quoted in Berman, *The Tragedy of Vietnam*, p. 52.

103. William Westmoreland, *A Soldier Reports*, p. 128.

104. Handwritten notes of McGeorge Bundy, Johnson Library: National Security File, McGeorge Bundy files, Luncheons with the President folder, in Gibbons, *The U.S. Government and the Vietnam War*, Part III, p. 194.

105. November 16, 1978, Congressional Research Service interview with General Andrew Goodpaster, quoted in Gibbons, *The U.S. Government and the Vietnam War*, Part III, p. 166. McNamara also cites this source, as well as his own recollection, in confirming the 500,000 figure (McNamara, *In Retrospect*, p. 177).

The full report presented by General Johnson upon his return from Vietnam on March 12 remains classified. (See also interview with Andrew J. Goodpaster by Fred I. Greenstein on October 31, 1984, in John P. Burke and Fred I. Greenstein, *How Presidents Test Reality: Decisions on Vietnam, 1954 and 1965*, p. 161.)

106. The specifics of the CIA proposal remain classified, but a useful description can be found in Gibbons, *The U.S. Government and the Vietnam War*, Part III, pp. 191–192. There is no evidence as to whether President Johnson saw the proposal, although McGeorge Bundy did. Johnson did see a report from CIA director McCone on March 31 that included summaries of some of the same CIA recommendations.

107. McNamara was quoted by McGeorge Bundy in a March 6, 1965, memo from Bundy to the president, Johnson Library: National Security File, McGeorge Bundy Memos, Box 3, vol. 9—March 6, 1965, p. 2.

108. For an excellent summary of the dissenting military views on ground force deployment see Gibbons, *The U.S. Government and the Vietnam War*, Part III, pp. 168–173.

109. March 14, 1965, "Report on Survey of the Military Situation in Vietnam," Tab B, pp. 11–12, in U.S. Army Center for Military History, as quoted in Krepinevich, *The Army and Vietnam*, p. 142.

Chapter 5

Americanizing the War

THE TOP OFFICIALS SEARCH FOR A POLICY

There were a few attempts in March within the government to encapsulate the objectives for U.S. actions in Vietnam. Assistant secretary of defense John McNaughton came up with a draft memo of American war aims that was circulated among the top policymakers a number of different times between March and July 1965:

70%—To avoid a humiliating US defeat (to our reputation as a guarantor);
20%—To keep SVN (and then adjacent) territory from Chinese hands;
10%—To permit the people of SVN to enjoy a better, freer way of life.
Also—To emerge from crisis without unacceptable taint from methods used.
Not—To help a friend, "although it would be hard to stay in if asked out."[1]

While not stated U.S. policy, McNaughton's draft reflected the attitude in Washington that the United States was primarily interested in doing just enough to prevent the collapse of South Vietnam because of international prestige as well as domestic politics (not "losing" Southeast Asia and avoiding attack by conservatives). He believed that the key consideration was the following: "It is essential—however badly SEA [Southeast Asia] may go over the next 1–3 years—that the US emerge as a 'good doctor.' We must have kept promises, been tough, taken risks, gotten bloodied and hurt the enemy very badly."[2]

Such goals would be very hard to translate into military terms. How much of a military effort was required to appear as the "good doctor"? McGeorge Bundy had voiced a similar sentiment a few days before. He asked, "In terms of U.S. politics which is better: to 'lose' now or to 'lose' after committing

100,000 men? Tentative answer: the latter."[3] That was rather an extraordinary admission and showed that deploying 100,000 U.S. forces was an end in itself, almost irrespective of their military value on the ground. Winning or losing was secondary to maintaining American prestige and avoiding the perception that America was a paper tiger.

With no consensus among Johnson's top foreign and military advisers in March on the most effective use and numbers of combat forces and disagreement on political tactics in the United States, questions and frustrations in the administration began to mount. The U.S. role in Vietnam had entered a new phase, but it was not clear to U.S. officials what the long-range policy was. When the president's advisers stepped back and looked at the whole picture, many times they felt that U.S. policy was not working. But such analysis was very rare. Usually, policy on Vietnam was simply reactive.

In July 1965 McGeorge Bundy reviewed the history of recommendations for increased U.S. forces in Vietnam and wrote the president that in March "initially we all had grave objections to major U.S. ground force deployments." Bundy noted that once combat troops were introduced, "these deployments did not give us bad reactions, and *it became easier* for Westmoreland to propose, and for us to accept, additional deployments."[4] Each new investment of American troops would increase the stakes considerably. No longer was just American reputation on the line. Once there were many U.S. soldiers in Vietnam, the military thrust was as much toward protecting American boys as preventing the collapse of South Vietnam. This also gave the military a greater say in Vietnam policy. George Ball continually argued that each decision to escalate made ground forces "a necessary follow-up." But as Ball later remarked: "Nobody was prepared to concede that any particular step would require any further step. This was kind of a standard assumption which I kept repeating again and again was a false assumption . . . . You go forward with this further step, and you will substantially have lost control. Finally, you're going to find the war is running you, and we're not running the war."[5]

Robert McNamara noted, "All of us should have anticipated the need for U.S. ground forces when the first combat aircraft went to South Vietnam—but we did not. The problem lay not in any attempt to deceive but rather in a signal and costly failure to foresee the implications of our actions."[6] But McNamara was referring to what he feels was no deception by the military in proposing small increments of troops in order to get the hundreds of thousands more they supposedly desired. He ignored the pattern of deception with respect to acknowledging what American actions and the implications of American policies were in Vietnam. In addition, neither McNamara nor President Johnson can claim that he had no way of foreseeing what would happen down the road. General Harold Johnson and others had claimed that considerable numbers of combat forces were necessary simply to turn the tide, which was the basic objective. As McNamara noted, the president believed that combat troops were the most effective means of military response.

CONGRESS AND THE MILITARY BUDGET

At the same time as the initial ground forces went into Vietnam, and as further deployments were considered, top Pentagon officials were on Capitol Hill testifying for a military budget that reflected almost nothing on Vietnam. In fact, as a result of Robert McNamara's attempt to make defense spending more cost-effective and eliminate waste, the military budget presented to Congress in February and March 1965 cut expenditures from the previous year. Although the Bureau of the Budget did not work this out per se with the Pentagon, it was applauded by the White House because the savings could certainly be put to use in the domestic arena. As the military budget was finalized before being presented to Congress, there was a steady stream of correspondence back and forth between the Budget Bureau and the Pentagon. There was not a single reference to Vietnam.[7] The increasing prospects of escalation in Vietnam were simply not addressed in the FY 1966 budget.

In late February and early March, Secretary McNamara went before the House and Senate appropriations and armed services committees to testify on behalf of the military budget.[8] Even though Vietnam was rarely mentioned by the defense secretary, what little that was discussed about the conflict indicated that the administration was not focused on the long-term consequences of military escalation. The many other military and civilian officials who testified about the military budget were also not forthcoming about just what the policy was with regard to Vietnam. Their testimony was proof that the FY 1966 budget had not at all accounted for the deteriorating situation in Vietnam in February 1965, much less a long-term military commitment.

The Defense Department estimated its expenditures to be $52.6 billion, a reduction of $400 million from FY 1965 and $2.1 billion from FY 1964.[9] McNamara's prepared statement was read February 24 before the Senate Armed Services Committee and the Appropriations Subcommittee on the Department of Defense and March 2 before the House Subcommittee on Defense Appropriations. He opened his discussion on Vietnam by stating, "The present situation in South Vietnam is grave but by no means hopeless." McNamara emphasized that the South Vietnamese armed forces had been strengthened and the United States was providing only military advice and support. He devoted only a page and a half of the total of 54 pages to Vietnam and described the military mission in this manner: "U.S. military personnel now in South Vietnam continue to carry out their complex advisory and support missions, in headquarters and in the field, with the skill, dedication, and bravery we have come to expect of our Armed Forces."[10] He gave no indication of the plans for escalation and greater deployment of U.S. forces under discussion at the White House. Thus, it was hard to make any useful evaluation of the economic and budgetary impact of the conflict at this time.

It is important to note that when the United States first escalated in Vietnam, the military drew upon resources and "inventory in pipeline" (matériel already procured, built, or appropriated as part of the bureaucratic process). The result was that the Pentagon, while devoting many more resources to Vietnam by the beginning of February 1965, simply reprogrammed its allocations, thus reducing other programs in the budget, and did not have to ask Congress for any new appropriations. In many ways, the 1966 military budget bore no relation to the current Vietnam policy decisions. The administration trumpeted major military savings while more and more of the military resources and programs were devoted to Vietnam.

Secretary of the army Stephen Ailes insisted that even as the military situation changed there should be no need to alter the defense budget: "The major thing we have done is to increase the number of people we have in Vietnam. But they have come from within our Army resources. We have simply deployed units which have been deployed in [the continental United States] or in the Pacific area previously; these do not necessarily involve a change in the troop structure of the Army . . . . When we deploy additional equipment, we normally do it from Army stocks."[11] Ailes, when pressed by Congressman Robert Sikes about what would happen in the case of a major escalation (not just in Vietnam), replied that "our budgeting requirements would be changed to a very marked degree." He emphasized the high payroll costs that would be involved if forces were increased as well as construction costs and other areas needed to meet the demands of increased personnel. But he stated that no one anticipated such an escalation: "[T]his budget does support the force which in our judgment should be maintained to enable us to play the proper Army role in any of these eventualities."[12] Ailes was arguing that the conflict in Vietnam could be managed and supplied with what the U.S. military already had in stock; it was merely a matter of reprogramming or reallocating resources and inventories. An additional problem with Ailes' thinking on this point was that it ignored the economy as a whole. Military needs could be met easily because the Pentagon's budget cuts created more capacity in most of the defense production industries—but not without a price in the civilian economy, which would soon begin to feel inflationary effects.[13]

Ailes also admitted that the military budget did not reflect "the increased consumption of equipment in Vietnam" such as helicopters. But this did not concern him because at that time the United States had not lost too many helicopters. The military line was that the proposed budget, even with its cuts, was sufficient to meet the current level of American engagement in Vietnam. But one could also see from the testimony that the Pentagon really did not know what effect the conflict in Vietnam was having. They were relying on old numbers until a true assessment of the growing military requirements in Vietnam could be made. Ultimately, the testimony of the military officials created the sense that they were stalling until they could recalculate those requirements. Ailes referred to a Department of Defense study in progress that was to determine aircraft needs and reassess equipment losses: "The decision with respect to aircraft was to hold this rate until we get a firm prediction of what our needs are as a result of this study."[14] But, as Alain Enthoven and Wayne Smith noted, not until 1966 did the Pentagon develop a "crude Vietnam program budget" as well as models and estimates of the cost implications of additional deployments in Vietnam.[15]

NO CHANGES IN THE BUDGET ARE REQUIRED

During his testimony on March 2, McNamara stated, "The budget was submitted to Congress on January 25 and I do not believe that any event since that time, or since the decisions were made which were reflected in that budget, require any change in the defense portion of the President's budget."[16] This statement came in the wake of the Pleiku attack, the beginning of the Rolling Thunder campaign, and the authorized deployment of 3,500 American combat troops to Danang. Some congressmen and senators seemed concerned, as the situation in Vietnam heated up, especially in light of the new sustained bombing campaign, that the administration had not budgeted enough for any escalation. McNamara responded that the budget provided for "increasing ground force strength" in two ways: one, by increasing logistical support and two, by making it possible to move the ground forces to the conflict area in the time required. However, he noted:

[S]hould it later develop that we need still larger numbers of people and other expenditures, we have authority under certain contingency provisions in the budget to expend funds for that purpose. . . .

I don't know whether additional funds will be required above what we have requested for fiscal year 1966, and I don't want to try to make a guess, because it is so difficult to look ahead 12, 15, 18 months, to the end of fiscal year 1966. I only point out that it will be our policy to supply in the form of military aid whatever South Vietnam requires to carry out effectively its counter-insurgency program without fiscal limitation. In order to carry out that policy, we need the authority we have requested, to increase our military aid if that should prove necessary . . . . There is no fund limitation affecting our support for South Vietnam or our present preparation for whatever lies ahead in the southeast Asia area.[17]

So McNamara left himself an out if more money was needed. But he discussed only an increase in American military assistance to South Vietnam, not any contingencies that involved direct American military engagement.

The defense secretary then stated that there would be no dramatic upward surge in the defense budget unless there were unexpected developments in the international arena. But he clearly downplayed the possibility of a major change in the American involvement in Vietnam: "I do not believe that American troops can be used to substitute for South Vietnamese troops on the ground in South Vietnam to counter the guerrillas operating in the country. I think it would be a mistake to use them for that purpose. We do believe that we can assist the South Vietnamese logistically, with advisory service, and very recently because of a change in the tactics and level of Viet Cong activity, we have been using U.S. aircraft in South Vietnam against the guerrillas themselves."[18] Yet, McNamara had already approved Westmoreland's request for U.S. ground forces (and by this time, President Johnson had also just approved the initial deployment).[19] The Joint Chiefs of Staff and the military command in Saigon were asking for even more soldiers. McNamara painted a picture that was, at best, accurate only when the budget had been put together at the end of 1964.

While it was unlikely that McNamara or anyone else knew in early 1965 just how great an economic burden the war would be, there had to be serious concern in the Pentagon that the proposed defense budget would not be adequate for the military needs in Vietnam in fiscal year 1966. Yet, while General Creighton Abrams, army vice chief of staff, acknowledged that things in Vietnam could change, "every cost that we are capable of identifying with validity at this time is reflected and is covered [in the FY 66 budget]."[20] The Defense Department seemed focused only on the costs of current contingencies and activities. Congressional testimony and the pending military budget appeared to be at least two or three months behind the reality of what was happening in Vietnam even as American combat forces were wading ashore at Danang. Secretary of the navy Paul Nitze admitted that, "there have been no changes in this budget since our problem became more complicated."[21] Yet, neither he nor anyone else from the Pentagon expressed concern that the budget did not reflect the complications in Vietnam.

A few testified that the budget might not be adequate. Admiral David L. McDonald, chief of naval operations, stated that even with an increase in funds for fleet material readiness, "with the increase in the tempo of operations, particularly in the southeast Asian area, our requests might prove to be inadequate."[22] But McDonald, along with Nitze and Marine Corps commandant General Wallace Greene, agreed that at present there was little doubt that any changes in Vietnam could be met with reprogramming that would divert resources from some other program.

All of the military witnesses contended that the changes in Vietnam in February and March 1965 did not alter their budget needs. They did not foresee any need for supplemental appropriations. Nitze was asked by Congressman Sikes, "[D]oes this budget provide a strong and sound and sure springboard from which we can rapidly expand if there should be further escalation of conflict?" He replied: "I believe it does, sir."[23] Admiral McDonald added that a significant early escalation would make things more complicated and increase the needs of the military. If there was a major escalation (including the possibility of Chinese intervention), he stated: "I would want a great deal of money . . . . About all I could get my hands on . . . . I would be reluctant to call up the Reserve, Mr. Chairman, but I guess if it were really serious, I would."[24] But, for the current situation, Greene and McDonald continued to claim that any future contingencies that they could imagine would be easily handled through reprogramming.[25]

Only the air force gave a more pessimistic, or realistic, outlook. Major General Duward L. Crow, budget director and comptroller of the air force, stated that while for the present time the air force planned on reprogramming, the fiscal 1966 budget did not reflect the anticipated requirements for a step-up in activities in Vietnam. He noted that "if there were any substantial increased activity above the present level, we unquestionably would have to come in for a supplemental appropriation."[26] Congressman Sikes then inquired: "You would have to come in for a very great increase, would you not?" Crow replied: "It would depend on the nature of the expansion, but as a general statement in reply to your question, yes, sir." Because of the Rolling Thunder bombing campaign, the air force knew perhaps more than the other military services about what escalation might require, especially since the sustained bombing campaign was considered ineffective at that time, and the air force wanted to increase the level and scope of the bombing. But, as General Crow pointed out, the Pentagon budget process lagged behind the military reality: "The general guidelines for the development of the 1966 budget did not anticipate increased activity in Southeast Asia."[27]

Only once did a military witness foreshadow where U.S. policy in Vietnam was leading. After a week of testimony about the budgetary estimates by the military, General Harold K. Johnson, army chief of staff, indicated that the United States could not win the war in the foreseeable future. When asked what he meant, his reply was: "I believe it would take as long as 10 years. I believe that one of the—I would not want to term it a mistake—but one of our errors has been looking forward to success in the course of the next year, or 2 years. I think that we have to raise our sights materially, plan for the long term and if it occurs sooner than that, fine."[28] This statement was in sharp contrast to McNamara's. Surprisingly, though, no one asked him what a 10-year war might require and how that would affect the budget. He did not expand on his answer, nor was he requested to. While General Johnson talked of 10 years, neither he nor anyone else ever mentioned the prospect of deploying 500,000 American soldiers. In fact, a ground war was never discussed at all.

During their congressional testimony in February on the budget, none of the Administration's top economic advisers warned of any adverse economic effects of the war. Economic and defense planners alike believed they had room for growth in the military budget. Kermit Gordon, testifying before the Joint Economic Committee on February 23, talked about defense spending and the military budget without mentioning Vietnam except to say:

[T]he 1966 budget did not contemplate a substantial step-up in operations in South Vietnam. However, we do believe that the amounts in the 1966 Defense budget request could provide adequately for a range of possible conditions in Southeast Asia in the coming year. Furthermore, recognizing that as the year unfolds, developments may occur which cannot now be estimated with any confidence, the budget includes a substantial allowance for contingencies for defense as well as non-defense programs totaling $650 million in new obligational authority and $400 million in expenditures. These amounts are larger than is customary. If, however, international conditions—in Southeast Asia or elsewhere—did change to a degree that was not covered by the budget estimates, the necessary financial requirements would have to be sought from Congress via a budget amendment or supplemental appropriation.[29]

He stressed that defense expenditures had been reduced from FY 1965 and added that in the coming months the Pentagon hoped to be able to identify more savings in its long-term budget projections through FY 1968.

The congressmen and senators were most concerned that McNamara's budget cuts were too deep and that such cuts and a reliance on reprogramming for Vietnam needs had eroded the military's ability to deal with present security needs other than Vietnam. The military men, in particular, McNamara, simply assured them that American security would not be jeopardized. Through most of the hearings on the FY 1966 military budget, much of the focus in Congress was primarily on issues such as specific weapons and personnel, with almost no mention of the long-term economic situation. The one contingency that caused some concern was if the communist Chinese became involved militarily, but even that was not discussed much. Otherwise, those in Congress and the military were confident about the American ability to handle the Vietnamese communists.

Senator John Stennis (Democrat of Mississippi and a member of both the Armed Services and Appropriations Committees) later stated in 1967 that the defense budgets of 1965 and 1966 were simply inadequate and "made sound overall budgetary and economic planning difficult, if not impossible." He specifically discussed the FY 1966 budget: "This budget had been finalized in the fall and winter of 1964. It was essentially a peacetime budget. In no way did it take into account or fund for the large demands on our military resources and assets which resulted from our greatly increased involvement in the war in Vietnam. It was clearly apparent that, since the budget had been put together, the cost of the war had gone up and up in every respect."[30]

Secretary McNamara said nothing to change the focus of that debate to a full discussion of long-term American military escalation and the resulting economic requirements—and, quite frankly, neither did most members of Congress. As McNamara testified, the Johnson administration was prepared to do whatever was necessary in Vietnam, including requesting more money down the road. While some witnesses testified that the budget was inadequate for any major escalation, there seemed little concern from either the Administration or Congress that such escalation was possible. That lack of concern foreclosed any debate about goals and priorities in Vietnam within the context of debate on the overall American budget. Such a debate could have provided the opportunity to discuss and compare all the goals and priorities that the Johnson administration wanted to pursue, both at home and abroad, so that hard policy choices could be made. At the same time, the Pentagon was committed to whatever it would take to do the job in Vietnam. The military did not want its mission inhibited by the costs, and the president wanted to pay only minimal costs. But, above all, no one really wanted to discuss the costs.

THE APRIL NATIONAL SECURITY COUNCIL MEETINGS

At the end of March, the Westmoreland/JCS request for three ground force divisions was the primary focus of the president's top civilian advisers on Vietnam. When Ambassador Taylor returned to Washington on March 29 for consultations on Vietnam, a high-level NSC meeting was scheduled to discuss the military request. He continued to argue against the further deployment of ground forces, and in early March he had gotten them restricted to the defense of U.S. bases and coastal installations only. But Westmoreland and the JCS formally requested a change so that the soldiers could go on the offensive.

In preparing for the scheduled April 1 NSC meeting, McGeorge Bundy wrote a memo for the president in which he recommended that the president hold off on Westmoreland's request and instead deploy "two additional Marine battalions and one Marine Air Squadron and associated headquarters support elements" while increasing U.S. military support forces by some 18,000–20,000 men. He also recommended a gradual intensification of Rolling Thunder.[31] At the April 1 meeting, the president followed Bundy's advice and authorized two more marine battalions for Danang and Phu Bai, along with 18,000 to 20,000 logistical troops, and increased Rolling Thunder raids.[32] He also granted Westmoreland's request that the troops be able to patrol the countryside, authorizing "their more active use." Now the soldiers would go on the offensive. William Bundy later remarked that the period of escalation in March and April "was an important series of build-up decisions made in part on what seemed clear cases of individual need, and in part to lay a groundwork for whatever might be needed in the future."[33]

The NSC met again on April 2.[34] Chairman of the JCS General Earle Wheeler stated that the logistics for further deployment were in place and that there would be an early deployment of the two marine battalions. According to Chester Cooper's notes, the president "indicated that he didn't think the sending of U.S. military forces to Vietnam would require a new congressional resolution."[35] In addition, McGeorge Bundy suggested that until there was a new presidential speech or press statement, everyone should be guided by the president's press conference of the previous day. In his public remarks, Johnson had stated, in response to a reporter's question about whether "U.S. bombings of North Vietnam are bringing any results": "We have a commitment to the people of South Vietnam . . . . We seek no wider war . . . . So we will try to take such measures as are appropriate and fitting and measures that are calculated to deter the aggressor."[36] Bundy then emphasized in the National Security Council meeting: "Under no circumstances should there be any reference to movement of U.S. forces or other future courses of action."[37] Ambassador Taylor then "indicated the line he would take with the press: no dramatic change in strategy; we will try to do better what we are doing now."

During the meeting, John McCone expressed the view of CIA analysts that the communist position was actually hardening as a result of the air strikes and that any future policy decisions, especially in connection with sending additional troops to South Vietnam, should take that into account.[38] The CIA believed that the South Vietnamese armed forces were no longer willing or able to provide the necessary defense against the Viet Cong. Thus, the United States would be moving into a vacuum and by necessity have to take on the bulk of the fighting.

McCone opposed the limited bombing measures and the gradual introduction of ground forces. He felt both played into the hands of the communists. He advised against the deployment of ground forces since not enough was being done to deter the North from escalating: "I think what we are doing is starting on a track which involves ground force operations which, in all probability, will have limited effectiveness against guerrillas, although admittedly will restrain some VC advances. However, we can expect requirements for an ever increasing commitment of U.S. personnel without materially improving the chances for victory . . . . In effect, we will find ourselves mired down in combat in the jungle in a military effort that we cannot win, and from which we will have extreme difficulty in extracting ourselves."[39] Along with Ambassador Taylor and Admiral U.S.G. Sharp, commander in the Pacific, McCone felt that the bombing needed to be harder, and more frequent and inflict greater damage.

McCone's cautious language about being mired down in the jungle was similar to George Ball's argument, even though the CIA head was quite a hardliner. McCone's dissent was not considered very critical because he was due to retire in a few weeks. But there was now strong opposition against gradual escalation from two sides—those who wanted to go harder against the North, like McCone, and those who wanted to get out, like George Ball. For them, the incremental process appeared worse than no escalation at all. Throughout the spring and summer of 1965, there were numerous cases of disagreement with particular actions or policies. But the disagreements never coalesced against one particular decision. There was always someone who had qualms about a certain action and feared the consequences. But because no decision at this time seemed irreversible, they gave in.

NSAM 328: THE MISSION CHANGES IN VIETNAM

The decisions of the April 1 NSC meeting were formalized in National Security Action Memorandum (NSAM) 328. Authorization for the increase in combat troops was written as follows: "The President approved a change of mission for all Marine Battalions deployed in Vietnam to permit their more active use under conditions to be established and approved by the Secretary of Defense in consultation with the Secretary of State."[40] As the authors of *The Pentagon Papers* noted, NSAM 328 "was a pivotal document. It marks the acceptance by the President of the United States of the concept that U.S. troops would engage in offensive ground operations against Asian insurgents."[41]

President Johnson had told the press before the NSC meeting on April 1, "I know of no far-reaching strategy that is being suggested or promulgated."[42] Yet the president had already received the requests for three divisions, and the focus of the meeting he was about to go into was the question of a significant increase of American ground forces. Johnson then provided the authorization at the meeting for U.S. forces to go on the offensive for the first time. Administration officials were clearly instructed in NSAM 328: "The actions themselves should be taken as rapidly as practicable, but in ways that should minimize any appearance of sudden changes in policy . . . . The President's desire is that these movements and changes should be understood as being gradual and wholly consistent with existing policy."[43]

The president made it clear that "premature publicity be avoided by all possible precautions."[44] The administration went far beyond preventing premature publicity, however. It was a campaign of deceit and denial to downplay the military decisions. Instructions in a cable from the State and Defense Departments to Taylor regarding NSAM 328 made it clear that by keeping publicity "low-key" it would not look as if there was any significant escalation: "Pacing of deployments is of critical import as we do not repeat not desire give impression rapid massive build up but intent is to accomplish deployment of Marine forces earliest feasible after Ambassador Taylor secures permission GVN. Desire indicate we continuing on course previously set and gradual build up proceeding according to plan. In keeping this policy deployments, other than Marines, will be spaced over period time with publicity re all deployments kept at lowest key possible."[45] The debate still focused primarily on when and where to send in combat troops and how they should be deployed, not the long-range consequences of continuing escalation. William Bundy later argued: "As one looks back on it, the whole period from February through July falls into a consistent pattern of minimizing the significance of each separate move and letting the total speak for itself. This was surely the aim of early April, and the sense of the memorandum [NSAM 328] as it was understood by those who acted under it."[46]

Bundy discussed the "intense controversy" that later arose about the decisions of April 1 and whether they were a commitment to ground force combat on an open-ended basis. Were there deliberate concealment and misrepresentation, especially in the language of the memorandum? He noted that NSAM 328 was the first formal decision to authorize military units to engage in active combat. He argued that given what occurred in the next four months, this was "a new and unlimited course, while concealing or withholding the full picture of future steps that were foreordained and for all practical purposes decided." Yet, Bundy argues that this was not how those in the April 1 NSC meeting viewed the decision, except perhaps for McNamara and the Joint Chiefs, who, in Bundy's view, realized that a great deal more troops would be required down the road. This was not a decision to go to war, but it was clearly a major escalatory step that was done in a continuing pattern of deception, as Bundy noted: "But to say this hardly gets around the question of concealment. *Any* decision for American combat missions, it may be argued, should have been at the very least disclosed to the Congress and seriously discussed with its leaders. Even if the carrying out of the authority was well off in the future—two months would elapse before it was invoked—the Congress and perhaps the public as well, had a right to know and to be consulted . . . . Suffice it, for the present, that the decision was in essence part of the President's earlier February posture, that he was not changing a basic American policy. As such, it was not debated in early April."[47]

Ambassador Taylor felt at the time that the decision taken on April 1 was a strategy of gradual experimentation with an offensive mission for the marines. There was to be no rush into a major deployment of combat forces until there was an incontrovertible need. Taylor was quite pleased after the meeting that Johnson had not given in to the military and seemed to be moving cautiously. But upon his return to Saigon, Taylor began to sense "an eagerness . . . to rush in troops now that the initial official reluctance had been breached."[48]

THE PACE OF ESCALATION QUICKENS

President Johnson had now Americanized the war, and, he threw himself into the planning and decision making with great vigor. With the dispatch of ground forces, Johnson now became more personally involved with military decisions and had now taken on the task of primary decision maker regarding troop commitments. The president's prodding produced a flood of new ideas in mid-April, including additional troops, incorporating Americans into South Vietnamese units, and the notion of using "civil affairs" units from the U.S. military to assist in pacification.[49] In fact, Johnson seemed as anxious as anyone to continue putting more men into South Vietnam. McGeorge Bundy seemed to question in a memo to the president on April 14 just how far he wanted to go: "I am *not* sure that you yourself currently wish to make a firm decision to put another 10,000–15,000 combat troops in Vietnam today. As Taylor says, we were planning when he left to use the Marines already on the scene in combat roles and see how that worked. It is not clear that we now need all these additional forces."[50] Yet the day before, as the two additional marine battalions arrived in South Vietnam, Johnson had already authorized a Westmoreland request for the deployment of the 173d Airborne Brigade, the first regular army combat units.

After Taylor's return to Vietnam, senior officials in Washington began to freeze him out of the process. McGeorge Bundy went so far as to urge the president to restrain McNamara from sending Taylor implementing orders, noting that they would be "very explosive right now because he will not agree with many of them and he will feel he has not been consulted."[51] Upon learning inadvertently of the decision to deploy the 173d Airborne from a JCS message to CINCPAC, Taylor cabled to McGeorge Bundy: "This comes as a complete surprise . . . . [and shows] a far greater willingness to get into the ground war than I had discerned in Washington during my recent trip."[52]

CONTINUED PUSH FOR THE GREAT SOCIETY

For much of March and April, as the United States committed itself on the ground in Vietnam, Congress was consumed with Great Society legislation, in particular the Voting Rights Act. In the first two weeks of March, President Johnson had to deal with a major civil rights crisis as the Selma, Alabama, marches to register black voters had put voting rights squarely on the national agenda. Both the massive black push for voter registration and the southern white reaction brought the voting issue to the fore. Until that point, Johnson had postponed any new civil rights legislation in 1965. Other key components of the Great Society legislative programs had already been sent up to Congress, and, as Eric Goldman noted: "He sought time for the South to digest the Civil Rights Act of 1964, and feared that a second pro-Negro move so soon would provoke a Senate uproar snarling all other legislation."[53] Also, the president wanted to avoid the perception that he was pushed into anything, and, in March especially, he did not want "a hasty display of federal force" at the behest of the civil rights activists.[54] He wanted to avoid coming down too hard on the South. But in the meantime, slowly and quietly, Johnson had already put his attorney general to work on a draft of a new Voting Rights Act. So, when the events in Alabama took hold, the president was quickly able to take advantage of the renewed national clamor to deal with the voting discrimination in the South.

Lyndon Johnson's political response to the Selma marches was one of the high points of his presidency. He held off on sending in federal forces until both the civil rights advocates, who wanted protection for the marchers, and Alabama governor George Wallace, who claimed he could not afford to protect or ensure their safety, were in favor. At the same time, he had the Justice Department finish the draft bill on voting rights and then decided to present it personally to Congress. Before a joint session that was televised throughout the nation during prime time, he became the first president since 1946 to appear before Congress to lobby for a domestic bill. It was a dramatic moment, and the reception for the president's speech was overwhelming. Eric Goldman described the thunderous approval of the chamber and how many in the gallery "wept unabashedly" at the conclusion of the speech.[55]

The bill that was presented to Congress had been very carefully constructed and was the combined product of the White House, Justice Department, Senate majority leader Mike Mansfield, and Senate minority leader Everett Dirksen. The president had made it a point to include Dirksen and praise him at every turn. As with the Civil Rights Act of 1964, Dirksen was the key to getting the bill out of committee (on the Judiciary Committee, Senator James Eastland of Mississippi was determined to kill it) as well as ending any filibuster by southern senators. However, the president well understood the political reality in the South and was therefore willing to let the southerners go through the paces of opposing the bill as long as they did not kill it and no amendments were made to gut it. The debate over the Voting Rights Act was quite strong for the next four months, until August 6, when it was signed into law by President Johnson. One of the interesting sidelights to the civil rights agenda in 1964 and 1965 was that many black leaders either gave their support to the president for his Vietnam policies or at least toned down their opposition.[56]

From March through May, many of the Great Society initiatives were in critical stages up on Capitol Hill. Only two previous Congresses in the twentieth century were notable for the amount and scope of legislation passed: the opening congressional sessions during the first terms of Woodrow Wilson and Franklin Roosevelt.[57] The attention given by the White House to the

legislative   program   was   remarkable   for   its   organization   and
comprehensiveness.   The Legislative Liaison Office under White House aide
Larry O'Brien maintained flowcharts to keep up with the course of each bill,
whether it was in subcommittee, being marked up, or on the House or Senate
floor.   O'Brien and his staff kept daily head counts on congressional votes.
They prepared weekly comprehensive reports for the president.   Each cabinet
department and executive agency also prepared weekly status reports on
pending legislation—each department had its own congressional liaison staff—
and there were also reports on enrolled legislation currently being
implemented.[58] Before Vietnam became an overriding concern in late 1965,
half of each cabinet meeting dealt with reports on pending legislation and
strategy to gain needed votes.   This remarkable effort was in notable contrast to
the secrecy of the Vietnam decisions that were being made and being
downplayed.   The separation of domestic and foreign policy resembled a
sleight-of-hand trick: keep all the energy and the spotlight focused on the
domestic agenda and keep the military policy off in the shadows.   But this also
highlights a difference between domestic and foreign policy; a president can
simply bypass the Congress and avoid a debate in ways virtually impossible
with domestic issues, at least in the short term.

As the push for the domestic agenda increased, an undercurrent of
dissatisfaction with the Johnson administration began to appear as serious
domestic protest against the administration's Vietnam policies began to form in
March and April.   While a distinct, but increasingly vocal, minority, these
liberal dissenters represented much of the intellectual core and strongest
supporters for the president's Great Society program.   The dissent focused
primarily on the bombing campaigns and the lack of any movement toward
negotiations.   President Johnson's coalition and broad mandate were now
splintering.   Exacerbating this was that the American people did not feel much
warmth for the president.   The press had also grown very wary of Johnson and
now only reluctantly praised him at all.   Some of this was due to his
personality, and some was due to the fact that while major strides were made on
the domestic front, he was increasingly criticized on international issues,
particularly Vietnam.   As the president himself remarked, his support was "like
a Western river, broad but not deep."[59]

By the spring of 1965, Lyndon Johnson had become the dominant force with
respect to Vietnam policy as well.   The administration was pursuing what the
country wanted: a better, more prosperous society and a halt to communist
aggression.   But Johnson ultimately failed in his desire to have both on his
terms—the country paid a great price in how the goals were pursued in trying
to have it all.   The president won so many battles but would lose the wars, both
domestically and in Vietnam.   Johnson unlocked many of the barriers to civil
rights and anti-poverty and social welfare legislation.   However, he never
rallied the society behind either war—not against Vietnam or against poverty.
Other than his great moment with the voting rights bill, Johnson did not go to
the people to enlist their support and sacrifices for the wars at home and in

Southeast Asia. Much of what he accomplished was done in back rooms, by political horse trading and cajoling or secretively and deceptively, as in the case of Vietnam. He was able to outflank his opposition—southerners on civil rights, liberals on foreign affairs. He was able to twist arms and exhort his staff and congress, but he did not really inspire the American people.

THE JOHNS HOPKINS SPEECH

In the last week of March and the first week of April, a growing concern had developed on Capitol Hill about where U.S. policy was headed in Vietnam. Some, such as Senate majority leader Mike Mansfield, felt that Vietnam was not a vital interest of the United States. Many others, including Senators J. William Fulbright, Frank Church, and George McGovern and even Republicans like Senator Jacob Javits, were most concerned that as the United States became more involved, no attempts were being made to talk to, or negotiate with, the communists. While there was a growing outcry against the bombing, little concern was exhibited in March and April by most members of the press or the Congress about the use of ground forces. Scarcely an eyebrow had been raised when the first U.S. marine battalions were sent ashore at Da Nang. With the exception of a few liberal members of the press and senators such as Mansfield and Wayne Morse, sending a few battalions of combat forces was not viewed as either irreversible or a sign that many more men were to follow. This belief persisted since few thought the president would willingly embroil the country in another Asian land war. Americans had learned that lesson in Korea.

Soon after the first marines went ashore, an unnamed presidential adviser soothingly said to a reporter: "Don't worry, this President is not about to get involved in a land war in Asia. He is just not going to do it."[60] Few people doubted otherwise, whether in the administration, Congress, or the press. Only a few prominent voices, including newspaper columnists such as Walter Lippmann and Joseph Kraft, warned against the prospect of a major war. But most criticism focused on the bombing campaign and the lack of negotiations. On April 2 Canadian prime minister Lester Pearson urged the president during an address at Temple University to pause in the bombing of North Vietnam in order to create conditions for negotiations.

To answer his critics, in late March the president had his staff work on a major address on Vietnam. Johnson chose to deliver the speech on April 7 at Johns Hopkins University, after many revisions of the text. He had his staff provide previews of the speech in the days before its delivery and even brought critics such as Lippmann and Senators Fulbright and Mansfield to the White House for their opinion of the text. In the first few drafts, there was a modest appeal for peace in the middle of the text. The speech was revised, and the following was placed up-front: "We will never be second in the search for such a peaceful settlement in Vietnam . . . . We have stated this position over and over again, fifty times and more, to friend and foe alike. And we remain ready, with this purpose, for unconditional discussions with the governments concerned."[61]   It was not much noticed that the phrase "governments concerned" would de facto exclude the Viet Cong, who were doing almost all of the fighting in the South. The first half of the speech discussed the reasons the United States had made a commitment in South Vietnam. The president added that when the United States reacted to the stepped-up attacks on South Vietnam with an increased military response, including bombing the North, this was "not a change of purpose. It is a change in what we believe that purpose requires."

The primary thrust of the speech was a proposal, along the lines of the Great Society, for major aid projects and financial assistance for a future Vietnam (although there is no evidence that this idea was previewed with anyone in Southeast Asia). Thus, Johnson had combined his concern for "reputation," as McNaughton had put it in his March 24 draft memo, with an attempt to provide a better life for the people of South Vietnam and make that country safe for democracy. Johnson proclaimed that to "leave Vietnam to its fate would shake the confidence . . . in the value of an American commitment." The speech was widely hailed in the press and on Capitol Hill. William Bundy noted that the president's call for discussions "landed on the press and public like water on parched ground—a measure, no doubt, of the frustration Americans instinctively felt that their country seemed to be doing nothing in Southeast Asia except bombing."[62] While both of the dissenters from the Tonkin Gulf Resolution, Senators Gruening and Morse, were critical of the speech, most of the negative reviews came from the political Right, some of whom accused the president of trying to buy peace in Southeast Asia.

THE QUESTION OF NEGOTIATIONS

President Johnson had often stated privately his belief that the communists had to be forced to come to the bargaining table. So any peace overture was primarily for domestic consumption. The possibility of serious negotiations had no role at this point in Johnson's strategy to end the conflict in Vietnam. While he sincerely believed that the United States, with its vast resources and democratic tradition, could transform Vietnam, he knew that the communists were winning the war. Changing that was of paramount importance.

In early March, Secretary McNamara had stated that it was important to "find a way to have real talks in an international meeting."[63] But others in the administration were less anxious to get to the bargaining table; Rusk and McGeorge Bundy felt that there was no great hurry since the United States could negotiate whenever necessary. For some, like John McNaughton, a strong rationale for the deployment of ground forces had been to create a bargaining chip. McGeorge Bundy had also consistently stated that ground forces would strengthen the U.S. bargaining position. George Ball believed that the negotiation efforts of 1965—including the president's expressed willingness for "unconditional discussions" in his Johns Hopkins speech—were genuine but doomed "because we weren't prepared to make any real concessions. Negotiation at that time still consisted pretty much of saying to

Hanoi, 'Look, let's work out a deal under which you will capitulate.'. . . the problem was that while people say they desperately wanted to negotiate, they never were prepared to make any real concessions."[64] William Bundy felt there was a consensus in the administration "that the U.S. should not be too forward in stating peace positions. It was a position that the administration was to cling to for too long, and at some cost to the credibility of its efforts for peace."[65]

But to blunt the criticism that he was not seriously pursuing negotiations, Johnson made a show at Johns Hopkins of being willing to go to the bargaining table without preconditions. However, as William Bundy stated, there was a "false note [in] the President's subsequent claim that this had, in effect, been the American position all along" because it had not been so in February. It "was perhaps part of the President's strong urge to claim that all the elements of his policy were simply logical extensions, not changes."[66] On the other hand, Johnson's call for unconditional discussions "helped greatly to stem the attacks on the Administration that were rapidly rising at the time. Then, and for many months to come, the American position toward negotiations seemed to most, though far from all, reasonable and considerably more forthcoming than that of North Vietnam."

On April 8, North Vietnam took the initiative. Perhaps in response to the president's Johns Hopkins speech, the North proposed a "Four Points Program" as the basis for a solution to the Vietnam conflict. The basic points were:

1. Recognition of the basic national rights of the Vietnamese . . . the U.S. Government must withdraw from South Vietnam U.S. troops, military personnel, and weapons of all kinds, dismantle all U.S. military bases there, and cancel its military alliance with South Vietnam . . . . the U.S. Government must stop its acts of war against North Vietnam and completely cease all encroachments on the territory and sovereignty of the DRV;
2. . . . the military provisions of the 1954 Geneva Agreements must be strictly respected;
3. The internal affairs of South Vietnam must be settled by the South Vietnamese people themselves in accordance with the program of the NLF [National Liberation Front] without any foreign interference;
4. The peaceful reunification of Vietnam is to be settled by the Vietnamese people in both zones, without foreign interference.[67]

Even though the purported rationale behind the American escalation, in particular, the sustained bombing of the North, had been to bring North Vietnam to the bargaining table, the White House categorically rejected Hanoi's overture. The United States did not even reply to the initiative, although the North Vietnamese never stated that the four points were the only basis for a solution but rather "a basis" for solving the conflict. President Johnson was not interested in unconditional discussions anymore than the communists were.

The third point, which stated that the situation must be settled in accordance with the NLF program, was completely unacceptable to the U.S. government. However, McGeorge Bundy wrote to the president that he, Ambassador

Llewellyn Thompson (ambassador at large and former ambassador in Moscow), and acting CIA director Ray Cline felt that the proposals were "at least a hint of real interest from Hanoi in eventual discussions."[68] Bundy also noted four days later: "If we choose to make them so, [the] proposals could provide the basis for a negotiating dialogue."[69] White House aide Richard Goodwin sent President Johnson a memo that argued that the four points may not have been preconditions for discussions but staking out an opening negotiating position.[70] As such, he recommended that the United States pursue this further. It was also reported a week later that North Vietnam was prepared to enter peace talks without prior withdrawal of U.S. forces if a cease-fire could be established first. Again, nothing came of this.[71] George Ball also urged Johnson on April 21 to explore the North Vietnamese points because they provided a basis for negotiations.[72] A month later, on May 18, Mai Van Bo, a North Vietnamese diplomat in France, passed on a message to Washington via the French Foreign Ministry: "The four points of April 1965 should not be considered as prior conditions but rather as working principles for negotiations."[73] But Johnson was uninterested in exploring whether Hanoi's four points provided any opening for negotiations.

There were clear reasons that the president rejected any discussions. First, Johnson felt that any eagerness to negotiate would be a sign of weakness—that the United States lacked the will to stay the course in Vietnam. Second, according to consultant to the president Eric Goldman, the president felt that "his hurrying to the conference table would produce a tide of hawk feeling that would be difficult to control."[74] Thus, the United States simply ignored the Four Points Program without comment. Ultimately, the president could placate critics on the Left by appearing moderate and diplomatic with a speech that proclaimed the United States second to none in searching for peace while actually taking no initiative other than maintaining a stronger military commitment in order to appeal to the Right. With the speech behind him, Johnson began to move toward greater military escalation on the ground.

THE HONOLULU CONSENSUS

In early April, there were four battalions of ground forces in Vietnam, all marines. The administration had insisted in March that the mission of the marines was to provide "local close-in security." In order to protect the Da Nang air base, the U.S. forces had to patrol a perimeter around the base that was well within the range of Viet Cong mortar fire. And, in order to secure the area from mortar fire, the patrols would need to cover an area of some 16 square miles. So it was unavoidable to meet up with the enemy. Westmoreland was aware of this when he made the request for the marines. The president and his advisers were aware of it when he approved the combat troops.

Over the next few months, each shift in the mission for the American forces in South Vietnam was subtle: for example, in April "close-in support" became "combat-support" once the Americans and Viet Cong had tangled. This was a modification of the initial strategy of limited combat action from secure enclaves. The military continued to urge a greater offensive strategy, including sending U.S. troops into the highlands in pursuit of the enemy. Soon, offensive operations became policy as the instructions on April 14 from CINCPAC to the military command in Saigon indicated: "As I understand the JCS directive, the Marines are to engage in offensive counterinsurgency operations earliest. The mission outlined in Ref A should be strengthened . . . as follows: 'In addition, undertake in coordination with RVN I Corps, an intensifying program of offensive operations to fix and destroy the Viet Cong in the general Danang area.' Ref D indicates the offensive phase may not be reached for several weeks. If I read the messages properly, this is not what our superiors intended. Recommend you revise your concept accordingly."[75] Westmoreland later noted that by mid-April American units were at times "engaging in full-scale offensive operations."[76]

Robert McNamara, accompanied by William Bundy and McNaughton, met with Taylor, Wheeler, Westmoreland, and Admiral Sharp on April 19–20 in Honolulu. Taylor's disagreement with the ideas and instructions he had received from Washington was a major reason that the conference was convened. He came prepared to argue against the ground forces deployment, but upon finding himself greatly outnumbered, he capitulated and "came aboard."

The result of the meeting was the unanimous recommendation, proposed by McNamara to the president on April 21, for a major increase in U.S. forces. There were then 33,500 U.S. forces already in Vietnam, and a level of 40,200 had been authorized. The Honolulu group recommended doubling the level of forces to 13 U.S. combat battalions and 82,000 men and acknowledged that many more might be needed.[77] McNamara presented this to Johnson as a way "to break the will of the DRV/VC by depriving them of victory."[78]

But there was little optimism. As Westmoreland later acknowledged, "[N]obody saw any immediate hope of dramatic improvement in the ground war."[79] *The Pentagon Papers* noted: "The conferees appear to have realized not only that the forces they had recommended be deployed to Vietnam might not be enough, but also that it would be unwise to attempt to affix any time limit to the war."[80] They were clear that "[i]f the ground war is not to drag indefinitely, they consider it necessary to reinforce GVN ground forces with about 20 or more battalion equivalents in addition to the forces now being recruited in SVN. Since these reinforcements cannot be raised by the GVN they must inevitably come from U.S. and third country sources."[81]

The consensus that emerged in Honolulu for additional ground forces was the "new" necessary number to prevent defeat in the South. McNamara stated that they believed it would take from six months to two years to convince the North Vietnamese and the Viet Cong that they could not win in the South. This was reported to the president, although among themselves they had agreed that no time limit could be affixed.[82] Yet no one could really say whether 90,000 American men would be nearly enough. The Honolulu "consensus" was pure speculation and reflected the view that eventually American superiority—in terms of technology and resources—would carry the day. But when and under what circumstances would North Vietnam realize it had "failed"? What evidence did the Pentagon have that it would take from six months to two years? American officials continued to underestimate the will of the communists and still viewed the war as a short-term problem even as they were acknowledging that many more troops would probably be needed in Vietnam.

Evidence continued to mount that the conflict in Vietnam was going to be long and require even greater escalation. The CIA, even after McCone had departed, continued to offer pessimistic analyses. McCone himself argued that if a guerrilla war develops "and lasts several months or more, I think world opinion will turn against us . . . and indeed domestic support of our policy may erode."[83] An April 30 report asserted that "the general outlook remains dreary and in some respects the dangers of the situation have increased. There will be constant danger that the war-weary people of South Vietnam will let the US assume an even greater share of the fighting. There will also be danger that increased US troop commitment will lead more South Vietnamese to accept the communist line that US colonialism is replacing French. This could turn increasing numbers of Vietnamese toward support of the Viet Cong effort to oust the US."[84] Thus, the United States was faced with a need to correct the crumbling situation in the South as well as stop the communist military advances. In both Washington and Saigon, U.S. military force was seen as the answer to both problems. One of the key outcomes of the Honolulu meeting (especially as a follow-on from the April 1 NSC meeting) had been the unstated conclusion that a ground war in Vietnam was the key to the U.S. ability to halt the communist advances. The immediate concern was no longer convincing the communists they could not win but staving off defeat. Therefore, as Maxwell Taylor later noted, additional combat troops were necessary "to give the required impetus to the ground campaign in South Vietnam where the decisive action lay."[85] Ground forces were viewed no longer as simply troops to augment and protect the bombing campaign but as the key to U.S. policy in Vietnam.

CONTROLLING INFORMATION

As troop deployments continued, and the military mission changed, efforts to control public opinion increased. Cables were constantly sent back and forth from Saigon to Washington to determine the most appropriate public posture. The president was increasingly worried when information came out of the U.S. Embassy in Saigon that seemed to go further than White House statements. On April 10 McGeorge Bundy sent a memo to Rusk and McNamara that stated: "The President has directed me to emphasize again his continuing concern for more careful control of military information on operations in Vietnam . . . . The President is also dissatisfied with the rapidity of release of information respecting further troop reinforcements to Vietnam and does not understand why there should have been an announcement on this subject from Saigon. This announcement seems to him inconsistent with the decisions reached on April 1 [NSAM 328]."[86] Bundy specifically mentioned paragraph 11 of NSAM 328, which warned against any "premature publicity" and the need to "minimize any appearance of sudden changes of policy."

James Greenfield, assistant secretary of state for public affairs, responded sharply to Bundy's memo. He cautioned that "efforts to hold back on disclosing this kind of information would immediately open up the Administration to the charge of withholding or 'managing' the news."[87] Greenfield argued that a lack of disclosure did more harm overall than the actual news stories: "We must do everything possible to avoid lending support to allegations that we are 'hiding the truth' or 'suppressing news,' even when disclosure produces temporary embarrassment." Bundy sent a copy of the memo to the president, noting, "I think on the whole, he makes an annoyingly good case."[88]

It was clearly policy to obscure the truth. Ambassador Taylor cabled Greenfield in late April to explain the current instructions for on-the-record press statements: "[W]e believe that the most useful approach to press problem is to make no repeat no special public announcement to the effect that U.S. ground troops are now engaged in offensive combat operations, but to announce such actions routinely as they occur."[89] While there was no decision to lie, hiding the truth meant that the press would have to determine American policy on its own. Taylor concluded, "Eventually, of course, fact that Marines or other ground troops are engaged in offensive combat will be officially confirmed. This low-key treatment will not repeat not obviate the political and psychological problems . . . but will allow us to handle them undramatically." According to *The Pentagon Papers*, "The long official silence between the sanction for U.S. offensive operations contained in NSAM 328 and the final approval [which came in June] of the conditions under which U.S. troops could be committed was not without cost. The President had admonished each of the NSC members not to allow release of information concerning the provisions of the NSAM, but the unduly long interregnum inevitably led to leaks."[90] Such leaks served only to fuel the growing perception that the White House was less than candid about Vietnam.

When President Johnson approved the Honolulu recommendations on April 22, he effectively doubled the number of combat forces in South Vietnam with no public announcement. However, news stories about a significant escalation and apprehensions about a major war began to surface. Many in Congress urged a clarification of American policy toward Vietnam.[91] On April 30 Dean Rusk testified on Vietnam in an executive session of the Senate Foreign Relations Committee: "We have there now about 34,000. It is very much under contemplation that it might be necessary to add to those forces additional forces."[92] This response was typical of administration dissembling, as the president had already authorized an increase to 82,000 and was contemplating an additional 42,000 increase. Rusk added, in response to whether another congressional resolution was contemplated, "We do not at the present time have in mind such a change in the scale of the forces I think to raise that question as an immediate problem."

CONTINUED ECONOMIC "PROSPERITY"

Arthur Okun of the Council of Economic Advisers noted that at the same time as President Johnson approved NSAM 328, the change of military mission in Vietnam, on April 1, 1965, he was also agreeing to stimulate the economy further with the CEA's proposed excise tax cut. Economic prosperity was the linchpin around which all the domestic legislation turned. President Johnson talked about this to the cabinet on April 20, 1965: "All of us realize, I am sure, that one of the strongest factors contributing to the success of the program this year has been the vigorous health of the economy. Thirty years ago it was the failure of the economy that inspired Congress and the country to undertake new and necessary measures of reform and progress. Today it is the success and stability of the economy that is encouraging Congress and the country to buckle down to the unfinished business on our domestic agenda."[93]   It is also important to note that in 1965 there were few budget battles between Congress and the White House. They would begin in earnest during 1966 with the FY 1967 budget. But in 1965 Congress gave the president only slightly less than what he asked for—$107 billion instead of $109.4 billion in authorizations.[94]

Throughout March, April, and May, the president's key economic advisers were increasingly optimistic about the economy. CEA Chairman Gardner Ackley reported to the president and cabinet on March 25, "There is need for, and there is room for, continued brisk expansion . . . . Our prosperity is sound, healthy, and pervasive and the prospects for it continuing in that way remain promising."[95] In fact, economic optimism was on the rise, even greater than it had been at the beginning of 1965. The cuts in military spending were a key part of this. On March 31 the Troika sent a memo to the president that stated that there would be a revised deficit projection: "The new estimate of the deficit for fiscal 1965 showed a decrease of about $1 billion, largely due to 'reduced or deferred defense spending.'"[96] The Troika then recommended a stronger fiscal stimulus on March 31 and again in June. Even as the U.S. military mission changed, there was still no concern at all about an expanded military effort in Vietnam. As Gardner Ackley later noted, "In the spring of '65 the references to the economy 'overheating' was not an actual problem at all. The economy was still well below what we considered full employment in the beginning of '65."[97] There was no thought that a sudden increase in military spending might create more growth and employment.

The consensus was that there was still room to grow, although there was a little nervousness as to whether the economic expansion would finally level off or even go into a recession. But the news remained quite positive, and the economic experts continued to urge even more fiscal stimulation. The April 20 CEA report to the cabinet emphasized that the GNP continued to increase (in fact, the increase in GNP since the first quarter of 1961 had been 30 per cent by early 1965) and that housing construction reversed its decline, which had begun in early 1964.[98] Congress approved the president's $4.7 billion excise tax cut package in June. In effect, the measure was a repeal of excise taxes initiated during the Korean War. This would be a financial stimulus that hit just as major defense increases also occurred.   Okun noted that no one who was in on the tax cut meeting was in the NSC meeting. He later questioned whether there was a connection on the timing and the fact that only Johnson was aware of both the economic and military decisions.   He surmised the following:

There are two hypotheses. LBJ may have been sitting there saying, "If these guys knew that defense spending was going up, they might not be as enthusiastic about an excise tax cut. I want an excise cut that's on page 1 and therefore they don't have to know what's going on in defense spending, and I don't have to get flak from my subordinates. In this way I keep control." That's not my bet as to what was going on in his mind. My bet is that he did not really put these two things together in a concerted way. He had a Vietnam problem and he had domestic prosperity; he wanted to capitalize on the domestic prosperity and, if anything, he may have thought, "Gee, if people are going to get bad news on defense spending, then they'd damned well better get good news on tax cuts." But I don't see that as a conscious, carefully constructed decision that "I know what's best," taking all things into account.[99]

Okun's analysis is interesting and illuminating. With either explanation, Johnson wanted to keep Vietnam and domestic decisions far apart. However, the fact that the president purposely kept the Vietnam decisions of early April secret lends strength to Okun's first hypothesis. Johnson kept his economic advisers in the dark for most of 1965 on the long-range preparations for war in Vietnam. Okun might have been correct in saying that the economists may well have argued against a tax cut in the face of NSAM 328. He added: "There was a remarkable degree of compartmentalization between the national security and the domestic policy operations . . . . [Johnson] wanted it that way. Several explicit decisions had been made for escalation along the course of the Vietnam fiasco and at no time were we ever brought in on one of those decisions until early in March of 1968."[100]

Therefore, economic forecasts were based on false assumptions. According to the Council of Economic Advisers, "The Troika forecasts [in the spring and early summer of 1965] still pointed to only moderate advances in the economy and were based on fiscal policy assumptions far different from those that emerged after Vietnam defense outlays jumped."[101]   But the administration continued to make assurances that increased activity in Vietnam was not a financial problem. During congressional testimony in early May, Robert McNamara stated, "We have financed the war to date, if you will, without additional funds. We have been able to do it by making cost reductions greater than anticipated at the time we submitted the budget to Congress." When asked by Senator Proxmire, "So that despite the fact that you have had to step up the operation in Vietnam, you have been able to compensate for the increased cost of the war out there by savings elsewhere?," McNamara replied,

"[Y]es." He also noted that the savings from FY 1965 exceeded Pentagon expectations—so those savings have been utilized "to finance these increases required [in Vietnam]."[102]

The result of this assured defense savings was apparently that defense needs and the military budget went unchallenged and unexamined by the rest of the administration. There was much discussion in cabinet meetings about preparing budgets and legislative programs but not on defense spending. Vietnam policy as a topic was usually covered only by a secretary of defense briefing. But there is no evidence that the Defense Department submitted written briefs and policy reports for cabinet meetings as other departments and agencies did.

Recommendations and plans for new legislation and initiatives in late 1965 and 1966 to go before Congress were continually being developed by the Bureau of the Budget. It provided assessments of how much money should be appropriated and how any new programs would impact financially. But none of the material passed on to the cabinet and the White House staff by the Budget Bureau took into account increased military spending or questioned the level that the Pentagon had budgeted for the war. The budget officials must have known that the Defense Department figures were based on the situation at the end of 1964, but there was still no discussion of increased military spending or new defense requirements. During May and June the Budget Bureau prepared a number of briefs on bringing the administration goals and programs and those of the various departments in line with the FY 1966 budget. Military spending and the Defense Department seemed to be completely out of the policy and budget loop. During a May 14, 1965, Bureau of the Budget FY 1966 Legislative Program Proposal, which included an entire section on foreign affairs, the goals for foreign aid, East–West trade, export promotion, adjustment assistance, and the Asian Development Bank were discussed in terms of the FY 1966 budget. There was no mention of defense needs or Vietnam.[103]

THE SUPPLEMENTAL APPROPRIATIONS BILL

The increasing congressional and public concern about Vietnam policy was overtaken by events in the Dominican Republic. On April 24 fighting broke out on the island between government and rebel forces, which purportedly had some communist elements. By April 28 U.S. marines had gone ashore, under the pretext of protecting American lives. Within a few days, some 20,000 U.S. soldiers were dispatched to the Dominican Republic. While this crisis was to consume most of Washington's attention for the next 10 days, it also served to disillusion further the liberal wing of the Democratic Party. There were few lasting effects, as the Dominican Republic did not prove to be a long-term problem, but the timing was important, as it added fuel to those who criticized the president for his policy in Vietnam. Many critics felt he reacted precipitously, based on misinformation, and many questioned Johnson's credibility.

In the midst of the Dominican crisis, President Johnson decided to go to Congress for a show of support on Vietnam. On May 4 he sent to Capitol Hill a $700 million supplemental appropriations bill for Vietnam to run through June 1965, the remainder of the fiscal year. Most of the request would go toward construction, consumable supplies, operations and maintenance costs (petroleum, repairs, etc.), ammunition, bombs, tube artillery, and aircraft and helicopters. While the Bureau of the Budget signed off on the May Supplemental Appropriation bill, there was no economic analysis done on the specifics of the $700 million request or on the economic impact. Although the request covered only an eight-week period, no one thought to question the spending needs for FY 1966, which was to begin in July. Accompanying the request was a statement from the president: "This is not a routine appropriation. For each Member of Congress who supports this request is also voting to persist in our effort to halt communist aggression in South Vietnam. Each is saying that the Congress and the President stand united before the world in joint determination that the independence of South Vietnam shall be preserved and communist attack will not succeed."[104] Johnson immediately brought the congressional leadership to the White House for a pep talk (and included the press for the first part of the meeting). There was little discussion of how the money was to be used, only that it was urgent for the next two months and critical that a firm and unified stance be demonstrated to the world.

Many congressmen and senators were upset not only by the sudden timing of the request but by the fact that they felt boxed in politically. A number of them reluctantly supported the appropriations but did not want their votes seen as an indication of support for U.S. policy in Vietnam. Many on Capitol Hill proclaimed that the bill was no substitute for a congressional resolution on policy. Typical of the reaction of those who had growing doubts about U.S. policy in Vietnam was that of Senator Joe Clark of Iowa. McGeorge Bundy noted in a memo to the president: "Clark is furious at our supplemental for VN, but he thinks he will probably vote for it."[105] The debate did not last long, and the bill passed the House on May 5 with only seven no votes and the Senate on May 6 with only three no votes.

William Bundy later wrote that the bill was Johnson's reaction to growing congressional pressure for a new resolution on Vietnam. Bundy stated that it could be described only as a "gimmick": "In effect, the President sought to make the appropriation of a relatively small sum—not in fact related to any specific program or its costs—into a small-scale new Tonkin Gulf Resolution."[106] As Secretary McNamara admitted in his Senate testimony, the bill was not even needed. The administration had the authority to replace stocks under emergency provisions in both the defense budget and the Military Assistance Program. Yet, he also stated he could make no pledges that he would not be back in a few months for more money in FY 1966, thus sending more mixed messages.[107] Clearly, the White House wanted a referendum on Vietnam policy, and McNamara implied as much on Capitol Hill. When asked whether passing this bill would be a reaffirmation by Congress of the Tonkin

Gulf Resolution, he replied that one important objective of the bill was to allow Congress "an opportunity to reappraise U.S. policy in Southeast Asia, and hopefully, to endorse it with a ringing vote of confidence."[108]

The consequences of this bill were even more far-reaching because H.J. Resolution 447 was, in effect, the first congressional action on Vietnam since the Tonkin Gulf affair. While the president claimed to be taking the "necessary steps," as provided for in the Tonkin Gulf Resolution, the vote in early May was not on whether the United States should be in a land war in Southeast Asia. Congress was presented with a fait accompli: there were 34,000 American forces in Vietnam and thousands more on the way. The United States was also conducting severe bombing raids into the North. Therefore, the only issue before Congress was whether to provide additional support, matériel, and manpower for those boys who were, in fact, already engaged in combat. Congress was simply left with a decision on whether to appropriate money to support the military decisions being made in the White House and in the field—decisions about the scope of which Congress was greatly unaware.

With its power of the purse, Congress could have made the bill a referendum on the president's policies, but it would have been very difficult politically to hold such a debate in the context of providing for American soldiers whose lives were at risk 5,000 miles away. Even so, it is through the budget and congressional appropriation process that Congress has the greatest impact on military policy. But most on Capitol Hill found it politically untenable to vote against providing for men in the field as a way to influence military policy. A good example of this congressional caution was Senator George McGovern, who had grave doubts about U.S. policy in Vietnam as early as 1965 and soon became an outright opponent of the American role there. However, his first vote against military appropriations for Vietnam did not occur until 1969.[109]

In signing H.J. Resolution 447, President Johnson remarked: "To our own boys who are fighting and dying beside the people of South Vietnam, this resolution says to them: 'We are going to give you the tools to finish the job.'"[110] Those words, within the context of a request that covered only two months, implied a short-term military commitment. But no one in the government admitted publicly that the administration was unsure of what it would take "to finish the job," and so the amount of resources needed was unknown. Johnson's phrase "finish the job" created the impression that the United States was after a victory when, in fact, he and his advisers were first trying to prevent a collapse in South Vietnam and then over the next six months to two years hoped to convince the communists that they could not win. This fits with the phrase the Honolulu conferees used in April to describe the goal of "breaking the will of the DRV/VC by denying them victory"—it was disingenuously called the "victory strategy."[111]

THE BOMBING PAUSE

Another White House move with political motives was undertaken on May

12, when the United States halted its bombing of the North, in return for which the Administration expected a significant reduction in military activity by the Viet Cong. Although not announced publicly, its purpose was conveyed to Hanoi via the Soviet Union. A message was delivered to the North Vietnamese Embassy in Moscow but was returned unopened and unanswered.[112] The message conveyed nothing regarding negotiations or conditions for negotiations—Hanoi was simply expected to make a significant reduction in the communist military activities. It was a one-sided proposal. The North had to halt communist activity in the South while the United States would stop the bombing. No mention was made of American and South Vietnamese military activities in the South.

There were those in the administration who felt that the White House was simply engaged in a "grandstand play—a piece of 'crisis management' for the world audience—intended to demonstrate Johnson's statesmanlike magnanimity and reasonableness, intended to fail, and intended to be followed, 'regretfully, but unavoidably' with air strikes against DRV."[113] Johnson could then claim that the United States had tried to gain peace, but the communists prevented any progress. Communist intransigence would be used to justify any further escalation. William Bundy, who along with his brother had drafted the message to Hanoi, admitted that some in the administration criticized the tone and content of the message. He admitted, "It was a crisp, kind of lawyer's document . . . not well handled."[114] In fact, it was never released publicly or even acknowledged by the administration until Hanoi Radio broadcast it in December 1965.

The president himself admitted that blunting domestic criticism was a major motive; it was a means to quiet the Left: "We tried out [Mansfield and Fulbright's] notion and got no results . . . . We have stopped in deference to [them], but we don't want to do it too long else we lose our base of support."[115] But the conservatives were the ones Johnson truly feared and ultimately deferred to. George Ball agreed that Johnson was consistently nervous about a conservative backlash against him: "[Lyndon Johnson] was always very suspicious of the bombing pauses for a reason that is hard fully to appreciate at this time. He was deeply convinced, I think, that the real danger to American public opinion was the hawkish right-wing, that they were all the time pushing him into things that he was doing his best to resist . . . . But the big consideration in his mind was the one of the play of forces on the domestic scene. I think he was deeply and very honestly concerned at the fact that this would give a very big advantage to the very extreme hawks."[116] Ball later stated that the pause was little more than a "hiccup," and, according to Ball, the North Vietnamese foreign minister claimed it was "'a deceitful maneuver to pave the way for American escalation'—which I thought a perceptive appraisal."[117] Not surprisingly, the bombing quickly resumed on May 18.

THE COMMUNISTS ESCALATE

Meanwhile, in spite of the increase in American combat troops and the sustained bombing raids, the North responded with its own escalation. Not only were the communists undeterred by the American actions, but they displayed even greater resolve. On May 11 the Viet Cong attacked Songbe (some 50 miles north of Saigon), using more than a regiment of troops and shortly thereafter began a significant military offensive in the northern provinces of South Vietnam.

For the first time, units of North Vietnamese regulars were used. On April 21 the CIA and the Defense Intelligence Agency had confirmed that a regular North Vietnamese army battalion (from the 325th People's Army of Vietnam [PAVN] division) has been deployed in the South, perhaps as early as February.[118] The lack of a strong case that the North had a significant presence in South Vietnam and the weakness of the February white paper suggested that Hanoi responded to the U.S. military actions (particularly the bombing) in 1965 by sending many soldiers, including regulars, and weapons into the South. There had also been a tacit understanding that so long as the United States refrained from bombing the North, Hanoi would keep its regular army units out of the South.[119] The evidence remains sketchy at best, but it appears that whatever North Vietnamese forces were present in the South, they were fairly minor, especially in light of the number of northern regulars who were to come South in late April and May, two months after the bombing began.

In May, when the communist offensive began, many units of the South Vietnamese army either melted away or did not account themselves well in battle, suffering very high casualties. Some U.S. forces became more involved in the fighting, and on a few occasions American military advisers actually took over command of South Vietnamese forces in the midst of a battle. The price for American involvement was now mounting: in April and May there were 200 American casualties, with 18 killed.[120] In response to the mounting American casualties recorded by eyewitness accounts from reporters in Vietnam, a large cry had erupted from the press about the apparent lack of candor from the administration regarding U.S. policy in Vietnam. There were also warnings that the United States was committed to the deployment of many more soldiers. On May 19 Hanson Baldwin of the *New York Times* commented that 500,000 men and many years of fighting would be needed as part of an "inkblot" strategy that called for combat troops spreading out from secure enclaves.[121]

Even as American troops engaged in combat operations, the administration continued to go to great lengths to deny that there was any change at all in their military mission. This fiction continued, even as more and more combat units were sent into Vietnam. By the beginning of June, there were over 50,000 American soldiers in South Vietnam, with another 15–20,000 already authorized and on the way. Even more disturbing was that by the end of June American troops and advisers began to fight the communists independently of the South Vietnamese armed forces.

WESTMORELAND SPARKS A POLICY DEBATE

On June 7, as the South Vietnamese armed forces continued to suffer setbacks, General Westmoreland requested a major increase in U.S. and third-country forces as soon as possible: 34 American battalions and 10 from other countries. He also requested that all offensive restrictions on the American forces be lifted. The significance of the "44-battalion request," beyond the numbers, was that the United States would take on many of the offensive roles that heretofore had been undertaken only by the South Vietnamese forces. American units would no longer remain in reserve. To prevent the defeat of South Vietnam, the American military would now have to take up the fight against the Viet Cong and their North Vietnamese allies. As *The Pentagon Papers* authors wrote: "[I]n such a move the spectre of U.S. involvement in a major Asian ground war was there for all to see. With no provision for quick withdrawal . . . the long-term implications for the U.S. in terms of lives and money could not be averted."[122]

Westmoreland's request arrived as Johnson and his key advisers were grappling with the very real possibility of the collapse of South Vietnam. A very pessimistic report from Ambassador Taylor noted that the Viet Cong, reinforced by North Vietnamese regulars, were regrouping and equipping themselves for a major offensive. It stated that "it will probably be necessary to commit U.S. ground forces to action."[123] No one was very optimistic; graduated escalation was not yielding any positive results. The bombing campaign seemed to have no effect on the enemy's morale or capabilities; the introduction of 75,000 American forces had not improved the situation. As the outlook worsened considerably in June, it appeared that, at best, to turn the balance in the United States' favor would require a major commitment to a ground war over the next few years. William Bundy recalled that when the president asked point-blank, "How do we get what we want?" all the answers embodied "a defensive and long-term strategy" but still "premised on the rational belief that a frustrated and pained Hanoi must in time call it off."[124] But Westmoreland's request immediately placed the prospect of a ground war in Southeast Asia squarely on the policy agenda. The dilemma facing Johnson and the top U.S. policymakers was no longer just finding the right equation as to how extensive the bombing should be or how many more soldiers needed to be sent to Vietnam. The real question was whether the administration wanted to commit the United States—its manpower, its resources, its economy, its people—to a land war in Southeast Asia.

SOUTH VIETNAM CONTINUES TO DETERIORATE

The Joint Chiefs immediately supported Westmoreland's request: "[T]he ground forces situation requires a substantial further build-up . . . at the most rapid rate feasible on an orderly basis."[125] Events on the ground seemed to confirm Westmoreland's analysis. The South Vietnamese army continued to fall back in the face of mounting communist pressure. On June 14

Westmoreland cautioned that the 44-battalion request should be seen as "no force for victory but as a stop-gap measure to save the ARVN from defeat."[126] The JCS relayed the following question from the president to Westmoreland: Would 44 battalions "be enough to convince the VC/DRV that they could not win?" The general responded: "The direct answer to your basic question is 'No.'" He continued, "[T]here was no evidence that the VC/DRV would alter their plans regardless of what the U.S. did in the next six months . . . . If the U.S. was to seize the initiative from the enemy, then further forces would be required into 1966 and beyond."[127] Because there was no guarantee that the large number of forces he had requested would be enough, Westmoreland also suggested that some kind of limited mobilization was "clear and pressing." So even if the United States could prevent the collapse of the South, many more men would be required next year.

William Bundy recalled that the situation greatly deteriorated in late May and June 1965: "That was the most successively, utterly depressing, six weeks of action I can recall, . . . you just got the feeling very rapidly and progressively that the Rot had really set in."[128] Then the political situation in Saigon collapsed. On June 11 there was another military coup in Saigon. This one installed General Nguyen Cao Ky as prime minister and General Nguyen Van Thieu as chief of state. William Bundy recalled that Ky and Thieu "seemed to all of us the bottom of the barrel, absolutely the bottom of the barrel!" He added, "It had to stop here, there wasn't any place to go after that. The civilians had failed, the military had not done it well up to that point . . . this was the last holding point, you might say, in the government. So this was the backdrop for the set of thinking that went into the July 28 final decision."[129]

"LYNDON JOHNSON LETS THE OFFICE BOY DECLARE WAR"

Another part of the "backdrop" was that the administration greatly strained its credibility on Vietnam policy in early June. During a background briefing session for reporters on June 8, the State Department's chief spokesman, Robert McCloskey, let slip that American soldiers were engaged in offensive action: "President Johnson has authorized his commanders in Vietnam to commit United States ground forces to combat if their assistance is requested by the South Vietnamese Army."[130] He was actually just reiterating what General William DePuy, Westmoreland's deputy, had said in Saigon three days previously. But President Johnson was so livid at McCloskey's "leak" that he fumed at Rusk, "He'll be giving his future briefings somewhere in Africa."[131]

It had already become apparent to correspondents in South Vietnam that in the past month U.S. forces were no longer just in defensive positions but were going out after the Viet Cong forces. Stories from Saigon consistently hinted at this. Pressed by reporters, McCloskey had already tried to finesse the issue three days previously when he admitted that U.S. forces occasionally engaged in combat while patrolling defensive perimeters. But he emphasized that the U.S. forces remained in their capacity as advisers. The real significance of McCloskey's June 8 statement was his reference to presidential authorization, remarking that it had "developed over the past several weeks"—thereby putting any sense of dissembling directly at the president's feet. The *New York Times* stated: "The American people were told by a minor State Department official yesterday, that, in effect, they were in a land war on the continent of Asia. This is only one of the extraordinary aspects of the first formal announcement that a decision has been made to commit American ground forces to open combat in South Vietnam: The nation is informed about it not by the President, not by a Cabinet member, not even by a sub-Cabinet official, but by a public relations officer."[132]   I. F. Stone titled his column the next day, "Lyndon Johnson Lets the Office Boy Declare War."[133]

The following morning, White House press secretary George Reedy issued a statement that emphasized, "There has been no change in the mission of United States ground combat units in Vietnam in recent days or weeks. The President has issued no order of any kind to General Westmoreland recently or at any other time."[134] But then the White House appeared to confirm the substance of what McCloskey had, in fact, said: "If help is requested by the appropriate Vietnamese commander, General Westmoreland also has the authority within the assigned mission to employ these troops in support of Vietnamese forces faced with aggressive attack when other effective reserves are not available and when, in his judgment, the general military situation urgently requires it." That seemed a rather open-ended policy of offensive combat, left to Westmoreland's discretion.   Reedy's press release was also rather deceptive, even though it was technically true.   The change of mission (NSAM 328) occurred in the beginning of April, so it was not recent; the press only sensed it recently.   NSAM 328 was addressed to the secretary of state, secretary of defense and director of the CIA, so the president never issued an "order" to Westmoreland.

The problem with the White House policy of distortion and denial on the military mission in Vietnam was that it was easily exposed. Reporters in the field could see that the mission had changed when they witnessed soldiers engaged in offensive warfare.   More significantly, as a result of misleading statements by the administration, increasing numbers in Congress, in academic circles, and especially in the press began to feel that Johnson was lying to the American people. This was part of a continuing pattern in which the White House gave evasive statements every time there was an expansion of the U.S. role in Vietnam. As a result, a growing pattern of deception and suppression of news seemed to be developing. All of this increased the credibility problem for the president.   William Bundy argued that one of the key factors that contributed to the credibility gap was the administration's reluctance in May and June—and he attributed this to a "Presidential order"—"to disclose that our forces were really engaged in combat."[135]

NOTES

1. Johnson Library: March 24, 1965, McNaughton draft memo, "Annex—Plan of Action for South Vietnam," in McNaughton Files, Box 1, File 4.

2. Ibid. p. 6.

3. March 21, 1965, handwritten outline of U.S. interests in Vietnam, apparently for a presidential speech on March 26. Johnson Library: Papers of McGeorge Bundy.

4. July 24, 1965, memo from McGeorge Bundy to the president, "The History of Recommendations for Increased US Forces in Vietnam," Johnson Library: National Security File, Vietnam Country File, Box 11, Tab 3a, p. 2.

5. Johnson Library: George Ball Oral History, p. 31.

6. Robert S. McNamara, *In Retrospect: The Tragedy and Lessons of Vietnam*, p. 175.

7. See correspondence in the National Archives: RG51, series 61.1a, Box 148, M2-1/1, Budget and Financial Management folder.

8. The key defenders of the military budget were from the Defense Department, not the Bureau of the Budget. Neither the BOB director nor the Treasury secretary talked about military spending in his congressional testimony in early February 1965 regarding the FY 1966 budget.

9. National Archives: Bureau of the Budget. *The Budget in Brief: Fiscal Year 1966*, p. 24. Of the $52.6 billion, $51.6 would come out of the administration budget, and the other $1 billion from trust funds. (These figures are in absolute dollar amounts.) See also pp. 7–8 in *Military Procurement Authorizations, Fiscal Year 1966*, Joint Hearings before the Senate Committee on Armed Services and the Subcommittee on Department of Defense of the Senate Committee on Appropriations, February 24, 1965.

10. See *Department of Defense Appropriations for 1966*: Hearings before the Subcommittee on Department of Defense Appropriations House Appropriations Committee, 89th Congress, First Session. Part 3. March 2, 1965, pp. 13–14, or Senate Hearings, *Military Procurement Authorizations, Fiscal Year 1966*, pp. 16–17.

11. *Department of Defense Appropriations for 1966*, March 8, 1965, p. 554.

12. Ibid. p. 556.

13. Committee for Economic Development, *The National Economy and the Vietnam War*, p. 18.

14. *Department of Defense Appropriations for 1966*, March 8, 1965, p. 560. One problem with the study on aircraft needs was that they still did not know what the wear-out rate was. (Ibid. p. 563.)

15. Alain Enthoven and K. Wayne Smith, *How Much Is Enough?*, p. 293.

16. *Department of Defense Appropriations for 1966*, March 2, 1965, p. 71.

17. Ibid. p. 94.

18. Ibid. pp. 63–64.

19. McNamara did state that the United States had gone beyond 23,500 men in South Vietnam and that another 1,500 soldiers were on their way to Vietnam. None of the congressmen picked up on this or discussed it further. (Ibid. p. 108.)

20. *Department of Defense Appropriations for 1966*, March 8, 1965, p. 554.

21. *Department of Defense Appropriations for 1966*, March 11, 1965, p. 696.

22. Ibid. p. 678.

23. Ibid. p. 696.

24. Ibid. p. 696.

25. Ibid. p. 763.

26. *Department of Defense Appropriations for 1966*, March 15, 1965, p. 851.

27. Ibid. p. 852.

28. *Department of Defense Appropriations for 1966*, March 24, 1965, p. 918.

29. Statement of Kermit Gordon before the Joint Economic Committee, February 23, 1965, p. 19. Office of Management and Budget Records Division: Accession No. 51-79-121, Box 77 - FY 1966 Defense Budget, "Congressional Action" folder. See also National Archives: RG51, Series 61.1a, Box 131, 1965 E3-1/3, "Joint Economic Committee" folder.

30. April 25, 1967, statement of Senator Stennis before the Joint Economic Committee. (Joint Economic Committee. *Economic Effect of Vietnam Spending*, p. 70.) During the hearings on the FY 1966 military budget Stennis served as acting chairman of the Committee on Appropriations and the Subcommittee on Defense Appropriations in place of Senator Richard Russell who was ill.

31. April 1, 1965, Memo from McGeorge Bundy to the president, "Key Elements for Discussion, Thursday, April 1," Johnson Library: National Security File, NSC History—Deployment of Forces.

32. The April 1 meeting was attended by the president, Rusk, McNamara, McGeorge Bundy, Taylor, McCone, William Bundy, Cyrus Vance, McNaughton, and General Wheeler.

33. Johnson Library: William Bundy unpublished manuscript, chapter 25, p. 1.

34. At this second NSC meeting, which was shorter and more of a briefing than the one on April 1, in attendance were the same men from the previous meeting, plus secretary of the Treasury Henry Fowler, United States Information Agency (USIA) director Hobart Rowan, Agency for International Development (AID) deputy director William S. Gaud, White House aides George Reedy, Bill Moyers, and Jack Valenti, and Chester Cooper. At these two critical meetings on Vietnam policy, George Ball, the most eloquent opponent of escalation, was attending a North Atlantic Treaty Organization (NATO) meeting in Paris.

35. Chester Cooper's April 5, 1965, memo, summary of April 2, 1965, NSC meeting, in Johnson Library: NSC History File, vol. 3, Box 1, Tab 33.

36. April 1, 1965, press conference, in *Presidential Press Conferences: Lyndon Johnson*, vol. 1, p. 291.

37. Chester Cooper's April 5, 1965, memo, p. 2.

38. Ibid. p. 3.

39. April 2, 1965, memo from McCone to secretary of state, secretary of defense, assistant for national security affairs, and Ambassador Maxwell Taylor, in Johnson Library: NSC History, Box 41, Tab 135.

40. NSAM 328, April 4, 1965, in *The Pentagon Papers*, Gravel edition, vol. 3, p. 703. The memo was written by McGeorge Bundy and addressed only to Rusk, McNamara, and McCone.

41. *The Pentagon Papers*, Gravel edition, vol. 3, p. 447.

42. April 1, 1965, press conference. See *The Johnson Presidential Press Conferences*, vol. 1, p. 294.

43. See NSAM 328 text.

44. Ibid.

45. U.S. Department of State, Central File, Pol 27 Viet S, Washington to Saigon 2184, April 3, 1965, quoted in William Conrad Gibbons, *The U.S. Government and the Vietnam War: Executive and Legislative Roles and Relationships*. Part III: January–July 1965, p. 202.

46. Bundy manuscript, chapter 23, p. 24.

47. Ibid. chapter 23, p. 23.

48. Maxwell Taylor, *Swords and Plowshares*, p. 341.

49. Johnson Library: April 14, 1965, cable to Rusk from Taylor, NSC History, vol. 3, Tabs 173, 176.

50. Johnson Library: Memo from McGeorge Bundy to the president, April 14, 1965, National Security File, McGeorge Bundy Memos to the President, vol. 9, Box 3.

51. Ibid.

52. April 17, 1965, cable to McGeorge Bundy from Taylor, ibid. Tab 176.

53. Eric Goldman, *The Tragedy of Lyndon Johnson*, p. 318.

54. Lyndon Baines Johnson, *The Vantage Point*, p. 162.

55. For an excellent account of the speech and its reception, see Goldman, *The Tragedy of Lyndon Johnson*, pp. 319–322.

56. See Steven F. Lawson, "Civil Rights" in Robert A. Divine, *Exploring the Johnson Years*, pp. 108–109. Both Whitney Young of the Urban League, who criticized white liberals for getting worked up over Vietnam and Roy Wilkins, executive secretary of the National Association for the Advancement of Colored People (NAACP), who worked to give the anti-Vietnam cry a minimal profile in the Civil rights movement, were worried that anti-Vietnam activities would drain energy and workers away from civil rights. Nor did they want to lose the critical support of the president. It wasn't until the war was in full swing by mid-1966 and 1967 that many began to realize the devastating effect the war was having on the liberal, civil rights, and antipoverty programs. Not until 1967 did Martin Luther King, for example, split completely with President Johnson over Vietnam.

57. Goldman, *The Tragedy of Lyndon Johnson*, pp. 333–334. The first session of the 89th Congress passed 89 administration-sponsored or administration-backed measures. Johnson lost only three bills: appropriation for rent supplementals; Washington, D.C., homerule; and the repeal of a section of the Taft-Hartley Labor Act.

58. In the Johnson Library, the massive paper flow and the attention paid to each bill can be traced in the Pending Legislation Files, Enrolled Legislation Files, and Legislative Background and Domestic Crises Files.

59. As quoted in Goldman, *The Tragedy of Lyndon Johnson*, p. 336.

60. Marvin Kalb and Elie Abel, *Roots of Involvement*, p. 185.

61. For a detailed discussion of the genesis and writing of the speech, see Kathleen Turner, *Lyndon Johnson's Dual War*, pp. 111–33.

62. Bundy manuscript, chapter 23, p. 29.

63. Quoted by McGeorge Bundy. This was stated in a meeting on March 5 between McNamara, Bundy, and Rusk. (Johnson Library: National Security File, McGeorge Bundy Memos, Box 3, vol. 9—March 6, 1965, p. 3.)

64. Ball Oral History, p. 39.

65. Bundy manuscript, chapter 22, p. 12.

66. Ibid. chapter 23, pp. 36–37.

67. April 8, 1965, from Hanoi Radio on April 13, 1965. Quoted in George McT. Kahin, *Intervention: How America Became Involved in Vietnam*, p. 326.

68. April 20, 1965, memo from Bundy to the president, in ibid. p. 327.

69. April 24, 1965, memo from Bundy to the president, in ibid. p. 326.

70. Richard Goodwin memo to President Johnson, April 27, 1965, as quoted in Turner, *Lyndon Johnson's Dual War*, p. 134.

71. *Washington Post*, April 24, 1965, p. A1.

72. See Johnson Library: NSC History, vol. 3, Tab 187.

73. Alan E. Goodman, *The Lost Peace: America's Search for a Negotiated Settlement of the Vietnam War*, p. 29.

74. Goldman, *The Tragedy of Lyndon Johnson*, p. 406.

75. Cable from CINCPAC to RUMSMA/COMUSMACV, April 14, 1965, pp. 1–2. Johnson Library: NSC History, vol. 3, Tab 171.

76. William Westmoreland, *A Soldier Reports*, p. 135.

77. McNaughton's "Minutes of April 20, 1965, Honolulu Meeting," in Johnson Library: McNaughton File XV, Appendix H, Box 7, pp. 1–2.

78. April 21, 1965 memo from McNamara to the president, in *The Pentagon Papers*, Gravel edition, vol. 3, p. 706.

79. Westmoreland, *A Soldier Reports*, p. 132.

80. *The Pentagon Papers*, Gravel edition, vol. 3, p. 457.

81. See Appendix II, "Minutes of April 20, 1965, Honolulu Meeting—Instructions to Ambassador Taylor," in Johnson Library: McNaughton File XV, Appendix H, Box 7.

82. April 21, 1965, memo from McNamara to the president, in *The Pentagon Papers*, vol. 3, p. 706.
The so-called consensus presented to the president was a bit less than it seemed. Admiral Sharp wrote some years later that McNamara's report was "a distortion of the view I took at that conference. However, as with most conferences that Secretary McNamara attended, the published results somehow tended to reflect his own views, not necessarily a consensus." (See U.S.G. Sharp, *Strategy for Defeat: Vietnam in Retrospect*, p. 80.)

83. Final letter from McCone to the president before he left the CIA, in Johnson Library: April 28, 1965, letter from John McCone to President Johnson, NSC History, Box 41, Tab 134.

84. CIA, Office of National Estimates, Special Memo #12-65, April 30, 1965: "Current Trends in Vietnam," in Johnson Library: NSC History, vol. 3, Tab 211.

85. Taylor, *Swords and Plowshares*, p. 405.

86. April 10, 1965, memo from McGeorge Bundy to the secretary of state and the secretary of defense (cc: LBJ), in Johnson Library: National Security File, McGeorge Bundy Memos to the President, Box 3, vol. 10.

87. Johnson Library: National Security File, McGeorge Bundy Memos to the President, Box 3, vol. 10.

88. May 4, 1965, covering note by McGeorge Bundy, also in Johnson Library: National Security File, McGeorge Bundy Memos to the President, Box 3, vol. 10.

89. Cable from Taylor to Greenfield, April 26, 1965, in Johnson Library: National Security File, NSC History, vol. 3, Tab 202.

90. *The Pentagon Papers*, vol. 3, p. 460.

91. See *Washington Post*, April 24, 1965, p. A9; and I. F. Stone, May 12, 1965, column, "The Forms of Democracy But No Longer the Reality," reprinted in I. F. Stone, *In a Time of Torment, 1961–1967*, pp. 231–34.

92. U.S. Congress, Senate Committee on Foreign Relations, unpublished executive session transcript, April 30, 1965. In Gibbons, *The U.S. Government and the Vietnam War*, Part III, p. 239.

93. Johnson Library: Cabinet Papers File, Box 2, Cabinet Meeting agenda folder, April 20, 1965, Item 2.

94. Authorization figures are higher than the actual projected spending for fiscal year 1966: the budget figure of $99.7 billion. Such authority would allow spending that would extend beyond the fiscal year for some multiyear programs.

95. Gardner Ackley's report to the president and cabinet: "The Economic Situation by the Council of Economic Advisers," March 25, 1965 (Cabinet Meeting), Johnson Library: Cabinet Papers, Box 2, March 25, 1965, Folder 1, pp. 3–4.

96. Johnson Library: Bureau of the Budget Administrative History, p. 62.

97. Johnson Library: Gardner Ackley Oral History, Interview 1, p. 26.

98. Johnson Library: Report to the President and Cabinet on the Economic Situation by the Council of Economic Advisers, Meeting Notes File, Cabinet Papers, Box 2, p. 1.

99. Interview with Arthur Okun, in Erwin C. Hargrove and Samuel A. Morley (eds.), *The President and The Council of Economic Advisers: Interviews with CEA Chairmen*, p. 279.

Okun cited *The Pentagon Papers* as his source for knowledge of the April 1 NSC meeting. So he may have been unaware of the later declassified material (including NSAM 328) in which the president emphasized the secrecy of the decision to deploy more troops and change the mission of the ground forces.

100. Ibid. p. 279.

101. Johnson Library: Council of Economic Advisers Administrative History, Box 1, vol. 1, Folder 1, Chapter 2, p. 44.

102. Hearings before the Senate Appropriations and Armed Services Committees on "Supplemental Appropriations for Department of Defense, 1965, Emergency Fund, Southeast Asia," May 5, 1965, p. 28.

103. White House Confidential File, Box 61, section LE: Legislation 1963–65. See also Johnson Library: CEA Report to the president and cabinet, May 13, 1965—Report to the President and Cabinet on the Economic Situation by the Council of Economic Advisers, Meeting Notes File, Cabinet Papers, Box 2.

On June 3, 1965, a "Preliminary Annotated Checklist" of new budget priorities was prepared by the Bureau of the Budget, Council of Economic Advisors, and the Office of Science and Technology. This checklist included a number of substantial new proposals and programs to be tackled in FY 1966. These included proposed new cabinet departments such as Transportation and the possibility of an Education Department. Concerns were expressed for tax reduction and reform, a balance of payments program, and temporary tax reductions. They wanted to guard against a recession. But nowhere was there any mention about the impact of increased defense spending or the escalating situation in Vietnam. Yet, the Bureau of the Budget had a major impact on what every other department was doing in the administration. (See Johnson Library: *1966 Legislative Program Proposals* in White House Confidential File, Box 61, section LE: Legislation 1963–65.)

104. Johnson Library: Pending Legislation Folder 89-18: HJ Resolution 447.

105. May 5, 1965, McGeorge Bundy memo to the president—"My Talk with Senator Joe S. Clark," Johnson Library: National Security File, McGeorge Bundy Memos to the President, Box 3, vol. 10.

106. Bundy manuscript, chapter 25, pp. 18–19.

107. McNamara's testimony in Hearings before the Senate Appropriations and Armed Services Committees on "Supplemental Appropriations for Department of Defense, 1965, Emergency Fund, Southeast Asia," May 5, 1965, pp. 2–3, 12.

108. Ibid. p. 21.

109. A later analysis of congressional records revealed that "from 1965, when the first Vietnam supplemental was enacted, through the end of 1972, between 95 and 96 percent of the members of Congress present and voting approved the war-related appropriations bills on final passage." (*The Congressional Quarterly Weekly Report*, January 27, 1973, p. 119; Johnson Library: BDM Corporation, *A Study of Strategic Lessons Learned in Vietnam*, vol. 4, pp. 5–20.)

110. Johnson Library: Pending Legislation Folder 89-18: HJ Resolution 447.

111. Notes of John McNaughton, as quoted in *The Pentagon Papers*, New York Times edition, p. 407.

112. For the text of the message see *The Pentagon Papers*, Gravel edition, vol. 3, p. 369.

113.   Quoted from someone 'in the Defense Department—most likely in McNaughton's office, although not McNaughton himself—who wrote a scathing criticism of the bombing pause and the U.S. approach to discussions with Hanoi. It was undated and unsigned, entitled "Criticism of the Initiative by the 'Unsympathetic.'" (Johnson Library: McNaughton File, vol. 15, in Gibbons, *The U.S. Government and the Vietnam War*, Part III, p. 255.)

114. William Bundy Oral History, May 29, 1969, p. 28.

115.   Valenti Notes of May 16, 1965, meeting on Vietnam in Johnson Library: Meeting Notes File, Box 1.

116. Ball Oral History, p. 7.

117. George Ball, *The Past Has Another Pattern*, p. 404.

118. *The Pentagon Papers*, Gravel edition, vol. 3, p. 410.

119.   Roger Hilsman, William Bundy's predecessor as assistant secretary of state, had made it clear in a memo to secretary of state Rusk that if the United States bombed the North, Hanoi would unleash 10 regular army divisions, and if the North sent the divisions into South Vietnam, then the United States would bomb the North. (Roger Hilsman, *To Move a Nation*, pp. 526ff.) Hilsman's memo used the specific phrase "tacit understanding," (April 15, 1990 letter from Roger Hilsman to the author.)

120. *The Pentagon Papers*, New York Times edition, p. 410.

121. *New York Times*, May 19, 1965, p. 19.

122. *The Pentagon Papers*, Gravel edition, vol. 3, p. 462.

123.   June 5, 1965, cable from Taylor, #4074, in Johnson Library: National Security File, NSC History, vol. 5.

124. Bundy manuscript, chapter 26, p. 6.

125.   Memo from General Earle Wheeler to McNamara, "US/Allied Troop Deployments to South Vietnam (SVN) (S)," June 11, 1965, p. 2, in Johnson Library: National Security File, NSC History, vol. 5. According to newly appointed assistant secretary of defense Alain Enthoven and his assistant K. Wayne Smith, "[T]he JCS made virtually no independent analysis of the Vietnam War. (See Enthoven and Smith, *How Much Is Enough?*, pp. 299–300)

126.   Westmoreland cable to the JCS, June 14, 1965, "Concept of Operations— Force Requirements and Deployments, South Vietnam," Johnson Library: National Security File, NSC History, vol. 5.

127.   See *The Pentagon Papers*, Gravel edition, vol. 4, p. 291.   Also see Westmoreland, *A Soldier Reports*, p. 141.

128. Bundy Oral History, May 29, 1969, p. 30.

129. Ibid.

130. *New York Times*, June 9, 1965, p. A1.

131.   Dean Rusk, quoted in Thomas J. Schoenbaum, *Waging Peace and War: Dean Rusk in the Truman, Kennedy, and Johnson Years*, p. 440.

132. *New York Times*, June 9, 1965, p. 46.

133. June 9, 1965, column reprinted in Stone, *In a Time of Torment*, pp. 58–61.

134. *New York Times*, June 10, 1965, p. 2.

135. Bundy Oral History, May 29, 1969, p. 30.

Chapter 6 _____

In Pursuit of a "Stalemate"

NO MORE ILLUSIONS

Even as pessimistic reports that South Vietnam was on the verge of military collapse continued to come in from Saigon, President Johnson was reluctant to grant General Westmoreland's request for 44 battalions. The decision Johnson now faced was whether to commit to war in Southeast Asia. At an NSC meeting on June 11, Johnson said: "We must delay and deter the North Vietnamese and Viet Cong as much as we can, and as simply as we can, without going all out. When we grant General Westmoreland's request, it means that we get in deeper and it is harder to get out . . . . We must determine which course gives us the maximum protection at the least cost."[1] It appeared that Johnson was still searching for a cheap way to escalate without getting into a land war. The prospect was not an all-out war with everything in the American arsenal—for that risked a superpower or nuclear confrontation—but a conventional land war. Westmoreland's request would bring the number of American troops in Vietnam to over 175,000 (over 200,000 if non-U.S. forces were not part of the component), over half the deployment during the height of the Korean War.

A CIA analysis of June 10 strongly agreed that ground forces should be increased in order to prevent the collapse of South Vietnamese morale and military capabilities. Many of these analyses were done hastily because, as assistant secretary of state William Bundy noted, "Steps seen at the April Honolulu conference as likely to hold at least through the summer were already revealed as insufficient."[2] Bundy added: "Any idea that Hanoi would come around in 'perhaps a year or two' should likewise have been dead." The CIA also argued that "the arrival of US forces in these numbers (150,000) would not change the Communists' basic calculation that their staying power is inherently superior to that of Saigon and Washington."[3] Moreover, the CIA questioned how many American soldiers would be enough and just how well 150,000 U.S. soldiers would do in the Vietnamese jungles: "We do not know how the test of combat would come out at the level of US involvement now being considered."

Some State Department and CIA officials also questioned the urgency of Westmoreland's request. When Ambassador Taylor returned to Saigon, he confirmed Westmoreland's estimate of the situation but underscored, "There was no intent . . . to state or to imply 'that there is a serious danger of complete military collapse within a relatively short period of time.'"[4] So initially, the only part of Westmoreland's request the president approved was the deployment of the 1st Air Cavalry Division (about 28,000 troops, including support personnel).

George Ball strongly underscored to the president that by raising the U.S. commitment from 50,000 to 100,000 or more men and deploying most of the increment in combat roles, the country was on the verge of a new war: "the United States directly against the Viet Cong."[5] Ball opposed the Westmoreland request and cautioned: "Perhaps the large-scale introduction of American forces with their concentrated fire power will force Hanoi and the Viet Cong to the decision we are seeking. On the other hand, we may not be able to fight the war successfully enough—even with 500,000 Americans in South Vietnam—to achieve this purpose. Before we commit an endless flow of forces to South Vietnam we must have more evidence than we now have that our troops will not bog down in the jungles and rice paddies—while we slowly blow the country to bits."

Ball wanted to limit the number of forces and maintain freedom of action because "the more forces we deploy in South Vietnam—particularly in combat roles—the harder we shall find it to extricate ourselves without unacceptable costs if the war goes badly." In one way, Ball's assessment was not much different than that put forth by the CIA on June 10. The CIA pointed out that the resources—in terms of manpower, matériel and even the political commitment—required to do the job might be far greater than envisioned.[6] The agency did not draw any conclusions as to whether the United States should follow a specific course but noted that the means and numbers were not necessarily compatible with the goals. Clark Clifford, one of the president's most trusted friends and advisers had written on May 17 to the president that "a substantial buildup of U.S. ground troops . . . could be a quagmire. It could turn into an open end commitment on our part that would take more and more ground troops, without a realistic hope of ultimate victory." The words of both Ball and Clifford were quite prophetic. However, neither man became aware of the other's ideas about the war until the president invited Clifford to sit in on a meeting to discuss Vietnam on July 22.[7]

McNAMARA EXPLAINS THE AMERICAN POLICY

On June 18 defense secretary Robert McNamara briefed the cabinet on

Vietnam. He explained the American goals in Southeast Asia but downplayed the growing debate within the president's circle of military and foreign policy advisers. He then outlined the administration's military objective in Vietnam:

> by moving toward a stalemate, convincing [the communists] that the situation in the South will not lead to a military victory, that they can't win while the stalemate continues, they are being forced to absorb the penalty in the North as a result of our bombing of their military targets. So that is our basic strategy. We think that if we can accomplish that stalemate, accompanied by the limited bombing program in the North, we can force them to negotiations, and negotiations that will lead to a settlement that will preserve the independence of South Vietnam. The basic question, the military question is how can we accomplish a stalemate, and how can we move from a situation which they believe they are winning to one in which they see that there is no hope for the victory that they are endeavoring to accomplish.[8]

After describing some of the military moves the United States had made up to that point, McNamara continued:

> But it is very clear that these actions are not enough, 100,000 men added to 550,000 [ARVN] won't lead to a total that will effectively counter 65,000 guerrillas. The mobility . . . and firepower we are providing have not satisfactorily offset the increase in the Viet Cong strength. There's only one remaining answer, and that is to send in outside ground combat troops, and this we are doing . . . . We currently have 9 battalions there, and 6 more are moving there at the present time. That will lead to a total combat strength of about 21,000, a total U.S. military strength in the country of between 70,000 and 75,000.
>
> Will this be enough? I don't know. [9]

McNamara had already acknowledged this during a June 5 meeting with the President when he remarked: "We're looking for no more than a stalemate in the South. Can we achieve it? I don't know." The defense secretary acknowledged the same point made by George Ball and the CIA: there seemed no way to know how many troops would be enough, even to achieve a stalemate.[10] McNamara then emphasized to the assembled cabinet that major escalation could lead to a ground war with the Chinese, which no one wanted: "What are the alternatives? There really are none. We can escalate, and we do have the power to escalate, we can destroy from the air all of North Vietnam, and we can destroy much of China. But it is very clear that that will lead to a ground war in Asia which we couldn't win in any meaningful sense of the word, and which would destroy the lives of hundreds of thousands of Americans."[11]

The only alternative was withdrawal from the region, which was unacceptable. So, a stalemate was the middle ground between international humiliation and an Asian conflagration. When McNamara completed his presentation, the following exchange ensued:

Health Education and Welfare Secretary Anthony Celebrezze: I question the wisdom from a psychological point of view of telling the American people about a stalemate. Is that all we are going to tell the American people, that all we are getting is a stalemate?

McNamara: I didn't tell that to the American people. I wanted you to understand that our military program is directed to that end, and it is this which underlies our measured application of power. It is by this measured application of power that we seek to avoid the risk associated with rapid escalation.

The word "stalemate" is a colored word and the word "victory" is a proper word to use here but there shouldn't be any misunderstanding on your part as to what we are doing and how we are measuring the quantity and power to apply it.

Celebrezze: I think that we should use that, and I just wanted to make sure that everybody understood we didn't start using the word "stalemate" publicly, because we would be in difficulty.[12]

The deception of the American people was now the Johnson administration's policy. McNamara's presentation and response to Celebrezze demonstrate that the president and his Vietnam advisers were less than honest in two ways. First, they were not up-front with the public that the military goal was a "stalemate," not a victory. Second, while admitting to the cabinet and domestic advisers the policy of a stalemate, they did not inform them of the likelihood that a significant military escalation would probably be required to achieve that stalemate. Neither McNamara nor any other top military or foreign policy official mentioned that Westmoreland's request for hundreds of thousands of American soldiers was at that moment awaiting a presidential decision.

During the June 18 cabinet meeting, there was also a discussion of the preliminary estimates for the FY 1967 budget. The president sharply noted that the costs of the initial program goals and objectives submitted to the Budget Bureau "cannot conceivably be fitted into a reasonable budget total for fiscal 1967. The excess costs of your program submissions over any kind of realistic budget total is about twice what it was at this stage of budget-making last year."[13] He noted that budget outlays would rise sharply due to a number of causes, including the second-year costs of that year's new legislation. There would also be less budgetary leeway than in the past because, in part, the "declining defense expenditures . . . may not be with us in 1967." It was time to turn to the domestic budget for needed savings. As a way to avoid a guns-or-butter battle, Johnson specifically urged his domestic and economic advisers in June to cut sharply any nonessential, low-priority programs and also increase efficiency.[14]

The president emphasized to the cabinet that a moratorium on new programs or program improvements was no answer and that new ideas would have to be created by "a tough and hard-headed weighing of priorities among existing programs—weeding out the obsolete and the lower priority activities" and "a thorough and continuing search for more efficient means of carrying out ongoing activities." Johnson then made a rather ironic statement in light of how he made decisions regarding Vietnam: "The Budget Director tells me that while there have been some improvements in this regard, the preview submissions still do not fully reflect the kind of *hard choices* which we are going to have to make."[15]

WEIGHING THE OPTIONS

Shortly thereafter, Johnson authorized further deployments of ground forces. On June 26, 11 days after deploying the 1st Air Cavalry Division, he approved three more marine combat units, over 10,000 men.   In response to Westmoreland's desire for a free hand to maneuver troops around the country, Johnson also gave him additional authority to commit U.S. troops to combat "independently of or in conjunction with" the South Vietnamese armed forces.[16] Westmoreland was essentially given the authority to do as he saw fit. William Bundy had also emphasized that "we want to depict the present decision not as a new and separate escalation decision by the U.S., but as the essential response to increased VC strength and DRV involvement."[17]

President Johnson soon turned his attention to Ball's June 18 memo and allowed the undersecretary of state to present his arguments at a meeting on June 23 to discuss Vietnam. This discussion focused primarily on how many forces should be deployed to Vietnam in light of Westmoreland's request. There was general agreement that more forces would be needed, but no consensus on how many. After Ball and McNamara, who had come to support the JCS/Westmoreland increase, made their cases, Johnson asked both of them to prepare studies in support of their respective positions.

From June 24 to July 1, Ball and McNamara put together their proposals for the president. These papers were written in an atmosphere of secrecy and amid growing speculation about the administration's policy in Vietnam.   The military situation was now in the press daily, although the policy debate remained under wraps. William Bundy noted that any revelation that Ball advocated withdrawal would have been a bombshell—he was thought to be just a moderate voice by those outside the inner circle. In addition, because Bundy, who was initially assisting Ball, could not agree with Ball's proposed early American withdrawal, he wrote a third paper,which advocated holding on through the summer at roughly 85,000 men. McNamara sent his first draft (primarily written by McNaughton) to the White House on June 26, while Ball presented his paper at a White House meeting on Vietnam on June 29.[18]

Ball's June 29 paper, "Cutting our Losses in South Viet-Nam," evoked strong debate in the meeting.[19]   At the beginning, Ball emphasized that the paper was based on "the premise that we are losing the war." For Ball, South Vietnam was politically a lost cause, and "a deep commitment of United States forces in a land war in South Viet-Nam would be a catastrophic error. If ever there was an occasion for a tactical withdrawal, this is it." Neither expanded air attacks nor a major expansion of U.S. combat forces in South Vietnam, nor a combination of both, would achieve the U.S. objectives. Ball believed that because the United States could not succeed, it should either withdraw or at least limit the U.S. deployment. Ball emphasized: "This is our last clear chance to make this decision." The consensus among the president's other advisers was that withdrawal was completely unacceptable.

In McNamara's draft of June 26, he strongly urged the deployment of 44 battalions within the next few months.[20]   Some of the sharpest criticism for McNamara's position actually came from McGeorge Bundy in a memo to the defense secretary on June 30. As on previous occasions, Bundy gave excellent reasons against escalation: "It proposes a doubling of our presently planned strength in South Vietnam, a tripling of air effort in the north, and a new and very important program of naval quarantine.   It proposes this new land commitment at a time when our troops are entirely untested in the kind of warfare projected. It proposes greatly extended air action when the value of the air action we have taken is sharply disputed. It proposes naval quarantine by mining at a time when nearly everyone agrees the real question is not in Hanoi, but in South Vietnam. My first reaction is that this program is rash to the point of folly."[21] Bundy also emphasized that he saw "no reason to suppose that the Viet Cong will accommodate us by fighting the kind of war we desire . . . . this is a slippery slope toward total US responsibility." He then underscored the point by noting that McNamara's plan "omits examination of the upper limit of US liability.   If we need 200 thousand men now for these quite limited missions, may we not need 400 thousand later?"[22] He wanted to wait, saying that it was not clear that the United States should make such decisions to escalate in early July without more evidence. McGeorge Bundy had raised excellent and often uncomfortable questions and punched holes in the actions and policies being considered but without much apparent conviction behind his criticism. As he admitted, this memo was "designed to raise questions and not to answer them."   He was often perceptive enough to see the long-term consequences of escalation but never offered alternatives. In his June 30 memo to McNamara, Bundy saw many of the same pitfalls as Ball had, although he felt that the large numbers of American troops would not so much bog down as be ineffective and "lightly engaged."[23]

On July 1 the president actually received four separate memoranda on Vietnam: from Rusk, McNamara, William Bundy, and Ball. McGeorge Bundy, in presenting the four memos to Johnson, advised him in a covering note that he should "listen hard to George Ball and then reject his proposal" and then "move   to   the   narrower   choice   between   my   brother's   course   and McNamara's."[24] In a second note, he summarized the two main alternatives: "George Ball's preference for a negotiated withdrawal, and Bob McNamara's recommendation of a substantial increase in the military strength with a call-up of reserves during this summer."[25] McGeorge Bundy emphasized that the July 2 meeting to discuss the memos was not for decisions but to sharpen the issues.

Rusk's memo made no particular military recommendation. His points were broadly political. He insisted that the Viet Cong were not winning and could be denied a victory. But the key to any decision was that the president had to maintain the "integrity of the U.S. commitment [and] . . . if that commitment becomes unreliable, the communist world would draw conclusions that would lead to our ruin and almost certainly to a catastrophic war."[26] Rusk was also interested in shoring up the Saigon government and wrote of the South Vietnamese: "They must be told bluntly that they cannot take us for granted but must earn our help by their own performance." No one questioned the political commitment that Rusk emphasized, but the immediate issue was how much of a greater U.S. military commitment Johnson should make.[27]

Ball's memo, "A Compromise Solution for South Viet-Nam," was a reworking of his June 29 paper. In it he recommended that U.S. force levels be held at 72,000 men, with their mission restricted to base security and as a reserve to the South Vietnamese army. He urged that the United States limit "its liabilities in South Viet-Nam and try to find a way out with minimal long-term costs."[28] He continued: "The alternative—no matter what we may wish it to be—is almost certainly a protracted war involving an open-ended commitment of US forces, mounting US casualties, no assurance of a satisfactory solution, and serious danger of escalations at the end of the road." Ball concluded his memo with a recommended program for negotiations.

McNamara's position was that the United States should "expand substantially the US military pressure against the Viet Cong in the South and the North Vietnamese in the North and at the same time launch a vigorous effort on the political side to get negotiations started."[29] He did not respond to any of McGeorge Bundy's criticisms. McNamara quoted Westmoreland as saying that the 44-battalion plan "should re-establish the military balance by the end of December." But how did anyone know that? The defense secretary had told the cabinet two weeks before that he did not know how many troops were required for a stalemate. According to McNamara, Westmoreland acknowledged that the military "cannot now state what additional forces may be required in 1966 to gain and maintain the military initiative," so "there may be substantial US force requirements." Westmoreland later stated, "It was virtually impossible to provide the Secretary with a meaningful figure [on] how many additional American and Allied troops would be required to convince the enemy he would be unable to win."[30] In other words, it should have been clear to all who read McNamara's proposal that thousands more soldiers would probably be required. McNamara also urged the call-up of U.S. reserves (up to 100,000 men) and extension of tours of duty in all services.

Even though casualties would increase, and the war would continue for some time, McNamara claimed that this program would have popular support because it was "likely to bring about a favorable solution to the Vietnam problem." There was no basis for stating this, especially considering that toward the end of the memo, he unambiguously stated that "the war is one of attrition and will be a long one." Had the policy been presented to the American public in the same manner in which it was given to President Johnson, it is doubtful that the support McNamara described would have been so forthcoming. John McNaughton commented a few weeks later that even in the event of American "success," it was "not obvious how we will be able to disengage our forces from South Vietnam."[31] The bottom line was that the United States would be engaged militarily in Vietnam for many years to come, either as combatant or occupying power. With a call-up of the reserves and a likely war of attrition, McNamara admitted that "the test of endurance may be as much in the United States as in Vietnam."

The defense secretary also acknowledged that the proposed number of U.S. troops was too small to make much of a difference in a guerrilla war. However, he claimed that a "'Third Stage' or conventional war in which it is easier to identify, locate and attack the enemy" was now evolving in Vietnam.[32] Many top military officials were convinced that sending enough American soldiers to get the communists into a conventional war was a key to turning the tide in South Vietnam. Once the conflict turned from guerrilla warfare to conventional warfare, the U.S. military could then force the communists to admit the impossibility of winning a conventional conflict. Ball strongly disagreed: "[W]e have no basis for assuming that the Viet Cong will fight a war on our terms when they can continue to fight the kind of war they fought so well against both the French and the GVN."[33] A CIA analysis of June 29 noted, "While more intensive than in the past, this larger scale commitment of Viet Cong forces in combat reflects no marked change as yet in the essential guerrilla character of the Viet Cong military effort."[34] McNamara admitted that even in the face of setbacks in the South, the communists might choose to escalate rather than negotiate. No one in the Pentagon mentioned any escalation threshold beyond which the United States would not go. This worried some civilian advisers who wanted a ceiling or at least to know, as McGeorge Bundy consistently put it, "the upper limit of US liability."[35]

William Bundy's "Middle Way" proposal (which had the support of what his brother called "the second-level men in both State and Defense") was not optimistic about the prospects in Vietnam. It reflected a strong bureaucratic reluctance to increase to 44 battalions or call up any reserves until a clearer picture of the military situation was possible. Thus, the proposal argued for holding on with 85,000 men for the next few months: "This is a program . . . to test the military effectiveness of U.S. combat forces and the reaction of the Vietnamese army and people to the increasing U.S. role."[36] The "middle way" also rejected withdrawal or negotiating concessions in any form. The main point was, "[W]e lose little by waiting, compared to the risks."

THE PRESIDENT AND HIS ADVISERS DELIBERATE

After getting the July 1 memos and convening a meeting on Vietnam the next day with the authors of the four proposals, the president apparently set a late July timetable for decisions. There are discrepancies about whether Johnson had already made up his mind. He seemed inclined to escalate but had not decided on the pace and scope. He appeared unsure about an all-out war effort that would include calling up the reserves, deploying even more men in 1966, and perhaps a tax increase. The president had three very different choices in front of him, but only two of the three were truly up for consideration. Ball's proposal did not get wide circulation. Even before the July 2 meeting, Rusk and McNamara had called Ball's position "dangerous" and not to be argued in front of others.[37]

It was clear that giving the military what it wanted meant continued expansion of the war through 1966. From mid-June through mid-July Westmoreland and Admiral U.S. Sharp, the head of CINCPAC, consistently made the point that many more U.S. forces (beyond the 44-battalion request) would probably be needed. They could not predict how many, but they certainly made it clear to McNamara that it would be a long war. In addition, Westmoreland strongly urged a complete national commitment to the war. He had sent a cable declaring, "It is difficult, if not impossible, for me to imagine how we can commit and sustain U.S. forces . . . , without backing them up for the long pull by mobilization of manpower, industrial and training resources at least to a limited degree."[38] He also noted that it would be difficult to maintain troop morale "while the average U.S. citizen enjoys his butter at no inconvenience." It is important to note that the 44-battalion force recommendation was the limit of what could be prepared and absorbed by the end of 1965, not any firm estimation that only 175,000 men would be needed. To Westmoreland, these forces would be part of a first phase, to run through 1965, geared toward preventing a communist victory. He then hoped to begin an offensive in high-priority areas during the first half of 1966, resume pacification, and in one or two years destroy the rest of the enemy's main forces.

Johnson continued to defer the decision. He wanted further study and advice, although he did authorize the deployment of 10,400 support troops (as distinct from combat troops) on July 10. The president admitted at a press conference that the situation in Vietnam "will get worse before it gets better."[39] He added, "Whatever is required I am sure will be supplied. We have met and taken action to meet the requests made by General Westmoreland, and as other needs appear, we will promptly meet them." Public opinion was clearly a concern in the White House. An "Outline of Public Justification for Increased Military Support in Vietnam," which had been prepared for the president in late June, noted the "legitimate public concern over this unhappy situation."[40] Most of the president's advisers wanted him to be up-front with the American public. As it was, the press and Congress were now aware that Westmoreland had made a substantial military request, but differing figures were tossed about in Washington, mostly in the 100,000 to 200,000 range. Expectations of war grew.

President Johnson then asked McNamara to go to Saigon in order to examine the military situation firsthand. The secretary's trip was accorded a great deal of weight in Washington because he had last visited Vietnam in April 1964. Westmoreland saw the visit as simply a fact-finding mission that was part of the decision process on the 44-battalion request.[41] But it appeared that Johnson and McNamara wanted not only to resolve the immediate decision but, in recognizing the implications of expanding the war, to get some idea of how much more would be required.

McNamara cabled Taylor that the purpose behind the visit was to receive recommendations on the military needs (both men and matériel) through 1966. He stated that there were two basic questions to answer before expanding U.S. forces[42]:

a) . . . what assurance do we have that with the resulting force level we can prove to the Viet Cong that they cannot [win] and thereby force them to a settlement on our terms?
b) will large increases in the number and involvement of U.S. combat units and military personnel in South Vietnam cause the Vietnamese government and especially the army, to let up; will it create adverse popular reactions to our presence in the country?

McNamara concluded, "Upon our return, we expect that important policy decisions will be made. These may well require major legislative and executive action (including possibly the declaration of a national emergency, calling up of reserve forces, large additions to the budget, etc.) for which we wish to be fully prepared." He clearly envisioned a major war commitment.

The expectation among almost all of the president's senior foreign policy and military advisers was that the reserves would be called up and that the president would have to go to Congress. A memo from Rusk to new CIA director William Raborn showed what decision the president was expected to make. The CIA was asked to "provide an assessment of major reactions to a substantial increase in our force structure in South Vietnam":

The following should be the major assumptions for your assessment: 1) U.S. forces would be increased from their present level of approximately 75,000 to 175,000 by Nov. 1; 2) In order to achieve this build-up without weakening our overall force structure and deployment of forces, legislation would be requested to permit call-up of reserves and permit extension of tours. Under this legislation, some 225,000 reserves would be called up, and tours would be extended, at the rate of 20,000 a month cumulatively for a year (subject to review at the end of that period); 3) in order to permit a release of reserves and determination of extended tours, the regular strength of the armed services would be increased by 400,000 men over the next year. Draft calls would be increased by 100%; 4) a budget supplement of between $2 and $3 billion would be sought in order to support this build-up.[43]

At the same time, the Pentagon was still trying to figure out the right combination of numbers and time to do the job. McNaughton put together a set of projections over the next three years.[44] He concluded that a compromise solution offered the best chance of success:

The Options: Assuming maximum ingenuity on the all-important political side, the estimated probabilities of the 5 combinations of outcomes/efforts are as indicated below. (Notice that, of the "tolerable options," only B1 looks promising.)
The estimates for "success/inconclusiveness/collapse" were as follows:

Outcome/Effort Combinations[45]	By 1966	By 1967	By 1968
A1 (win with 200–400,000+ US)	20/70/10	40/45/15	50/30/20
A2 (win with 75,000 US)	10/70/20	20/50/30	30/30/40

B1 (compromise with 2–400,000+ US)	40/50/10	60/25/15	70/10/20
B2 (compromise with 75,000 US)	20/60/20	30/40/30	40/20/40
C3 (capitulate and withdraw)	0/0/100	0/0/100	0/0/100

McNaughton continued:

Outcomes/efforts/collapse costs. There has been no decision taken putting on the same value scale (a) desirability of various outcomes, (b) undesirability of various efforts, and (c) undesirability of having tried and failed. For example:
- Is a collapse at a 75,000 level worse than an inconclusive situation at a 200–400,000+ level? Probably yes.
- Is a 60% chance of a "compromise" better than a 40% chance of "winning"? Probably yes if the compromise is tolerable.
- Is a 40% chance of "compromise" in 1966 better than a 40% chance of "winning" in 1967? Query.

Of course, one has to wonder how McNaughton arrived at these probabilities. There was no cost accounting for each of the scenarios either; that is, what were the costs in terms of financial expense, needed matériel and resources, and lives lost? McNaughton's work showed both how complex the decision facing the president was and that the whole business was very muddy and lacked clear-cut rationales. He also made a remarkable admission: an American withdrawal and compromise after committing up to 400,000, as the French carried out due to their defeat at Dien Bien Phu, were preferable to an American withdrawal in the summer of 1965.

By mid-July it appeared that President Johnson had made up his mind. Deputy secretary of defense Cyrus Vance sent a memo on July 17 to McNamara in Saigon that relayed Johnson's "current intention to proceed with [44] battalion plan."[46] When Vance asked the president whether McNamara's proposed call-up of the reserves and extension of tours of duty "would be acceptable in the light of his comments concerning domestic program . . . [Johnson] stated it would." However, the president had some serious political concerns. As Vance noted in the cable, Johnson felt he could not go back to Congress for more than $300 or $400 million as a military supplement before next January. Vance added, "If a larger request is made to the Congress, he believes this will kill domestic legislative program." Despite Johnson's concerns, William Bundy interpreted Vance's cable as a message to McNamara that he "forget all other possible courses, and submit a straight action plan for the 44-battalion force, including congressional approval on a reserve call-up."[47] Johnson had not yet made a specific decision but he seemed committed to escalation. He was, however, quite concerned about the costs and congressional reaction.

GEARING UP FOR WAR

Preparations continued apace in anticipation of a major presidential decision on Vietnam. Key advisers began to make plans as to how the president's decision to escalate would be presented to the public, to Congress, and to key U.S. allies. Public support was a particularly important concern. William Bundy had raised this issue in his July 1 memo: "While military effectiveness is the basic reason for holding at about 85,000, we must also reckon the Congressional and public opinion problems of embarking now on what might appear clearly to be an open-ended ground commitment."[48] McGeorge Bundy had posed the following question to the president when he presented him with the four memoranda: "What would a really full political and public relations campaign look like in both the Bundy option and the McNamara option?"[49] For Bundy, whatever policy the president chose, how to explain it and sell it was a critical decision.

The president's advisers assumed he would soon make a major announcement and declare a national emergency. McGeorge Bundy informed Johnson that "Vance has gone ahead with planning for the reserve call-up, the extension of tours, and the increased draft calls which are foreshadowed in the military planning." Bundy then outlined a plan of action for Johnson on July 19, the day before McNamara's return from Saigon.[50] The Pentagon had put together a first draft of a presidential statement, which was sent to the State Department for input. The administration's best speechwriters were to be brought in on the subsequent drafts. Drafts of congressional legislation were readied. The whole weight of the foreign policy bureaucracy was now preparing to go to war. William Bundy had compiled a checklist that included a draft of a major presidential statement, preparations for committee testimony in Congress, consultations with the congressional leadership and international leaders, and a strategy for gaining public support.[51]

The White House staff was also working on the best method to call up the reserves. Henry Rowen, assistant director of the Bureau of the Budget, was apparently tasked by the NSC to explore different methods for a call-up. His memo to McGeorge Bundy stated that reserves may be called up by executive order; however, "the President must first declare a new national emergency."[52] Alternatively, reserves could be called up by the service secretaries "in time of war or of national emergency declared by Congress." Rowen recommended the congressional route: "It assures Congressional participation and support and avoids the problems involved in declaring a new national emergency." But if the President wanted to avoid a major debate on Vietnam and keep Congress' attention focused primarily on the domestic agenda, neither a request for a congressional resolution nor an executive declaration of a national emergency seemed desirable.

This developed at a time when Congress was nervous about the possibility of escalation. Speculation about Vietnam in the press and on Capitol Hill was widespread, especially in anticipation of McNamara's return from Vietnam. In addition, Senator John Stennis had been loudly proclaiming in the past month that the administration had not budgeted enough money for military needs and was diverting too much to domestic programs.

THE ILLUSION OF ECONOMIC OPTIMISM

Just as the foreign policy machinery was gearing up for war, the domestic advisers were bringing all their efforts to bear on winning final authorization and appropriations for the president's ambitious domestic policy agenda. The highly prosperous economy was to fuel and finance Johnson's plans. Former CEA chairman Walter Heller, who remained a consultant to the CEA in 1965, later noted that, "indeed, without any significant step-up in inflation, the cash budget *fleetingly* came into balance just before the July 1965 escalation in Vietnam."[53] In that respect, Johnson escalated at the most optimal time, since the economic policies remained very successful in July 1965. It would have been difficult for any president not to be seduced by the economic prosperity he had achieved, especially when it allowed him to be a strong warrior and halt the spread of communism while continuing to expand the economy and build a Great Society.

As the president and his advisers debated the extent of American escalation in July 1965, the administration's domestic and economic planners concentrated fully on the Great Society agenda, giving little thought to Vietnam. During the two monthly Quadriad meetings (the "Quadriad" was the Troika plus the chairman of the Federal Reserve Board) in May and June, neither Vietnam nor defense spending was put forward as an agenda issue.[54] At the cabinet meeting on June 18, the Council of Economic Advisers presentation noted that the economic outlook remained good. In fact, if the CEA had to revise the forecast, it would revise it upward.[55] President Johnson met regularly with the Troika and the Quadriad and individually with the economic advisers. So he had the opportunity to be up-front with his escalation plan and get advice on the economic consequences.

The problem with the continual upbeat assessment of the American economy was not that no case could be made for it but that the Council of Economic Advisers and other administration domestic planners made their assessments based on false assumptions. When the economic advisers finally began to turn a watchful eye toward foreign policy and especially the escalating situation in Vietnam, they still did not know what the scope of the war would be. They did not even consider the escalation in Vietnam an issue worth questioning or exploring, much less one that would unleash an overheated economy and require economic caution. While the conflict in Southeast Asia was certainly an important foreign policy issue, it was not seen as a significant economic issue.

With the cabinet, President Johnson discussed the Vietnam conflict in terms of months, not years: "We don't really anticipate that the prospect is good for settlement or for arriving at any agreement, certainly until the [fall] monsoon season is over . . . . Our problem is largely one of trying to protect our national interest in the next three or four months, hoping that the conditions and the atmosphere will be better for our position in the fall."[56] Vietnam was presented as a short-term problem, and the goal, as McNamara stated to the cabinet on June 18, was a stalemate.

Walter Heller later noted the illusions economic planners had: "We were moving under the more or less gentle zephyrs of the tax cut. We were moving so nicely toward full employment, and with very little price inflation. What there was . . . was almost all in farm prices, which is not a function of overall aggregate demand . . . . The Vietnam escalation just knocked things into a cocked hat because it superimposed about $25 billion of expenditures that no one had factored into the economic plan on a program that was essentially a full employment program to begin with."[57] The primary fear in the summer remained that the economy might weaken or slow down. In June 1965, about a month before the key decisions to escalate, there were signs of weakness in the economy. As a result, the president and the CEA discussed the need for a small income tax cut for lower-income people in case the economy got soft.[58]

The economists had begun to worry that the 50-month prosperity could boomerang in the future, but they were undecided as to how that might happen. Gardner Ackley noted the two main fears. First: "There is the danger of expanding too fast—of letting the growth of demand push too hard against the growth of our ability to produce, engendering inflationary pressures."[59] That is essentially what did happen, beginning in the fall. But he added a second caution: "Prosperity . . . can also just run out of gas." So there was fear of a recession also. This created a rationale for the belief that the economy might need further stimulation. Talk of another tax cut emerged for just such a purpose.

Ackley later noted that even after the economists got Johnson to agree to the removal of excise taxes initiated during the Korean War, they still felt "it would be desirable to have a somewhat larger expenditure budget than the President's guidelines had provided."[60] So in early 1965 Ackley and Schultze had urged a couple of billion dollars more in expenditures, primarily for education and Social Security. Since the President, as he had in the past, wanted to keep expenditures down on the domestic side in order to appear fiscally responsible on Capitol Hill, the economists appeared to believe that a modest stimulation to the economy, even in the form of a small increase in military spending, was not an altogether bad prospect.

But for the most part, even at the height of the summer of 1965, the economists continued to see defense spending as an area for savings, not a drain, in the budget. In the July report of the interdepartmental "Committee on the Economic Impact of Defense and Disarmament," chaired by Ackley, the only mention of Vietnam was in the introduction:

Recently, we have been in another major period of transition. This transition has been characterized by a roughly stable level of defense expenditures—and, therefore, a significant decline in the share of defense of our gross national product and in employment—together with a sizable shift in the composition of defense spending. To what extent this transition will be interrupted or postponed by the needs of the war in Vietnam is not yet clear.

However, neither the shifts from one kind of defense spending to another (for example, from strategic weapons to weapons of limited war), nor the resumption of the gradual shift away from defense presents major problems for our economy.[61]

Even as the president and his military advisers were committing to major escalation in Vietnam, the economic planners were still thinking in terms of a decrease in defense spending. The Budget Bureau and the Treasury Department published their joint year-end statement in July of budget results for fiscal 1965, which stated that as a result of decreases in defense spending, the $3.5 billion in the administrative budget was "the smallest deficit in five years."[62] At this point, prior to the beginning of FY 1966, one analyst noted that "the Budget Bureau estimated that the additional costs of Vietnam were $100 million or less a year, a rather insignificant factor in a $50 billion military budget and a $700 billion economy."[63]

But were the economic advisers getting an accurate picture? As Gardner Ackley later noted, at first the Council of Economic Advisers did not have "all the facts about the extent of the Vietnam buildup . . . but I think increasingly as 1965 wore on, we were becoming pretty clear about what was going on."[64] One could argue that the economists should have challenged their optimistic assumptions if only because of what they read in the newspapers each day—or, at the least, they should have questioned the war's impact on the economy during cabinet briefings or meetings with the president.

Defense indicators began to show a rise in certain key areas in the spring. For example, in January 1965, after declining for four consecutive quarters, the Federal Reserve Board's index of "defense equipment" began a steady rise. In March the decline in army uniformed personnel reversed, and the number of uniformed personnel in all services sharply increased in June.[65] But there seemed to be a consensus within the administration that the American economy still had enough slack to absorb any modest increase in defense spending, so the reversals in those defense indicators were not taken seriously. In looking back on the period, however, it would seem that very careful attention should have been paid to the area of defense economics because reduced military spending had been one of the keys to the prosperous economy and was a critical factor in increased government spending for domestic programs.

McNAMARA'S PROGRAM: NO TURNING BACK

Robert McNamara returned from South Vietnam to deliver his report to the president on July 20. As he was departing Saigon, he stated: "The overall situation continues to be serious. In many aspects, it has deteriorated since 15 months ago when I was last here."[66] That statement increased the war speculation, and most observers now expected that the American war effort would enter a new phase, especially in light of McNamara's comments. Johnson had created many of those expectations during a July 13 press conference when he announced that when McNamara returned from Saigon, he would carefully consider his recommendations, "and we will do what is necessary." The *New York Times* observed, "Public thinking is being prepared for a build-up of American military strength in Vietnam to something in the neighborhood of 200,000 men and there is no certainty that even that will prove enough."[67]

White House aides had already said that there would be an increase in U.S. forces in Vietnam. The question then was how many and under what conditions more troops would be deployed, as well as what sacrifices the president would ask of the American people. The series of policy meetings the president was to hold on Vietnam from July 21 through July 27 would be front-page news each day. As the week of deliberations on Vietnam progressed, the press grew more anxious, speculating on the urgent and secret meetings going on at the White House. On July 25, The *New York Times* wrote, "There is little question in Saigon that the U.S. is preparing to take over the main burden of the ground war from the South Vietnamese."[68]

When McNamara returned from Vietnam and met with the president on July 21, he once again pressed his recommendation for 44 battalions, emphasizing that it was even more urgent. Claiming the support of Taylor, Lodge, Westmoreland, Wheeler, and Sharp, McNamara asked for a total of 175,000–200,000 American personnel (the latter number if South Korea did not come through with their expected nine battalions). He then warned that the military might need another 100,000 troops by January 1966. Therefore, in order to carry out this program, he urged the call-up of 235,000 men in the U.S. Reserve and National Guard and an increase in the regular armed forces by some 375,000. This would require an expansion of the draft and extending the tours of duty of men already in the service. McNamara wanted to make available "approximately 600,000 additional men" by mid-1966.[69] The military had pushed this greater offensive posture all along, but McNamara's on-the-scene assessment gave it real weight. His proposal was based on the following: "Expand promptly and substantially the US military pressure against the Viet Cong in the South and maintain the military pressure against the North Vietnamese in the North."[70] The key new element was the proposed expansion of U.S. military activity in the South: in essence, a ground war.

McNamara also added "that success against the larger, more conventional, VC/PAVN [People's Army of Vietnam] could merely drive the VC back into the trees and back to their 1960–64 pattern—a pattern against which US troops and aircraft would be of limited value but with which the GVN, with our help, could cope." In other words, U.S. forces would right the military situation, drive the communists back into the jungles, and then hand the fighting back over to the South Vietnamese. In pressing his case, McNamara admitted the following about his proposed expansion: "This alternative would stave off defeat in the short run and offer a good chance of producing a favorable settlement in the longer run; at the same time *it would imply a commitment to see a fighting war clear through at considerable cost* in casualties and material and would make any later decision to withdraw even more difficult and even more costly than would be the case today."[71] The secretary of defense was blunt; the bottom line was that once in, there was no turning back.

Even though McNamara believed that the United States had a good chance of achieving its goals in Vietnam, anyone who read the memo had to realize that the country would pay a very high price in terms of lives and resources. As McNamara himself admitted in the report, "[E]ven in 'success,' it is not obvious how we will be able to disengage our forces from Vietnam." In fact, he did not provide any dates or timetable for the president. With no ceiling on troop levels or time limit, the escalation would be open-ended. On July 22 chief of naval operations Admiral David L. McDonald claimed, "By putting more men in it will turn the tide and let us know what further we need to do."[72] That was a stopgap measure, put forth by military men whose only certainty was that thousands more U.S. forces would be needed.

However, despite the costs, McNamara still felt escalation was the only acceptable alternative and the least expensive. He argued that withdrawal was out of the question because of the cost to American effectiveness, prestige, and commitments worldwide. To delay would make the costs only higher down the road and lessen the chances for success. At the core of his proposal was that the United States had to bite the bullet and plunge headfirst into Vietnam. McNamara also acknowledged that by the end of 1965 his program might lead to a rise in the number of American soldiers killed to "the vicinity of 500 a month" but assured the president that the American public could be counted on to support this "sensible and courageous military-political program."[73] One can only surmise that he made this prediction of domestic support for American deaths based on an anticipated frank public admission by the administration that the United States was going to war.

THE QUESTION OF COSTS

Unlike in the spring and early summer, in July there was a concern about the costs of the military moves now contemplated. McGeorge Bundy raised some of McNamara's concerns in a memo to the president on July 21:

Bob [McNamara] is carrying out your orders to plan this whole job with only $300–400 million in immediate new funds. But I think you will want to know that he thinks our posture of candor and responsibility would be better if we ask for $2 billion to take us through the end of the calendar year, on the understanding that we will come back for more, if necessary. Bob is afraid we simply cannot get away with the idea that a call-up of the planned magnitude can be paid for by anything so small as another few hundred million. Cy Vance told me the other day that the overall cost is likely to be on the order of $8 billion in the coming year and I can understand Bob's worry that in the nature of things, these projected costs will be sure to come out pretty quickly, especially if he looks as if he was trying to pull a fast one.[74]

In asking for a call-up of the reserves, an increase in the regular armed forces, and supplemental appropriations (immediately and at the beginning of 1966), McNamara's report clearly recommended that the country go on a war footing. Also, although not mentioned in the final report, a significant issue in the background was whether a tax increase might be needed. McNamara had personally gone to Johnson and requested, in strong terms, a tax increase, but to no avail. The president "flatly refused my advice to increase taxes to pay for the war and thus avert inflation. I submitted my spending estimate and proposed tax increase in a highly classified draft memorandum known to only a handful of people. Not even the treasury secretary or the chairman of the Council of Economic Advisers knew about it."[75]

The question of a tax hike was raised for the first time publicly when Gardner Ackley stated before the Joint Economic Committee: "If our opportunities or responsibilities—particularly in defense—should mount sufficiently, we might even have to think in terms once again of tax increases. It is much more probable, however, that the growth of Federal expenditures will not exhaust the potential growth of our revenues and that tax reductions will again need to be considered."[76] Ackley did acknowledge, "The big question mark which confronts us today in thinking about fiscal policy for fiscal 1967 is the size of the defense budget. I think until we have a clearer fix on that, it is very hard to make any judgments about the need for tax reduction or tax increase."[77] Many economic analysts point to this passage as proof that the economists knew there was a danger that greater defense spending would overheat the economy and lead to inflation.[78]

However, this interpretation implies that Ackley ignored some kind of warning or danger signal from increased defense budget figures. It is also important to emphasize that Ackley was pointing to the question of defense spending in FY 1967, the middle of 1966, a year away. The next day, treasury under secretary Joseph Barr remarked, "At this time, I personally believe that we have enough slack in the balance of this calendar year and in the first half of next year to say that we don't need any tax increases." But he added that, "no one knows at this time if an expenditure increase in connection with Vietnam will be required."[79] Barr noted further "that all we know about Vietnam now indicates two things. There is enough capacity so that there will not be pressures on inflation . . . . There is enough taxing power so there would not have to be an increase in taxes."[80]

The day before McNamara's return, McGeorge Bundy had addressed the issue of paying for the war when he provided the president with arguments for avoiding a billion-dollar appropriation in Vietnam. His reasons were as follows:

1. It would be a belligerent challenge to the Soviets at a time when it is important to do only the things which we have to do (like calling reserves).
2. It would stir talk about controls over the economy and inflation—at a time when controls are not needed and inflation is not that kind of a problem.
3. It would create the false impression that we have to have guns, not butter—and would help the enemies of the President's domestic legislative program.
4. It would play into the hands of the Soviets at Geneva, because they could argue that it was a flagrant breach of the policy of "mutual example" on defense budgets.
5. It is not needed—because there are other ways of financing our full effort in Vietnam

for the rest of the calendar year, at least.[81]

The memo was returned to Bundy with a handwritten note from the president: "Rewrite eliminating 3." He seemed to want no acknowledgment of the guns-versus-butter dilemma. Four days later Bundy returned it with the third point deleted, and, interestingly, the phrase "like calling reserves" in point 1 was also gone.[82]

The president had believed ever since he received McNamara's proposal of July 1 that he would have to go to Congress for additional authority in Vietnam to call up the reserves.[83] He affirmed this belief to Vance on July 16. McGeorge Bundy was opposed to a reserve call-up, but it seemed a foregone conclusion and was never debated much. General Wheeler later noted that there were two compelling reasons to call up the reserves. First, "your manpower units in other areas would be spread thin because of the Vietnam situation." Second, "it would be desirable to have a reserve call-up in order to make sure that the people of the United States knew that we were in a war and not engaged in some two-penny military adventure."[84] Calling up the reserves meant higher immediate costs because of the rank of those called up, the hiring structure, and high pay per man. Thus, the reserve option would have been more expensive than extending tours of duty and instituting large draft calls. Relying entirely on extended tours of duty and on a draft was significantly cheaper, especially in immediate costs. Therefore, at some point in the final 10 days of deliberation, the president decided to go against the Pentagon's wishes and would not submit any request for the reserves to Congress. The decision to cut back on the scope of the war measures and downplay the escalation seemed strictly a personal one taken by Johnson with almost no debate. The president wanted the cheapest road to escalation.

THE DECISION TO ESCALATE

As the president and his advisers deliberated in June and July over Westmoreland's request for 44 additional battalions, they clearly faced much higher military costs for the buildup in Vietnam. During this period, the major assumptions made by the Vietnam planners were that American forces would be increased from 75,000 to 175,000 by November 1. The reserves would be called, and tours of duty would be extended. The regular strength of the services would increase by 400,000 men over the next year, and draft calls would increase by 100 per cent. Finally, a $2–3 billion budget supplement would be sought in order to support the buildup.[85] There is, however, no evidence that these assumptions were passed on to the domestic planners.

On July 22 the president met with many of his top military advisers on Vietnam. Admiral David L. McDonald, chief of naval operations, summarized the military recommendation as follows: "1) Supply force as Westmoreland has asked for; 2) Prepare to furnish more (100,000) in 1966; 3) Commensurate building of air and naval forces, step up air attacks on NVN [North Vietnam]; 4) Bringing in needed reserves and draft calls."[86] The president then asked,

"Any ideas on costs of what this would be?" McNamara replied: "Yes—$12 billion—1966."[87] On July 21 Cyrus Vance had told McGeorge Bundy that the overall costs for Vietnam would likely be $8 billion in the next year, so Johnson should not have been surprised at the high price tag; nor did he challenge the number at this point in the deliberations.[88] When the president asked what effect the $12 billion figure would have on the economy, McNamara claimed, "It would not require wage and price controls in my judgment. Price index ought not go up more than one point or two." The secretary of defense had just put a substantially high price tag on the decision the president was about to make and concluded that it would have little economic impact. Yet, that was the total extent of the discussion; no one challenged, questioned, or even followed up on McNamara's answer. This is especially striking in light of the fact that most of Johnson's advisers acknowledged that they did not know how many men would be required to turn the tide against the communists in Vietnam. No one asked the economic advisers the same question that the president asked of McNamara, What impact would a $12 billion escalation over the next year have on the economy?

While McNamara was optimistic about the minimal effect his proposal would have on the economy, Johnson clearly worried about its political and economic consequences. A heavy price tag would create havoc with his domestic policy agenda. Yet in none of the meetings in which costs of military escalation and economic consequences were discussed, however briefly, were any administration economists or domestic planners present. The cost estimates did not seem to mean that much because later that afternoon, without most of the military men present (except Wheeler), McNamara came back to the president and stated: "The services have submitted budget requests of $12 billion. We can cut this down by half or more."[89] Again, no one bothered to ask McNamara how he arrived at the cost figure and what military scenario it reflected. So the president was now told that the job could be done in the neighborhood of $6 billion or less in 1966. In his memoirs, McNamara would later claim that his estimation was $10 billion and implies that the president was the driving force behind keeping the appropriations requests far below that figure.[90] It is, therefore, unclear whether McNamara's halving of the initial estimates for FY1966 was simply a response to what he knew Johnson wanted or whether he was providing a best-guess estimate.

Johnson also had to take into account the costs of the Great Society programs. In July 1965, however, there were very few fixed costs of his domestic agenda. In July Johnson had two dilemmas domestically. First, about one-third of his proposed legislative agenda of Great Society programs had not yet been passed into law by Congress. Second, many of the programs, although enacted into law, had yet to begin, so that the costs remained on paper. Would those costs need to be adjusted as they were put into place? The president could not yet answer that question, but he was now faced with superimposing a major military escalation onto the American economy.

NOTES

1. Bromley Smith's notes of NSC meeting June 11, 1965, in Johnson Library: NSC Meetings File, vol. 3, Tab 34, Box 1, p. 2.

2. Johnson Library: William Bundy unpublished manuscript, chapter 25, p. 27.

3. CIA memorandum, June 10, 1965, "US Options and Objectives in Vietnam," sent from CIA director Admiral Raborn to McGeorge Bundy, in Johnson Library: National Security File, NSC History, Vol. 5.

4. June 18, 1965, cable from Taylor to the State Department, in Johnson Library: NSF Vietnam Country File, cited in William Conrad Gibbons, *The U.S. Government and the Vietnam War: Executive and Legislative Roles and Relationships*, Part III: January–July 1965, p. 293.

Taylor and deputy ambassador U. Alexis Johnson strongly believed that the current deployments of U.S. forces should be given a chance to prove their value in an enclave strategy. However, by this time, their views carried little weight in the White House. In many ways, the U.S. Embassy in Saigon, so long at the forefront of U.S. policy in Vietnam, was no longer relied on by Washington for ideas and information. The military was now the primary source of information, and policy was being generated from Washington. (*The Pentagon Papers*, Gravel edition, vol. 3, p. 472.)

5. June 18, 1965, memo to the president from George Ball, "Keeping the Power of Decision in the South Vietnam Crisis," in Johnson Library: National Security File, NSC History, vol. 5, Tab 317.

6. CIA memorandum, June 10, 1965, "US Options and Objectives in Vietnam."

7. Johnson Library: National Security File, Vietnam Country File, Box 11, Tab 14.

8. Johnson Library: Cabinet Papers File, Box III, Cabinet Minutes, June 18, 1965, p. 43.

9. Ibid. pp. 47–48.

10. Robert S. McNamara, *In Retrospect: The Tragedy and Lessons of Vietnam*, p. 187.

11. Cabinet minutes, June 18, 1965, p. 51.

12. Ibid. pp. 52–53.

13. Statement of the president to the cabinet on the budgetary situation, June 18, 1965, in Johnson Library: Cabinet Papers File 1, June 18, 1965, Box 3.

14. See U.S. Congress, Joint Economic Committee *Hearings before the Subcommittee on Fiscal Policy: "Fiscal Policy Issues of the Coming Decade,"* July 20, 1965, p. 29.

15. Johnson Library: Cabinet Papers File 1, June 18, 1965, Box 3, emphasis added.

16. *The Pentagon Papers*, Gravel edition, vol. 3, p. 471. See also Lyndon Johnson's unanalytic description of this in *The Vantage Point*, pp. 142–143.

17. June 23, 1965, memo from William Bundy to McGeorge Bundy, in Johnson Library: National Security File, Vietnam, Box 14, Tab 332.

18. According to William Bundy, there was a very narrow circle of people who were working on the McNamara and Ball memos to the president. He stated that "this narrowing of the circle was undoubtedly very frustrating to those at the fringe, and has contributed to highly misleading accounts of the reality of the process." He specifically referred to James Thomson and Chester Cooper of the NSC staff. Bundy claimed, "[They] were not privy to the papers of late June, or to the discussions of the whole month of June. Their impressions of the superficiality of decisions already made seems to derive from the large meetings of late July. By that time, indeed, . . . the main decision had been made, and Ball's main arguments considered and rejected. June and

early July, the crucial first phase of decision, were a different story, and debate was very much 'for real.'" (Bundy manuscript, chapter 26, p. 25.)

Ball confirmed this when he argued that he felt that he was taken very seriously in June and early July; again, that was not the case in late July, when many, not just Ball and William Bundy, felt the policy meetings were simply staged.

19. For complete text, see Johnson Library: National Security File, NSC History, vol. 5.

20. In the Johnson Library, there is a memo from McNamara to the president dated June 26 but revised July 1, so one cannot be sure what was in the original, as there is no copy of that. However, one can clearly infer from a memo sent by McGeorge Bundy to McNamara on June 30 in response to the June 26 draft that the 44-battalion request was in that first draft. Bundy talked of putting in 40–50 battalions in his memo.

21. McGeorge Bundy memo to McNamara, June 30, 1965, p. 1, Johnson Library: National Security File, NSC History, vol. 5.

22. Bundy felt that a much tougher and expanded air war should be considered. He also referred to "larger action" in the following manner: "If General Eisenhower is right in his belief that it was the prospect of nuclear attack which brought an armistice in Korea, we should at least consider what realistic threat of larger action is available to us for communication to Hanoi." This was probably not a veiled hint at using the threat of nuclear weapons; instead, severe strikes at the North, rather than greater U.S. deployment in the South, should be explored and might be more successful. (Johnson Library: National Security File, NSC History, vol. 5, McGeorge Bundy memo to McNamara, June 30, 1965, p. 2.)

Bundy later told Neustadt and May that, in addition to voicing to McNamara misgivings that he was hesitant to expose to President Johnson, he was probably responding to someone in the Pentagon—perhaps McNaughton, an old friend—who had asked him to help McNamara pose hard questions to Westmoreland and the JCS. (Richard Neustadt and Ernest May, *Thinking in Time*, p. 80.)

23. The CIA also responded to McNamara's draft and supported his call for more ground forces in order to prevent the collapse of the South Vietnamese army but felt that his proposal to increase air attacks in the North would be futile because "the issue must ultimately be settled in the South." William Bundy noted that during this period, late June and early July, the CIA did not put forward any of its own analysis, only comments on the draft papers. In his manuscript, there was a crossed-out sentence with a footnote that read "R. [Raborn] simply had no weight." (Bundy manuscript, chapter 26, p. 25.)

24. Johnson Library: National Security File, NSC History, vol. 5, July 1, 1965, memorandum for the president, p. 1.

25. July 1, 1965, memo for the president from McGeorge Bundy, "Meeting Friday Morning on Vietnam," in Johnson Library, National Security File, McGeorge Bundy Memos to the President, Box 4, vol. 12.

26. July 1, 1965, Rusk memo, "Vietnam," in Johnson Library: National Security File, NSC History, vol. 5, p. 2.

27. William Bundy later argued that the Rusk memo, ignored to some extent by later analyses because it did not focus on the military question at hand, may have had a significant impact on the president's thinking:

One memorandum may have been of greater weight than any of the much longer ones from others. In terse language, in a rare direct memorandum not shown the others before its submission, the Secretary of State advised the President to do whatever was necessary to fulfill the American commitment to South Vietnam. [He continued:] So Dean Rusk, skeptical in the fall of 1961 and uncertain in January of 1965 that South

Vietnam had the political cohesion to be worth going all out for, had now concluded that to walk away from an American commitment, to temporize in our actions to meet it, to do anything short of all we possibly could, was to pose the greatest possible danger to world peace. General war must be, if necessary, risked, for such a risk would be less than the risk of general war which would arise if the communist world concluded the U.S. would not carry through on an undertaking once it became difficult. It was the quintessence of the Secretary's point of view, laid down in this hour of decision, to be repeated over and over in the coming years of trial.

(Bundy manuscript, chapter 27, pp. 11–12)

28. July 1, 1965, memo from George Ball, "A Compromise Solution for South Viet-Nam," in Johnson Library, National Security File, NSC History, vol. 5.

29. June 26, 1965, memo for the president (revised July 1, 1965), "Program of Expanded Military and Political Moves with Respect to Vietnam," in Johnson Library: National Security File, NSC History, vol. 5.

30. William Westmoreland, *A Soldier Reports*, p. 142.

31. July 13, 1965, Draft, "Analysis and Options for South Vietnam," in Johnson Library: McNaughton File, Box 1, File 4.

32. June 26, 1965, memo for the president (revised July 1, 1965).

33. Ball July 1, 1965, memo.

34. June 29, 1965, CIA memo, "Developments in South Vietnam during the Past Year," SC No. 07353/65 in CIA Central File. In early July army chief of staff General Harold Johnson criticized Westmoreland's deployment strategy in Vietnam. He stated that the proposed plan of operations focused "too much on the conventional and not enough on the unconventional and related aspects of the conflict." (July 7, 1965, memo from the Army Chief of Staff to Deputy Chief of Staff for Operations, "Commander's Estimate," in National Archives, RG 319, quoted in Gibbons, *The U.S. Government and the Vietnam War*, p. 358.)

35. Bundy used the phrase both in his June 30, 1965, memo to McNamara and in his July cover memo to the president.

36. July 1, 1965, William Bundy Memo, "A 'Middle Way' Course of Action in South Vietnam," in Johnson Library, National Security File, NSC History, vol. 5.

37. July 1, 1965, memo for the president from McGeorge Bundy, "Meeting Friday morning on Vietnam", in Johnson Library, National Security File, McGeorge Bundy Memos to the President, Box 4, vol. 12.

38. June 20, 1965, cable from Westmoreland in Westmoreland Papers, Center of Military History, cited in John P. Burke and Fred I. Greenstein, *How Presidents Test Reality: Decisions on Vietnam, 1954 and 1965*, p. 247fn.

39. July 9, 1965, press conference, in *The Johnson Presidential Press Conferences*, vol. 1, p. 334.

40. Johnson Library: National Security File, NSC History, vol. 5, Box 42, Tab 326.

41. Westmoreland, *A Soldier Reports*, p. 141.

42. July 7, 1965, cable from the secretary of defense for Ambassador Taylor in Johnson Library: National Security File, NSC History, vol. 6, Tab 378; copies were also passed on to CincPac and Westmoreland.

43. July 15, 1965, memo for the director of CIA from the secretary of state, in Johnson Library: National Security File, NSC History vol. 6, Tab 387.

44. July 13, 1965, Draft, "Analysis and Options for South Vietnam," in Johnson Library: McNaughton File, Box 1, File 4.

45. McNaughton defined "win" as "defeating the VC (a la Malaya/Philippines); compromise with the VC (a la Laos 1962/Vietnam 1954); capitulate to the VC (a la [France in] Algeria)."

46. U.S. Department of Defense, Files of the Office of the Secretary of Defense, DTG 172042Z Washington to Saigon. Quoted in Gibbons, *The U. S. Government and the Vietnam War*, Part III, p. 381. (34 was the U.S. component of the 44-battalion request.)

47. Bundy manuscript, chapter 27, p. 14.

48. July 1, 1965, William Bundy memo.

49. July 1, 1965, McGeorge Bundy memo.

50. July 19, 1965, memo from Bundy to the president, "Vietnam Planning at Close of Business, July 19," in Johnson Library: National Security Files, McGeorge Bundy Memos File, Box 4, vol. 12.

51. July 17, 1965, William Bundy Memo, "Checklist of Actions," in Johnson Library: National Security File, NSC History, vol. 6, Tab 390. McNamara would later call Bundy's preparations for an announcement "a superb program." (McNamara, *In Retrospect*, p. 205.)

52. July 22, 1965, memo from Henry S. Rowen to McGeorge Bundy, "Alternative Methods of Call-up of Reserve Forces" in Johnson Library: National Security File, McGeorge Bundy Memos to the President, Box 4, File 12.

53. Walter Heller interview, in Erwin C. Hargrove and Samuel A. Morley (eds.), *The President and the Council of Economic Advisers*, p. 206. Cash budget is a method of budgeting federal expenditures that includes all government accounts, including those of which the government does not consider itself the sole owner, for example, Social Security, highway, and housing programs.

54. See "6/9/65 Memo to the President from Gardner Ackley. Subject: Background for Thursday's Quadriad," in Johnson Library: Council of Economic Advisers Administrative History, Box 1, vol. 2, Part I, Folder 2.

55. Johnson Library: Minutes of June 18, 1965, cabinet meeting in Cabinet Meetings File, Box 3, Folder 1, June 18, 1965, p. 4.

56. Ibid. p. 9.

57. Johnson Library: Walter Heller Oral History, Interview 2, November 21, 1971, pp. 40–41.

58. Ibid. p. 41.

59. Remarks by Gardner Ackley before the World Congress on Marketing, June 16, 1965, in Johnson Library: Cabinet Meetings File, Box 3, Folder 1, June 18, 1965.

60. Gardner Ackley interview, in Hargrove and Morley, *The President and the Council of Economic Advisers*, pp. 245–46.

61. "Report of the Committee on the Economic Impact of Defense and Disarmament, July 1965," CEA Administrative History, Box 3, vol. 2, Part IV, Folder 3. This was one of the few references to Vietnam and the budget in the Johnson Library files for the period prior to the preparation of the FY 1967 budget in late 1965.

62. Johnson Library: *The Bureau of the Budget During the Administration of President Lyndon B. Johnson, November 1963–January 1969*, vol. 1: *Administrative History*, p. 63. The Budget Bureau revealed that "receipts had gone up $1.8 billion from the January estimates, while expenditures had dropped $1.0 billion, largely reflecting decreases in defense." The new estimate of the FY 1965 deficit showed a $1 billion decrease, largely due to "reduced or deferred defense spending." (Ibid. p. 62.)

63. Murray Weidenbaum testimony before U.S. Congress, Joint Economic Committee Hearings, *Economic Effect of Vietnam Spending*, April 26, 1967, p. 176.

64. Johnson Library: Gardner Ackley Oral History, March 7, 1974, p. 2.

65. William Bowen, "The Vietnam War: A Cost Accounting," *Fortune*, April 1966, p. 120.

66. *New York Times*, July 21, 1965, p. 1.

67. Ibid. p. 36.

68. *New York Times*, July 25, 1965, section 4, p. 1.

69. Meeting on Vietnam, July 21, 1965, notes recorded by Jack Valenti in Johnson Library: Meeting Notes Files, Meetings on Vietnam Folder: July 21–27.

70. July 20, 1965, memo from McNamara to the president, "Recommendations of Additional Deployments to Vietnam," in Johnson Library: National Security File, NSC History, vol. 6, p. 4.

71. Ibid; emphasis added.

72. July 22, 1965, morning meeting on Vietnam, Jack Valenti's notes, July 21–27.

73. Ibid.

74. Memo from McGeorge Bundy to the president, July 21, 1965, "Timing of Decision and Actions in Vietnam," in Johnson Library: National Security File, McGeorge Bundy Memos to the President, Box 4, File 12. (There is no documentary evidence in the Johnson Library of any "orders" to keep escalation at $300–400 million to which Bundy refers, but Johnson did initial this memo.)

75. McNamara, *In Retrospect*, p. 205.

76. "Fiscal Policy Issues of the Coming Decade" hearings, testimony of Gardner Ackley, July 20, 1965, p. 11.

77. Ibid. p. 32.

78. See, for example, James L. Cochrane, "The Johnson Administration: Moral Suasion Goes to War," p. 239; and James E. Anderson and Jared E. Hazleton, *Managing Macroeconomic Policy: The Johnson Presidency*, p. 124.

79. Testimony of Joseph W. Barr during "Fiscal Policy Issues of the Coming Decade" hearings, July 21, 1965, p. 51. Most likely, the slack he was referring to was the $7 billion of additional tax revenues.

80. Ibid. p. 53.

81. July 19, 1965, "The Reasons for Avoiding a Billion Dollar Appropriation in Vietnam," in Johnson Library: Memos from McGeorge Bundy to the President, National Security File, NSC History, vol. 6.

82. July 23, 1965, "Reasons for Avoiding a Big Military Appropriation in Vietnam," in Johnson Library: Memos from McGeorge Bundy to the President, National Security File, NSC History, vol. 6.

83. He had said this to former president Eisenhower in their July 2 phone call. Eisenhower Library, "Memorandum of Telephone Conversation: 10:55 A.M., July 2, 1965," quoted in Gibbons, *The U. S. Government and the Vietnam War*, Part III, p. 344.

84. Johnson Library: Earle Wheeler Oral History, August 21, 1969, pp. 19–20.

85. July 15, 1965, memo for the director of CIA from the secretary of state, in Johnson Library: National Security File, NSC History, vol. 6, Tab 387.

86. Jack Valenti's notes, July 22, 1965, morning meeting on Vietnam, Johnson Library: Meeting Notes Files, Meetings on Vietnam Folder, July 21–27.

87. Valenti notes, July 22, 1965, morning meeting.

88. Memo from McGeorge Bundy to the president, July 21, 1965, "Timing of Decision and Actions in Vietnam," in Johnson Library: National Security File, McGeorge Bundy Memos to the President, Box 4, File 12.

89. Valenti's notes, July 22, 1965, afternoon meeting.

90. McNamara, *In Retrospect*, p. 205.

Chapter 7 _____

The Low-Key Decision for an Asian Ground War

THE FINAL DELIBERATIONS ON ESCALATION

President Johnson spent much of the period from July 21 to July 27 conferring with his key advisers. Yet, neither the president nor his advisers were really considering all the alternatives. The question was not whether to send in more troops but how many and when. There was to be no rethinking of the basic rationale for an American presence in South Vietnam; escalation was a foregone conclusion. Most importantly, President Johnson was willing to pay the price for putting more American soldiers at risk: "I feel it would be more dangerous to lose this now, than endanger a greater number of troops."[1]

The Pentagon cannot be accused of misleading the president about the implications and costs of this request. It was made clear to Johnson that he was being asked to commit to a substantial deployment that would need to be supplemented with more soldiers and more money over the course of the next few years. When the president asked about the costs of the Westmoreland request, McNamara had given him a figure of $12 billion. General Wheeler noted that it was unreasonable to expect to win in a year regardless of the number of U.S. troops involved. However, "we might start to reverse the unfavorable trend in a year and make definite progress in three years." General Wallace Greene, the commandant of the Marine Corps, stated that success might require five years and 500,000.[2]

The president understood that if he approved the Pentagon's request, he was for the first time making a long-term military commitment in Vietnam. Johnson asked his advisors, "[W]hat will happen if we put in 100,000 more men and then two, three years later you tell me you need 500,000 more?. . . And what makes you think if we put in 100,000 men, Ho Chi Minh won't put in another 100,000, and match us every bit of the way?"[3] No one protested that 500,000 men was unlikely, and General Wheeler noted that the odds were 50/50 that North Vietnam would respond to an American deployment by sending in more soldiers. He actually looked forward to the latter prospect because he felt that if the North sent down its army, that would give the United States the opportunity to destroy it (which it could not do then, because to attack the North would risk Chinese intervention). Wheeler added that if the communists escalated, "This means greater bodies of men—which will allow us to cream them."[4] They would be forced out of the jungles to fight on American terms. He also gave another argument: with an increase in U.S. forces there would be proportionately fewer casualties, and "[t]he more men we have the greater the likelihood of smaller losses."

After McNamara's return from South Vietnam, Johnson appeared more cautious. The president was positioning himself to minimize the decision, but he also appeared to have doubts—not about escalating but about the full-scale escalation proposed by the military. Johnson was quite blunt with his military advisers: "But you don't know if 100,000 men will be enough. What makes you conclude that if you don't know where we are going—and what will happen— we shouldn't pause and find this out?" He also wondered: "Are we starting something that in two to three years we simply can't finish?"[5]

However, most of his advisers felt that the timing was critical; the United States had arrived at a choice point where it must decide whether to get out or pour in more men. The decision could not be deferred any longer, in their view. To each of Johnson's questions, his military advisers maintained a "can-do" attitude, even if it were to take five years and 500,000 men. One must ask whether the situation in Vietnam truly demanded a decision or whether the president took action because Westmoreland forced the issue with his recommendation. Much of the pressure to escalate immediately was predicated on a communist offensive during the monsoon season that would not materialize near the level predicted by the military. Nonetheless, the president, in agreeing to escalate, may have undercut the military because he was unwilling to pay the price.

An additional question that is hard for any analyst to answer is whether the president and his advisers underestimated the Viet Cong and North Vietnamese to such an extent that they threw about figures such as 500,000 men and five years without truly believing them.[6] There was no limit or fixed policy on the numbers. The military and civilian advisers predicted a long, hard war, but as a superpower, did they really conceive of such a prospect? It is probably an unanswerable question, but there is no question that the communists were vastly underestimated, as was the difficult nature of a guerrilla war. Discussion continued, often with little debate and many seemingly rhetorical questions. Such a procedure struck some participants as being staged, that a decision had already been made. William Bundy later stated about the July 21 meeting: "It was a bit of a set piece though, I have to say. I don't feel that this was where the decision was being made in all honesty . . . You had the feeling that I think

McNamara had already reported at dawn to the President and gone over it—you felt it had been scripted to a degree."[7]

HOW TO PRESENT THE ESCALATION

The policy was decided by July 22. As William Bundy later noted: "It was the end of the debate on policy, and the beginning of a new debate on tactics and above all on presentation to the country."[8]   Some of President Johnson's advisers emphasized how critical it was to be up-front about what the escalation would mean. General Wheeler strongly urged, "We need to make clear this is a somber matter—that it will not be quick—no single action will bring quick victory."[9]   George Ball had cautioned: "It is one thing to ready the country for this decision and another to face the realities of the decision. We can't allow the country to wake up one morning and find heavy casualties. We need to be damn serious with the American public."[10]   McNamara ventured that it was time to make clear to the country that American troops were already in combat and on the offensive.[11]

While the administration could no longer deny what was occurring in Vietnam, one of the president's chief concerns was how to make the decision to escalate acceptable to the American public.   Johnson was understandably reluctant to go before the American people and echo the words of his advisers: that this would be a war of up to five years and could involve over 500,000 American soldiers. He pointedly asked, "Do all of you think the Congress and the people will go along with 600,000 people and billions of dollars 10,000 miles away?"[12]   The only response from his advisers was that polls indicated that the public supported the administration's "commitment" in Vietnam (however, the polls did not reflect the scenario that had been laid out before the president). President Johnson retorted, "But if you make a commitment to jump off a building, and you find out how high it is, you may withdraw the commitment."[13]

In hindsight, it seems remarkable that McGeorge Bundy argued "there will be time to decide our policy won't work after we have given it a good try"—in effect, claiming that the United States could always pull out.[14] This was the opposite of McNamara's belief that once in, it would be hard to get out. William Bundy later wrote that the predominant thinking in June and July was that, "even if the chances of early failure were very substantial, as we took them to be . . . you *had* to make the try."[15]   His brother had also recommended that since the United States was already pursuing the war in Vietnam, the Administration should play down the escalation decision. This would avoid making it look too "dramatic" and thereby alarming the American public. As NSC adviser, Bundy was situated in the White House and so was probably more sensitive to the president's political concerns than his other Vietnam advisers. He was also against calling up the reserves because of the dramatic impact such a decision might have.   McNamara, on the other hand, seemed far more interested in taking the case to the people and being up-front with them. This was a key issue, as McGeorge Bundy's first item from a set of talking points for

Johnson at the July 22 afternoon meeting showed: "How big a change in policy is this and how do we explain it—in political and military terms?"[16]

Others in the administration also urged a "low-key" military increase. assistant secretary of state for international organizations Harlan Cleveland suggested to Rusk that downplaying the escalation to some degree would be best: "The American people have looked hard at two major policy changes—the decision to bomb North Vietnam and the decision to move from an advisory to a combatant role. A doubling of our forces in Vietnam does not, it seems to me, need to be played as a third major policy change."[17] How to "play" new and critical decisions seemed almost as important as the decision itself. But Cleveland's assumption was flawed; the American people never had the opportunity to look hard at the decision to move into a combat role because the White House constantly claimed there was no change of policy.

A July 20 CIA memo on the communist reaction to U.S. escalation stated, "If the announcement were made in piecemeal fashion and with no more high level emphasis than necessary, the development of a crisis atmosphere might be mitigated."[18] The CIA concluded, however, that "the reactions of the Communist powers, particularly in the military field, would not be basically changed by the method of announcement." So there was little reason from an international standpoint to keep the expansion "low-key."

Robert McNamara told President Johnson directly, "This is a major change in U.S. policy. We have relied on SVN to carry the brunt. Now we would be responsible for a satisfactory military outcome."[19] The president then asked McGeorge Bundy to give a summary of the criticism to be expected. Apparently, Johnson introduced him by saying, "What Bundy will now tell you is not his opinion or mine (I haven't taken a position yet) but what we hear." Bundy's presentation was:

Argument we will face: for ten years every step we have taken has been based on a previous failure. All we have done has failed and caused us to take another step which failed. As we get further into the thing we get deeply bruised. Also we have made excessive claims we haven't been able to realize. Also, after 20 years of warnings about war in Asia we are now doing what MacArthur and others have warned against.

We are about to fight a war we can't fight and win, as the country we are trying to help is quitting.

The failure on our own to fully realize what guerilla war is like. We are sending conventional troops to do an unconventional job.

How long—how much? Can we take casualties over five years—or are we talking about a military solution when the solution is political? Why can't we interdict better—why are our bombings so fruitless—why can't we blockade the coast—why can't we improve our intelligence—why can't we find the VC?[20]

After reading this, a simple question arises, Why didn't Bundy and the rest of the president's advisers attempt to answer such critical questions long before arriving at such a major decision? As it was, Bundy's points were not addressed at the top echelons of the government before the president announced the deployment. A key point to consider is whether President Johnson downplayed the escalation because neither he nor his advisers could sufficiently answer Bundy's questions—a failing that would have been exposed had a true debate over Vietnam policy developed.

Throughout the administration's discussions between July 21 and 27 on Vietnam, the question of costs was purposely deferred. McGeorge Bundy felt the administration could take a different tack in financing the escalation that was not so disruptive. The key to Bundy's plan and the basis for President Johnson's ultimate decision were to defer financing decisions until January 1966, which would be much less "dramatic" than making a full-scale commitment in the summer.[21] One reason it would have been important to avoid a major debate in Congress over costs at this point was the overall status of Great Society programs on Capitol Hill. While most of the authorizing legislation for Johnson's new programs for the War on Poverty, health care, and education had been enacted, many of the necessary appropriations had not yet been passed. It would have been over appropriations that a major guns-versus-butter battle would be fought.

THE IMPACT OF A MILITARY BUILDUP

Like most of the country, the economic advisers were also anxious during the week of July 20 through July 27. They were likewise relieved at President Johnson's announcement to escalate moderately. Gardner Ackley later noted, "Until perhaps October 1965, the best guess of the Council of Economic Advisers had been that the strategic Vietnam decisions that the President had made in July would add only moderately to government expenditures during calendar year 1966."[22]

One analyst made the point that while the economists were not informed of the extensive plans for escalation, they were also "not attuned to the special way in which a rapid military buildup affects the economy."[23] That may be an unfair assessment because once the administration's economists understood the scope and rapidity of the expansion, they warned the president in December that he risked major inflation and that he should take strong war-time measures, including a possible tax increase. Had they known of the planned escalation in the summer, they may also have prompted a similar economic debate. But there is no question that most economists maintained a casual attitude toward the apparent modest increase in military spending because they believed that the current pace of industrial and economic activity was about to slow down. They no longer expected continued economic growth, so they were less inclined to worry about inflation as a result of a rise in defense spending.[24]

A note of caution was raised that summer from a prominent source: Federal Reserve Chairman William McChesney Martin. He gave a speech on June 1 that made the business community as well as the press and the administration take note. In his remarks, Martin raised the danger of inflation but did not point the finger at rising defense obligations or spending. His primary concern was the danger of "over-inflating the money supply" and the seriousness of the balance of payments, which could lead to inflation and other excesses.[25]

The speech brought out into the open a debate that had been bubbling within the administration for a few months. With the domestic economy operating at such a high level and the balance of payments out of balance (i.e., the United States was spending and investing more abroad than it was taking in), Martin believed that a tightening of credit and a rise in interest rates were in order as cautionary measures. The nation's balance of payments had fallen in the last quarter of 1964. Possible measures to reduce the balance-of-payments deficit had been actively debated within the administration.[26] So Martin wanted to rein in the economy a bit, remarking that the recent "rise in Government expenditures even in times of advancing prosperity threatens to make it difficult to be more expansionary should a serious decline in business activity require it." On the other side of the debate was the Council of Economic Advisers, which wanted greater fiscal stimulation and feared that the Federal Reserve's approach could slow the expansion or bring on recession. Ackley claimed that the efforts to counter inflation through a policy of tightening the money supply during the Korean War had failed greatly.[27] The CEA wanted to rely on a flexible policy with, for example, further tax cuts that could be utilized in the event of recession. But most of all, the CEA and the president continued to push for policies that would expand the economy further.

Both the White House and the CEA issued "no comments" after Martin's speech.[28] Treasury secretary Henry Fowler claimed that he and secretary of commerce John Connor agreed with Martin in light of the need for a balanced expansion that would "neither run out of gas nor run out of control."[29] The attempt by Martin to dampen overenthusiasm appeared to take hold—which is probably all he wanted—at least for a little while. While economic caution emerged for a time in June and July at the prospect of a major war, that caution disappeared with the president's announcement of moderate escalation.

Because of the unparalleled growth from 1961 to 1965, resulting in the American economy operating at close to full capacity, little room was left for economic maneuver by mid-1965, when the military escalation spiraled. Business was so good and production was so high that when the war in Vietnam began to heat up, military requirements took resources and labor away from the strong domestic sector. There was no room for maneuver because there was little surplus labor or resources since the economy was running close to full capacity. This was in marked contrast to the beginning of World War II, when the tremendous surge in military output drew upon a labor force that was vastly unemployed and resources that were greatly underemployed.

The military planners were not concerned with the economy, and the economists were unconcerned with the war. Neither was aware that the other area was at a critical juncture. The president, responsible for the overall picture, did not want to admit that the war and the economy might be in conflict. He did not want to face any cuts in either domestic or military affairs.

President Johnson remarked at a cabinet meeting on July 27:

Over the past several weeks we have been giving particular attention to our next budget. I've made clear my conviction that our next budget will be the critical and crucial test for the future of our Administration's programs—and all that we are striving to do.

This past week was the most productive legislative week in the 35 years I have been in Washington. I believe it was the most historic legislative week of this century.

But I am sure the advances we made—and will continue to make in this session— would not come except for the effort we have made to reduce costs, tighten our spending belt and assure the Congress and the people that we are giving a full dollar's value for every dollar spent.[30]

He appeared to see no interrelation between domestic and foreign/military affairs or that they had an overlapping impact on each other. An increase in military activity would have its first impact in the private sector, not in the government budget, so the president was able to buy time to continue the momentum for domestic programs. It is important to emphasize again that Vietnam was discussed in cabinet meetings only in terms of briefings by McNamara or Rusk. Even in late July, as the president was making a significant commitment in Vietnam, there is no evidence of any cabinet discussion of the impact of the escalation in Vietnam on the U.S. domestic economy. In fact, after a thorough review of all the cabinet meeting notes for 1965, it appears that the first time the issue was raised occurred during the November 19 cabinet meeting.[31] As William Bundy noted, too much of the overall picture remained only in Johnson's hands: "I think the President ran the war on the theory that whatever the military in the field wanted was theirs. And I don't think that the field served him well in the sense of coming in and saying exactly what difference it would make, but you really can't expect that. But it wasn't pulled together and somebody saying, 'Look, how about the cost of this? How about the whole—? . . . It was not a coordinated operation; it wasn't coordinated that I could detect really in the strategy. The President took it *all* in his own hands. All the threads ran only to him and not sideways to others, or at least to many of them."[32]

The economists believed the defense buildup would be slow. They were assured on this point by the Pentagon officials, who consistently claimed that any increase in Vietnam needs could be handled by reprogramming. However, there are some basic financial ramifications of a military buildup. Raising more men would lead to significantly higher pay and training costs. There would also be lost ammunition and equipment as well as the need to equip additional units.

But the administration sought only the identifiable $1–2 billion (requested as a $1.7 billion supplemental on August 4) and waited until January 1966 to ask for the balance from Congress. As the president told the congressional leadership on July 27, they would "get the bill later." Four days earlier, deputy secretary of defense Cyrus Vance wrote Senator Richard Russell, chairman of the Senate Appropriations Committee, that the Pentagon believed that the approved appropriations "will generally be adequate to finance the programs contemplated in the President's Budget for FY 1966."[33] He added that "we are presently reviewing our requirements in Southeast Asia. If required we will submit to the Congress our recommendations for additional appropriations as needed." But at that time, the requirements were essentially known; and the figure of $12 billion cited by the military services was ultimately the added costs for FY 1966.

There was, however, a built-in assumption that seemed to have misled many of the economists and, perhaps, some of the military advisers. Ever since the Korean War, the U.S. military had maintained a peacetime deployment and a level of readiness and equipment on hand that had never been achieved prior to any other military conflict in American history. The country was fully armed. Therefore, a huge military buildup was viewed as unnecessary, unlike with Korea or the two world wars. It was assumed that the United States could quickly respond to any contingency and deploy forces wherever necessary— with little need for a major buildup and additional financial sacrifice.

Even though the Defense Department had cut its spending over the past two years, many believed that, given the overall percentage of government spending (between 9 and 10 per cent of GNP) devoted to military needs, the Pentagon was sufficiently prepared to deal with a military conflict like the one in Vietnam without much disruption to the American economy. Arthur Okun observed that: "the Vietnam conflict found us well prepared and required a relatively small buildup in total military procurement."[34] Yet, that small buildup was quite significant, especially when no wartime measures were taken and given an economy that had little room to maneuver as it moved toward full employment, all of which was compounded by the expectations for more expansive domestic programs. Defense and economic planners such as Okun may have deluded themselves that a strong defensive posture during peacetime would limit the disruption to the civilian economy if war came. War still consumes great numbers of resources. From 1960 to 1965 military spending rose from $45 billion to $50 billion. However, from 1966 to 1969 it rose from $50 billion to $78 billion.[35]

More significantly, there was a complete lack of overall economic coordination; domestic and military policies were simply kept apart. No one was responsible for looking at the big picture. The president never asked his economic advisers for specific analyses of the military escalation. On July 27 the president held an "off-the-record" cabinet meeting. An hour before the meeting, Charles Schultze was invited to the meeting by Johnson and asked, in the words of presidential aide Horace Busby, to "present some material which you submitted to him recently on government employment figures."[36] Schultze was not asked to prepare anything else for the meeting. The economic or budgetary implications of the escalation in Vietnam to be announced the next day were apparently not an agenda item. It was not until a request for 200,000 more U.S. forces by Westmoreland in late 1967 that Johnson finally asked for an evaluation by the CEA on what the economic realities were.[37] The economists were never provided with an accurate portrayal of the military scenario. One reason this was particularly damaging was that almost all fiscal action taken by the Johnson administration came from a Troika recommendation.[38] Thus, to keep defense information from the Troika or provide it with misleading numbers was to undermine greatly the quality of its recommendations.

So while the president and his military advisers were considering in July a major expansion of America's involvement in Vietnam, economic officials and outside consultants were meeting to discuss the economy. The CEA staff and planners were already considering ways to stimulate the economy in FY 1967 in order to prevent a slowdown in the expansion. It appeared that the economists believed they could switch financial stimulation on and off rather easily. However, it turned out that by the time they realized the extent of the defense needs, it was quite difficult to apply any restraint.

AVOIDING A GREAT DEBATE

As the decision to escalate drew closer, the president had two worries with respect to his domestic agenda. First, there was still outstanding Great Society legislation that was winding its way through Congress. Second and more important, he would need the continued cooperation of Congress in order to fund the Great Society programs that had been enacted into law. William Bundy added:

Johnson knew his Congress, and knew that the practical majority he held in 1965 was a precarious one. Once the Congress got itself involved in direct responsibility for the Vietnam War, conservatives would move from sufferance to opposition and to harsh cutting of domestic funds, and moderates from unstinting support to sympathy for the economy. The result, over time, would be to make the program ineffective. My liberal reader may again exclaim, "But this is exactly what did happen."" And so it did, from 1967 onward. But the point is that in 1965 and 1966 Lyndon Johnson went to extraordinary lengths that it should not happen in those formative years. History must judge him on this basis, and the decision not to seek a great debate in July 1965 was a crucial part of his actions.[39]

An exchange during his July 28 press conference echoed the debate Johnson wanted to avoid:

Q: Mr. President, from what you have outlined as your program for now, it would seem that you feel that we can have guns and butter for the foreseeable future. Do you have any idea right now, though, that down the road a piece the American people may have to face the problem of guns or butter?

The President: I have not the slightest doubt but whatever it is necessary to face, the American people will face. I think that all of us know that we are now in the 52nd month of the prosperity that has been unequaled in the Nation, and I see no reason for declaring a national emergency and I rejected that course of action earlier today when I made my decision . . . . At the moment we enjoy the good fortune of having an unparalleled period of prosperity with us, and this Government is going to do all it can to see it continue.[40]

Lyndon Johnson had told the American people that communist expansion could be halted in Vietnam without having to sacrifice anything at home. There would be no debate. William Bundy noted the following about the July 28 announcement: "[T]he upshot was a resubmission of the same decision [to escalate] but in a form that didn't require a great debate, and just put a different cast on it. And that the Presidential statement would do the work and there would not be a great debate."[41] He then added that this was consistent with the bombing in February and the initial deployment of ground forces: "Suppose you had gone to the country and gotten a real mandate, as I think you would have got; but suppose it would have cost you thirty or forty percent—say these were ten key Great Society measures and you lost three or four overboard—I think there's no doubt the President wanted the best of both and this was his way of trying to get the best of both."

As Lyndon Johnson stated, he did not want to go the "full congressional route now."[42] It can be argued, as William Bundy has argued, that because of his concern to avoid a debate, "the President sent Secretary McNamara back to the drawing board, because he had looked in the eye the consequences of a course of action involving taking the matter, on you might say a decisive and great debate basis, to the Congress at that particular moment of time."[43] So there would be no reserve call-up, no tax increase, and no admission of the significant costs of the authorized escalation. The President would not even allow such an admission within the rest of his Administration. When Johnson asked McGeorge Bundy to eliminate in his July 19 memo the sentence, "It would create the false impression that we have to have guns, not butter—and would help the enemies of the President's domestic legislative program," this indicated a desire to avoid a guns versus butter argument even within internal government debates.[44]

In mid-July, when McNamara argued that without a tax increase the war would lead to a budget deficit, the president responded: "You know so goddamned much about it, you go up there and you get it [a tax increase] and you come back down here and give me the names of the people who will vote for it. Obviously you don't know anything about politics. I'll tell you what's going to happen. We'll put it forward; they are going to turn it down. But in the course of the debate they'll say: 'You see, we've been telling you so. You can't have guns and butter, and we're going to have guns.'"[45] The president clearly wanted to avoid a debate on Capitol Hill in which Congress would force him to choose between guns and butter. Senator Mansfield had warned President Johnson in June against another congressional resolution because a major debate would almost surely ensue: "A request [for congressional support] at this time could set off a wave of criticism and of demands for inquiries which, in the end, even though a resolution were overwhelmingly approved, would not in any way strengthen your hand, render your task easier or make your burden of responsibility lighter."[46] According to McGeorge Bundy, the president's "own priority was to get agreement, at the lowest level of intensity he could, on a course that would meet the present need in Vietnam and not derail his legislative calendar."[47]

Although the president was increasingly under attack by liberals for his Vietnam stand, it was the conservatives who really worried him. When Charles

Schultze testified on July 22 before the Subcommittee on Fiscal Policy, Republican senator Jack Miller wondered, if Congress was asked to increase military appropriations (he cited a figure of $1 billion), whether it would not "be proper to, if not suspend, then reduce some of the expenditures being proposed or already proposed in the fiscal 1966 budget for some of these Great Society programs? For example, the proposed increase in the expenditures for the Office of Economic Opportunity and its activities, which I understand are about double what they were last year." He continued, "[I]t seems to me the highest priority must be to get on with the fighting and winning of the war . . . . If that is so, something has to give somewhere along the line. [To Schultze:] What Congress needs from you people is some priorities."[48] Miller added that he did not think social programs ought to be canceled but certainly suspended: "We cannot fight a war and do everything else at the same time. I think if we try to do it, we are going to lose both ways."

Schultze responded that an increase in military spending did not mean that social programs had to be cut: "I don't want to leave the impression that each dollar of additional military spending necessarily must be accompanied by a reduction elsewhere, because this economy is such that it is precisely in a situation to absorb and still produce what we need for the military and to provide the manpower we need for the military." This exchange between Miller and Schultze was an excellent example of one of President Johnson's greatest fears: conservatives would sacrifice Great Society programs in order to fight the war, and it reinforces the idea within the administration that both guns and butter were possible. Another example of Johnson's concerns occurred when Senator Strom Thurmond criticized the lack of sufficient appropriations for the military during the hearings on the 1966 defense budget: "To be trying to save money in the Defense Department to spend on Appalachia and the poverty programs, and all of these things, does not make sense to me."[49] Johnson later described the scenario: "Once the war began, then all those conservatives in the Congress would use it as a weapon against the Great Society . . . . Oh, they'd use it to say they were against my programs, not because they were against the poor—why, they were as generous and as charitable as the best of Americans—but because the war had to come first."[50]

In addition, Republicans were beginning to criticize the president more frequently. The president received a legislative report from his staff in June that stated: "The Republican minority took violent exception to the majority's position, stating that in the light of the increased tempo of operation in Southeast Asia, the '66 Budget was clearly inadequate since it was based on planning which did not include the increased costs of Southeast Asia operations."[51] This would have fueled his concern that Republicans wanted to reorient U.S. economic priorities toward Vietnam and defense needs and away from domestic programs.

As Republicans raised their voices, many Democrats began to close ranks behind the president. Johnson actually used the specter of the Republican Right to gain support from Democrats who had grave doubts about his Vietnam policies. In addition, when Johnson claimed that he was holding the line against conservative elements in the military and civilian bureaucracies, even the *New York Times* came to the president's aid when it criticized Republicans in an editorial on July 9: "[S]ome in Congress have made it clear that they will be doing their best to embarrass and harass the President in his effort to prevent the war from escalating too dangerously."[52]

As William Bundy noted, "All through this summer, Lyndon Johnson had to keep the congressional scorecard in his head, and to imagine what would happen to his most deeply felt new plans if the Congress were diverted to a big debate on the Vietnam War. It was not a factor he ever argued, or even noted, in my presence . . . . One could sense its vital significance, however, simply by instinct."[53]   The decision not to seek a major debate was a crucial part of Johnson's decisions on how to escalate, on how to present it to the country and the Congress, and on avoiding a war footing only at the last moment so as to preempt any dissent among his advisers.

OPTING FOR A "LOW-KEY" DECISION

When President Johnson remarked on July 22, "I don't think that calling up the reserves in itself is a change of policy," Dean Rusk replied that "moving from 75,000 to 185,000 men is a change of policy."[54]   But the secretary of state then agreed with McGeorge Bundy's view that "[m]uch is to be said for playing this low key." McNamara added: "We can stay away from 'change of policy' but it is a change in risk and commitment. We need to explain why it is in our interests to do it."[55]   White House aide Horace Busby warned the president of the propensity for a low-key approach: "Your advisers have 'the habit' of downplaying our role in Vietnam. Hence, a tendency is present to insist that whatever is done is, actually, only an extension of all we have been doing. This may be self-deceptive."[56]

But Johnson did not follow the advice of those who wanted him to go before the people with a major statement or discussion of Vietnam. His close aide Jack Valenti urged a prime-time television address to enhance Johnson's image.[57] Yet the president appeared to want his actions in Vietnam to speak for themselves without mapping out his overall policy. He noted on July 21 that House minority leader Gerald Ford had demanded that he testify before Congress and explain why the reserves must be called up. Ford had also indicated that he would oppose a reserve call-up.

On July 23 the president seemed to have made up his mind about the reserves and the need to avoid declaring a national emergency. McNamara had presented him with three alternatives:

1) Authorization for an increase to 175,000 by November 1 and another 100,000 in 1966. In addition, Congress would be asked for a reserve call-up and a $2 billion addition to the defense appropriations bill;
2) This would authorize the same troop increases but delay the reserve call-up and requests for money until September;

3) The same troop increases would be authorized, but no reserves would be called (the draft would be increased and tours of duty extended) and only $1 billion would be requested.[58]

The first option was favored by McNamara; Johnson chose the third option. He had accepted McNamara's recommendation on the timing and number of U.S. forces, but there would be no reserve call-up, and Congress would be asked for less money. Tours of duty would be extended, and the draft would be increased.

It is important to note that while the military had determined what was needed to get the job done in Vietnam, the choice of how the United States would escalate was clearly the president's. "Low-key" was, indeed, the watchword—decided by the president, apparently with little debate.[59] This was a critical decision that had far-reaching consequences, both for U.S. policy in Vietnam and for domestic policy. George Ball explained at a State Department meeting on Vietnam that the president "was anxious to present the decisions which might be made in the next few days in a low-key manner in order a) to avoid an abrupt challenge to the Communists, and b) to avoid undue concern and excitement in the Congress and in domestic public opinion."[60] William Bundy later noted that Johnson's approach was not challenged within the key decision-making circles: "What were the pros and cons, from a foreign policy standpoint, of a 'loud and clear' Presidential decision and announcement, accompanied by major Congressional action and a Great Debate, versus a 'low key' announcement without such action or Debate? On this question, there was never a separate debate in the concluding July week between the 21st and 28th."[61] This may have been because Johnson did not reveal his decision to go the low-key route until the last few days; everyone assumed that the decision would be a major move. The State Department, NSC staff, and White House staff had drafted speeches and legislation to call up the reserves. It is clear that the machinery for a major announcement was in place; most of Johnson's top civilian and military advisers had made preparations to forge a unified war effort and were ready to put the country on a war footing. The choice not to do so was the president's.

Over the weekend of July 24 and 25, McNamara joined the president at Camp David. He assured him that the reserves would not be needed for the proposed escalation and that the increased draft and extended tours of duty would suffice. McNamara seemed to be responding to Johnson's apprehensions about the political effects of the multibillion-dollar costs and the reserve call-up. In response, McNamara had slashed the cost estimates of the services from $12 billion to less than $6 billion and reoriented the source of manpower from the reserves to the draft. By alleviating the president's concerns, the fanfare surrounding Johnson's escalation decision could be significantly decreased.

At a July 27 NSC meeting, Johnson described the option he had decided upon: "We have chosen to do what is necessary to meet the present situation, but not to be unnecessarily provocative to either the Russians or the communist Chinese. We will give the commanders the men they say they need and, out of existing matériel in the U.S. we will get them the materiel they say they need.

We will get the necessary money in the new budget and we will use our transfer authority until January. We will neither brag about what we are doing or thunder at the Chinese communists and the Russians."[62] The reference to the Russians and Chinese provided a useful rationale for a moderate tone, but they were rarely discussed in the deliberations of the previous week.[63] McGeorge Bundy later observed that his notes of July 27 "record my own feeling that the President's unspoken objective was to protect his legislative program—or at least this appeared to be his object in his informal talk as late as Thursday and Friday of the preceding week—July 22, and July 23."[64]

There was no response when the president asked whether anyone in the room opposed the course of action he favored. According to David Halberstam's account of the NSC meeting, the "key moment" was when Johnson turned to General Wheeler and asked whether he agreed with the choice of option five. Wheeler nodded agreement, even though "[e]veryone in the room knew Wheeler objected, that the Chiefs wanted more, that they wanted a wartime footing and a call-up of the reserves; the thing they feared most was a partial war and a partial commitment."[65] Johnson had undercut his military officials by portraying his decision as giving the commanders what they wanted, while undercutting his economic advisers by not informing them of his military plans.

Later, on July 27, President Johnson met with many leaders of Congress. He brought them in to sell them on what he had already decided. He had done the same thing with the cabinet earlier that day; he convened a meeting to inform them of his decision on Vietnam and then get a consensus on the administration's policy.[66] The president explained to the congressional leaders that he felt the low-key escalation route was the one that made the most sense. So Johnson left the impression that his policy was to provide the military with immediate needs and then see what happened. But the president never mentioned the specific number of troops that would be authorized by November (175,000) or the number for 1966 (an additional 100,000). Therefore, the long-term military commitment and implications were not made clear. The specifics of Westmoreland's requests and White House approval (including a later proposal for 440,000 troops in December 1965) were made public for the first time only in June 1966.

McNamara pointed out that the administration would ask for $1.5 billion immediately and then "[c]ome back to Congress in January with clear understanding."[67] McGeorge Bundy referred to this as "give you the story now and the bill later." His notes also recorded that Johnson did not want to go through "a big process" then but instead deal primarily with what was needed between July and the end of the year. McGeorge Bundy's notes of the July 27 meeting with the congressional leadership recalled that the president said again that under the other alternative, "he would have to get a new bill and a great big reserve plan and go through a big process." With his preferred option, we would simply put "$1.8 billion or whatever into the appropriation bills on the Senate side and then get in an order for January." The secretary of defense said that under the first option "we would be asking for a blank check because we did not know what would happen," while under the second, "we would ask for what we see clearly between now and January." The second option was presented as the more fiscally responsible one, even thought McNamara had claimed it would have a $12 billion cost a few days earlier.

As President Johnson explained his decision to escalate, he was less than candid about the specifics. When asked by Senator George Smathers whether this was a change of policy, he replied: "As aid to the VC increases, our need to increase our forces goes up. There is no change in policy."[68] Johnson then informed the leadership: "You'll have a good, sizeable supplemental in January—a few billion dollars."[69] That would be "the bill" Bundy referred to in his notes. So in the course of a week, the cost of the proposed escalation had fallen from $12 billion to $6 billion to a few billion dollars—not for any sound economic or military reasons but because the president wanted a low-key escalation for political reasons. He did not just mislead Congress as to the likely costs they would face in January; but more importantly, he precluded a debate on his policy. Congress could not very well disagree with his moderate goals. As David Halberstam noted, the president presented his decision as the "centrist, moderate one: only Lyndon Johnson could go to war and be centrist and moderate."[70]

Most of the senators and congressmen present agreed with the president's decision as it was explained to them, and they liked the "story now, bill later" policy. Only Senator Mansfield, who had already made known his disagreement with administration policy, voiced dissent. After the leadership meeting, the president met again with his key advisers. According to McGeorge Bundy, "The President remarked that we were prolonging the agony for 90 days and that he wanted a statement of 700 words, the essence of which would be that he was giving Westmoreland what he needed."[71] On the morning of July 28, the president held a briefing with 33 key members of Congress in order to explain his escalation decision before he publicly announced it at noon that day. He emphasized the modest nature of his decision and noted, "There are military men who'd like to go a lot further."[72] The president could argue that he was not really committing to a major war yet was still making a strong stand against communism. Congressional reaction was generally sympathetic. Six of the Senate's most senior and powerful members (Democrats Russell, Mansfield, Fulbright, and Sparkman and Republicans Aiken and Cooper) sent a 19-point memorandum to Johnson on July 27 that was quite moderate in tone. The preface spoke of a "general sense of reassurance that your objective was not to get in deeply and that you intended to do only what was essential in the military line until January, while Rusk and [United Nations ambassador Arthur] Goldberg were concentrating on attempting to get us out."[73]

THE UNITED STATES QUIETLY GOES TO WAR

On July 27 the White House announced that the president would make an opening statement on Vietnam at an afternoon press conference the next day. For a number of press people this was a significant clue that the expected decision might be less drastic than expected. In two previous crises, the Tonkin Gulf incident and the deployment of U.S. Marines to the Dominican Republic, Johnson had made evening addresses to the nation.

At the press conference, Johnson gave a brief overview of why the United States was in Vietnam and then stated: "I have asked the Commanding General, General Westmoreland, what more he needs to meet this mounting aggression. He has told me. We will meet his needs. I have today ordered to Viet-Nam the Air Mobile Division and certain other forces which will raise our fighting strength from 75,000 to 125,000 men almost immediately. Additional forces will be needed later, and they will be sent as requested."[74] He noted that the monthly military draft would be doubled but emphasized that there was no need to call up the reserves. A limited appropriation would be asked of Congress until a formal supplemental request could be presented in January. Although negotiations had hardly been discussed during his Vietnam deliberations, Johnson added that the United States was willing "to begin discussions with any government, at any place, at any time."[75] He then followed his Vietnam presentation with two additional and important announcements: the appointment of John Chancellor as head of the Voice of America and the nomination of Abe Fortas to the Supreme Court.

Johnson mentioned only 125,000 troops without stating that he had actually authorized 100,000 more forces by November for a total of 175,000 and another 100,000 in 1966. He discussed the Air Mobile Division, but that unit had been authorized a month before. He gave no cost estimates. When asked how long the war would continue, Johnson replied, "I would not want to prophesy or predict whether it would be a matter of months or years or decades. I do not know that we had any accurate timetable on how long it would take to bring victory in World War I. I don't think anyone really knew whether it would be 2 years or 4 years or 6 years, to meet with success in World War II."[76] But Johnson had been given estimates by his military advisers that the tide would be turned within two years and that it would probably take at least five years to convince the communists they could not win. Furthermore, his use of the term "victory" was misleading because the administration's concept of victory was a stalemate.

The president was trying to have it both ways: a modest, nondisruptive expansion while pointing to the type of "victory" achieved in the two world wars. In those wars the United States was prepared to do whatever it took to defeat the enemy, however long it took. In Vietnam Johnson was prepared to send enough troops to Indochina to convince North Vietnam to stop supporting the communist guerrillas in the south. The president was clear about why the United States had to fight in Vietnam, but he was not at all candid with the American people about both the extent of the military commitment and the limitations to American military action.

President Johnson emphasized that he had rejected a call for a national emergency and proclaimed that the conflict in Vietnam would not disrupt the nation's economic prosperity. Then, he was asked the following: "Mr.

President, does the fact that you are sending additional forces to Viet-Nam imply any change in the existing policy of relying mainly on the South Vietnamese to carry out offensive operations and using American forces to guard American installations and to act as an emergency backup?" The president responded, "It does not imply any change in policy whatever. It does not imply any change of objective."[77] This was a masterful answer. The administration had consistently claimed that its policy had not changed since the beginning of the year. But the questioner asked about a policy change in reference to the perceived military mission—that is, reliance on the South Vietnamese for the bulk of the fighting, which was not how the administration interpreted its policy. The only U.S. "policy" was to prevent a communist victory. All else was just tactics. So President Johnson replied only to the phrase "change of policy" without addressing what the questioner really meant by that. The military role or strategy, as implied in the question, had clearly changed, but that is not what the president responded to. Johnson continued to downplay and obfuscate what he was doing.

William Bundy later acknowledged that when President Johnson stated that sending 50,000 more troops to Vietnam did not "imply any change in policy whatever," he was technically correct: "[N]either the American objective nor the basic strategy for achieving it had altered. But it was stretching a point, as the President had done in February, in April, throughout 1965, to say that there was 'no change in policy,' in the ordinary meaning of those words. Particularly with a distinctly offensive concept for the use of American forces in mind, the role of the United States in the conflict was clearly altered to the point of constituting a 'change in policy.'"[78]

There was great relief at the moderate nature of the president's decision.[79] Even most of the critics of his Vietnam policy hailed the decision, including Senators Mansfield, Fulbright, Church, Nelson, Cooper, and Aiken.[80] Most pointed to the decision not to call up the reserves and Johnson's avowal to seek a resolution through the United Nations as the key components of a modest and reasoned approach. To many, the president appeared to have established a consensus that the fighting in Vietnam should remain limited. The *New York Times* reported that Johnson had tried since mid-June to convince liberals such as Fulbright that he and McNamara were resisting the strong pressures from the Pentagon for an expanded war.[81] So when the expansion was much less than the public expectations, he was able to regain the support of most liberals (with Senators Morse and Gruening the exceptions). Also, Republicans rallied around the president in order to present a unified front to the world, even though some favored much greater bombing in the North and a total victory objective.

The prospect of a limited war fell into line with the wishful thinking of many on Capitol Hill. E. W. Kenworthy of The *New York Times* theorized that "a majority of Congress still sees our commitment in the limited and conditional terms set forth by President Kennedy."[82] Most of the media applauded the speech. The *New York Times* editorialized, "The President made it very clear yesterday that he intends a controlled and severely limited operation on the part of the United States; and this is as important a point as could be made."[83] The *Washington Post* talked of the president's "sincere desire to substitute the conference table for the battlefield."[84] Most observers concluded that this would not be a repeat of Korea. But William Bundy has argued that even though Johnson downplayed his decision, "[t]he 28 million Americans who listened to their President that Wednesday noon can have been left no doubt that a new and much larger American involvement was under way."[85] The deployment was clearly big, but when the president of the United States bluntly states there are no national emergency and no change of policy, can 28 million Americans be blamed for their wishful thinking? Thus, the question arises, Did the credibility gap result from false preconceptions and the mistaken interpretations of the press and other observers who failed to hear what the president said, or did Lyndon Johnson truly deceive them?

William Bundy concluded about the July 28 decision:

So in the end what was a profoundly important and far-reaching decision—recognized as such by a great many, and by almost all sophisticated observers—was presented in the most moderate possible form. This had advantages and disadvantages, neatly balanced, in terms of the war itself . . . . But, to repeat, the President's basic reasons for acting as he did were domestic in character, directly related to his reform legislative program. His hope, and gamble, was that by gradual rather than abrupt techniques of leadership the country and the Congress could be brought to support to the full both war and domestic reform—or that the war would develop in line with the more optimistic predictions given to him, and thus reduce the choice. It was a fateful action decision.[86]

While Johnson gave the military the needed men and matériel, neither the American economy nor society in general was mobilized behind the war effort. While fighting in the jungles of Southeast Asia escalated, business would remain as usual back home. The military services, however, had anticipated a much greater war commitment. General Wheeler sent a message to Admiral Sharp and General Westmoreland on July 27: "Do not be surprised or disappointed if the public announcement does not set forth the full details of the program, but instead reflects an incremental approach."[87] The decision not to put the nation on a war footing would be a major criticism by military men in their later analyses of the American failure in Vietnam.

For the next two and a half years, the United States continually escalated within the framework of a limited war. Before Walter Lippmann wrote his column on the decision, he called George Ball to confirm whether his assessment was correct that, although Johnson "had repeated the grand formulae of a great war, in fact his decision as of now is to fight a limited war." Ball's reply was that this was true and that "[t]he President is still in control of the situation. Things were not yet in the saddle."[88] That seems the most telling argument to show that Johnson knew what he was getting into; he simply wanted to maintain control over the commitment to a war in Southeast Asia and a Cold War policy of containment that he felt he had inherited and that had him trapped. He rejected the advice of his most senior military and civilian officials to go on a war footing because he was not yet willing to pay the price for that war. The dissembling and deception could buy his programs time, perhaps enough time so that they became embedded in the American social and economic fabric.

What Johnson had done was simply to defer the hard consequences of military escalation—rallying the public to get behind the necessary sacrifices (both at home and in the lives of young soldiers who would be lost on the battlefield), tax increases, and a shift of resources from the domestic sector to the military sector—so that he would not have to pay the price at that moment. He was not straight with the public about what he knew to be in store down the road. But there could be no question that the president and the nation would have to pay a significant price down that road, and the first area where Lyndon Johnson got trapped was with the economy, because just as the public was misled as to the nature of the U.S. military commitment, so, too, were the country's top economic officials.

NOTES

1. Johnson Library: Jack Valenti notes of July 21, 1965, meeting on Vietnam, Johnson Library: Meeting Notes Files, Meetings on Vietnam Folder, July 21–27.

2. Valenti notes of July 22, 1965, morning meeting on Vietnam.

3. Valenti notes of July 21, 1965, meeting on Vietnam.

4. Ibid.

5. Valenti notes of July 22, 1965, morning meeting.

6. See Richard Neustadt and Ernest May, *Thinking in Time*, p. 84. Gelb and Betts agreed, arguing that when figures such as 500,000 or more men were used by the military, few of the key advisers, and least of all the president, "seemed to pay much attention to [the] upper estimate, or to take it seriously." (Leslie Gelb with Richard Betts, *The Irony of Vietnam: The System Worked*, p. 127.)

7. Johnson Library: William Bundy Oral History, Tape 5, June 29, 1969, p. 41. Chester Cooper and George Ball also agreed with this.

8. Johnson Library: William Bundy unpublished manuscript, chapter 27, p. 33. Neustadt and May stated that an unnamed aide of the president's later told them, "It was his [LBJ's] custom . . . to reach a decision inwardly and *then* organize the process for making that decision appear the result of consultation and debate." (See Neustadt and May, *Thinking in Time*, p. 79.) Thus, no one can be sure when the president actually decided to escalate, but this supports Bundy's contention that these meetings were staged.

9. Valenti's notes of July 21, 1965, meeting.

10. Ibid.

11. Johnson Library: Chester Cooper notes for July 21, 1965, meeting: Meeting Notes Files, Meetings on Vietnam Folder, July 21–27.

12. Valenti's notes of July 22, 1965, morning meeting.

13. Ibid.

14. Bundy's remarks were paraphrased in Chester Cooper's July 21, 1965, notes.

15. William Bundy Oral History, p. 35.

16. Memo from McGeorge Bundy to the president, "Possible Items for Discussion" —July 22, 2:30 P.M. meeting, in Johnson Library: McGeorge Bundy Memos to the President file, Box 4, File 12.

17. July 22, 1965, memo to Dean Rusk from Harlan Cleveland, "Subject: Vietnam," Department of State Central File, FAIM/IR, as quoted in William Hammond, *Public Affairs: The Military and the Media, 1962–1968*, p. 183.

18. July 20, 1965, CIA memo, "Communist and Free World Reactions to a Possible U.S. Course of Action," in Johnson Library: National Security File, NSC History, vol. 6, Tab 398.

19. Valenti's notes of July 22, 1965, morning meeting.

20. Ibid.

21. See Johnson's remarks during July 27, 1965, NSC meeting in Bromley Smith's notes, "Subject: Deployment of Additional U.S. Troops to Vietnam," in Johnson Library: NSC Meetings File, vol. 3, Tab 35, Box 1.

22. Letter from Gardner Ackley to *Newsweek*, September 6, 1978—included in the beginning of Gardner Ackley Oral History File in Johnson Library.

23. Robert Warren Stevens, *Vain Hopes, Grim Realities: The Economic Consequences of the Vietnam War*, p. 71.

24. See "Business Roundup" in *Fortune*, September 1965, p. 28.

25. June 1, 1965, speech to Columbia University alumni, excerpted by *New York Times*, June 2, 1965, p. 69.

26. The balance-of-payments situation would seriously deteriorate in 1966, primarily due to U.S. commitments in Vietnam. Godfrey Hodgson noted that a decline in the balance of payments was one key negative consequence of the Vietnam escalation: "The decision to escalate the war in 1965, which had both directly and indirectly a negative effect on the balance-of-payments position, came at the moment when a long-standing imbalance . . . would otherwise have been cured by the successful economic policies." Godfrey Hodgson, *America in Our Time*, pp. 254–55.

27. See *New York Times* story accompanying the Martin speech, June 2, 1965, p. 69.

28. President Johnson was actually seething at Martin. The speech apparently led the White House to inquire into whether the president had the power to remove a member of the Federal Reserve or to designate another chairman prior to the expiration of the current chairman's term of office. (See James E. Anderson and Jared E. Hazleton, *Managing Macroeconomic Policy: The Johnson Presidency*, p. 123.)

29. Fowler quoted by columnist James Reston, *New York Times*, June 4, 1965, p. 34. Reston made an interesting observation, noting that Ackley was Lyndon Johnson's "spur," while Martin was his "anchor."

30. Johnson Library: Cabinet Papers File, Box 4, File 1—July 27, 1965.

31. Johnson Library: Cabinet Papers File, Box 4, November 19, 1965, meeting.

32. Johnson Library: William Bundy Oral History, Tape 5, June 2, 1969, interview, pp. 10–11.

33. July 23, 1965, letter from Vance to Senator Russell. Office of Management and Budget Records Division: Accession No. 51-79-121, Box 77 - FY 1966 Defense Budget, "Congressional Action" folder.

34. Interview with Arthur Okun, in Erwin C. Hargrove and Samuel A. Morley (eds.), *The President and the Council of Economic Advisers: Interviews with CEA Chairmen*, p. 279.

35. See Johnson Library: *The Economic Report of the President, 1973*, p. 278.

36. July 27, 1965, note from Busby to Schultze in the National Archives: RG51, series 61.1b, Box 10, Cabinet Meetings (July 1965–December 1965) folder.

37. See David Halberstam, *The Best and the Brightest*, p. 740.

38. Anderson and Hazleton, *Managing Macroeconomic Policy*, p. 54.

39. Bundy manuscript, chapter 30, pp. 22–23.

40. *The Johnson Presidential Press Conferences*, vol. 1, p. 354.

41. William Bundy Oral History, May 29, 1969, pp. 43–44.

42. See Lyndon Baines Johnson, *The Vantage Point*, p. 150.

43. William Bundy Oral History, May 29, 1969, p. 43.

44. July 19, 1965, "The Reasons for Avoiding a Billion Dollar Appropriation in Vietnam" and July 23, 1965, "Reasons for Avoiding a Big Military Appropriation in Vietnam," in Johnson Library: Memos from McGeorge Bundy to the President, National Security File, NSC History, vol. 6.

45. This quote is cited by William Conrad Gibbons as a confidential Congressional Research Service interview, February 1, 1979. (See William Conrad Gibbons, *The U.S. Government and the Vietnam War*, Part III: January–July 1965, p. 389.) McNamara recounted a similar exchange in his memoirs. (Robert S. McNamara, *In Retrospect: The Tragedy and Lessons of Vietnam*, p. 205.)

46. Memo to the president from Senator Mansfield, June 9, 1965, in Johnson Library, National Security File, Name File: Mansfield.

47. Letter from McGeorge Bundy to Larry Berman, quoted in Larry Berman, *Planning a Tragedy*, p. 145.

48. Joint Economic Committee, Congress of the United States. Hearings before the Subcommittee on Fiscal Policy, *Fiscal Policy Issues of the Coming Decade*, July 22, 1965, pp. 90–91.

49. U.S. Senate, *Department of Defense Appropriations for 1966*, Hearings before the Subcommittee of the Committee on Appropriations, July 16, 1965, p. 546.

50. Lyndon Johnson quoted in Doris Kearns, *Lyndon Johnson and the American Dream*, p. 252.

51. June 18, 1965, memo from David E. McGiffert, assistant secretary of defense for legislative affairs, to Larry O'Brien, special assistant to the president, "Report on Major Legislation," in Johnson Library: Reports on Legislation, June 21, 1965, Folder. McGiffert's memo was passed on to the president.

52. *New York Times*, July 9, 1965, p. 28.

53. Bundy manuscript, chapter 27, pp. 14–15.

54. Valenti notes of July 22, 1965, afternoon meeting.

55. Ibid.

56. Busby memo to the president, July 21, 1965, in Gibbons, *The U.S. Government and the Vietnam War*, Part III, p. 405. One wonders whether Busby was not subtly reminding him of the president's own tendencies in this regard.

57. Kathleen Turner, *Lyndon Johnson's Dual War*, p. 148.

58. Johnson Library: July 24, 1965, memo to the president from McNamara; see Gibbons, *The U. S. Government and the Vietnam War*, Part III, pp. 414–415.

59. At the top of his agenda sheet for the July 26, 1965, meeting, McGeorge Bundy's handwritten notes are the following:

1) Hold for additional info.
2) Give Arthur chance at UN
3) Keep low-key if *possible*!
What's the Hurry—War Will Go On!
At the bottom he wrote again: "Keep Low Key!!—*We Must Stay*.

(Johnson Library: Files of McGeorge Bundy, Boxes 18/19—Luncheons with the President, vol. 1, Part I.)

60. Notes of July 23, 1965, State Department meeting in Johnson Library: National Security File, Country File: Vietnam.

61. Bundy manuscript, chapter 30, p. 15.

62. NSC Meeting, July 27, 1965, Subject: Deployment of additional U.S. troops to Vietnam, Bromley Smith's notes in Johnson Library: NSC Meetings File, vol. 3, Tab 35, Box 1.

63. Notes from the meetings between Johnson and his advisers showed that the possibility of Chinese and Soviet intervention was a minor consideration, although it played a much greater role as a post hoc rationale for downplaying the decision. Notes of the two meetings, July 27 and July 28, with congressional leaders confirmed the same thing.

64. Bundy wrote a memo on November 2, 1968, from notes dated July 27, 1965. He noted that the memo "strictly relates to what the notes themselves contained; there is no reliance on memory." The memo was sent to Tom Johnson at Lyndon Johnson's office in Austin on August 5, 1969—Johnson Library: Meeting Notes File, Box 1, July 27, 1965, NSC meeting; Joint Leadership Meeting Folder.

65. Halberstam continued, "But Wheeler was boxed in; he had the choice of opposing and displeasing his Commander in Chief and being overruled, anyway, or going along. He went along." (Halberstam, *The Best and the Brightest*, p. 728.)

66. Johnson Library: Cabinet Meetings File, July 27, 1965, Folder—Other than the agenda, no other records could be found in the Johnson Library.

67. Johnson Library: Meeting Notes File, Box 1—Folder NSC meeting File, Joint Leadership Meeting of July 27, 1965.

68. Valenti notes of July 27, 1965, meeting.

69. McGeorge Bundy notes of July 27, 1965, meeting. Valenti's notes recorded Johnson's statement as follows: "We have the money. 50 billion plus 800 million. When you come back in January you'll have a bill of several billion dollars." (Valenti's notes of July 27, 1965, meeting.)

70. Halberstam, *The Best and the Brightest*, p. 728.

71. Johnson Library: Meeting Notes File, Joint Leadership Meeting of July 27, 1965, Box 1, NSC meeting folder.

72. McGeorge Bundy notes, in Gibbons, *The U.S. Government and the Vietnam War*, Part III, p. 437.

73. Cited in George McT. Kahin, *Intervention: How America Became Involved in Vietnam*, p. 391.

74. *The Johnson Presidential Press Conferences*, p. 349.

75. Ibid. p. 350.

76. Ibid. p. 353.

77. Ibid. p. 355.

78. Bundy manuscript, chapter 30, p. 30.

79. In the *New York Times* a lead story noted, "Most members of Congress received President Johnson's statement on the Vietnam crisis with a sense of relief." (July 29, 1965, p. 1.) A second story began, "Wall St. heaved a sigh of relief." (July 29, 1965, p. 35.)

80. Apparently, many of the senators and congressmen who met with the president felt they had an important impact on his decision to move cautiously in expanding the war. A statement read by Mansfield at the July 27 meeting was cited in the *New York Times* as being persuasive with Johnson. (ibid. July 30, 1965, p. 3.)

81. See *New York Times*, June 16, 1965, p. 1.

82. Kenworthy's article provides an excellent summary of congressional views at the time, especially why most on Capitol Hill were so reluctant to criticize publicly the administration's Vietnam policy. (*New York Times*, July 25, 1965, section 4, p. 1.)

83. *New York Times*, July 29, 1965, p. 26.

84. *Washington Post*, July 29, 1965, p. A16.

85. Bundy manuscript, chapter 30, p. 30.

86. Ibid. chapter 30, p. 33.

87. Wheeler cable to Sharp and Westmoreland, July 27, 1965, in Westmoreland Papers, Center for Military History, as quoted in John P. Burke and Fred I. Greenstein, *How Presidents Test Reality: Decisions on Vietnam, 1954 and 1965*, p. 230.

88. *Washington Post*, July 30, 1965; Telcon, July 30, 1965, Ball Papers, Box 7, as quoted in Lloyd C. Gardner, *Pay Any Price: Lyndon Johnson and the Wars for Vietnam*, p. 251.

Chapter 8

The Confusion over Military Costs

AN INADEQUATE MILITARY BUDGET

While the key military decisions regarding Vietnam were being made in June and July 1965, the economic planners remained in the dark. Walter Heller described the misapprehension economists faced in the fall of 1965: "We had no concrete idea how much Vietnam was going to cost. First, I think fundamentally it was being underestimated to begin with. And, second, some of the estimates were somehow or another not getting across the Potomac from the Pentagon to the Executive Office Building, at least not to the Council's part of the Executive Office Building. Anyway, the Council was operating partially in the dark."[1]

By the end of July, given the expected escalation in Vietnam, it had become clear to the economic planners that the war would have some impact on the economy and that the size of the defense budget would continue to be the key to more economic prosperity. Budget director Schultze noted just before the president's decision to escalate that military spending in FY 1966 "will clearly be higher than the President estimated in January."[2] Yet, regardless of the uncertainty in July about the president's plans for Vietnam and in spite of a number of indicators that projected military spending was increasing, the economists were working with a FY 1966 budget before Congress in the summer of 1965 that projected a decrease in defense spending and a decline in total uniformed personnel. When the budget was sent up to Capitol Hill in January, administration spokesmen had trumpeted the military savings. Kermit Gordon emphasized that the Pentagon had realized savings of $1.4 billion in 1963 and $2.8 billion in 1964. He added that the goal for FY 1966 was "a cost reduction goal of $4.1 billion."[3] At the same time, the Pentagon insisted that America's defense posture was as strong as ever. The savings were the result of greater efficiency and the consolidation or discontinuance of 95 defense installations.[4] In fact, closing military bases upset some members of Congress, who began to question whether the defense budget was being unnecessarily sacrificed, and others who were also concerned that some of their constituents would lose jobs as a result.

In May and June 1965 Bureau of the Budget economists tinkered with the defense budget based on a few revised estimates. As a result of the $700 million May supplemental for Vietnam, new defense and military assistance requirements (including Vietnam costs and pay increases) would total $48.6 billion for FY 1965. The supplemental was the only defense increase, however, and there would still be a $900 million savings over the previous year's budget. FY 1966 re-estimates by May 19, 1965, called only for an "excess over $100 million in 'contingencies'" for Vietnam military needs.[5] That was all. While the Budget Bureau based its recalculations on figures it got from the Pentagon, they got these numbers in such a piecemeal fashion that there was little sense of what was coming down the road, even as ever greater numbers of American forces were deployed in Vietnam.

By June, however, the administration's economic planners were forced to begin to respond to a growing concern in Washington about the potential for a major war in Vietnam. A few key congressmen and senators began to worry publicly that military spending was far too low in light of a possible expansion of the war. On June 25 Senator John Stennis stated on the Senate floor that the entire FY 1966 defense budget was inadequate.[6] A struggle between some members of Congress and the executive branch over estimates of the costs of the Vietnam War began to emerge.

Senator Stennis held hearings on "U.S. Army Readiness" before the Preparedness Investigating Subcommittee of the Senate Armed Services Committee during May and June. These hearings were the first congressional attempt to come to grips with the military expenditures and needs for the Vietnam conflict. The main reason for the hearings was the concern that the crises in Vietnam and the Dominican Republic undermined American military readiness elsewhere and that the Pentagon was draining too many resources away from its regular programs to build up operations and units in Vietnam. At the beginning of the escalation the war was financed through "reduced readiness"—that is, men and matériel were diverted from other programs, which left fewer trained men and smaller stocks of war matériel to deploy or use in other contingencies.[7] Therefore, any immediate wartime sacrifices could be deferred. The war reserve of "combat consumables" was drawn down; that is, new equipment and spare parts that would have gone elsewhere were diverted to Vietnam. The necessary army equipment and soldiers for Vietnam were taken from the existing 22 divisions of the U.S. Army that had already been programmed and budgeted for. The army planned for the needs of equipping 22 divisions, not for specific contingencies. Therefore, when a crisis arose, such as Vietnam or the Dominican Republic, the military commanders drew from those 22 divisions what they needed, leaving them at less than full strength. In May Senator Stennis became aware of this and opened his Military Preparedness hearings. Almost all of the testimony and evidence gathered for the subcommittee came from military sources, not government economists.[8] The subcommittee's professional staff concluded that diversions of aircraft to Vietnam particularly weakened the main armed forces back home.[9]

During June and July 1965 the Senate Subcommittee on Defense Appropriations was attempting to finalize the fiscal year 1966 budget. In order to report it out of committee, hearings that began in February resumed. These hearings, also under the chairmanship of Senator Stennis, were held during the last two weeks of July. At the outset, Stennis reiterated his point from June 25: the FY 1966 defense budget was inadequate since it included no additional requests for the Vietnam War. Therefore, he insisted that "more realistic budget estimates [be] furnished to us before these hearings are closed."[10]

Stennis criticized the Pentagon and cited McNamara personally for not putting together the necessary information so that the Senate could quickly appropriate whatever was needed for the U.S. armed forces in light of the Vietnam conflict.[11] Noting that he and McNamara disagreed as to the urgency and timing, Stennis wanted to resolve the question of the military's needs during these final budget hearings. As it was, the subcommittee fully expected the secretary of defense to present a clear picture of American military needs in Vietnam when he returned from his mission to Saigon on July 20. In the meantime, witness after witness from the Pentagon admitted that their budget figures had been finalized in November and December 1964. They claimed that an accurate estimate of the Vietnam conflict's effect on their budget requests was impossible to assess until McNamara's return. The Defense Secretary was not expected to bring back a specific cost estimate but rather a final determination as to what the specific military needs would be to get the job done in Vietnam.[12] The costs would then depend on the degree of escalation authorized by President Johnson, who would presumably base his decision on the recommendations of McNamara and the military commanders. So everything was on hold. It should be noted that although the military officials were very vague in their answers about costs for military operations in Vietnam, they were assuming that once McNamara returned, and the president granted Westmoreland's request for additional troops, the whole picture would change, and the country would move to a war footing, making the concerns of Stennis and others somewhat moot.

Both of the Stennis hearings were making quite a bit of noise on Capitol Hill, and it appeared that the senator's goal was to force the administration to go on some type of war footing so that military needs in the United States, Europe, and elsewhere were not sacrificed for Vietnam.[13] The administration was clearly concerned, and the military's allies in Congress became an increasing factor for the President in his political calculations. White House legislative director Larry O'Brien warned the president of the increasing pressure that had coalesced on Capitol Hill for a stronger public military commitment.[14]

Stennis did not want the Senate later accused of not providing everything the military needed. His concern was evident as he noted that if the reserves were called up, "and the people find out they do not have enough equipment, ammunition, supplies, ordinary items, they are not going to blame the Army, they are going to blame us. They will not blame the Congress as a whole. They will blame the Armed Forces and the Appropriations Committees."[15] The senator from Mississippi felt that the defense secretary and the civilian advisers in the Pentagon had jeopardized the military by making unwarranted cuts that left the services far below what they needed. While the military representatives of the three service branches agreed that they had asked for more money when the FY 1966 budget was prepared, not one of them claimed that his respective service was unprepared or underfunded as a result. One reason for this was probably that the services routinely padded their budget requests at the beginning of the defense budget process in the expectation that the nonlessentials would be cut.[16]

Senator Henry Jackson expressed concern that "for a time now we have been drawing on our assets and within existing divisions and existing Army units to meet the situation in Vietnam, in lieu of going direct to the Congress for funds in order to maintain the requirements previously laid down by the Army as proper goals."[17] For that reason, General Abrams replied, there was a strategic reserve, and Vietnam was an emergency contingency for which that reserve was being used. The eventual need for a supplemental appropriation was also raised during the hearings. Abrams remarked: "We do feel that we may have to recommend to the Department of Defense a supplemental action in fiscal year 1966. We are not certain of that at this time."[18] Abrams' words, however, had captured the discrepancy between the administration's public posture and the military reality. The White House and the Pentagon were preparing for a long war while publicly terming it "an emergency contingency."

It is striking that as the United States got more involved in Vietnam, almost everyone—from the Pentagon to the economic councils—continued to assert that Vietnam was not significant enough to have any adverse impact on the administration's programs and policies. McNamara continued to insist that the Pentagon was a source of budget savings. He wrote the president in mid-July, "Savings of $4.6 billion were actually realized during FY 1965, $2.1 billion more than estimated. Savings of $6.1 billion a year by FY 1969 and each year thereafter have been set as our new long-range goal—an increase of $1.5 billion per year over the previous objective." McNamara then emphasized, "Again, I want to assure you that these savings are being accomplished without any adverse effect on our military strength and combat readiness."[19] The entire 14-page memo was very upbeat about the future of continued cost reductions in the Pentagon, and nowhere did McNamara mention Vietnam. McNamara's memo and others like it may well have hurt McNamara's credibility with the president when a little over a week later he tried to make the case that Westmoreland's request would cost upward of $12 billion in additional spending and that the country must consider tax increases, calling up the reserves, and possibly wage and price controls. Johnson's advisers—military and domestic—provided him with a lot of ammunition to believe that escalation would not necessarily mean he had to sacrifice butter for guns. The economic advisers seemed to have been in the dark; McNamara, it would seem, should have known better.

THE KOREAN ANALOGY

One possible explanation for the administration's lack of candor about Vietnam lay in concerns about military and economic parallels with the Korean War. When the conflict in Korea began, the country had to move quickly to get millions of men under arms. The immediate increase in appropriations greatly exceeded the increase in actual expenditures. Much of the appropriated money was not used for several years as a result of poor estimates of the financial and equipment requirements.[20] In 1965 military and economic planners alike were wary of the mistakes of Korea. According to the Pentagon comptroller, during the Korean War "the Department of Defense attempted to make immediate best guesses as to the size and duration of the conflict, even during its earliest stages. This procedure led to severe estimating problems."[21] Therefore, the Pentagon seemed much more reticent about providing cost estimates and resource requirements (certainly to Congress; perhaps to the economists as well).

Admittedly, the immediate escalation in Korea resulted in a severe inflationary surge, and the government had to resort to price controls. However, after the initial surge in prices in late 1950 and 1951, inflation was marginal during the rest of the Korean War. In 1965, most of the administration's economic and military planners did not see a parallel to Korea because, in their view, the economy could handle any escalation, and there were built-in safeguards that did not exist during the Korean War. The force level in 1965 was much greater, so it would seemingly not require drastic measures (it was at the highest peacetime level in U.S. history). Since the Korean War, the United States maintained an up-to-date military arsenal and a high level of defense expenditures due to the Cold War. Arthur Okun, a member of the CEA, argued that unlike World War II and the Korean War, the Vietnam conflict "did not require a major reshaping of America's global military strategy."[22] From 1954 to 1962, 9–10 percent of GNP was spent on defense; in 1949 and 1950, only 5 percent of GNP. Some economists saw the high military budget as reason that escalation would not hamper the economy and was cited by the Council of Economic Advisers in the 1966 Economic Report of the President.[23]

Budget director Charles Schultze pointed out that "one of the accomplishments over the past 4 years has been to build a military force with the capability of moving into a situation like this, giving us time to make the appropriate evaluation."[24]   This probably led many to assume that the war could be handled adequately without going on a war footing. Robert Komer later wrote that "the Kennedy/Johnson buildup of nonnuclear general purpose forces did facilitate the kind of U.S. military intervention undertaken in Vietnam.   Capabilities naturally shape strategy and tactics, as well as vice versa."[25] He quoted one Pentagon official as saying, "If McNamara hadn't increased our conventional capability all along the line, we probably wouldn't have gone into Vietnam because we couldn't.'"

Another Korea parallel that the Defense Department wanted to avoid was that at the end of that war there was a huge quantity of military stocks still on hand, far beyond anything needed at the time. So as the Vietnam conflict escalated, the Pentagon wanted to combine a drawing down on existing stocks with supplemental appropriations so that if the war was resolved quickly, they would not be stuck again with a huge surplus. Since the Pentagon did not want to get out too far in its Vietnam planning, McNamara cut back on the service budget requests with the understanding that if the initial estimates of their needs were correct, the military could then draw upon existing inventories or return to Congress for additional funds.[26] This clearly worried many on Capitol Hill and led to the sharp criticism by Senator Stennis. McNamara actually admitted that he purposely asked for funds "at the last possible moment" in order to avoid "over-buying" and piling up surplus materiel at the end of the war.[27]

Clearly, the "lessons" of the Korean War had a significant impact on the way in which the Pentagon expanded its role and budgeted its programs in Vietnam. But one should note that the parallels that military and economic officials drew between Vietnam and Korea were based upon quite dissimilar circumstances. Not only was the Korean conflict relatively short, but there was actually a starting point. The economy was operating below capacity prior to the Korean War. In addition, nondefense spending by the federal government decreased between 1950 and 1952. Truman did not attempt to have both guns and butter. Even if there were some legitimate reasons to be concerned about estimating problems and overstocked equipment, the resulting deception and downplaying of what the United States was doing in Vietnam helped to ensure that the war was poorly planned and not strongly supported or understood by the American people.

While Truman also did not seek a declaration of war from Congress, the North Korean invasion was a very distinct act of aggression, and the resolution by the United Nations Security Council was viewed by most as a declaration of war. In addition, Truman mobilized the reserves, and sought price controls and tax increases, while cutting or putting on hold domestic programs. The country went on a strong war footing. Many in the Johnson administration believed that the abrupt escalation and dramatic shift into a war economy had negative political consequences for President Truman, even though the public strongly supported the initial decision to go into Korea. Also, many of Truman's domestic programs, including Great Society ideas like Medicare, were killed by the Korean War. So there was a historical rationale to downplay the decision to escalate in Vietnam, even though there was a nearly-unanimous consensus that further deployments were necessary and that the conflict would be a long one.

Since the Pentagon was determined not to follow the Korean path of overordering and since defense officials placed new orders only as needed, the economists seemed to be watching the wrong signals and therefore got a false sense of the military expansion. They were waiting for a sudden burst of major military activity, like Korea, not an incremental, unannounced escalation. The economists believed that unless the Vietnam conflict approached the size of the Korean War it was doubtful that all-out production for any defense-related items (which would push demand and overheat the economy) would result.

BUTTER AND GUNS

The problem with the belief that the escalation could be graduated and that payment for the war could be deferred was that neither military planning nor the economy remained on hold or even at a gradual pace. The announced escalation and the military plans, even before the cost of the war was accounted for in the January 1966 budget, had a significant impact on the U.S. economy, including an inflationary effect in the fall. Before the administration ever went to Congress in January 1966, the government had greatly increased its military orders. As a result, a buildup began: labor was hired, raw materials purchased, commitments made, all contributing to a major expansion in the economy in the last four months of 1965.

These were signs and warnings that major increases in military spending were imminent at rates much higher than widely expected. As economist Murray Weidenbaum noted, "The Government would increase its orders in September, October, November of 1965, no reflection whatsoever in any current budget, but those orders were obviously immediately escalating the economy."[28] He noted, therefore, that a key factor to watch was new obligations, which includes both government payrolls and contracts with private firms: "The actual amount of new obligations incurred during fiscal year 1966 was somewhat in excess of $67 billion, or almost one-fourth greater than in 1965. Actual expenditures increased at a much slower rate during the same period—17 percent. In other words, obligations are the more sensitive lead indicator."[29]

Another economic analyst observed that in 1965, while overall purchases and expenditures were increasing at .2 percent and 2.0 percent, respectively, all of the leading indicators pointed to significant increases in defense activity: "Gross obligations incurred increased by 6.0%. Military prime contract awards increased by 12.4%. Manufacturers' new orders for defense products increased by 19.9%. Pentagon progress payments advanced by 21.9%."[30] This is particularly significant because these key indicators of defense obligations had remained fairly steady from 1962 through 1964. The increases in 1966 were to be even far greater.

Further analysis showed that military contracts increased substantially in 1965 (after a significant decline in the second half of 1964), while military production rose at a more gradual rate.[31] Defense obligations for hard goods (these are major equipment items such as aircraft, ships, missiles, tanks, ammunition, etc. as well as spare parts) had dramatically increased in the second quarter of 1965.[32] They subsided a bit in the late summer and then shot up again in the fall. However, since the biggest rise had occurred in April, May, and June, the economists might have looked at the consequences more thoroughly.

Key defense-related businesses and industries were feeling the effects of greater U.S. involvement in Vietnam even before Johnson announced the escalation on July 28. In mid-July many military contracts received add-ons, and businesses were urged to hustle their deliveries. Tires for military vehicles were directly airfreighted to Vietnam; orders for fuses used on helicopter rockets were rushed; there were large increases in orders for machine gun spare parts.[33] Ordnance and munitions makers were alerted to expect significant new orders shortly. The most dramatic rise in military orders was for helicopters, but the army was also short on communications equipment, grenade launchers, trucks, and spare parts.

Deputy defense secretary Cyrus Vance had informed the Bureau of the Budget in January 1965 that part of the Pentagon's military budget of $51,739,414 in total obligational authority "anticipates the early enactment of necessary authorization. The estimates for major procurement programs are included in the anticipation of the authorization for funds to be appropriated for the procurement of aircraft, missiles and naval vessels."[34] The Defense Department had anticipated a rise in its need for hard goods. In using the phrase "early enactment" Vance implied that the Pentagon anticipated that need would be quite soon in the fiscal year, perhaps in the late summer or early fall. The numbers were not high, but the prospect of major orders of hard goods early in the new fiscal year was noteworthy and should have provoked the economists to question whether or not this would add a significant stimulus to the economy or at least question the numbers and the economic impact of the policy objectives in Vietnam. One economic analyst has made the point, however, that information on such key indicators as prime contract awards, defense industry new orders, backlogs and inventories, and manpower data "was not customarily made available in one place, even within the Department of Defense."[35] The economists would have had to work hard to get hold of all the relevant indicators within a short time period.

Another economist supported the view that "orders" were critical: "In the second half of calendar 1965, Defense Department prime contract awards ran $3.3 billion ahead of the corresponding period of 1964—$6.6 billion at an annual rate. In contrast, the Defense Department estimates fiscal 1966 *expenditures* for the Vietnam war at only $4.6 billion. Anyone trying to catch an intimation of things to come might do well to keep an eye on *orders*, rather than expenditure estimates."[36] The increased demand squeezed industries that were already at full capacity because of the domestic expansion. So, plants were expanded, and wages were raised, fueling an inflationary buildup. Less than a month after the July escalation, many defense-related businesses were reporting that the "pace of orders occasionally is approaching frenetic proportions."[37]   If the administration economists had understood better the scope of the military expansion, they might well have predicted the immediate jump in defense contracts and orders in the fall of 1965. Thus, they could have foreseen and prepared sooner for inflation and the significant rise in government spending when it inevitably occurred by mid-1966.   As it happened, they had to work backward; it was only through economic indicators, not from any information supplied by the White House, that they began to comprehend the nature of the escalation in Vietnam and thus revise their economic assessments.

But immediately after President Johnson's announced escalation, most observers in the economic and business communities were quite upbeat.   In early July many economic observers had predicted a recession by the first of the year. One perceived economic benefit to the expansion in Vietnam was that the extra money for defense needs would be injected into the economy just as a Social Security tax increase was due to hit on January 1, 1966. So the defense spending would help alleviate the expected economic drag from the tax increase.   As an August 7 article in *Business Week* stated: "In a cold mathematical view, the Vietnam build-up thus far ordered by President Johnson changes the economic outlook for the better."[38]   Fears of overheating were allayed by the mildness of the buildup, and fears of a slowdown were quelled by increased spending.   The article proclaimed that the economy was healthy enough to provide both guns and butter.

The most immediate effect of the escalation was felt primarily in the civilian sector of the economy, not the military sector.   One of the first signs of trouble was the rise in the consumer price index in the second quarter of 1965.[39] Economist Murray Weidenbaum also noted, "To some extent, the inflationary pressures of the Vietnam buildup were accentuated by a liberal monetary policy in 1965, some of the results of which continued to be felt in 1966."[40]   One of the major consequences of this monetary policy was that the American economy had little slack when the military expansion hit, thus laying the ground for inflation and an overheated economy.

Some economists have pointed out that the administration's economic goal of a growing, high-employment economy created an "inflationary bias."[41] Thus, a significant increase in military spending would have an even greater impact within an economic system that was operating with such an "inflationary bias."   This meant that the economy was prone to inflation when there was excess demand, that is, when overall demand surged beyond production capacity.   An expanding war in the absence of a slack in the economy would mean rapid and possibly large rises in the cost of living.

The overall CEA plan had been based on the achievement of 4 percent unemployment with an accompanying price increase rate of only 2 percent.[42]

In mid-1965 financial markets were well balanced, long-term interest rates were stable, and credit was readily available.[43] So when there was an increase in prices to a small degree, there was little concern in Washington because it was all part of the plan. The administration economists had enough confidence in the economic information they had at their disposal and faith in their pro-growth policies that the administration could continue along the path of fiscal stimulation while publicly standing for anti-inflation measures. Logically, it would seem that the combination of a reduction of excise taxes, the first supplemental budget increase for FY 1965 ($700 million in May), increased Great Society spending, and increased military expenditures would have alerted the economists to moderate their fiscal policies.[44] But they were misled about the extent of the military buildup, and, it is important to emphasize, the negative economic effects were not felt quickly. There were important shifts in some key economic indicators, but in light of what they thought they knew about the military plans, the economic officials were not overly concerned, and there was no political imperative because overall the American society was benefiting from the fiscal policies in mid-1965.

Even in the fall of 1965, the economists believed that the economy could absorb the Vietnam War spending increases, because as late as November, expectations within the government for the January Vietnam supplemental were in the neighborhood of $4 billion, possibly more than $6 billion at the highest end.[45] One of the key numbers that gave the economic community reason for optimism was $7 billion, which was the projected yearly increase in federal receipts at the current rate of economic growth.[46] In other words, the economy was generating $7 billion of additional tax revenues. Therefore, the economy could absorb spending increases (on Vietnam and domestic programs) up to $7 billion. If it went over that optimistic scenario, then something would have to give: domestic spending or military spending.

THE DANGERS OF INFLATION

One of the key economic consequences of the escalation was the inflationary impact on the economy—a significant inflationary surge in late 1965 and the first half of 1966. The inflation that took root was both long-term and felt throughout almost all sectors of American society. The *New York Times* called 1966 the "year of the economic goof"—if that is the case, then 1965 was the year that created the economic confusion and laid the trap. Later, the recognition of the economy's sensitivity to abrupt changes in defense expenditures led in 1967 to the establishment of the cabinet committee on Post-Vietnam Economic Planning in order to plan for the transition to peace.[47] There were six main stages to the inflation: (1) demand soared; (2) employment climbed; (3) wages increased; (4) labor costs spiraled; (5) consumer prices rose; and (6) "real" spendable earnings leveled off.[48] As earnings leveled off, less tax revenues were generated. With the demands of a war, governmental expenditures on military needs are injected into total spending in the economy. There results a competitive money demand for goods and services. The demand for war goods often squeezed consumer goods, and thus prices rose.

The legacy of the economic decisions and the lack of honest military costs were fairly devastating within a few years. From 1965 to 1970 interest rates rose steadily. As a result, the net worth of many Americans declined, and purchasing power was greatly eroded. As economist Eliot Janeway noted after the initial overheating, "Uncontrolled, the American economy staggered under the burden of a wartime buildup that, for the first time in American history, cramped and pinched the economy instead of spurring its expansion.[49] Over the same period, the deficit grew to $25.2 billion by 1968. The balance of trade surplus began to decline in 1965 and subsequently declined each succeeding year until 1970. Then, after a rise in the surplus, trade began to run a deficit in 1971 and 1972.[50] Inflation was to reach even greater historic heights in 1973 and 1974. One of the most devastating results of the Vietnam conflict was the combination of rising inflation *and* rising unemployment. Inflation became entrenched in the economy, and unemployment reached drastic levels, contrary to the tenets of Keynesian theory, to which the Johnson administration economists subscribed.[51] Ultimately, this led to an international crisis over gold as much of the rest of the world lost faith in the dollar as well as the American economy, the cornerstone of the post–World War II economic order.

There have been a couple of alternative reasons put forth to explain the inflation. One is that the war had little impact; rather, governmental spending in other nondefense areas led to the inflation. However, as Charles Schultze noted at a November cabinet meeting, domestic spending was higher, in large part due to "rising interest rates on expenditures for interest."[52] The rise in interest rates was fueled by the effect of the military escalation on the economy. A second explanation, which came from Arthur Burns, chairman of the Council of Economic Advisers under Eisenhower (later appointed chairman of the Federal Reserve Board by Richard Nixon), was that the expansionary economic policy of 1964 to 1966 was overly concerned with economic growth, thus unleashing the inflation.[53] But the catalyst was the military escalation: "If the government had foreseen how rapidly the cost of the Vietnam War would mount and if it had taken promptly the restraining measures needed to keep the aggregate demand for goods and services from outrunning the nation's capacity to produce, the new round of inflation that we have experienced since 1964 could have been prevented."[54] One has to question why the government did not foresee the rapidly escalating costs of the war.

The Pentagon later attempted to show that the inflation of late 1965 and beyond was not simply the result of the Vietnam War: "It has been said that the buildup in Defense in FY 1966 and FY 1967 caught the economic policymakers by surprise. Perhaps, but there were unforeseen increases of comparable magnitude in other Federal spending at the same time."[55] According to the Pentagon, defense "spending" for FY 1966 was estimated to be $52.5 billion in January 1965 and was actually $58.5 billion, a 6 percent increase. All other spending was estimated to be $74.9 billion and was actually

$79.3 billion, an increase of 4.4 percent. In January 1966, FY 1967 defense estimates were $61.4 billion and actually were $71.3 billion, a 9.9 percent increase. For all other spending the figures were an estimated $83.6 billion and $89.6 billion actually spent, a 6.0 percent increase.[56] The Pentagon point was that the increase in nondefense spending was almost never mentioned as a key factor in the acceleration of the American economy then.

But even restricted to simple quantitative figures, such analysis does not go very far. It ignores the impact of unexpected military costs and the lack of wartime economic measures. In addition, even though there was a significant rise in nondefense spending, the total impact on the entire economy, not just government spending, must be analyzed. For example, the rise of defense obligations and outlays accounted for nearly 25 percent of the increase in GNP in 1966.[57] The economy as a whole was hurt by the war, and so were the financial markets that helped propel the inflation and a money crunch. Because the negative consequences of the war's costs had a rippling effect through the entire economy, domestic programs were certainly affected, and their costs increased. Thus, the planned Great Society was quickly becoming more expensive and overbudget as a result of the inflation.

According to a 1968 Treasury Department internal study, there were after mid-1965 a "serious financial imbalance, sharply rising interest rates, and an eventual reduction of credit availability heavily concentrated in the mortgage market."[58] The economists did not recognize what was happening until the end of the year. The "absence of firm information on the future of defense spending" resulted in the Troika's inability "to revise its projections of future activity in adequate fashion."[59] In late summer 1965 the Treasury Department's Economic and Financial Policy Group "saw that the possibility of a bulge in federal spending had introduced a new element into the short-term business outlook and began to give thought to the counter-measures that could be taken if serious inflationary pressures were to develop."[60] But no one acted because there were no definitive Defense Department figures. By waiting so long, countermeasures were bound to become reactive rather than preventive.

THE DEFENSE DEPARTMENT ACCOUNTING

In July and early August, as Congress continually tried to get a fix on what the costs of the expansion in Vietnam would be, the Defense Department avoided any realistic military figures. On a few occasions McNamara talked of the price tag that would come in January, but only with foreign policy and military advisers. There were no firm numbers. At the beginning of the July 21–27 Vietnam deliberations, he talked of $12 billion to meet Westmoreland's military requests, but by the end of that week the figures he noted were $3–5 billion.[61] The economic advisers were not privy to those discussions and could admit only that they did not know what the impact of Vietnam would be. The $12 billion figure was, as McNamara has admitted, "highly classified" and was deliberately kept from the Council of Economic Advisers and the Treasury Department.[62] The economists had left all military spending questions to the

Pentagon and simply waited until McNamara provided them with clear-cut budget requests.

Even as military orders mounted, it was difficult for the Pentagon to cost out the war effort. This problem did not just occur at the beginning of the escalation. When pressed during testimony before the Senate Armed Services Committee in 1967, McNamara admitted that he was unable to give a monthly breakdown of Vietnam costs: "It is almost impossible to do it on a yearly basis, and it is really impossible to do it on a monthly basis. I can tell you how much we are spending in total for defense per month of course, but splitting that into Vietnam and non-Vietnam is honestly almost impossible."[63] But at the very least in 1965, he knew there would be a major increase in military spending, and the economic advisers did not.

As the country waited for McNamara to return from Saigon in order to find out how the United States would expand the war, so, too, did the Pentagon and Congress wait for the plan of escalation in order to attach some cost estimates to the war effort. During the final congressional hearings in July on the FY 1966 defense budget, which began while McNamara was in South Vietnam, military officials stated that once decisions regarding Vietnam operations were made, they could quickly come up with budget estimates. These budget analysts from the three service branches could, perhaps, be accused of overstating their cases before Congress when they proclaimed that the cost projections could be done within hours (in the case of the navy) to a week (in the case of the air force).[64] Perhaps there was too much of a "can-do" attitude in these attempts to reassure Congress that once the defense secretary gave the go-ahead, providing a budget would be fairly simple. Nevertheless, it was clear from the testimony of its own budget analysts that the Pentagon could have presented specific figures to Congress in early August. How reliable they might have been is speculative.

But the president handicapped McNamara upon his return from Vietnam. There would be constraints on how the country went to war, so the Pentagon had to work within a policy of gradual escalation. As a result, the budget figures would most likely have to be sent up to Congress incrementally as well. However, the Pentagon had given Congress the impression that if any of the defense estimates changed, they would be informed. Cyrus Vance, in a letter on July 23 to Senator Richard Russell, chairman of the Subcommittee on Defense Appropriations, claimed that current defense appropriations were "adequate."[65] This, combined with the testimony of the Pentagon budget analysts, led the appropriations committee to believe that the $1.7 billion supplemental request on August 4 was an accurate reflection of the extent of the escalation costs. Vance's letter was sent the day after McNamara and the top military commanders had told President Johnson that the immediate costs for Vietnam would be $12 billion.

So, although the Pentagon could have made estimates and made clear what the criteria were, it would have been politically difficult to put a price tag on the war since President Johnson had not announced the full extent of the escalation he had authorized in late July. While the military went ahead with planning through 1966, their current cost estimates were relevant only to the early fall of 1965. Many in Congress were slow to respond. This was especially true in the House. Even in the middle of June most Democrats remained satisfied with the proposed defense budget for FY 1966.[66] After Johnson's announcement of July 28, the Pentagon was increasingly reluctant to put a price tag on the war. One Pentagon official, in direct contradiction of the Defense Department's budget analysts, commented: "We have no intention of cost-accounting the war in Vietnam. Our business is to support the conflict there. Our business is not cost accounting. We have no estimates of costs. It's not practical to say the war has cost x dollars to date."[67]

The Pentagon plan seemed one of asking for the appropriations that were needed immediately while waiting until 1966 to get a better long-term cost accounting. Then, once the Pentagon judged the battle situations, more accurate and efficient accounting could be done. But some have questioned whether the military was actually prepared to make any accurate cost analysis. There had been no detailed advance planning for deployments of the size force that Westmoreland requested.[68] While the Pentagon's Systems Analysis personnel did work with the military planning staffs to convert the huge catalog of units requested by General Westmoreland, the results, in spite of the testimony by the service budget personnel, were mostly crude deployment tables. The first systematic attempt to analyze the cost implications of additional deployments was not undertaken until 1966, when Systems Analysis first developed a Southeast Asia cost model.[69]

Initially, the military covered the escalation by drawing down from existing equipment and manpower. In the short run that could be done easily, but there was little thought as to what the spring escalation compelled in terms of manpower and resources down the road (if only to get those men back home if the United States withdrew over time). At one point during the congressional hearings in July, the air force comptroller admitted that the air force had reduced its military personnel from 855,802 to 828,000 within the last year and was still scheduled to cut down to 809,134 over the next year.[70] Many of the senators were somewhat incredulous that this was going on as the country was getting deeper into a military conflict. In fact, military personnel had begun to increase. The numbers reflected a major drop in personnel until the spring. Nevertheless, that the air force was still scheduled to reduce its numbers may have been true on paper, even though that did not reflect the reality.[71] What emerged was a confusing picture of a country preparing for war. Even though the United States had by mid-July sent 75,000 troops into South Vietnam (and 25,000 more were on their way), the country was not at war; neither the bureaucracy, the economic infrastructure, nor even the military itself had in any way geared up for a war.

THE $5 BILLION FIGURE

During the deliberations on Vietnam at the end of July, there arose a perception in the press that major escalation would cost $5 billion. An article in the *New York Times* noted that in addition to opposing a reserve call-up, Johnson chose the option that would "give the congressional leadership the story now and the bill later" instead of the option of "the full congressional route now," because "[t]he $5 billion figure required by [the latter] Option would have to be provided in a separate appropriation that might set off a sharp debate."[72] So, the public and congressional perception was that a $5 billion bill had been avoided.

Somehow, $5 billion became fixed in the minds of economists and businessmen alike. There was a belief that $5 billion was the upper limit of an increase in Vietnam expenditures for the FY 1966 budget. *Fortune* magazine specifically cited the figure in an analysis of the uncertain effect of a rise in Vietnam spending: "even if expenditures of Vietnam rose to $5 billion." This phrase implied that such an amount was the highest imaginable.[73] A month later, the magazine's economists began to view the $5 billion figure as the most likely "rate of defense spending by next spring" in an article entitled, "A Pivotal $5 Billion."[74] But the *Fortune* analysis claimed that once the defense rate hit $5 billion, it would then flatten out. The scope of the military expansion remained hidden as the article stated that defense outlays could hardly build up to a figure of $10 billion, "unless Washington comes to new decisions—a second troop buildup or another re-equipment program—in effect to escalate the Asian war further." *Fortune* noted that if the buildup did get to $10 billion, "the nation would have to begin to sacrifice some butter. On the present outlook for a $5-billion rise, however, this will not become an issue."[75] Thus, there was a strong misimpression among government economists and domestic policy advisers, the media, Congress, and the business community that $5 billion was the upper limit of the extra costs of the war.

McNAMARA AND THE AUGUST $1.7 BILLION SUPPLEMENTAL

On August 4, 1965, President Johnson sent up to Congress an amendment to the appropriations bill for FY 1966 requesting $1.7 billion as an Emergency Fund for Southeast Asia.[76] That same day, Secretary McNamara appeared before the Defense Subcommittee of the Senate Appropriations Committee. A number of key members of the Senate Armed Services Committee also joined the hearings. This was the first congressional appearance by the defense secretary to explain the president's new Vietnam decisions. One of the most noticeable features of McNamara's testimony was that he, like the president, did not reveal the extent of the decision made on July 28. He explained to the senators that Westmoreland would get what he needed without specifically noting that what was agreed to were deployments of 175,000 American troops by November and another 100,000 in 1966.[77]

But one figure was public, and not much attention was paid to it: the 340,000 men McNamara planned to add, through the draft and extended tours, to the nation's armed forces. Was this number not a clue that future demands on the military would require 340,000 more soldiers? As *The Economist* noted, "This figure was not plucked from the air."[78] McNamara did not say how many would be going to Vietnam, where the increased fighting would cost much more money than if they were to be deployed elsewhere around the world, but simply stated that "it is very difficult to develop a detailed and precise budget estimate." In addition, the mission of the American forces was downplayed. McNamara noted that "the central reserve of the South Vietnamese Army has been seriously depleted in recent months. The principal role of U.S. ground forces will be to supplement this reserve in support of the front line forces of the South Vietnamese Army."[79]

McNamara pointed out that the overall goal of the emergency fund was to prime the military machine: "The $1.7 billion amendment to the bill now before the committee which we are proposing at this time will provide the additional financing needed through January to gear up the production machine—to accelerate the delivery of essential items already in production and to initiate the production of new items required for the support of our forces in southeast Asia, as well as the construction of the most urgently needed facilities."[80] This sounded like quite a mobilization of the military-related industries. One has to wonder how much attention the administration economic planners paid to McNamara's words or whether they continued to see a slow buildup that may or may not last long. Economists tended to focus on how the Pentagon was going to reflect military spending in the budget while ignoring how the private sector was gearing up for the war.[81] Lack of attention to this by the administration economists contributed to their getting caught off guard by the subsequent inflation.

Senator Stennis asked McNamara how he could expect his subcommittee to mark up the defense appropriations bill for FY 1966 without at least some estimate of the future costs. He also made the point that it would make more sense to finance the war through congressionally authorized appropriations up-front rather than emergency supplementals along the way. McNamara's reply was that the Pentagon could not give a proper estimate at that time and would have a much clearer picture by January, noting that "we will be in a much better position next January to provide these details and to state our additional requirements for the balance of fiscal year 1966."[82]

When Stennis persisted, McNamara finally relented that he would submit a "very, very rough approximation" for the record. He later entered the following into the record:

Based upon current projections as to the possible requirements for supplemental appropriations in January of fiscal year 1966, it is estimated that approximately $400 million will be required to be obligated under the "Military Personnel" appropriations during the first 7 months of fiscal year 1966 (through January 31, 1966) over and above the contemplated rate of obligational .03 availability as provided in the President's budget for the Department of Defense for fiscal year 1966 under the same appropriations.

Due to the absence of definitive program requirements under the "Operation and Maintenance" appropriations, it is not feasible at this time to provide a comparable estimate of the supplemental obligations that probably would be incurred under the "Operation and Maintenance" appropriations during the first 7-month period of fiscal year 1966 (through January 31, 1966).[83]

It is important to keep in mind that McNamara was estimating how much over and above the budget figures the military's requirements would be. Yet the only concrete figure he gave was a $400 million figure, which was of little use to anyone, except it implied that the economic impact would be almost negligible.

McNamara then added that the Pentagon did not have a method of allocating Vietnam-related costs other than the military assistance program and estimated that the Vietnam costs were $800 million in FY 1965; but that was a rate from the spring.[84] But he then added, "What the $1.7 billion will do is provide an input equal to the anticipated output in the next year, or year and a half . . . . It is to replace that consumption that we are proposing the $1.7 billion primarily for procurement . . . . What the $1.7 billion, in addition to the basic fiscal year 1966 budget, does is not only replace consumption as it occurs but keep up the upward trend on bombs and ammunition."[85]

McNamara went on to say that this supplemental would be sufficient for the rest of the calendar year, but if the military were expending combat consumables at an escalating rate, "we will have to come back in January and ask for a supplemental, a formal supplemental to the 1966 budget."[86] As McNamara explained it, the $1.7 billion was a projected rate of expenditure for Vietnam over the next year. Admittedly, that rate could, and probably would, increase by January 1966. But even if it tripled, that would be $5.1 billion, a figure that most economists were comfortable with. Therefore, McNamara lowered expectations to such a degree that even pessimistic analyses would be off in their worst-case projections. Because the Pentagon started at such a low base rate ($1.7 billion), no one could conceive of a $12 billion supplemental in January.

Yet, the whole issue of the supplemental request was somewhat misleading. Although McNamara claimed that the $1.7 billion request was a rate of expenditure, it was not a limitation upon what the Pentagon could actually spend between August 1965 and January 1966. The supplemental had to cover outlays that had already been arranged; just as the outlays made and planned for in the fall of 1965 would then have to be covered by the next supplemental in January 1966. So the August supplemental was actually economic confirmation that major military escalation had begun in the spring.

The Defense Department also took advantage of Section 512c of the appropriations act, which allowed it to commit itself to outlays for operation, maintenance, and personnel (new draftees and increased training) without any prior appropriation by Congress. This was planned when the decision to escalate was made in July.[87] In August McNamara had pointed out that section 512 (which was written into each defense appropriations bill since 1961) allowed the administration to "[s]pend a disproportionate amount of the budget in the early months of the year."[88] The Pentagon could spend the money faster than had been planned or projected at that point. Therefore, they could front-load their military spending from what was appropriated in the budget and then come back to Congress for a huge supplemental in January. So there was really no financial limit to the spending then. On October 12 President Johnson exempted 18 categories of military appropriations for personnel (as a result of the major troop increases) from the spending schedule in order to "permit spending on an accelerated basis."[89] This was due to "increased activity in Southeast Asia and the recent military pay increase." The exemptions were to remain in effect through the end of the fiscal year. Therefore, as early as October the administration began to draw on money to be apportioned over the entire fiscal year. This was a major clue that the size of the January supplemental would be quite substantial.

It is important to remember that for FY 1965 the Pentagon asked for $49.0 billion in defense spending. However, due to cost-cutting and delays in procurement, actual outlays were projected at only $47.4 billion when the FY 1966 budget came before Congress in February. The $1.6 billion savings in the FY 1965 defense budget was a significant factor in keeping the FY 1966 budget down. However, by the spring of 1965 the escalation had increased to a point where the "savings" were used up, and supplementals were needed in May and August. In fact, military spending jumped dramatically from the third quarter of FY 1965 to the fourth quarter.[90] So, one could argue that by August 1965 the Vietnam War had cost the sum of the two supplemental requests, $0.7 billion and $1.7 billion, along with the lost $1.6 billion in savings, for a total of $4 billion.[91] This should have set off alarm bells in Washington, especially among the economists, but it appears that these factors did not begin to register until late September and October.

On Capitol Hill the senators were displeased with McNamara's vague presentation. Stennis expressed his frustration that the Pentagon could not "give us some kind of estimate for the supplemental request" in January. He added, "We are entitled to know more than we now do about it. I do not want to tell the Senators on the floor that you said you had no idea about it."[92] But Stennis could not embarrass or shame McNamara into giving the Senate anything more (nor would they get anything more during the fall). The lack of information on the costs of the war would continue to plague relations between the administration and Congress for the next few years.

In July 1967 the Joint Economic Committee would strongly criticize the administration, noting that, "the lack of accurate expenditure data during calendar 1966 handicapped the Congress seriously in reaching appropriate tax, spending, and other economic policy decisions."[93] The same could be said for the lack of data in 1965. There have been numerous analyses of how the administration deceived Congress in putting together the fiscal year 1967 budget; the main charge has been that Johnson and McNamara's figures were based on the war ending by June 1967. But there has been little discussion of the administration's decision to provide Congress with such a low rate for the initial escalation in Vietnam. The Pentagon did not honestly know how much the war would cost (they had a much better idea in 1966), but McNamara knew full well that $1.7 billion was far too low. Few in Congress and none of the President's economic advisers challenged McNamara or pushed for specific figures. This was noted with surprise and even a sigh of relief in the White House after the hearings. As assistant secretary of defense for legislative affairs, David E. McGiffert, wrote to White House aide Larry O'Brien, "Both the Senate Committee and the House Appropriations and Armed Services Committees during the later McNamara testimony, avoided any thorough exploration of how much the January amount might be."[94]

McNamara's language gave no indication of the expectations that were discussed in the many meetings on Vietnam during the week from July 21 to 27. When asked whether he expected escalation or acceleration of the conflict, McNamara replied: "I would rather not say expectation but we are planning higher rates. Whether those are required, it is difficult to say."[95] That answer was masterful deceit. Had any of the senators attended the key Vietnam meetings, they would have gotten a far different impression; the question was not at all "whether" a higher rate of escalation of the conflict would occur but how much. It was clear from the defense secretary's testimony that the United States was escalating, but it was not at all evident what the true rate and extent of that escalation would be. No limits to the escalation were discussed; the country would just have to wait until January. In the meantime, the president had already committed the United States to fighting a war in Vietnam.

NOTES

1. Johnson Library: Walter Heller Oral History, p. 42.

2. Testimony of Charles Schultze, U.S. Congress, Joint Economic Committee, *Hearings before the Subcommittee on Fiscal Policy: "Fiscal Policy Issues of the Coming Decade,"* July 22, 1965, p. 61.

3. Statement of Kermit Gordon before the Joint Economic Committee, February 23, 1965, p. 19, Office of Management and Budget Records Division: Accession No. 51-79-121, Box 77 - FY 1966 Defense Budget, "Congressional Action" folder.

4. Johnson Library: Bureau of the Budget Administrative History, Appendix 14, p. 6.

5. See May 19, 1965, memo from McCandless to Schultze on "1966 Budget Expenditures Estimate," in the National Archives: RG51, Series 61.15, Box 37—"1966 Budget Expenditure Estimates and Guidelines" folder.

6. "Fiscal Policy Issues of the Coming Decade" hearings, July 22, 1965, p. 89.

7. William Bowen, "The Vietnam War: A Cost Accounting," *Fortune*, October 1965, p. 120.

8. U.S. Senate, "U.S. Army Readiness," *Hearings before the Preparedness Investigating Subcommittee of the Committee on Armed Services*, May 13, 1965, p. 22.

9. Ibid. pp. 25–26.

10. U.S. Senate, *Department of Defense Appropriations for 1966*, Hearings before the Subcommittee of the Committee on Appropriations, July 16, 1965, p. 225.

11. Ibid. July 14, 1965, p. 8.

12. In fact, General James Richardson, army deputy chief of staff for personnel, testified that in the FY 1966 budget army strength decreased by 10,000 men. When asked about the situation in Vietnam, he could only answer that the decrease would probably be eliminated and, in all seriousness, added that more men might be required but that it was still being studied. Again, one gets the impression from the budget testimony in July that neither he nor anyone else wanted to make any definitive statement until McNamara and the president decided what the new U.S. military commitment in Vietnam would be. (Ibid. July 14, 1965, p. 49.)

13. Stennis capitalized on the illness of Senator Richard Russell, who would have chaired the budget hearings. Russell was close to the president and much less inclined to criticize the administration. He was also much less of a hawk on Vietnam than Stennis. On the other hand, had Russell been the driving force behind these hearings, Lyndon Johnson's great respect for Russell might have persuaded him more on the inadequacy of the military budgets.

14. O'Brien received a cautionary memo from assistant secretary of defense David McGiffert in late June:

"Stennis' Preparedness Subcommittee is continuing its investigation of readiness in all three military Departments, stressing particularly the extent, if any, to which the demands of the Vietnamese conflict are prejudicing readiness of our forces elsewhere in the world . . . . I think we can expect increasing pressure and criticism, both public and private from the subcommittee during the rest of this session." (Memo from David E. McGiffert to special assistant to the president Larry O'Brien, June 28, 1965, in Johnson Library: Reports on Legislation File, Box 12, June 30, 1965, folder)

15. *Department of Defense Appropriations for 1966*, July 14, 1965, p. 134.

16. One Pentagon official involved in the budget process for the services noted that if (X) represented what a particular service needed, then "we came in with (X+5) billion and it was cut to (X) billion, which was about what we expected. Now if we'd come in with (X) billion we would have ended up with (X-3) or (X-2) billion. This would have been a very unacceptable budget from the [service's] standpoint. So we would be cutting our own throats by coming in with a realistic budget." (See John P. Crecine, *Defense Budgeting: Constraints and Organizational Adaptation*, p. 41.)

17. "U.S. Army Readiness" Hearings, May 13, 1965, p. 108.

18. Ibid. p. 102. One of the concerns the senators had was that the army wanted more men and equipment but was overruled by the Defense Department civilians and the secretary. The military witnesses were thus defending conclusions and cuts they did not believe in. One of the results that some senators apparently hoped to gain in these hearings was an admission by army officials that the army had been considerably weakened. Of course, publicly, the army men stood squarely behind their superiors at the Pentagon. (U.S. Army Readiness Hearings, June 3, 1965, pp. 154–55.) There is some indirect evidence that certain senators, in particular, Stennis, were secretly provided information in the summer and fall from military personnel who were disgruntled at McNamara's budget cuts. This was implied in the Council of Economic Advisers and Department of Treasury administrative histories in the Johnson Library.

19. July 12, 1965, memo from McNamara to the president, "Department of Defense Cost Reduction Program—Third Annual Progress Report," National Archives: RG51, series 61.1a, Box 148, M2-1/1—"Budget and Financial Management" folder.

20. See Alain Enthoven and E. Wayne Smith, *How Much Is Enough?*, p. 269.

21. Testimony of Robert N. Anthony, assistant secretary of defense (comptroller) before U.S. Congress Joint Economic Committee, Hearings on *The Economic Effect of Vietnam Spending*, April 24, 1967, p. 5. Anthony became comptroller in July 1965.

22. "National Defense and Prosperity," remarks by Arthur Okun before the American Ordnance Association, October 12, 1966, as reproduced in Joint Economic Committee, *The Economic Effect of Vietnam Spending*, p. 543.

23. See January 1966, *The Economic Report of the President, 1966*, pp. 60, 62.

24. Hearings on the "Fiscal Policy Issues of the Coming Decade, July 22, 1965, p. 89.

25. Robert W. Komer, *Bureaucracy at War: U.S. Performance in the Vietnam Conflict*, p. 49.

26. See Center for Strategic Studies, *Economic Impact of the Vietnam War*, p. 30.

27. McNamara quoted in Bowen, "The Vietnam War: A Cost Accounting," p. 259.

28. Murray Weidenbaum testimony during Joint Economic Committee Hearings on *The Economic Effect of Vietnam Spending*, April 27, 1967, p. 184.

29. Center for Strategic Studies, *Economic Impact of the Vietnam War*, p. 34.

30. Thomas Alan Riddell, "A Political Economy of the American War in Indo-China: Its Costs and Consequences," p. 258. He got the data from the U.S. Commerce Department, Bureau of the Census, *Defense Indicators* (monthly), 1968–73.

31. See Robert Warren Stevens, *Vain Hopes, Grim Realities: The Economic Consequences of the Vietnam War*, p. 70.

32. See March 7, 1966, Bureau of the Budget report, "Defense Obligations for Hard Goods and New and Unfilled Orders and Inventories in Durable Goods: Manufacturing Industries, Quarterly, 1947–1965," in Office of Management and Budget Records Division: Accession No. 51-79-121, Box 39, Economy in Government folder.

33. *Business Week*, July 24, 1965, p. 24.

34. January 30, 1965, memo from Cyrus Vance to Kermit Gordon in Office of Management and Budget Records Division: Accession No. 51-79-121, Box 75, Budget for 1966 folder #3.

35. See Stevens, *Vain Hopes, Grim Realities*, p. 71.

36. Bowen, "The Vietnam War: A Cost Accounting," p. 259.

37. *Wall Street Journal*, August 23, 1965, p. 7.

38. *Business Week*, August 7, 1965, p. 23.

39. From the second quarter of 1965 through the end of 1966 there would be a continuous increase in the consumer price index at 3 percent per annum. See the Committee for Economic Development, *The National Economy and the Vietnam War*, p. 19.

40. Murray Weidenbaum testimony before Joint Economic Committee, *Economic Effect of Vietnam Spending*, p. 177.

41. See Riddell, "A Political Economy of the American War in Indo-China," pp. 205–208.

42. Arthur Okun, *The Political Economy of Prosperity*, p. 50.

43. Johnson Library: Department of the Treasury Administrative History, Box 1—vol. 1, Part 2, Folder 1, Chapter 5, pp. 14–17.

44. See Anthony S. Campagna, *The Economic Consequences of the Vietnam War*, pp. 18–19.

45. See Gilbert Burck, "The Guns, Butter, and Then-Some Economy," *Fortune*, October 1965, p. 120.

46. See *Business Week*, July 31, 1965, p. 32.

47. Johnson Library: CEA Administrative History, Box 1, vol. 1, Folder 2, Chapter 5, p. 39.

48. *New York Times*, June 25, 1969, p. 18—Sources: Department of Commerce and Department of Labor.

49. Eliot Janeway, *The Economics of Crisis: War, Politics and the Dollar*, p. 286.

50. *1975 Economic Report of the President*, p. 350, cited in Riddell, "A Political Economy of the American War in Indo-China," p. 238.

51. See Donald Kettl, "The Economic Education of Lyndon Johnson: Guns, Butter, and Taxes," in Robert A. Divine (ed.), *The Johnson Years*, vol. 2: *Vietnam, the Environment, and Science*, p. 73.

52. Statement by Charles Schultze at November 19, 1965, cabinet meeting, in the National Archives: RG51, Series 61.1b, Box 10—Cabinet Meetings, "July 1965—December 1967" folder. Schultze noted two other factors in domestic spending. First, Congress was more liberal with civilian and military pay raises than expected; and second, there had been a faster rate of progress and spending in some federal programs, space, for example.

53. See Arthur Burns, *Business Cycle in a Changing World*, pp. 278–83.

54. Ibid. p. 317.

55. U.S. Department of Defense (Comptroller), *The Economics of Defense Spending: A Look at the Realities*, July 1972, pp. 23–24.

56. Ibid. p. 24.

57. See Center for Strategic Studies, *Economic Impact of the Vietnam War*, p. viii.

58. Johnson Library: Department of the Treasury Administrative History, Box 1—vol. 1, Part 2, Folder 1, Chapter 5, pp. 14–17.

59. Ibid.

60. August 1965 staff memorandum (no specific date), "Notes for Economic and Financial Policy Group on the Implications of a Defense Buildup for Overall Economic Policy," in ibid. pp. 14–17.

61. See McNamara discussion of costs during July 22 afternoon meeting on Vietnam. Jack Valenti's notes in Johnson Library: Meeting Notes File, Meetings on Vietnam Folder: July 21–27.

62. Robert S. McNamara, *In Retrospect: The Tragedy and Lessons of Vietnam*, p. 205.

63. Testimony on "Military Procurement Authorization for Fiscal Year 1968," before the Senate Armed Services Committee, 1967, p. 265, as quoted in Center for Strategic Studies, *Economic Impact of the Vietnam War*, p. 22.

64. See testimony of Major General B. F. Taylor, director of the army budget, during hearings on "Department of Defense Appropriations, 1966," pp. 74–75.

65. July 23, 1965, letter from Cyrus Vance to Senator Richard Russell in Office of Management and Budget Records Division: Accession No. 51-79-121, Box 77, FY 1966 Defense Budget—Congressional Action folder.

66. See June 18, 1965, memo to Larry O'Brien, special assistant to the president, "Report on Major Legislation," from assistant secretary of defense for legislative affairs, David E. McGiffert.

67. As quoted in Bowen, "The Vietnam War: A Cost Accounting," p. 122.

68. Enthoven and Smith, *How Much Is Enough?*, p. 271.

69. Ibid. p. 293.

70. 1966 Defense Appropriations hearings, p. 352.

71. See Bowen, "The Vietnam War: A Cost Accounting," p. 120.

72. *New York Times*, July 30, 1965, p. 3. (See also Lyndon Baines Johnson, *The Vantage Point*, p. 150.)

73. "Business Roundup," *Fortune*, August 1965, p. 28.

74. "Business Roundup," *Fortune*, September 1965, pp. 27–28.

75. Most of the same conclusions were shared by a sampling of economists and businessmen done by the *Wall Street Journal*, August 16, 1965, p. 1.

76. See Office of Management and Budget Records Division: Accession No. 51-79-121, Box 74, Budget Amendment for 1966 folder.

77. August 4, 1965, testimony of Robert S. McNamara, U.S. Senate, *Department of Defense Appropriations for 1966*, Emergency Fund for Southeast Asia hearings before the Subcommittee of the Committee on Appropriations, p. 776.

78. *The Economist*, August 21, 1965, p. 693.

79. McNamara testimony during *Department of Defense Appropriations for 1966*, Emergency Fund for Southeast Asia hearings, August 4, 1965, p. 768.

80. Ibid. p. 773. That was as specific as McNamara got regarding what the $1.7 billion would go for.

81. See Weidenbaum testimony in Joint Economic Hearings, *Economic Effect of Vietnam Spending*, vol. 1, pp. 177, 210.

82. *Department of Defense Appropriations for 1966*, Emergency Fund for Southeast Asia hearings, August 4, 1965, p. 773.

83. Ibid. p. 806.

84. *Department of Defense Appropriations for 1966*, Emergency Fund for Southeast Asia hearings, August 4, 1965, pp. 816–17. McNamara later supplied classified information to the subcommittee that he stated would be a better "rough guess." What he submitted remains classified for 50 years, according to the National Archives. But he could not have provided much in the way of specifics because he later admitted, when asked for a cost estimate on how much the war currently cost on a daily or monthly basis, "It is so difficult to know how to allocate the cost. I don't know of any meaningful way to give it to you, sir." (Ibid. p. 865.)

85. Ibid. p. 817.

86. Ibid. p. 818.

87. In a letter from McNamara to Charles Schultze asking that BOB forward the $1.7 billion supplemental request to Congress on July 30, 1965, the defense secretary wrote, "It is our plan that the additional costs to be incurred in the areas of military personnel and operation and maintenance will be financed under the authority of Section 512 of the Department of Defense Appropriation Act, 1966 pending the enactment of appropriations therefore subsequent to the reconvening of the Congress in January." (Office of Management and Budget Records Division: Accession No. 51-79-121, Box 74, Budget Amendment for 1966 folder.) So the American people would be charged for the military commitments made from August to December when the administration went before Congress in January.

88. *Department of Defense Appropriations for 1966*, Emergency Fund for Southeast Asia hearings, August 4, 1965, p. 797.

89. Memo from J. Sherick, Military Division, Bureau of the Budget to Charles Schultze, October 8, 1965. See also memo from the president to the director of the Bureau of the Budget, October 12, 1965. Both memos are in the National Archives: RG51, Bureau of the Budget, Series 61.1a, Box 148, Folder M2-1/1.

90. See Department of Defense and Department of Commerce figures in Center for Strategic Studies, *Economic Impact of the Vietnam War*, p. 23.

91. See Burck, "The Guns, Butter and Then-Some Economy," p. 121.

92. Department of Defense Appropriations for 1966 hearings, p. 875.

93. Joint Economic Committee, *Economic Effect of Vietnam Spending*, July 7, 1967, p. 3.

94. See memo from McGiffert to Larry O'Brien, special assistant to the president, "Report on Major Legislation," in Johnson Library: Reports on Legislation, August 10, 1965, Folder.

95. *Department of Defense Appropriations for 1966*, Emergency Fund for Southeast Asia hearings, August 4, 1965, p. 854.

Chapter 9 _____

The War Overheats the Economy

THE CEA AND THE "ECONOMIC ASPECTS OF VIETNAM"

At first glance, the economic policy of fiscal stimulation had worked in splendid fashion for 1964 and 1965. During the last quarter of 1965 and first quarter of 1966, GNP increased by $30 billion, which at the time was the most rapid advance ever for the American economy.[1]   At the same time, unemployment dropped to 4 percent and manufacturing capacity hit 90 percent. However, in achieving these lofty goals in a period of major military escalation, the economy greatly overheated, and inflation took root. By December the economists were urging President Johnson to reverse course and restrain the economy. When they also recommended a tax increase, it was hard to convince the president that stimulation was no longer good and that restraint was required.[2]   By the beginning of 1966, their good luck and invincibility shattered, the economists' stock fell at the White House.

In the summer of 1965 there was one attempt to analyze the economic impact the Vietnam War might have. On July 30 Council of Economic Advisers chairman Gardner Ackley sent a memo to the president entitled "Economic Aspects of Vietnam."[3]   It was not until a request for a 200,000 increase in U.S. forces by Westmoreland in late 1967 that Johnson would again ask for an evaluation by the CEA on what the economic realities were. The thrust of Ackley's memo was that there was little cause for concern. But it appears that the key to his conclusions evolved from estimates he received from Robert McNamara. While he did not state specifically what the figures were, the tone of the memo and the particular references to McNamara implied that the defense secretary must not have been forthcoming about the scope and length of the American military commitment in Vietnam but couched it in terms of a modest escalation. The whole basis upon which Ackley made his conclusions was the following: "The current thinking in DOD [Department of Defense], as relayed to me by Bob McNamara on a super-confidential basis, points to a *gradual and moderate build-up of expenditures and manpower.*"[4] McNamara clearly did not mention a cost estimate over $5 billion because Ackley expressed little concern over the figures he received from McNamara and stated, "*Only in the remote event that the defense step-up for the near future got into the $10 billion range* would we have to give serious thought to higher taxes, selective commodity allocations or (last of all) to direct controls on wages and prices." Ackley's conclusions about the economic impact of Vietnam were that while the situation in Vietnam had affected "speculative commodity and financial markets," it was unlikely that prices, output, and employment would be disrupted.

An extensive analysis of the economic situation followed. Ackley noted that even if expenditures "fall in the path that Bob McNamara now visualizes as likely," this would provide a strong stimulus activity during the first half of 1966, and "[o]ur economy has lots of room to absorb a defense step-up." Ackley was very glowing in his assessment of the state of the economy: "There is still a *$15–20 billion margin of idle industrial capacity and excessive unemployment; Our productive capacity is growing by $25–30 billion a year* (apart from any price increases), making room for more butter and, if need, more guns." He noted further that the Vietnam news had a significant impact on the stock market. There had been a 12-point drop in the Dow Jones Index on July 20, generally attributed to McNamara's appraisal of the Vietnam situation as "deteriorated." But the market then gained 14 points from July to July 30 in response to the president's escalation announcement in which no drastic measures were planned. Thus, Johnson's gradual escalation was reaping economic dividends.

Ackley seemed very anxious to reassure the president that there was nothing to fear from the escalation and that he could have guns and butter. He emphasized, "Nobody can seriously expect that the kind of [military] program you outlined is going to overheat the economy, strain industrial capacity, or generate a consumer buying boom. But speculative excitement inflames easily in the commodity markets, and we should be careful in what we say and do." That last statement could only contribute further to the president's desire to play down the scope of the escalation. How the policies and decisions were to be presented were just as important as the policies and decisions themselves.

Ackley also provided more ammunition for Johnson's incremental (and deceptive) escalation. He argued that in the first half of 1966, Vietnam's impact on output and employment would be more significant—that is, increase their rates—but it would also mean "*extra insurance against slowdown* or recession during that period (when payroll taxes will jump)—*not a threat of overheating.*" Ackley also did not see any kind of economic stimulus occurring until the first half of 1966. He did add a few cautionary notes, stating that budget planning for FY 1967 would be affected—more money taken from revenues for defense outlays would mean less money available for domestic programs or tax cuts. Although he noted that now the president would be less likely to want to recommend a tax cut for the next year, it should not be ruled out. The strongest statement he could muster against the escalation was, "We are certainly not saying that a Vietnam crisis is just what the doctor ordered for the American economy in the next 12 months. But, on a coldly objective analysis, *the over-all effects are most likely to be favorable to our prosperity.*"

The CEA was essentially endorsing Johnson's Vietnam policy based on McNamara's judgment of its costs. There was no independent study, and the economic analysis by the CEA seemed very shallow. No exploration of the rise in defense orders or the increased numbers of soldiers was undertaken. It is important to emphasize that within the Johnson administration there was such a great respect among economic planners for McNamara's abilities that they simply deferred to his judgment on military budget matters. They were also grateful for the defense largesse of the past two years that they could put to use in funding the Great Society programs. A week earlier, on July 22, budget director Charles Schultze talked of McNamara's "tremendous capability" in getting a cost reduction program to permeate throughout the entire Pentagon.[5] He then emphasized that the $4.3 billion increase in Great Society programs from 1964 to 1966 came primarily from cost reductions in the military budget.[6]

There is no record of the president's response to the Ackley memo, so it is not clear whether he simply saw the memo, as Ackley intended it, as an economic endorsement of his political desire for both guns and butter. Like those businessmen who he noted were fearful of much worse news regarding Vietnam, Ackley showed a sense of relief and a strong optimism that had been lacking 10 days before in his testimony to the Joint Economic Committee, when he mentioned the remote possibility of a tax increase.[7] His confidence had been restored by the apparent moderate escalation chosen by the president.

THE MISLEADING PENTAGON FIGURES

As Ackley noted, his optimism was based on the picture of the future escalation and military needs he received directly from McNamara. The chairman of the Council of Economic Advisers was later accused of being duped by both the defense secretary and the president in order to delay the hard economic choices. Analysts such as David Halberstam and Edwin Dale argued that the FY 1967 defense budget was seriously and deceptively underestimated in January 1966.[8] Thus, there was no compelling reason for a tax increase in March 1966, an action that might have prevented the devastating inflation that was to follow. According to Halberstam, "Lyndon Johnson did not give accurate economic projections, did not ask for a necessary tax raise, and did in fact direct *his own* military planners to be less than candid with *his own* economic planners, a lack of candor so convincing that his economic advisers later felt that Defense Secretary Robert S. McNamara had seriously misled them about projections and estimates."[9] Dale claimed that in the budget sent to Congress in January 1966, "the cost of the war in Vietnam was unnecessarily underestimated by $10 billion."[10] One of the main reasons was that McNamara based the FY 1967 defense budget on the false and misleading assumption that the war would be over by the end of that fiscal year.

In Gardner Ackley's defense of himself and the President against the charges raised by Halberstam that the economic advisers had been duped in late 1965 and in 1966, he made the point that what deception there was had occurred earlier in 1965. Ackley paraphrased the criticism in the following manner: "Halberstam's essential argument is that President Lyndon Johnson deceived his economic advisers (and the Congress and the country) about the cost of the Vietnam War ('One part of the government was lying to another part.'), and that this deceit was a major reason for the failure to raise taxes. This failure in turn led directly to the inflation of 1966–69, the momentum of which carried into 1971, and, indeed, still haunts us today   [in 1972]."[11] Ackley's rejoinder was that he and his colleagues did make the right policy recommendation: "Whether or not members of the Council of Economic Advisers, the Secretary of Treasury, and the Budget Director knew *all* the 'facts' about the cost of the war, our knowledge was quite sufficient to let us make—as early as November 1965—the unanimous recommendation which almost everyone (Halberstam included) *now* agrees was the correct one— namely, that personal income and corporate profits tax rates should be significantly raised as soon as possible after January, 1966. (They surely could not have been raised any sooner.)"[12]

Ackley also admitted that they did not have all the facts and turned to the issue of the president's deception: "There can be no question that Lyndon Johnson was secretive about 'the facts' of military spending—as he was about everything else relating to the future. His principle of operations was always to preserve his options to the maximum possible extent . . . . The President's view of what his professional or technical advisers needed to know in order to give their best advice may sometimes have been incorrect."[13] It seems clear that the president's habit of compartmentalizing most of his actions and his advisers reflected a desire to keep the economic advisers uninformed of his long-term intentions to escalate militarily in Vietnam, thus eroding the advice he received on economic policy.

Finally, Ackley attempted to dispute Halberstam's contentions by noting that only before October 1965 had he been in the dark—that was the key period of deception: "I believe (although I cannot be positive) that from July (or perhaps even April) until October 1965, my own private advice to him [President Johnson], as well as my public statements on the economic situation, were based on an incomplete or incorrect understanding of decisions which he may have already made. Thereafter, my position on the tax increase needed the support of no information that I did not already have."[14]

Donald Kettl argued that Halberstam's contention that Johnson and McNamara were deceitful is doubtful, according to the documentary record in the Johnson Library archives. Kettl stated that "in the early stages, guns and butter did not seem like incompatible choices."[15] In his view, the economic costs only later became known. Kettl contended that "the struggle over the tax surcharge was the keystone of Lyndon Johnson's tragedy." But, in putting forward this thesis, Kettl ignored the early significance of the economic and domestic confusion and the poor economic analysis that occurred while the administration was escalating militarily. He criticized Halberstam for claiming that the economic advisers were deceived in December 1965; and he is right, because by that time they had a fairly good idea of the costs of the escalation. But the critical period was the first three quarters of 1965, when the stage was set. The advisers were deceived as far back as early 1965 because they were not informed about the military preparations and the president's intention in 1965 to commit to a costly and long war—the costs of which his military advisers had very frankly put forth to him.

For Ackley, the key was his misunderstanding of the nature of Johnson's decision to expand the war. The crux of Ackley's response was that he did not deny he was misled. His defense remained that once the administration economists realized the significant increase in defense outlays by November, they made the correct recommendation at the right time anyway. But by then, the policy of gradual escalation was firmly entrenched, and the damage of the continued economic policy of fiscal stimulation had been laid. A year after his reply to David Halberstam, Gardner Ackley remarked that there was just "wholesale mis-guessing" on what Vietnam would cost. But he placed any blame for deception on the military: "The Halberstam view that McNamara and Johnson really knew all along precisely what it was going to cost and they just weren't telling seems to me to be ridiculous. It's true that maybe the generals had a clearer idea than anybody else of what it was going to cost; but, if so, I don't think they conveyed it fully to McNamara, nor McNamara to Johnson, nor Johnson to us. But I don't regard that as a plot to deceive people . . . . I think Johnson, as well as McNamara and all the rest of us were misled by [the military]. Whether we were deliberately misled by the military, I don't know."[16] This view, however, does not ring true for the time period (1965 and early 1966) under consideration because the military services urged more defense money as well as stronger wartime measures. As noted earlier, on July 22 the military told both McNamara and Johnson that the costs would be $12 billion. It was McNamara who later that afternoon told the president that the $12 billion figure could be cut in half. So Ackley's conclusion about the deception seems misplaced.

Had his economic advisers known what President Johnson wanted to do with respect to Vietnam in the summer, would it have made any difference? Perhaps not, but the chances of a debate within the administration as well as the Congress about the costs of the war would have been greater. The country might have realized that it was going to war and that sacrifices would be needed down the road. But, as Lyndon Johnson made clear, that was a debate he clearly wanted to avoid.

AFTER THE ESCALATION ANNOUNCEMENT

The economists were not operating in a vacuum. By late July they knew that the conflict was going to accelerate further and, if nothing else, that they would have to account for the Vietnam escalation, albeit moderate as it appeared to them, in some way in their economic and budget calculations. Military costs would have to be revised. On August 10, 1965, the Bureau of the Budget prepared two new sets of FY 1966 and FY 1967 expenditure levels for the president. The first estimates were $104 billion for FY 1966 and $108 billion for FY 1967; the second set of estimates were $104 billion and $112 billion.[17] The increase for FY 1967 in the second set of numbers reflected "the possible increase in defense expenditures in Vietnam." Because the original FY 1966 budget had been estimated at $99.7 billion, the economists foresaw the cost of Vietnam to be only an additional $4.3 billion. If there was to be a significant increase in military spending, it would come in FY 1967. Schultze soon felt that his $108 billion estimate could be revised down to $105.2 billion because of Budget Bureau re-estimates of "how rapidly new programs will get started." Thus, savings would come from the domestic side.[18] Coupled with this was a strong confidence about the budget figures. From FY 1963 to FY 1965, the differences between the January estimates and the actual expenditures never amounted to more than $1.5 billion a year.

By mid-October, the $104 billion figure for FY 1966 had not increased, and the Budget Bureau treated the numbers as a certainty. Yet, even this apparent modest increase was to be downplayed. Schultze's recommendation, seemingly in keeping with Johnson's political concerns, was to make the budget revisions public "after Congress goes home." Traditionally, the president issued a fall budget review, but when Schultze confirmed the news that FY 1966 expenditures would be $104 billion, $4.5 billion above the January budget, he argued against issuing a fall review.[19] This was seconded by McNamara. Schultze explained his strategy: "At this time military expenditures in Vietnam are still uncertain. The size of the January Department of Defense supplemental is still undetermined. Publication of an official estimate of DOD expenditures would raise more questions about the size of the January supplemental than we could really answer."[20] Schultze proposed only to give a few background interviews to the press after Congress had recessed, so speculation about Vietnam costs could be dampened.

A September CEA staff analysis had concluded that "a somewhat more rapid upward creep of prices was to be expected with a more fully employed economy."[21] But the CEA believed that basic prices would remain under the acceptable rate of 2 percent, so there was little danger of inflation. The economists were watching the wrong signs and ignored some true indicators of danger, in particular, increased demand within military-related industries. Ackley later admitted that the charge of an overheated economy "certainly began to be valid in a significant sense toward the very end of 1965; and 1966 was certainly a year in which things were heating up considerably."[22] He remarked that the changes in the economy during the fall were "partly the direct effect of the increased expenditures that were being made, but, even more important, at first, was the impact of the expectation of further increases in military spending on private investment in plant and equipment and on inventory building. Just about every part of the economy was really beginning to boom."[23]

Expectations play a key role in economic stability. As the United States sent more and more men to Vietnam, it altered the expectations of businessmen and bankers, particularly with respect to the defense industry. Ackley was well aware of the impact of expectations when he wrote President Johnson in April 1965 to assure him of continued economic expansion: "[T]he remarkable industrial price stability of this expansion [1960–1964], now stretching over four years, has finally broken the inflationary prices expectations that were so troublesome to our progress for so many of the postwar years. Business investment and inventory decisions are not being distorted by the anticipation of higher prices."[24] Within a few months that type of distortion would arise again; and the expectations of inflation and demand changed in the business community before they did within government circles.

But Gardner Ackley continued to deny that there were any dangers, even in the fall. A column by Rowland Evans and Robert Novak on September 2, 1965, claimed that "highly informal preliminary conversations" were taking place within the administration about "an election-year tax boost."[25] Ackley immediately sent President Johnson a memo entitled "Scare Talk on a Tax Increase." According to Ackley, the column was "an irresponsible and incompetent analysis" in its claim that the economy threatened to "over accelerate" and insistence that "we face a bitter choice between higher taxes and higher prices for 1966."[26] He also argued that it was "particularly unfortunate because it sounds terribly authoritative. It throws around a lot of specific but highly exaggerated Viet Nam numbers . . . . It's hard to believe they got any of this junk from anyone in the Administration."

Evans and Novak implied that their information came from Treasury Department sources. The first figure they cited was $5 billion, which "Administration officials admit privately" will be the minimum for added Vietnam costs in the current fiscal year. In addition, "extra defense spending caused by Viet Nam could exceed $12 billion." Clearly, the $5 billion figure should have been no surprise because Schultze had already informed President Johnson of revisions upward in the current budget of $4.3 billion. Ackley implied that even that might have been exaggerated. The $12 billion number, the same figure cited by military men to the president in July, was completely off the mark for Ackley, who remained in the dark about defense figures.

The Evans and Novak story may have reflected some rumblings within the administration's economic bureaucracy. A passage from an internal Treasury Department memorandum that discussed possible economic controls was, according to a later Treasury analysis, "indicative of the general tenor of Treasury thinking at the time." It stated: "Even now [August 1965] it is apparent that a more rapid economic advance may be in prospect during the next year or so. Under the stimulus of a defense buildup, federal spending may rise during calendar 1966 by more than the increase in fiscal stimulus which would otherwise have been deemed appropriate. In turn, the prospect of a sizable defense-oriented increase in federal spending may lead to a general scaling up of private expenditure programs . . . . However, any sizable and continuing expansion in federal expenditures could certainly place the economy under some inflationary stress and aggravate the balance of payments situation."[27] While this memo raised some worries and did not contain the optimism of the CEA, there still existed a wait-and-see attitude regarding how military spending would play out through the end of the year. There is no evidence that a tax hike was discussed, much less proposed.

Gardner Ackley's biggest concern in September was that the administration was not counteracting the rumors of exaggerated military costs such as those cited by Evans and Novak. He wrote the president that "the absence of even vague statements from the Administration has left the field open to the Stennises and others. This has created uncertainty and fears of 'overheating,' which have been damaging to financial markets."[28] Ackley proposed speaking out on behalf of the administration in order to allay those fears. Schultze agreed with Ackley, but apparently McNamara preferred that he say nothing. On September 9 Ackley made a major speech, with the president's prior approval, in which he remarked, "Figures sometimes quoted in the press—that run to $10 to $14 billion—can at this point only be pure figments of someone's imagination. The estimates we at the Council have put into our tentative projections do not even approach that order of magnitude."[29] He concluded that "the particular uncertainty that has aroused renewed fears of overheating, reflects the sudden notion that we may soon have to choose between guns and butter. I see no basis for this fear." Although Ackley had cleared the figures with McNamara, Ackley later acknowledged the speech was a "major mistake."[30] In October Henry Fowler stated publicly, "If I thought defense was going to add $10 billion to $15 billion to our fiscal 1967 budget, I'd be back in my office right now considering proposals for tax increases to pay for it."[31]

DIFFICULTY IN PROVIDING ECONOMIC ANALYSIS

By the fall of 1965 economic officials began to feel that they were receiving incomplete or inconsistent information regarding Vietnam. Most of them blamed the military. Henry Fowler later remarked:

So from July 1965 on, we simply had to rely in the Treasury on the estimates that were arrived at from the Defense Department as to what the proportions of increased expenditures would be; what the consequences of that would be in terms of the budget; in terms of the call on employment; the strain that it would put on the economy; the probabilities of an excess of demand that might be a consequence of this scaling up of the war effort. In other words, the scaling of what one did in the fiscal and monetary restraint field had to necessarily depend on an unpredictable. The only guidance we could get on the unpredictability was the scale of effort that the Defense Department and Joint Chiefs outlined . . . . I had to take the positions and information that came to me from those sources as the benchmark for my own actions.[32]

Assistant secretary of the Treasury Paul Volcker was concerned in the fall that he was unintentionally "lying" in his public comments about the economy and believed that the information he was getting from the Pentagon about the cost of the war was "phony."[33] Yet, no senior official seems to have made any effort to clear up the picture.

Unlike Volcker, Fowler did not believe that the Defense Department had misled him, because he assumed he was privy to the military information. He claimed that he sat in on the National Security Council sessions as an invited guest by the president; and his role in such meetings "was to try to see that other things were cut or their rate of increase was moderated, or that the financial policies of the government should be designed to support the war effort."[34] The documentary evidence suggests that Fowler's recollection did not reflect what occurred in 1965. In most of the NSC meetings on Vietnam in 1965, Fowler was not present and certainly would not have known about the extent of the escalation in July. His name did not appear on the list of attendees at any NSC meeting that summer. From March through July Fowler attended only the April 2 NSC meeting, which primarily confirmed decisions taken at the NSC meeting the previous day, which he did not attend, and was a more thorough discussion of policy and information regarding U.S. military action in Vietnam. The next NSC meeting he is listed as having attended was on November 18. In addition, none of the economic advisers, the secretary of the Treasury included, pointed out the economic consequences of the Vietnam effort until December 1965 because they did not become aware of the scope of the U.S. military commitment until then.

Throughout most of 1965, defense spending remained outside the purview of economic analysis. Charles Schultze observed that the Budget Bureau had a much smaller role as an "independent staff check" in foreign and military affairs than in the domestic arena.[35] Another point to consider was that the Great Society programs were beginning just as the war was expanding. The Budget Bureau may well have been spread too thin in the summer of 1965 as it tried to manage the Great Society agenda. There were some critics of the bureau, including many in Congress, who strongly believed that the BOB was at the heart of many of the problems of the executive branch and did a poor job of managing the Great Society programs. A 1966 task force on government organization would later note that the hundreds of domestic programs initiated in the Johnson administration had "put a great strain upon obsolescent machinery and administrative practices at all levels of government."[36] The Bureau of the Budget was, therefore, struggling simply to deal with the Great Society agenda, much less figure out what the budgetary impact of the military escalation in Vietnam might be.

Most of the economic advisers expected the Treasury Department to provide the necessary economic data, but in 1965 it appeared that Treasury officials had no better handle on the military situation than any other economists. By 1966, according to one analyst, "At the height of the 1966 financial crisis, both the Federal Reserve Board and the President's Council of Economic Advisers complained that they found themselves obliged to perform their functions in an analytical vacuum because of the failure of the Treasury to function as their conduit with the Pentagon."[37]   Treasury failed "to require the Defense Department to keep it continuously informed of the rate of increase in war spending."

Charles Schultze later stated that no one in the administration, in particular, the Pentagon, came to him whenever the conflict escalated and stated that so many troops were needed at a particular cost and needed the Budget Bureau's advice. He also pointed out that in addition to greater numbers of troops than expected, aircraft attrition and ammunition consumption were higher than projected. So, new cost estimates were made almost every month: "[W]hat I was getting from my staff, primarily, who were in constant contact with the Defense people, and my contacts with Secretary McNamara, were kind of continually revised estimates, admittedly even on their part horseback guesses because you're still guessing ahead."[38]

THE ECONOMIC SQUEEZE BEGINS

Even in mid-October, the economic advisers continued to remain optimistic. Gardner Ackley noted in a memo to Charles Schultze that while small increases in the industrial price index could not be ruled out, "there is now no evidence of impending price increases to upset the balance of the expansion."[39] A recognition that the extent of the Vietnam buildup was much greater than anticipated took hold slowly. No specific date or event made the escalation apparent, but, as Ackley later noted, "I think increasingly as 1965 wore on, we were becoming pretty clear about what was going on."[40]   In the fall, the economists still believed, in the words of Schultze, "that the economy in 1966 would continue to move ahead relatively nicely without inflationary surge . . . . up through maybe October I don't have a feeling that anybody was beginning to be worried about too much pressure on the economy."[41]

As the economic situation became cloudier in the fall, the administration economists began to think about a change in strategy. Because there were no concrete estimates of defense spending, no one was clear on what course to follow. Charles Schultze did not receive revised numbers on military spending until early November. The new estimate called for spending $58.9 billion, an increase of $10 billion above the January 1965 estimate and $8 billion above the actual FY 1966 budget.[42]   During most of the month of November there were many meetings among the economic advisers in which concern for the new military figures was the central focus. But not until early December did Ackley and, to a lesser extent, Schultze and Treasury secretary Fowler begin to worry that the economy was overheating.

The president seemed to be aware that an economic squeeze was possible. In early September he ordered Budget director Schultze to find more savings within the government for the FY 1967 budget that was in preparation and to be even harder on requests for new or expanded programs. He had already sent a memo to all departments and agencies asking them to implement the planning, programming, and budgeting techniques of the Pentagon to enhance cost-effectiveness. He also wanted a government-wide search for the most effective and least costly alternatives to achieve administration goals. By September the president had given up on any more savings from the military budget. Johnson eliminated the following passage from a draft statement on the economy that he was to make to the cabinet on September 13: "I am glad to note that the Department of Defense, which exceeded its own goal in Fiscal Year 1965 by $2.1 billion, has established a new goal of [figure left blank] for this year to add to the total of $4.6 billion [for FY 1965]."[43] No mention of defense savings was made in the statement at all.

By November inflation was a real possibility. But there was no consensus on what measures to take in response. In a memo circulated at the November 19 cabinet meeting, Treasury secretary Henry Fowler warned of the dangers of inflation because of the domestic expansion. While he acknowledged the increase in military expenditures, he still seemed unaware of the economic impact of the military escalation. In effect, Fowler argued that reduced domestic spending would reduce inflation:

The budgetary decisions this year will be crucially important. Unemployment has come down to 4.3% and industry-operating rates have been near 90% in recent months. Private demand is increasing at a healthy rate and defense expenditures are rising because of Vietnam at a time when the gap between demand and the available manpower and unused capacity has narrowed to the lowest point in this 57-month expansion.

The combination of a much narrower gap and the psychological and economic consequences of the Presidential decisions last summer on Vietnam places an unusual and unique pressure on the domestic expansion. That expansion could end in inflation unless the government takes budgetary action, without neglecting national needs, and finances new programs from savings on old ones to the maximum extent possible. It requires a budget that achieves all possible savings to offset greater defense needs by stretching out or deferring the impact on spending of some of the new and proposed civilian programs—without delaying basic authorizing legislation or otherwise unduly impairing important but longer-run objectives. [44]

Fowler was belatedly acknowledging the significance of the July escalation decisions and that the costs of Johnson's Vietnam policy could no longer be avoided. However, in mid-November, when Fowler sent the White House a draft of a speech outlining a warning about federal expenditures, he received a message from press secretary Bill Moyers that President Johnson thought the speech a "little too hard on Vietnam." Johnson did not want to say to the "business community that we have declared war in Viet Nam" or imply that the economy could not afford both guns and butter: "You don't say that. That is what he is trying to avoid."[45]

THE FEDERAL RESERVE BOARD

Unlike the economic Troika of the CEA, the Budget Bureau, and the Treasury Department, the Federal Reserve Board had expressed concern about inflation in 1965. Fed chairman William McChesney Martin had been very concerned about inflation even back in 1964, when the economy had sufficient room to grow. Because of the Fed's concern with monetary policy there was a natural sensitivity toward inflationary policies or the possibility of inflation down the road. But there was a sense within administration circles that Martin was always overly concerned about inflation. So his worries were not taken as a true reflection of the economy. Martin was viewed as a loose cannon and overly independent by many in the administration. The president's economists worried that, at Martin's direction, the Fed would act unilaterally and tighten credit prematurely. This concern increased in the fall of 1965 and actually came true in December, when the Federal Reserve raised the discount lending rate from 4 percent to 4.5 percent on December 6 (it was to go to 5.75 percent by August 1966). President Johnson was particularly upset by the decision.

The Fed was certainly ahead of most other economists, both in and out of government, in sensing danger for the economy. According to Dewey Daane, a member of the seven-man Federal Reserve Board, the Fed was concerned by the midsummer of 1965 that defense spending would accelerate. As a result, the Fed had contemplated raising the discount rate as early as July 1965. Daane stated that there was a perception that economic restraints were needed. He added: "There was uneasiness. Martin had some sort of pipeline to David Packard [a powerful industrialist tied closely to defense industries]. I had a gut feeling that the [defense] figures were going to accelerate a lot more and said so at a meeting. Martin called me into his office and said, 'You know, I've been talking to David Packard and you're right.' He said, 'These things are going to go way beyond what the administration has admitted.'"[46] Gardner Ackley reiterated this point: "There was a period of a couple of months—six weeks maybe—in the summer, in which there was, I think, a deliberate effort not to let anybody know what was going on. But the people in Defense knew it, and the people in Budget and Council [CEA] did not know it."[47] Daane emphasized that the Pentagon knew the costs were going to escalate considerably and remarked, "Martin claims that he had a number of go-rounds with Johnson directly on this."

On November 23, 1965, there was an all-day meeting of 20 outside economists and officials of key departments. According to Seymour Harris, senior consultant to the Treasury Department, "The major conclusion was that the economy would grow in 1966 with a rise of 4 per cent (real terms), somewhat less than in 1965. Rising defense expenditures would remove the need of additional stimuli . . . . With a few dissenters, there was no great concern that the economy was overheated and would require restrictive monetary policy."[48] At the time of this meeting, Martin was trying to convince the president and his economists of measures to slow the economy. The Fed was skeptical of the accuracy of Vietnam expenditure estimates.

Undersecretary of the Treasury Joseph Barr noted that the Fed was using the higher estimates of defense spending internally, observing that "they were paying attention to what Senator Russell and Senator Stennis were saying in the area of military spending and weren't paying any attention to what the Defense Department was saying."[49] The Fed had still not sold other economists on the need for restraint, and, according to Daane, Martin thought he had convinced the president in late November of the need for raising the discount rate because Johnson saw it as a way to avoid having to address the need for a tax increase. Arthur Okun later recalled that "Johnson had a couple of Quadriads and lectured Martin on how bad it would be to do that. Why did he want to destroy that nice prosperity?"[50] If Okun was right, the president still did not realize how much that prosperity was in jeopardy as the war continued to escalate. Finally, when Martin could wait no longer, at his urging, the Fed increased the discount rate by a 4 to 3 margin.

Although increasing the discount rate had been brought up as a possibility in Quadriad meetings during the past month, the economic advisers assumed that the Fed would hold off on any decision until the president's FY 1967 budget had been completed. They were not as concerned with the increase in interest rates as with the timing, because the overall economic picture was not yet in focus. Economically, as Daane noted, "the Fed moved too late on the need for restraint." But, politically, the Fed was viewed as having moved too soon because for many like Ackley, raising the interest rate should have been part of an overall, coherent program. But Daane claimed that there was no assurance that any kind of restraint program would have been implemented at the beginning of 1966, and, in fact, the Treasury Department in particular had not acknowledged even the need for any kind of restraint.[51] There were some who argued that a tax increase would have been easier to obtain in early 1966 if the Fed had not acted too soon.[52] Gardner Ackley talked of the irritation that he and the other administration economists felt: "[T]he question as to how we should meet the requirement for economic restraint should have been looked at *jointly* by the Fed and the administration, and all alternatives of monetary policy or fiscal policy or some combination ought to have been considered. Indeed, such discussions were underway, and we thought that the Fed had jumped the gun."[53]

DECEMBER 1965: THE PENTAGON PROVIDES DEFENSE NUMBERS

Three days after interest rates were raised, the Pentagon finally had some firm budget numbers. On December 9 McNamara presented the president with figures for both the FY 1968 defense budget and the supplemental financial requirements for Vietnam: $61.2 billion for FY 1967 and a $12.8 billion supplemental for FY 1966. He also estimated that a $9.8 billion Southeast Asia supplemental would be required in FY 1967.[54] As late as November 23 the Budget Bureau's estimates were in the area of $3 to $5 billion above the $49 billion for FY 1966.[55] McNamara stated that his budget figures were based on two key assumptions. The first was that there would be deployments to

Southeast Asia comprising 391,200 men in South Vietnam and 28,400 in Thailand by June 30, 1967. The second was that "[p]rovision was made for combat conception for all items through December 31, 1966 and for all the items by June 30, 1967. Thus, it shouldn't appear that the war would continue beyond December 31, 1966. Production costs might make necessary another supplemental appropriation in June 1966."[56] McNamara shortly revised the figures so that they were based on the war ending by June 30, 1967.

While the Pentagon was apparently unable to project its costs much beyond mid-1967, McNamara and Johnson were not going to bother to explain that to Congress. In addition, as McNamara noted in his memo, another $9.8 billion would be needed in FY 1967. The disingenuous nature of his proposal can be seen clearly when coupled with a memo written to the president on December 7 in which McNamara recommended a total of 600,000 American forces in 1967. At the same time, he offered no hope of winning: "[T]he odds are about even that, even with the recommended deployments, we will be faced in early 1967 with a military standoff at a much higher level."[57] No such picture was painted for the domestic advisers or for the American public.

Apparently, the economists were told only that the cost assumptions went to mid-1967 and to plan accordingly, even though, unbeknownst to them, more costs were foreseen by the military. A year later, on January 4, 1967, Gardner Ackley tried to explain to the president why the economists' forecasts were off for 1966: "What in fact occurred is that the FY 1967 budget was based on the assumption that hostilities would end by June 30, 1967. As a result, $10 billion more [close to McNamara's $9.8 billion] in defense spending was needed for FY 1967. In addition, tight money and high interest rates would add about $4 billion more and total spending would be around $127 billion (with revenues estimated at $116 billion, the deficit would be about $11 billion, up from $2.3 billion)."[58]

According to Budget director Schultze, McNamara "was not willing to submit a budget which explicitly provided—now this gets tricky—money in fiscal 1967 to buy the long lead time items needed to fight the war if it continued in 1968."[59] One reason Schultze cited was that McNamara did not want to give the military a blank check. For McNamara to keep control over the costs and the programs, the best course was to authorize money with little lead time. Ostensibly, that would make the military more cost-efficient and fiscally responsible. Waiting until 1967 to buy matériel needed for fighting in 1968 would better reflect what would be required for the war effort than buying in the summer of 1966. However, the budgetary assumption that the war would wind down or end after June 1967 did not reflect either military or economic reality. Once again, the administration was downplaying the extent of the costs of the war and the significance of the commitment that would require American sacrifices.

McNamara himself was at the time acknowledging that the war would be a long one and noted in his memoirs that he told President Johnson that increased escalation "would by no means guarantee success, that U.S. killed-inaction could rise to 1,000 a month, and that we might be faced with a 'no decision' at an even higher level of violence, destruction, and death."[60] McNamara may well have begun to doubt the wisdom of the military escalation, but in attempting to prevent the military from getting a blank check, he handcuffed the Budget Bureau's staff who proceeded on the assumption that the war would be over by mid-1967. This reflects a continued lack of coordination and communication between the Vietnam war planners, on one hand, and the economic planners, on the other hand. While both economic and military planners might have pushed for greater coordination, the ultimate responsibility was that of the most senior advisers, particularly the president and the secretary of defense.

In a memo to Schultze at the end of 1966, the Office of Budget Review stated: "In January 1966, we made the assumption that the Vietnam conflict would be over by the end of the next fiscal year . . . . events turned out quite different from our assumptions."[61] This was part of a response to a question from Schultze: "How do you explain that fact that expenditures are now expected to rise by $21 billion in 1967 when your original estimate anticipated an increase of only $6 billion, a difference of $15 billion?" The Office of Budget Review answered: "In short, simultaneously, with the unforeseen increase in spending for Vietnam, came a tight money policy which also had consequences for the budget. As the tempo of defense spending picked up, the Federal Reserve raised interest rates and restricted the supply of credit . . . . Together, costs of Vietnam and market effects account for almost the entire difference of $15 billion." As was pointed out, the market effects were a direct consequence of the increased spending for Vietnam. A later economic analysis based on interviews with chairmen of the Council of Economic Advisers strongly asserted that "the CEA did not even know the extent and cost of involvement, expecting the war to end in June 1967 and not become a long-term factor in the economy."[62]

THE ECONOMISTS URGE RESTRAINT

Johnson's economists had finally recognized the economic danger signals in December, soon after the Fed increased the discount rate, and McNamara submitted his budget figures. Further economic restraint was needed. On December 26, 1965, Gardner Ackley wrote the president: "The only conclusion I can reach is that an increase of individual and corporate tax rates should be planned, whatever the FY 1967 budget may be . . . . Tactically, it may only be feasible to propose higher taxes later in the year. *From an economic standpoint, it needs to be done as soon as possible.*"[63] But for Johnson, such measures carried political costs that he was not willing to pay. He would be asking Congress for unpopular measures during an election year while the House and Senate were considering needed funding for Great Society programs. He had been warned by his staff that if a tax increase request went up to Capitol Hill, many in Congress "would start tearing at the budget instead."[64]

Whether McNamara had any influence on Johnson's thinking regarding the tax increase is unknown. According to Ackley, McNamara's thinking was similar to the president's. McNamara "was against the tax increase . . . strongly against it, not on economic grounds at all but on political grounds. I think he realized—perhaps more than anybody else and perhaps sooner than anyone else—that the Vietnam War was going to be an awfully unpopular thing and that a tax increase would just make it all the more unpopular."[65]

While Johnson had no choice but to accept the Fed's decision to raise interest rates, he refused to consider raising taxes. At the same time, he chose not to seek specific congressional approval of the war. Once again he downplayed the costs of military involvement and avoided a debate over American priorities and objectives. William Bundy argued that "if any man contemplated a great debate at the turn of 1965/1966, he could have almost at once come to two conclusions: 1) as in July, the President would in the end have gotten overwhelming approval . . . ; 2) in the process, the true depth of the financial problem must inescapably have been revealed and in practical politics this would have meant serious damage to the Great Society. In December and January, the line of policy of all of 1965 came to its final and greatest test."[66] Bundy added that in sticking to this policy and downplaying the dilemma and the costs of the commitment in Vietnam, "the President took his greatest gamble." Charles Schultze later argued that a key motive for Johnson to pursue a limited war was "making sure [the] domestic programs got through."[67]

At the end of December Johnson was faced with another disagreement between his economic advisers and the secretary of defense. McNamara wanted a $60 billion defense budget, while Schultze pushed for one of $57 billion. McNamara's concern, according to Joe Califano, was for "our credibility both in budget terms and in terms of Vietnam if we go for the lower figure."[68] In Schultze's view, the lower defense figure would allow him to bring the overall FY 1967 budget in around $110 billion. The deficit would be only about $3 billion as a result. Schultze emphasized to the president, "This level of defense expenditures would have to assume that the armed forces return to their pre-Vietnam level by December 1966."[69] Otherwise, "If the fighting continues in Vietnam, a request for additional defense funds will be necessary in May or June. We don't know the magnitudes but a minimum of $6–8 billion in appropriations and $4–5 billion in expenditures is likely." Since the military escalation would obviously continue, Schultze strongly recommended that any defense supplemental be accompanied by a request for an across-the-board tax increase on personal and corporate incomes.[70] This was a tactic of tying two unpleasant economic realities together and secretly deferring them until after the FY 1967 budget had been approved.

Although he had followed McNamara's advice to avoid any tax increase, Johnson chose the $57 billion budget figure. The president proposed restoring the excise taxes that were reduced the previous summer. Graduated individual income tax withholding was also instituted, and corporate tax payments were accelerated.[71] But Johnson rejected the tax hike recommended by the administration economists, and without it the budget was nothing but a "bits-and-pieces revenue package," as Arthur Okun described it.[72] Once again, the president chose to downplay defense costs, preferring to pay for the war with supplementals. The budget looked more modest than it really was because another "bill" for Vietnam would come later.

President Johnson chose Schultze's lower figure without his recommended prescription of higher taxes. The budget director warned of the dangers of a smaller defense package in early 1966. If the administration figures did not assume the cessation of Vietnam hostilities by the summer of 1966, then it was obvious that a supplemental request would come before Congress in May or June. As Schultze put it, "[T]he Administration will be accused of deliberately presenting a 'phony' budget withholding facts from the public, etc."[73] Memos at the time indicate that there was a prevailing view that even the $60 billion defense figure was too low. Concerning the $110 billion and $115 billion overall budget figures, Gardner Ackley later stated that "we knew damned well that neither of these figures was in the least bit relevant, and the real figure they were talking about—that military program which had been approved—was represented by a substantially larger figure."[74] Budget decisions and hard policy choices were delayed; a debate about national priorities could continue to be avoided or at least deferred. Therefore, it became much more difficult to plan for the future and establish priorities, both militarily and domestically. As Charles Schultze remarked, "[I]t *was* hard to get [the president] to take a long-run view of the budget implications of anything."[75]

Why was Vietnam so unique? Military expenditures during wartime are often underestimated. All wars are costly, and Vietnam was no exception. In fact, the Korean War required supplemental requests of $45 billion—a greater sum in a much shorter span than Vietnam. But during the Korean conflict the Truman administration enacted many wartime economic measures. In contrast, the Johnson administration was not willing to admit the costs of the war or cut back on domestic spending. Charles Schultze did not see the costs themselves as the problem. Rather, "The real problem here was, for all sorts of reasons, an unwillingness to admit publicly the war was going to cost a lot more than this."[76] One analyst noted: "Vietnam, despite its escalation, remained a small war militarily. But it was a very expensive war. It taxed the country's financial resources more severely than it strained its physical resources."[77] For the first time, the United States was fighting a war without any controls on its economy.

JOHNSON'S FIRST PRIORITY: POLITICAL FEASIBILITY

Lyndon Johnson did not follow the advice of his economists for fiscal restraint because it was politically convenient to put the lower defense figure into the FY 1967 budget sent to Congress. Congress was reluctant to increase taxes. Johnson believed, therefore, that any request for a tax increase would be politically untenable on Capitol Hill. At best, a tax hike would be agreed to by Congress only at the expense of major cuts in his Great Society program. Most importantly, senators and congressmen were not given any rationale for raising taxes, because the administration would not acknowledge the accelerated costs and scope of the war. Johnson claimed that Congress would not go along with a tax increase in early 1966, but any reluctance was understandable on the part of Congress since the cost of the war was unknown. Where was the economic justification?

At the same time, Johnson was not willing to cut back on the military commitment. Thus, he avoided any hard economic choices in order to maintain political support, at least for the short term. The war required economic policies that were politically undesirable. According to Gardner Ackley, once he and his economic colleagues presented their advice to the president, the "question no longer was 'What would be the best thing to do?' but immediately, 'Is that feasible?'"[78] The president's first priority was whether he could get the necessary votes and what political maneuvers were necessary as well as how much he would have to give up to get it. Ackley noted that he once tried to convince Johnson that the tax increase proposal was politically feasible and could be sold to Congress. Johnson replied contemptuously: "Who makes the political judgments around here? I pay you to give me economic advice."[79]

By the beginning of 1966, either the war, the Great Society, or the economy had to give. Schultze noted that the president did not want to sacrifice his domestic programs, just as they were getting started: "It would have been a perfect excuse for the conservatives to say, 'Well, we're in a war economy. These are all great, but let's postpone them.'"[80] The tendency in Congress would have been to go after the new programs rather than the older programs with established political constituencies. Johnson later talked of his dilemma when he tried to get congressional support for a tax increase in 1967: "[I]n the case of the tax bill the Democratic party was split. On the one hand, many conservative Democrats were saying to me: 'We'll go with you on the tax increase, but only if you wrap it in the American flag as a wartime measure and use the revenue solely for military expenditures and not for your Great Society programs.' On the other hand, several liberals were saying: 'We'll go with you, but only if you use all the revenue to build the Great Society programs, not for any of your military efforts.'"[81]

Given the political commitment of previous administrations as well as Johnson's personal pledge not to "lose Vietnam" and his stake in the Great Society programs, the economy was inadvertently the victim. The long-term result of the economic problems was that much of Johnson's domestic agenda was weakened due to a lack of financial resources. Johnson had no intention of hurting economic prosperity, but he refused to take the medicine prescribed by his economists or to be straight with the country about the extent of the escalation. Often it is just easier politically to make policy by inaction than take a specific course of action such as tax increases, cutting back on programs, or reducing a military commitment. He hoped that continued economic prosperity would solve his dilemma and make it possible to afford both guns and butter. He had made it work until then, so it was politically difficult for Johnson to change course in spite of the growing economic evidence. One reason not to follow the prescriptive advice of his economists in late 1965 and 1966 was that a tax increase would slow down the economy. Those same economic advisers had advised him for the past two years that the economy needed continued stimulation. He had even been told that the expected increase in military spending was a positive development. The prosperity of his first two years had been built on fiscal stimulation, tax cuts, and tight budgets. Given Johnson's policy of both guns and butter, turning down his economists' advice was almost inevitable. He had boxed himself in with his policy of having it all.

Although Johnson was clearly concerned about the political feasibility of a tax increase, to argue that he deliberately chose to sabotage the economy rather than fight for higher taxes is mistaken. So is the notion that there was nothing he could have done about it. Anderson and Hazleton argued that "[Johnson's] refusal for a year and a half to seek a general tax increase was predicated on his belief that it could not be obtained from Congress: he perceived a clear lack of agreement of specific policy goals (which was compounded by other factors, especially the Vietnam War) such as reducing inflationary pressures by an income tax increase. In all, the struggle over the tax surcharge illustrated the importance of politics in macroeconomic policy management."[82] However, the problem that this analysis ignores is that Johnson was too often deceptive and hid information. So he handcuffed himself from trying to create any type of political consensus for economic policies. He never really tried to get any agreement on specific policy goals—either with the economy or with Vietnam. Had Johnson been willing to go before Congress and the American people and been honest about the scope and costs of the war, the necessary economic measures could have gained a political urgency that they never had in 1966 and 1967. Had he been forthcoming with his own economists in 1965 about the extent of the escalation in Vietnam, fiscal precautions might have prevented much of the subsequent economic damage. Also, President Johnson might have been able to sell the public on the necessary economic sacrifices.

The Post-Vietnam BDM Study argued, "The chain of events that occurred was not inevitable. Candid public discussion of the goals of the political/military programs, supported by a committed political constituency, could have resulted in early economic sacrifices (i.e., increased taxation) to pay for the war. It was the political judgment at that time, however, and probably with considerable justification, that the public might not have supported administration policies had they been candidly articulated."[83] Had that support not been forthcoming, perhaps the war effort would have been rethought, and the United States might have gotten out much sooner. Without public candor the people might have been fooled for a while, but as the administration's credibility eroded, so, too, did the political support.

Many have argued, including the president himself, that had he gone to Congress, he would have had to cut back on the Great Society if he wanted to fight in Vietnam. That may well have been the case. But it would seem that as a result the economy would have been in much greater shape so that down the road economic prosperity might have provided a stronger financial base for the ambitious social programs. Instead, as most economists agree, the Vietnam War had dire economic consequences for the United States. The resulting surge in inflation and the subsequent budget deficits destroyed much of the economic prosperity upon which the Great Society was to be built.

GUNS AND BUTTER

It is important to understand that from 1961 to 1965, the United States was able to have both guns and butter. Until 1965 a strong military and major social programs—guns and butter—were not incompatible policies. While there had been references to "guns and butter" in the press after the July 28 escalation decision, the public perception that President Johnson was pursuing a specific policy of guns and butter really came with his State of the Union address on January 12, 1966, when he asserted that the United States could afford both the Vietnam War and the Great Society programs: "I have not halted progress in the new and vital Great Society programs in order to finance the costs of our efforts in Southeast Asia."[84] At that point, most, like Henry Fowler, felt that "[t]he 'guns and butter' issues [sic] is one that has been under constant debate since the Vietnam War assumed the major proportions and the magnitude of, let's say, 1966."[85] But in terms of what the president and his administration were attempting to accomplish domestically and in Vietnam, guns versus butter was an overriding issue in 1965. It was just not much of a public issue until 1966. Until then, the strong economic optimism led almost everyone in the administration, from the president on down, to believe that they could have it all, especially when the war was expanded gradually, and the future escalation plans were downplayed. The BDM Study noted: "The truth of the matter was that the economy could have afforded guns and butter at the same time only not quite as much of each as Johnson tried to provide. Before expenditures were taken as a given, the administration had to choose between excessive demand (i.e., inflationary pressure), a cutback in either private sector spending or the government's domestic programs, or a 'pay as you go' tax base. Not coming to terms with these trade-offs soon enough led ultimately to the unfortunate combination of all three undesirable options: cut-backs in the War on Poverty and other Great Society programs, increased taxes, *and* inflation."[86]

The administration developed no plans either to finance a major war or to keep it small (in terms of a conventional conflict). At the same time, there was no plan to pay for the war either. Economic measures were enacted only in reaction to the situation, not with any forethought. Johnson would not stake his political clout and persuasion on getting Congress to go along with up-front financing of the war. As a result, in 1966 and 1967 the administration paid attention to the budget but not the economy itself. In the broad canvas of the Cold War, the Vietnam conflict was a sideshow—and, as such, the administration tried to finance it on the side. Eliot Janeway noted: "One of the advantages of secretiveness about the planned scope of the war had been presumed to be avoidance of inflationary speculation, crippling controls and market crisis. But when the anticipated benefits of a small war and a big boom turned into the actual burdens of a big war and a costly squeeze, the economy was whipsawed between the inflation of costs and the deflation of earnings."[87]

Johnson had been consistently concerned with the costs of the escalation. On June 11, 1965, he stated: "We must delay and deter the North Vietnamese and Viet Cong as much as we can, and as simply as we can, without going all out. When we grant General Westmoreland's request, it means that we get in deeper and it is harder to get out . . . . We must determine which course gives us the maximum protection at the least cost."[88] He wanted to escalate as cheaply as possible to preserve his political strength and maneuverability, thus allowing himself to have both guns and butter. McNamara and McGeorge Bundy argued privately that any admission of the war's true cost would severely cripple his domestic programs and doom any more Great Society legislation before Congress. It is important to remember that while the Great Society programs had been authorized by Congress, and much of the start-up costs appropriated, the major brunt of the spending would come down the road, so much of the President's domestic agenda remained at stake.

Gardner Ackley emphasized, "Clearly [LBJ] wanted to have both [guns and butter]; and he felt that it was wrong, not only in 1966, but also in 1967 and early 1968, to say that simply because you were having to spend more for guns that it would have to come out of programs for the poor, and out of education, and all the Great Society programs. This just really hurt."[89] Ackley added that there were "a lot of brave words about how our economy is strong and big, and how we can do what we need to do. When we helped to write those words, we always had in mind, 'Yes, but it may take a tax increase, probably will.' In which case it's absolutely correct: you can have both guns and butter if you are willing to pay for them. I guess he knew that."[90] That Johnson knew it only seemed to make him try harder to avoid the costs of both guns and butter. Clearly, he wanted to fight a war at the minimum cost so he could afford both.

As Charles Schultze noted, Johnson did a masterful job of creating the Great Society but then botched its financing and long-term implementation: "So, in one sense, Johnson laid the groundwork for years of progress at an immediate cost, and far be it from me to say that the benefits weren't greater than the costs. It is just frustrating as the devil. You get annoyed and mad and frustrated and disgusted at how chaotic and sloppy some of it was, precisely because you're laying Vietnam of top of it and trying to nickel-and-dime these programs."[91] Eventually, the president lost control of events and policies, in Vietnam and at home.

Not until December 1966 did Johnson admit that the Administration had underestimated the costs of the war by about $10 billion (which was about 10 percent of the total U.S. budget, comparable to an underestimation of well over $170 billion in today's terms). As the economy worsened, and inflation surged again after a brief slowdown in early 1967, Johnson finally asked Congress in

August 1967 for a 10 percent tax surcharge. It was eventually signed into law on June 28, 1968, but with a presidential commitment to cut $6 billion from domestic programs. Ultimately, Johnson was forced to do what he had tried so hard to avoid and at a considerable—and many would argue, much higher—cost. He became a victim of his own policy of downplaying the conflict and the U.S. military role in it.

NOTES

1. John W. Sloan, "President Johnson, the Council of Economic Advisers, and the Failure to Raise Taxes in 1966 and 1967," p. 92. See also Erwin C. Hargrove and Samuel A. Morley (eds.), *The President and the Council of Economic Advisers: Interviews with CEA Chairmen*, p. 218.

2. See Sloan, "President Johnson, The Council of Economic Advisers, and the Failure to Raise Taxes in 1966 and 1967," p. 93, for an expanded analysis of this argument. He noted, "For Johnson to have abruptly changed the direction of fiscal policy from stimulation to restraint in December 1965, the intellectual ground would have had to have been nurtured. The CEA failed to do this. Much to its regret, the CEA found that it had to educate Johnson about the problems of inflation in 1966 and 1967."

3. July 30, 1965, memo to the president from Gardner Ackley, "Economic Aspects of Vietnam," in Johnson Library: Council of Economic Advisers Administrative History, vol. 2, Part 1, Box 1.

4. Ibid.

5. Testimony of Charles Schultze, U.S. Congress, Joint Economic Committee, *Hearings before the Subcommittee on Fiscal Policy: "Fiscal Policy Issues of the Coming Decade,"* July 22, 1965, p. 76.

6. Ibid. p. 88.

7. See testimony of Gardner Ackley during hearings of Joint Economic Committee, *Hearings before the Subcommittee on Fiscal Policy: "Fiscal Policy Issues of the Coming Decade,"* July 20, 1965, p. 11.

8. David Halberstam, "How the Economy Went Haywire," *The Atlantic Monthly*, September 1972, pp. 56–60. Edwin L. Dale Jr., "The Inflation Goof," in *The New Republic*, January 4, 1969, pp. 16–17.

9. Halberstam, "How the Economy Went Haywire," p. 56.

10. Dale, "The Inflation Goof," p. 17.

11. Gardner Ackley. "LBJ's Game Plan," in *The Atlantic Monthly*, December 1972, p. 46. This was written as a reply to Halberstam's September 1972 article.

12. Ibid. p. 46.

13. Ibid. pp. 46–47.

14. Ibid. p. 47. One can only assume that Ackley meant that after October he then understood the extent of the Vietnam decisions and received the necessary information of which he had been ignorant prior to October.

15. See Donald F. Kettl, "The Economic Education of Lyndon Johnson: Guns, Butter, and Taxes," in Robert A. Divine (ed.), *The Johnson Years*, vol. 2, pp. 54–55.

16. Johnson Library: Gardner Ackley Oral History, March 7, 1974, pp. 13–14.

17. Johnson Library: Bureau of the Budget Administrative History, p. 61.

18. Ibid. p. 61.

19. October 19, 1965, memo from Charles Schultze to the president, "Fall Budget Review," in the National Archives: RG51, Series 52.3—"Midyear Review: 1966 Budget" folder.

20. Ibid.

21. Council of Economic Advisers Administrative History, Chapter 2, p. 12.

22. Ackley Oral History, Interview 2, March 7, 1974, p.1.

23. Ibid. p. 2.

24. April 28, 1965, memo from Ackley to the president, "Steel Report," in the National Archives: RG51, series 61.1a, Box 131, E3-1/1, "Council of Economic Advisers 1965" folder.

25. Rowland Evans and Robert Novak, "Inside Report . . . A Tax Increase?," *Washington Post*, September 2, 1965, p. A21.

26. September 9, 1965, memo from Ackley to the president in the Johnson Library: White House Files, Box 357, PR18, Folder August 1, 1965–September 11, 1965.

27. August 1965 staff memorandum (no specific date), "Notes for Economic and Financial Policy Group on the Implications of a Defense Buildup for Overall Economic Policy," in Johnson Library: Department of the Treasury Administrative History, Box 1—vol. 1, Part 2, Folder 1, Chapter 5, pp. 14–17. The Economic and Financial Policy Group was formed in early 1965 under the leadership of Frederick Deming, undersecretary for monetary affairs, to examine, on an informal basis, matters of interest to the Treasury in the economic and financial area.

28. September 8, 1965, note for the president from Gardner Ackley in the National Archives: RG51, series 61.1a, Box 131, E3-1/1, Council of Economic Advisers 1965 Folder.

29. Ibid.

30. Ackley interview, in Robert Warren Stevens, *Vain Hopes, Grim Realities: The Economic Consequences of the Vietnam War*, p. 69.

31. Quoted in Hobart Rowan, *Self-Inflicted Wounds: From LBJ's Guns and Butter to Reagan's Voodoo Economics*, p. 10.

32. Johnson Library: Henry Fowler Oral History, Interview 5, July 31, 1969, p. 3.

33. See Rowan, *Self-Inflicted Wounds*, p. 9.

34. Fowler Oral History, pp. 4–5.

35. Johnson Library: Charles Schultze Oral History, Interview 1, March 28, 1969, p. 27.

36. The Heineman Report, cited in Larry Berman, *The Office of Management and Budget and the Presidency, 1921–1979*, p. 86.

37. Eliot Janeway, *The Economics of Crisis: War, Politics, and the Dollar*, p. 280.

38. Schultze Oral History, Interview 2, p. 11.

39. October 11, 1965, Ackley to Schultze memo, "CEA Report on Price Situation and Outlook," in the National Archives: RG51, Series 61.1a, Box 131, E3-6, "Prices, Consumption, and Cost-of-living" folder. In his memo, Ackley did not mention the impact of Vietnam or defense spending at all.

40. Ackley Oral History, Interview 2, March 7, 1974, p. 2.

41. Schultze Oral History, April 10, 1969, p. 4.

42. November 8, 1965, memo to Charles Schultze from the Office of Budget Review, "New Obligational Authority, by Agency" in the National Archives: RG51, series 61.15, Box 37, 1966 Budget Review folder.

43. September 11, 1965, memo, "Notes on Cost Reduction for Cabinet Meeting of September 13, 1965," drafted by the Budget Bureau (apparently by Schultze) in the National Archives: RG51, series 61.1a, Box 265, F3-2—"Cost Reduction" folder.

44. November 15, 1965, memo from Henry Fowler in Johnson Library: Cabinet Papers File, Box 4, November 19, 1965, meeting, folder 2, pp. 1–2.

45. "Notes of a Telephone Conversation," November 18, 1965, Fowler Papers, Box 8B, as quoted in Lloyd C. Gardner, *Pay Any Price: Lyndon Johnson and the Wars for Vietnam*, p. 264.

46. Dewey Daane during interview of Gardner Ackley (Daane was an interviewer) in Hargrove and Morley, *The President and the Council of Economic Advisers*, p. 249.

47. Ibid.

48. Summary of November 23, 1965, meeting sent from Harris to Charles Schultze on December 16, 1965, the National Archives: RG51, series 61.1a, Box 265 - E3, "The Economy and Economic Affairs in General, 1965" folder.

49. Johnson Library: Joseph Barr Oral History, Tape 1, p. 25.

50. Okun interview in Hargrove and Morley, *The President and the Council of Economic Advisers*, pp. 295–296.

51. Ibid. p. 250.

52. See Kettl, "The Economic Education of Lyndon Johnson," p. 62.

53. Ackley interview, in Hargrove and Morley, *The President and the Council of Economic Advisers*, p. 248.

54. December 9, 1965, memo from McNamara to the president—Subject: Defense Dept. Budget for FY 1967 and Supplemental Appropriation for 1966, Johnson Library: Department of Defense Agency file in the National Security File, vol. 3, p. 1.

55. See November 23, 1965, Budget Bureau memo, "1966 Budget Situation (Background Information)," in National Archives, Series 61.15, Box 11, "Economic Assumptions" folder. It is not clear who wrote the memo but appears to have come from Schultze.

56. December 9, 1965, memo from McNamara to the president, pp. 1–2.

57. December 7, 1965, memo from McNamara to the president, "Military and Political Actions Recommended for SVN," in *The Pentagon Papers*, Gravel edition, vol. 4, pp. 623–624.

58. January 4, 1967, memo from Ackley to the president in Johnson Library: CF BE file, as quoted in James L. Cochrane, "The Johnson Administration: Moral Suasion Goes to War," in Crauford D. Goodwin (ed.), *Exhortation and Controls: The Search for a Wage-Price Policy 1945–1971*, p. 273.

59. Schultze Oral History, April 10, 1969, p. 8.

60. Robert S. McNamara, *In Retrospect: The Tragedy and Lessons of Vietnam*, p. 222.

61. December 17, 1966, memo from Office of Budget Review to director of the Bureau of the Budget, in the National Archives: RG51, Series 61.1—Defense Estimates, 1966 folder.

62. See Hargrove and Morley, *The President and the Council of Economic Advisers*, p. 219.

63. December 26, 1965, memo from Gardner Ackley to the president, in Johnson Library: Confidential File, FI2-4, Box 42. Fowler, Schultze, and Ackley had received a draft memo from three of their top aides, Charles Zwick (deputy director of the BOB), Arthur Okun (a member of the CEA), and Robert A. Wallace (assistant secretary of the Treasury). They warned that price increases would be much higher than expected. The memo then urged raising personal and corporate income taxes in 1966 to deal with the acceleration of price increases. (December 23, 1965, memo to Fowler, Schultze and Ackley in the National Archives: Series 61.1a, Box 265, E3-1 folder.)

At first, Fowler refused to sign Troika memos or joint memos with Ackley that urged tax increases. (See Arthur Okun interview in Hargrove and Morley, *The President and the Council of Economic Advisers*, p. 301.)

64. Telex from Larry Levinson to the president, December 29, 1965, in Johnson Library: White House Confidential File, FI 4 Folder in Kettl, "The Economic Education of Lyndon Johnson," p. 61.

65. Ackley Oral History, March 7, 1974, p. 42.

66. Johnson Library: William Bundy unpublished manuscript, chapter 33, p. 26.

67. Schultze Oral History, Interview 2, pp. 17–18.

68. Memo from Califano to the president, December 23, 1965, in Johnson Library: EX FG 110, December 4, 1965–January 26, 1966, File, as quoted in Cochrane, "The Johnson Administration," pp. 240–241.

69. December 27, 1965, memo from Schultze to the president, in Johnson Library: White House Confidential File, FI2-4, Box 42.

70. Ibid. Schulze also wrote: "I agree with Secretary Fowler . . . that proposing a general tax increase in January would not be wise. At the same time, I am firmly convinced that with defense expenditures in the $60 billion range a general tax increase will eventually be necessary. In these circumstances, a *two-stage fiscal strategy appears to be most appropriate.*"

71. James Cochrane noted, "The [accelerated corporate tax payments] caused many firms to go into the money market to raise cash for advance tax payments while the Fed was tightening the market, helping to set the stage for the 'credit crunch' of 1966." (Cochrane, "The Johnson Administration," p. 241.)

72. Arthur Okun, *The Political Economy of Prosperity*, p. 70.

73. December 27, 1965, memo from Schultze to the president, in Johnson Library: Confidential File, FI2-4, Box 42.

74. Ackley interview in Hargrove and Morley, *The President and the Council of Economic Advisers*, p. 248.

75. Schultze Oral History, Interview 2, p. 48.

76. Ibid. p. 12.

77. Janeway, *The Economics of Crisis*, p. 280.

78. Ackley interview, in Hargrove and Morley, *The President and the Council of Economic Advisers*, p. 224.

79. Ibid. p. 225.

80. Schultze Oral History, Interview 2, p. 17.

81. Lyndon Baines Johnson, *The Vantage Point*, p. 443.

82. James E. Anderson and Jared E. Hazleton, *Managing Macroeconomic Policy: The Johnson Presidency*, pp. 238–39.

83. Johnson Library: BDM Corporation, *The Strategic Lessons Learned in Vietnam*, vol. 4, section 4, p. 31.

84. *Public Papers of the Presidents, Lyndon Baines Johnson, 1966*, p. 4.

85. Fowler Oral History, Interview 5, July 31, 1969, p. 2.

86. BDM Corporation, *The Strategic Lessons Learned in Vietnam*, vol. 4, section 4, p. 2.

87. Janeway, *The Economics of Crisis*, pp. 295–96.

88. Bromley Smith's summary notes of NSC meeting June 11, 1965, in Johnson Library: NSC Meetings File, vol. 3, Tab 34, Box 1.

89. Ackley Oral History, Interview 2, March 7, 1974, p. 16.

90. Ibid. p. 42.

91. Schultze Oral History, Interview 2, p. 28.

Chapter 10

Guns or Butter and the Study of the Vietnam War

DOMESTIC POLITICS AND FOREIGN POLICY-MAKING

Many reasons for the U.S. failure in Vietnam have been put forth in the past 25 years. Some, in particular, have pointed out that *how* the war escalated was a major reason for the tragedy of Vietnam. The military was not given a free hand to prosecute the war to its fullest; strong domestic support was lacking, due, in part, to confusing war aims and due to the increasing lack of credibility by Lyndon Johnson and his administration; and the country was never placed on a war footing and society never rallied around the war effort. Many of these contributions to the American failure came about, in part, because of Johnson's attempts to have both guns and butter. It is clear from both the documentary evidence and the recollections of Johnson and some of his close advisers that domestic politics played a very important role in the president's decisions to escalate in Vietnam. I have tried to show that it is as important to understand how the United States went to war as it is to determine why the war occurred.

Most economists and economic analyses have concluded that the Vietnam War had very negative consequences for the economy. The economy overheated as a result of staying with the policy of fiscal stimulation too long. Many political analyses of the escalation of the war point out that the president's desire to protect his domestic programs and legislative agenda were very important priorities. The president and his top advisers kept the economic and domestic planners in the dark about the extent of the military expansion, and Johnson continually downplayed the decisions to escalate in order to avoid a major debate on governmental priorities. The escalation decisions of 1965 were downplayed to such an extent that Lyndon Johnson was able to buy the time he sought to have almost all his Great Society programs authorized and appropriated. Johnson's economic and social priorities were critical in those two years in shaping how the president took the country to war. He successfully avoided a national debate about how much of the nation's resources should be allocated to the war and how much to his domestic agenda.

In analyzing the way in which President Johnson chose to escalate American involvement in Vietnam, it is important to understand the forces and factors that influenced and shaped his actions. What circumstances limited the decision to expand the American military involvement? The choice to escalate, with all its antecedent forces and limitations, led to new decisions—certain doors opened, while others closed—and required implementation. Johnson had to contend with the key elements in domestic politics: the Congress, the press, public opinion, the bureaucracy, powerful elites, and interest groups. While all of these groups are critical to the political process and the ultimate shape of the policy, it is the President and the nature of his "choice" that usually put things in motion and set the national agenda. Many factors help shape the "choice" a president faces: the nature of the policy-making process; domestic political values; the decision maker's perceptions, values, and belief system; as well as the nature of the international system. Most of the primary evidence clearly demonstrates that the guns-and-butter dilemma played a crucial role in the president's decisions. Therefore it is important to emphasize the various factors and pressures that created or fed that dilemma. For Lyndon Johnson, his political goals—creating a legislative program that would build a Great Society at home and halting communist aggression abroad—were the greatest factors in determining the nature of his choice to escalate.

In their book on Vietnam, Leslie Gelb and Richard Betts made the following point: "[Decision makers] saw no acceptable alternatives to what they were doing. They really believed they had no choice . . . . To deduce lessons from this experience, one must ask what it was about the system of decisionmaking that took choice away."[1] Therefore, the fact that the United States went to war to stop the spread of communism in Southeast Asia was almost inevitable. They argued that the system did what it was supposed to: "produce a policy responsive more to the majority and the center than to the minority."[2] Most American politicians, bureaucrats, military men, business leaders, interest groups, members of the press, and the American public in general subscribed to the theory of containment. So, the act of fighting to save South Vietnam was the natural result of the containment consensus. Johnson was carrying out a policy for which there was great support in the country and in Washington. The country's containment consensus was a very powerful driving force in American foreign policy.

Therefore, Johnson felt that he had no choice but to commit American military forces to halting communism in Southeast Asia. As I have demonstrated, however, President Johnson was the key figure in the decision to go to war in Vietnam. Even if he seemingly had little choice about whether to go to war, as president he could assert his control over how the United States would fight such a war.

Johnson's dilemma was that an all-out pursuit of war in Vietnam while trying to achieve the Great Society would prompt a fight in Congress over priorities and resource allocations. From his days as Senate majority leader, Johnson knew that he would need the support of both liberal and conservative Democrats for his foreign policy goals and his agenda at home. He could not afford to have his domestic programs held up by those who wished a tougher stance in Vietnam; nor could he afford to give up being tough on communism for those who wanted more resources devoted to the domestic agenda. Johnson had many political flanks to cover. Former Pentagon official Daniel Ellsberg has written that one of the "paradoxical features of U.S. escalating decisions" was the "conflict between domestic political requirements on outcomes and domestic political constraints on means."[3] Therefore, Johnson tried to walk a fine line with Vietnam, appearing tough on communism without being a warmonger. He introduced troops into Vietnam incrementally and with no fanfare—conducting a war on the side yet never calling it a war as such. The initial investment of troops and money in 1965 ensured that Congress would continue to provide the needed resources in order to protect the men and lives already invested in the war effort. The sunken costs made it more difficult to retreat from further escalation.

Governmental decisions and policies are usually the product of a complex set of variables. Some lend themselves easily to explanations; others do not. But it is particularly important to understand the context within which a decision or policy is formulated. The international context was clearly important to understand American foreign policy in the mid-1960s and "why" the United States intervened in Vietnam and why Southeast Asia was considered of vital interest for the United States. In 1965 the strategic value of Vietnam and the overall foreign policy goals were questioned by only a few people in Washington. That the United States would have to use military force to deter the communists and protect South Vietnam was accepted at the end of 1964 by the president and most of his top advisers as inevitable. The ensuing debate was over how to use that military force; how many men to deploy and when; how much of a commitment the American people should be asked to make; and how the country should be presented with the war, its aims, and its requirements and sacrifices.

DECISION MAKING AND THE ECONOMIC PICTURE

In the end, Johnson did not ask for a nationwide commitment. General Westmoreland later stated, "As a result of this [the guns-and-butter policy]—contrary to Mr. Kennedy's charge 'we'll bear any burden, pay any price'—the only ones that bore a burden, paid a price and made sacrifice were those on the battlefields, who were mainly the poor man's sons, and their loved ones at home. The average American, the war didn't touch him; except he was exposed to the war through television."[4] A greater share of the fighting burden shifted to the young and poor because the Administration increased U.S. forces through the draft, not the reserves or the guard. The poor and unskilled bore the brunt of the war, in terms of not only deaths but also lost opportunities because of the cutbacks in the Great Society programs and because they got fewer jobs in war industries than skilled workers and were the first to lose jobs in the war-related recession of 1970–1971.[5] Only after the price of the war became known, in terms of lives and financial costs, did the Vietnam policy begin to lose public support. But the administration knew the extent of those costs early on.

The president's policy of downplaying the escalation resulted, in large measure, from his strong desire to insulate the economy and his legislative program from the political ramifications of a guns-or-butter choice. Because the economists and budget planners were isolated from the Vietnam policies, they had no true understanding of the nature of the escalation and its potential impact on the economy and the president's domestic program. Given the thrust of the economic policy—strong fiscal stimulation—it was important to have a complete picture of all the U.S. commitments and future plans because the risks were substantial if the economy overheated.

Economic officials were also hampered by the process of military planning and budgeting prior to the 1970s. Military policy was often outside the normal policy review and determination of the nation's priorities and resources. Thus, the Pentagon had a very powerful hold over policy making because of its draw upon resources and the nature of the budget process. This was unlike today's military budgets, which are part of an overall package presented to Congress by the Office of Management and Budget (OMB). Today, the director of OMB is viewed as the architect of an overall budget, of which military spending is an integral part. This was not the case in 1965, when the military budget, determined by the defense secretary after input from the military services and Pentagon agencies, was primarily an addition to the civilian budget. In 1965 neither the military nor domestic budgeting systems had caught up to the fact that a war was being fought, and there was a lack of both comprehensive and alternative thinking and analysis regarding Vietnam.

As powerful an agency as the Bureau of the Budget was in the Johnson administration—by creating, organizing, and evaluating proposals as well as coordinating the president's programs and agenda—its activities did not extend into foreign policy in general and the military budget in particular. In 1965 the defense budget was clearly McNamara's. There was little interaction between the Budget Bureau and the Defense Department. Robert McNamara noted in 1965 that the Bureau of the Budget was not making any decisions that had anything to do with the Department of Defense. As one analyst noted, "It was clear, at any rate, that the bureau did not have the hold on the McNamara Pentagon that it had on other agencies."[6]

Charles Schultze stated in 1967, "I do not and should not share responsibility for the determination of how many men we need in Vietnam, nor how many planes. That is not my responsibility. In translating those determinations into the budgetary impact, of course I do have a role."[7] But such a determination works only if the president asks that of his budget director, and the military gives the budget director useful estimates. Since realistic defense figures did not come out until December 1965, economic planners like Schultze were bound to give poor advice. Schultze noted that the key player was the president. Referring to the defense budget, he commented: "The Budget Bureau can effectively dig into and review what the President wants it to review."[8]

Lyndon Johnson believed in late 1964 that his administration had to take advantage quickly of his great election mandate. He felt he would never be as popular as he was in the immediate aftermath of his victory. He wanted to exploit that popularity—both at home and with respect to Vietnam. Johnson pushed very hard for his legislative agenda at the beginning of 1965. He could not afford to lose Vietnam, but he could at least buy time—keep the communists from winning in South Vietnam as he built his Great Society. Johnson felt the pressure of time and politics, so he wanted to create as much as possible as soon as possible, noting to his cabinet in January 1965, "Every day that I am in office, I lose part of my power."[9] This was a constant domestic theme throughout 1965 and into 1966. When Senator Mike Mansfield in early 1966 called on the administration to consolidate rather than send up another big program to Capitol Hill because of the tremendous financial costs of the war, Johnson replied, "Consolidation is another word for quitting. We can't quit now. This may be the last chance we have to get some of these things done."[10] So, even in the face of an overheated economy and a greatly escalating war, Johnson continued to claim that the nation could afford increases in defense and in domestic programs.

Throughout 1964 and 1965 administration economists promoted fiscal stimulation and growth in order to create more government revenues, which would, in turn, expand the economy and finance the president's domestic agenda. This new economic orthodoxy (which began under President Kennedy) emphasized that the economy as a whole should be in balance and de-emphasized whether the budget was in balance.[11] This decrease in attention to the federal budget, combined with the lack of information on defense spending, created a major blind spot for the administration's economists. They continued to stimulate the economy but did not question the consequences of the expanded war in Vietnam. Had the White House not kept the economic and domestic planners in the dark about the Vietnam policy, they most likely would have rethought the policy of growth and overstimulation and also questioned the long-range effects of a major commitment in Vietnam.

As it was, the expansion of the war in early 1965 planted the seeds for inflation and the competition for resources between domestic and military needs. The war machine was primed by the increase in military orders as early as the spring of 1965. While the negative effects of an overheated economy were not felt throughout society until 1966, the private sector began to experience the first pull of a guns-versus-butter competition in 1965. The military escalation occurred in a rapidly expanding economy with virtually no slack, so the economy overheated. Admittedly, the domestic and economic planners underestimated how much a military buildup affects the economy, but they had clearly been deceived about the extent of that buildup.

Johnson's policy of trying to have both guns and butter by isolating the economic decisions from the military decisions did not work because foreign and domestic policy making cannot be separated to such a degree. There are a mutual dependence and an interrelation between the two. He chose to keep the war and its costs "low-key" for political reasons. Johnson failed as a leader because he would not make hard policy choices, which is the essence of leadership. He also failed by his own standards: both the war in Vietnam and the Great Society were ultimately unsuccessful—and a significant factor in those failures was that he tried to have both at the same time and would not cut back on either. By the end of his term, over half a million American soldiers were in Vietnam, while at home there were cuts in the Great Society programs, tax increases, and inflation.

THE LIMITED MILITARY ESCALATION

Johnson tried to buy time with his incremental escalation in Vietnam—time to keep the economic growth intact and time to get his legislative programs appropriated (not just approved). Larry Berman has argued the following about the July 28 decision to escalate: "The primary source documents show that Lyndon Johnson was *not* misled by advisers, nor did he cow them into submission. Instead, he created conditions under which all options could be presented (but not analyzed) and then used his great talents to forge a marginal political and military consensus. He utilized the advisory process to legitimize what he knew would later be characterized as a 'butter and guns' decision. He did *not* act indecisively."[12] The butter-and-guns conflict seemed to dominate the president's approach to the conflict in Vietnam. His ambitious domestic agenda had a great impact on American policy in Vietnam—in particular, with the goal of avoiding the guns-and-butter dilemma that the war and Johnson's domestic goals made inevitable.

Johnson's intentions and decision-making process seemed consistent throughout 1965. The president wanted a war that was as cheap as possible so that there were no policy debate and little disruption of the U.S. economy. Admittedly, this flew in the face of increased combat forces rather than greater reliance on the air war, which was a cheaper military policy. But Johnson had little faith in the military efficacy of bombing, so he tried to get his military preference, ground forces (which would prevent the loss of Vietnam, in his view), on the cheap. Since he believed that he would be forced to turn to ground forces in any event, it made most sense to control how and when they were deployed—when the nation was not yet focused on events in Vietnam. So he scaled down the military requests and maintained the perception that the escalation of the war was limited. Ostensibly, the ends were the same, but Johnson pursued the conflict with limited means. His policies would be cheap and cost less economically and politically: economically, by avoiding raising taxes or paying the higher costs of the reserves and the guard; and politically, by avoiding a debate in Congress and in American society. William Bundy called it "an all-out limited war," meaning an open-ended commitment, but with restrictions on the nature of the war itself.[13]

Secrecy and downplaying the escalatory steps were consistent strategies throughout 1964 and 1965, beginning with the Tonkin Gulf affair. President Johnson was not tricked into escalating, nor did the United States stumble unwittingly into a quagmire. Almost every decision to expand both the nature of the American military role and the number of U.S. forces was taken after deliberation by the president with his military and foreign policy advisers. They discussed tactical questions, never challenging the necessity of the U.S. commitment. One might question whether the debate was very meaningful, but there is no doubt that the president was presented with clear evidence that escalation would be costly and lengthy in order to achieve even the smallest measure of success. The only occasion on which the Administration did not have much debate at all was the original decision to deploy the two marine battalions to Danang in early March.

The strategy of graduated escalation was, by definition, incremental and certainly compounded the guns-versus-butter dilemma, and the incremental nature of the ground force decisions seemed closely tied to political objectives. While civilian officials in the Pentagon may have thought they could simply turn up the air war a notch or two and find the threshold of deterrence that would cause North Vietnam to cease its support of the Viet Cong in the South, the president was concerned about the perception that the country would be in for a long war and the effect that would have at home, most particularly in terms of the economic costs, public opinion, and congressional support for his domestic policy agenda. At each point of escalation, the president chose to limit the perception of that decision, claiming there had been no change of policy.

In many ways in late 1964 and early 1965 the military tactics and strategic options that were debated had been generated by the military and foreign affairs bureaucracy as a matter of course. Nothing major occurred until the president, with his own preconception of what was needed and how to achieve that, entered the decision-making arena and steered the process in the direction he wanted to go in Vietnam. He wanted to control that process by making it incremental and secretive in order to minimize the economic and political impact of the decisions and policies with respect to Vietnam that his administration was undertaking. This was a very muddled and ad hoc decision-making process that did not allow for much analysis of the costs (in terms of American lives, matériel, economic resources, and popular opinion) that would have to be borne in order to keep the Viet Cong from winning.

There was almost a sense of resignation by late July 1965: "[Johnson] regretted that we were embroiled in Vietnam. But we *are* there."[14] This raises the issue of the sunken costs trap: American men and American prestige and credibility had been invested, so that investment must be protected. Given the containment consensus, and, as Johnson put it, "the word of three Presidents that the United States would not permit this aggression to succeed," the president believed that he had no choice but to escalate, as no one saw any viable alternative to maintaining the American commitment in South Vietnam. But there was still no accounting of the necessary costs to stick to that commitment. William Bundy later argued: "As one looks back on it, the whole period from February through July falls into a consistent pattern of minimizing the significance of each separate move and letting the total speak for itself."[15] Paul Kattenburg, then a State Department analyst on Southeast Asia, echoed Bundy's conclusion much more bluntly: "The ingenious (or disingenious?) mind of our restless and deceptive president considered it vital that the United States and especially the Congress not 'go to war,' but 'find itself at war.'"[16]

A SLIPPERY SLOPE TO MILITARY ESCALATION?

A policy in which the United States would make only a minimal investment, one that just might turn the tide in Vietnam, seemed to pervade almost every escalatory decision through July 1965. An increase in the bombing sorties, an expansion of the target sets, even an eight-week air campaign were all cheap when compared to the perceived loss of American prestige and domestic political support if the United States were to withdraw. The same can be said for the slow and steady introduction of American ground forces: the initial deployment of a few marine brigades and then the change in their mission from defensive perimeter to active ground combat. There was the off chance that these small-scale escalatory steps might, after all, work. If one subscribes to the theory that the United States unintentionally ended up trapped in the quagmire of Vietnam, then this policy shift was gradual and unintentional, the result of incremental decision making and stopgap measures.[17]   One presidential adviser was quoted as saying later: "It was almost imperceptible, the way we got in . . . . There was no one move that you could call decisive, or irreversible, not even very many actions that you could argue against in isolation. Yet when you put it all together, there we were in a war on the Asian mainland, with nobody really putting up much of a squawk while we were doing it."[18]

Because the first combat troops were sent to Vietnam so soon after the beginning of the Rolling Thunder campaign, there seemed a clear correlation between the bombing and introduction of ground forces. But was the bombing decision the catalyst or the pretext for deploying combat forces? The speed with which Johnson sent in combat forces affirmed his preference for conventional and anti-guerrilla warfare. The president had given his advisers their wish; he tried the bombing but it seemed to have little impact. Thus, it was easy to take the next step—use of combat troops, which he had already come to believe was necessary. Those who support a straight incrementalism theory or the slippery-slope argument saw sustained bombing as the main goal and the introduction of ground forces as simply a natural outgrowth of the bombing commitment. Ground forces became necessary only because the airfields would need greater protection. The bombing begat the ground forces.[19]

Robert Gallucci put forth another view when he argued that the bombing was necessary in order to justify sending in ground forces and the subsequent increases in the number of American fighting men in Vietnam: "For those who had to concern themselves with the bounds of public opinion, the function of air power was to fail openly so that large scale losses of American lives on the ground in Asia could be justified."[20] Under this argument, the campaign of sustained bombing was simply a transition or a necessary prelude to the introduction of U.S. forces. The decision to bomb was, in effect, the decision for ground forces. This argument posits that for political reasons President Johnson had to build a rationale upon which he could send American soldiers to Vietnam. It was important and expedient to create a context that would allow for the introduction of combat forces as merely a logical extension of ongoing policy. This was underscored when President Johnson sent General Harold Johnson to Vietnam in early March to explore further military options, emphasizing that a request for more men would be looked upon favorably. This belies the arguments of some that the first deployment of combat troops was a onetime decision to meet a specific need and that the "attention of the major decisionmakers was still focused on the impending air war against North Vietnam which was expected to yield an early North Vietnamese response."[21]

When the marines were deployed to Danang, there was no debate about Vietnam. While some voices were raised against bombing, Congress held no hearings on Vietnam in February and March. One had to question whether the dissent that did exist, both in the government and outside, was so focused on the bombing policy that little attention was paid to the initial deployments of ground forces, which appeared quite limited. As Burke and Greenstein noted, one of the main obstacles to "clearly joined policy discussion which was built into the Johnson advisory process" was "the absence of forums in which contradictory viewpoints could be clarified, studied and debated. The questions raised by such skeptics as Humphrey, Mansfield, Ball, Taylor, Clifford and McCone were dissipated and diffused rather than addressed."[22] Also, all the dissent came up at different times—it was uncoordinated, unfocused, and never marshaled for one policy meeting. This was something like incremental dissent (which may be the by-product of an incremental policy process).

Much of the strategy and rationale behind the president's policy of escalation lay in his strong desire to insulate the American people from the impact of the conflict in Vietnam. Thus, Johnson wanted a policy that was "cheap." Johnson, who had little faith in the long-range success of bombing, once admitted, however, that one benefit to bombing North Vietnam was that it provided the United States with "maximum deterrence at minimum expense."[23] The decision to introduce limited combat forces would allow him to institute seemingly small, but important, defensive measures instead of sending over large numbers of troops and going to war. The country ended up in the same place, a land war in Asia, but got there differently.

The "quagmire" or "slippery slope" argument tends to be forgiving of the decision makers—they made mistakes, but they were unintentional ones. Johnson and his advisers, the argument goes, did not mean to take the country into a bloody war that would end in failure almost a decade later. Somehow, in the words of Robert McNamara, "unanticipated events forced us off our planned course."[24] In McNamara's memoirs it is interesting to note that at the end of two of his chapters he wrote, "And thus we continued our slide down the slippery slope" (Chapter 4) and "We were sinking into quicksand" (Chapter 7).[25] This implies that there were forces beyond the control of the American government. In discussing the knee-jerk embrace of the containment consensus and its uncritical application to South Vietnam or the arrogance of a superpower in misunderstanding the effectiveness and relevance of its military power or even what is necessary for a nation to commit itself to a war, McNamara-is probably right to imply that the United States went blindly and ill prepared to war in a place where it should not have. But there was much about the tragedy of Vietnam that was brought about by deliberate deceit and an attempt to subvert the political process of free and open debate about whether to go to war and how the country's resources—in terms of both lives and economic assets—should be allocated.

McNamara's argument implies that the administration led the country down a path it did not intend and, once it started down that path, could not stop. But most of the documentary evidence shows clearly that Johnson, McNamara, and most of the senior officials knew what path they were taking by the end of 1964, if not earlier. It is true that there was no single decision to go to war, but the way in which the incremental decisions were taken, in order to avoid a national debate and defer the price to be paid for increased military escalation, was deliberate and calculated. As the United States headed down that path, the president and his advisers consistently worked to deceive the public, Congress, and many of their own colleagues on the domestic side as to what was going on in Vietnam. As McNamara himself noted, by July 1965 "the fact that the nation had embarked on a course carrying it into a major war was hidden . . . . The president understood the magnitude of the decision he had made—and the price he would likely pay for the way he announced it."[26] Lyndon Johnson and his closest colleagues not only subverted the American democratic process but badly damaged both their foreign policy and domestic objectives as a result.

THE ABSENCE OF A DEBATE ON NATIONAL POLICY PRIORITIES

Larry Berman asserted, "Lyndon Johnson *may* have staged the July deliberations as a smokescreen for buying time to ensure passage of domestic legislation through Congress."[27] Others, such as Philip Geyelin, believed that the president put on a big show to raise people's expectations in order to appear moderate when he finally announced a decision that was less than expected. As a result, he could get away with downplaying his decisions and thus avoid a guns-or-butter debate. Both scenarios are plausible and do not necessarily contradict each other. They clearly get to the heart of Johnson's deceit, what

Robert McNamara termed Johnson's "frequent efforts to dissemble."[28]   The evidence does seem fairly clear in showing that Johnson had already made up his mind about approving the military deployment component of Westmoreland's request. During the week of deliberations between July 21 and July 27, the choice was posed as one between "the full congressional route" and "the story now and the bill later"—both of which approved of the deployment (although with the latter, Johnson's choice, the president did not actually provide the full story, and he went against recommendations for a call-up of the reserves and a tax increase).

The lack of a true debate in the administration was important since there was then no discussion of the nation's policy priorities. The economic and domestic advisers were excluded from the deliberations on Vietnam, and the military representatives did not challenge Johnson and his civilian advisers on Vietnam over the limited nature of the war. They went along with this strategy, one with which they disagreed at the time. Perhaps they accepted the political rationale for downplaying the war, or they may have believed so much in the supremacy of U.S. military might that it really did not make much difference that the United States would not go on a war footing. One postwar study argued: "Politicians look at the short term—getting past the next election or the next sticky period with Congress. The media are impatient by nature and easily bored with unspectacular gains or long lead times for policy to bear fruit. It may put the burden on the military leadership to direct the attention of the political leadership toward the long-term military consequences of a decisive strategy which in turn is necessary for political coherence, media understanding, and public support—extremely difficult tasks for the military in the American political context."[29] But one thing the military leaders may have been unaware of as they acquiesced was that "winning" was almost secondary to the civilian advisers and to the president. The important thing was trying, that is, upholding the American commitment and American prestige without upsetting the domestic agenda and America's prosperity. As McGeorge Bundy noted in February 1965, "[E]ven if it fails the policy [of escalation] will be worth it."[30]

The president was also not challenged by Congress.   There was no consideration of a declaration of war that summer; congressional opinion was disparate and confused. Congress was unsure of what to do about the increasing combat force deployments. Senator Jacob Javits wanted a congressional resolution; Mansfield wanted no resolution; John Stennis wanted a greater military effort and honest defense budgets; Wayne Morse wanted to pull out; Richard Russell wanted to avoid a decision altogether; and most Republicans, who wanted greater air power and sea power, were proponents of bombing. Many on Capitol Hill continued to view the conflict as quite limited and agreed with Gerald Ford, who stated on July 1, "We question the logic of committing U.S. ground forces on a large scale to fight a war in Southeast Asia."[31] Most senators and congressmen continued to expect that they would be consulted but when it did not happen, they did not demand it or force the president to do so.

James Sundquist, an expert on Congress, has commented on Congress' weakness in foreign policy matters during this time: "Congress deliberately yielded supremacy in foreign policy after the Second World War. They recognized in the 1930s that when members of Congress tried to control foreign policy they made a mess of it . . . . Congress recognized that foreign policy was beyond its capacity and that the President had to manage it."[32] McGeorge Bundy, when asked why the president did not go back to Congress in 1965, commented: "He didn't want to disrupt his legislative program. He really had pre-positioned the Gulf of Tonkin Resolution in his own mind. The Congress wasn't asking him to come back. He must have thought . . . he had taken care of the . . . problem."[33]   The president tried to avoid the negative domestic consequences of dramatically going to war; and the authorization of 44 battalions on July 28 was, de facto, a decision for war. The deception by the president and the congressional acquiescence in the Vietnam policy later led to a shift in relations between the executive and legislative branches of government. Subsequent legislation, in particular, the War Powers Act, has attempted to make it more difficult for the president to engage in hostilities and commit American forces without specific congressional approval.

With the early 1965 push on domestic and economic matters, discussion of strategy and goals with regard to Vietnam was almost always confined to National Security Council meetings. A review of cabinet meetings in January, February, and March 1965 reveals little discussion of the situation in Vietnam other than an occasional report by Secretary Rusk or McNamara. Both of them would focus almost entirely on the current status of events in Vietnam. Thus, most of the other departments of the government gave the impression that things were under control in Vietnam and everyone turned back to the urgent domestic agenda. Few questions were asked about Vietnam by other cabinet officers and key advisers, and none of the premises put forth by the foreign and military advisers for a U.S. military presence in Vietnam were challenged.

The president did not encourage that type of challenging discussion and debate in cabinet meetings anyway. Cabinet meetings were used for status reports and briefings and rarely for the setting of policy. The major agenda item of almost every cabinet meeting in 1965 was pending legislation. According to Arthur Okun, a member of the President's Council of Economic Advisers, "I understand that the most open cabinet meeting of the Johnson Administration took place in May 1968—if that's the case, it tells me a lot about the other cabinet meetings that I hadn't attended in the earlier years. There wasn't really a very candid discussion of issues."[34]

This was not so much of a problem within the domestic sphere because the economic advisers and the Bureau of the Budget, in particular, had a good grasp of the overall economic picture and how all the different departments and areas fitted together. The White House Legislative Affairs group under Larry O'Brien was keeping track of the varied and massive requests moving through the Congress in early 1965. Vietnam (and most military and foreign affairs) were separate concerns that were handled away from the domestic and economic officials. Not only did the military and foreign policy advisers keep quiet about Vietnam, but the economic advisers never pressed for information on Vietnam. As the authors of a study in 1968 by the Committee for Economic Development (which included Kermit Gordon and Walter Heller) noted: "The economic decisionmakers did not correctly foresee what the size of the Vietnam effort would be. To some extent this kind of error of forecasting is inevitable when military objectives are subject to change and enemy responses are uncertain. However, it seems also to have been true that the possibilities which the managers of the military effort had in mind were not always made clear to the managers of official economic policy."[35]

The domestic and economic advisers had been frozen out of the national security process. Under the Eisenhower administration, NSC meetings were regularly held on Thursdays. The budget director or his deputy usually attended and was expected to report on the impact of plans under consideration on the national budget. This did not happen under Kennedy and Johnson. The NSC met on an ad hoc, irregular basis, and the budget director rarely attended (never in 1965). While there were lower-level NSC staff meetings that were attended by an assistant director of the Budget Bureau, many of the midlevel NSC staff members were also not privy to the decision making on Vietnam in the summer of 1965. According to Burke and Greenstein, "Johnson went for long periods without calling the NSC into session and then often used it for briefings rather than policy discussions. There were no NSC meetings from October 1964 to the eve of the Pleiku incident in February 1965. During the first eighteen days of February, there were six NSC meetings, all dealing with Vietnam, with half focusing on the response to Pleiku, then only four more in the period from February 18 through July." The NSC met 24 times in 1964 and 11 times in 1965 (so there was only one more meeting in 1965 after July; it took place in November).[36]

PUBLIC OPINION AND THE CREDIBILITY GAP

Lyndon Johnson was strongly driven by the specter of congressional and public opinion. By downplaying the nature of the expansion in Vietnam, Johnson hoped to control and stay ahead of public opinion. To do so, he consistently tried to determine beforehand how the public and Congress would react to a given course of action. Johnson was acutely aware of public opinion, and many of his choices were predicated not just on what domestic politics were at the moment but also on what he felt domestic opinion would be in the future. Therefore, a decision or policy had to be packaged properly for public consumption.

As many authors have pointed out, Lyndon Johnson was not comfortable with a freewheeling policy debate, and he never liked to be out in front of the political momentum. He wanted first to create a consensus and then, once that was achieved, move forward with determination and dispatch. He never wanted to reveal his hand until he was sure what cards he was playing and, to as great an extent as possible, what cards others held. Eric Goldman observed that President Johnson was fond of saying, "Never move up your artillery until you move up your ammunition."[37] As a result, "he readied public opinion, kept up a stream of congressional conferences and waited for the right moment." With respect to Vietnam, Pleiku provided the first such moment. Thereafter, he gave his Johns Hopkins speech right after changing the mission of the troops; he went to Congress for support in Vietnam in the midst of the Dominican crisis; and in July he let the expectations for escalation reach crisis proportions and then announced a modest increase after key domestic legislation had passed, and Congress itself was reluctant to get into a debate on Vietnam.

Johnson was obsessed about secrecy, rarely for any security reasons but because he did not want anything to preempt his intended actions until he was ready to reveal them on his terms, with his timetable.[38] Doris Kearns argued that deception had been a part of Johnson's political life: "In early positions of leadership Johnson found that he could move in contradictory directions, so long as he compartmentalized his leadership, and kept his dealings with one group a secret from the next."[39] She added: "Even in the search for votes, the process of campaigning permits, indeed requires, stressing some facts and minimizing others. The politician's talent, as Johnson interpreted it, was the ability to embrace and enter into the habits and ways of life of many different men. This required control over information . . . . And when his leadership proved effective, Johnson had been praised by the very Senate on which he had practiced his deceptions. The country, then, would also reward the President for 'pulling off,' as he described it, 'both the war in Vietnam and the Great Society at home,' even if he hadn't told them everything at the time." He did this not only with the Congress, the press, and the public but also within his own administration.

Johnson was often disingenuous when he replied to questions about policies or what he might do about some problem or another. Jack Valenti made the following observation: "When Henry Cabot Lodge was thought about in the newspapers as a replacement to go back to Vietnam, they asked the President at a press conference: 'Are you thinking about a replacement?' and he said, 'There's no thought given today to any replacement.' Now the President's attitude would be he told the truth, because he didn't give any thought that day because the previous day he'd already decided to send Lodge back. Now that's a finely tuned kind of a thing, but the press then felt like he'd cheated them."[40] The president and his senior advisers consistently sent mixed signals. One analyst observed, "The public was never promised that any given escalation would be the last; officials, in fact, would consistently say that additional forces would be needed eventually."[41] However, at the same time, the administration implied that the war was limited and under control. There was a great reluctance to discuss specifics, especially about future deployments and the possible length of the war. William Bundy added that deliberate obfuscation was very much President Johnson's style: "In this respect I think you'd have to say the President's policy of not biting the bullet at any point in a public sense, and saying, 'This is what we're doing and why we're doing it,' of not letting it be said even at a senior level, 'This is what we're doing,' sowed dragon's teeth in terms of this credibility gap charge. He played the cards so *very* close to his chest, and one is bound to say that this was *his* influence and *his* choice. . . this was very particularly his way of doing it."[42]

General Wheeler later pointed out that it was not just President Johnson who had a credibility problem: "Mr. McNamara, for example, got himself upbraided on more than one occasion for coming back in 1964–65 and saying that we can start withdrawing our troops by Christmas or words to that effect." Wheeler continued, "I might add that the chiefs were appalled that he had made any such statement, because it didn't look that way to us. But this light at the end of the tunnel business and that kind of thing, I think it did cause trouble."[43] The deception was government-wide, and many contributed to it. Whether the military was innocent of credibility problems is questionable, but Wheeler's point is valid to the extent that a recurring theme in regard to the administration's handling of the escalation was that increases in troops were consistently minimized. In order not to alarm the public, the long-range military situation was ignored, making it appear as if there was a light at the end of a rather short tunnel. Arthur Okun believed that it was much less intentional than many have claimed. In late 1965 and 1966, he noted that Johnson "always said: 'You guys keep sounding as though the war's going to last forever. I see that light at the end of the tunnel.' I really believe that he kidded himself more than he kidded the country . . . . The administration and the national security types did really talk themselves into that light at the end of the tunnel."[44]

From February to July the president was very reluctant to issue any public statements other than those that contained very broad language that referred back to past American commitments to South Vietnam and the consistency of his decisions. In February McGeorge Bundy agreed that it was important to avoid "a loud public signal of major change of policy."[45] In July he and other top advisers seconded the president's belief that the decision to escalate must be kept "low-key" and avoid the perception of a change of policy."[46] Even after the war, Dean Rusk continued to defend the president's claim that there had been no change of policy as the United States escalated on the ground in 1965. When asked about McGeorge Bundy's April 6 memo on NSAM 328, which stated that nothing must be done to make the change in military mission in Vietnam appear anything but consistent with existing policy, Rusk remarked: "That depends on what you mean by policy. Policy was to try to prevent South Vietnam from being overrun by the North. Then if it takes say 50,000 men the policy is the same. If it takes 400,000 men the scale or the effort changes but not the objective in view."[47] His answer typified the president's position as well during that period. Even accepting the rather large leap in logic, there was a clear effort to downplay the true extent of the military expansion.

President Johnson was driven by a desire to mute criticism while avoiding the dilemmas of having to face the American people with the news that a wider war was planned. He used the rhetoric of what people wanted to hear, but his policies and decisions often did not match the words. One analyst has argued that "Johnson thus found it necessary to engage in a continuous and often elaborate effort to manage the news, the purpose of which was to preserve an appearance of continuity and inevitability, to make each new step in the growing American involvement appear as though it constituted 'no change of policy' and hence required no public discussion."[48] In effect, the policy declared itself through U.S. actions in Vietnam. A constant refrain from the White House was, "Our actions speak for themselves, and there is no change in policy"—thus, avoiding debate internally and in the country.

WAR PSYCHOLOGY

Colonel Harry Summers, an infantry veteran of the Vietnam War, has strongly criticized Johnson's "conscious political decision not to mobilize the American people for war."[49] Dean Rusk would later agree with those military men who criticized the president for not rallying the country behind the effort in Vietnam. Rusk noted: "What we did not do was to take steps to create a war psychology in the United States . . . . Now that was an important decision. It was not made all at once, but it was a matter that we talked about on a number of occasions."[50] Downplaying the escalation was a clear-cut policy decision. According to Rusk, "The reason we didn't [create a war psychology] was because there's too much power in the world to let the American people become too mad. Public opinion could get out of hand if you went too far down that trail, and with nuclear weapons lying around it's better not to have that happen." His argument seemed, to put it more bluntly, to suggest that a war-frenzied public might force the Administration to use nuclear weapons.[51] Rusk added: "We did not go out to whip up the anger of the American people over Viet Nam. In retrospect that needs examination. It might be that we should have done more of that than we did, but we deliberately did not do that."[52] Instead, the Johnson administration deliberately deceived the American public. Robert McNamara noted that the consequences of that were a failure "to retain popular support in part because we did not explain fully what was happening and why we were doing what we did."[53]

Limited war fighting was a major feature of the new Pentagon strategy.[54] Thus, McNamara, Johnson, and most of his key advisers viewed limited war as an instrument of diplomacy and a way to bring pressure to bear on the other side, rather than an all-out struggle of people and resources for victory.[55] McNamara was quoted as saying that the Vietnam conflict was "developing an ability in the United States to fight a limited war, to go to war without the necessity of arousing the public ire."[56] This limited war was downplayed to such an extent that public support and patience were quite thin, believing that the Vietnam conflict was much more limited than it actually was. The public was given the impression that victory would not cost much; the cabinet was told that the goal was a stalemate so they would believe the war would not cost much and remain focused on the domestic agenda. Budget director Charles Schultze later observed: "[I]t's just hard as the devil to fight limited wars for limited objectives, and this is exactly what he ran into. And, this is, I think, way deep down inside, one of the reasons that [Johnson] kept holding down all the public symbols of how big the war was." Schultze also noted that one of the reasons Johnson rejected calls for a tax increase—first by military advisers in July 1965 and then by economic advisers in 1966—was that "he would have to admit that this was a major war."[57] Such an admission about the war would have led to the debate that the president dearly wanted to avoid.

By downplaying the war, the White House created public support that was very soft and unprepared for a long conflict or major sacrifices. The American people did not march to war with banners flying but supported it reluctantly because they believed in the rationale—namely, that communism must be defeated and that the United States could not go back on its word. However, the modest expectations that allowed President Johnson to avoid a debate on national priorities would soon lead to disillusionment and distrust as the war escalated, and U.S. casualties increased dramatically. Rusk had expressed concern in June 1965 that U.S. policy in Vietnam "will be frustrated by misunderstanding on the part of our own people of the kind that you see expressed sometimes on the floor of the House or the Senate, and sometimes in public debate in this country, or by the pressures of our allies, who fail to understand the risk to all of the free world if we withdraw from Southeast Asia."[58] But one has to ask why, if the risk was so great, little was done to level with the American people as to how far the United States was prepared to go in fulfilling that commitment. Why was the United States fighting a limited war if the fate of the free world was at stake? Why had Robert McNamara claimed that the administration had to prevent the public from learning that the real goal was a stalemate in Vietnam—not the pursuit of a military victory? On one hand, the administration trumpeted the reasons that the United States had to get involved in South Vietnam; on the other hand, it greatly downplayed what American forces were doing there militarily and what was required of the United States to achieve the goal of halting communism in Southeast Asia by creating a military stalemate.

DELIBERATE INCREMENTALISM

Analysts have often referred to the incremental nature of the escalation. The escalation was gradual and in stages; it appeared neither intended nor systematically planned out. President Johnson kept each military increase moderate. Because of domestic politics, he wanted to avoid the hint of a major policy change that could trigger a great debate over national and governmental priorities. Public and congressional opinion was manipulated in order to present the country with a fait accompli. U.S. policy was both reactive and limited. The president's desire to avoid a major debate over national priorities helps explain why Johnson was enthusiastic to send in the military but always cut down the numbers or scope of their requests. The key issue for Johnson remained how to apply his preferred means to his preferred objective while avoiding a major debate that could jeopardize his domestic agenda. He chose to escalate step by step, in conjunction with a strategy of downplaying the extent of the expansion and the costs of the war. Therefore, much of the debate and the focus that engaged the president and his advisers in late 1964 and 1965 was about the means, and was less about the ends—that is, less about the goal of halting communism in Vietnam through military escalation and much more about how to do so.

Incrementalism has been defined as "a strategy covering a whole sequence of decisions aimed at improving the present state of affairs gradually by means of small steps."[59] There is a desire for marginal, rather than dramatic, improvements, in the hope that marginal will be sufficient. As Alexander George has noted, "[I]ncrementalism can be dangerously myopic insofar as the actions taken to achieve short-term gains, as in U.S. policy in Vietnam, may turn out to be steps on a slippery slope to highly unfavorable outcomes."[60] As a result, options are foreclosed and narrowed by the decisions and policies of the past so that by the next choice point, there are few, if any, choices left.

However, unlike in George's definition, Johnson used incremental steps and downplayed his actions in order to preserve what he felt to be the most favorable outcome: not losing Vietnam to communism or having to cut back on the Great Society agenda. Johnson was prepared to go to war—he simply wanted to get there without the country realizing it and without starting a debate on priorities. He was aware of the future risks because his advisers continually noted that large numbers of American forces and many years would be needed to prevent a communist victory in the South. Therefore, it is hard to support the idea that the president was drawn down a slippery slope. Burke and Greenstein have argued that the post-Pleiku decisions made by the president "seemed like a caricature of the incremental process of unplanned decision making."[61] In fact, the incremental process served to help Johnson pursue the containment of communism in Vietnam by the means he could most control and that best served his political interests. It was easier and more politically expedient to deal with Vietnam on a short-term basis—that was the essence of the escalation decisions in the spring of 1965, the low-key announcement of July, and the continued refusal publicly to provide any cost assessment for the war or even acknowledge that it would go beyond June 1967.

During an exchange between Senator John McClellan and Robert McNamara in early August 1965, the senator asked whether the United States was prepared to end this conflict or was instead "just going along and reacting more or less to what the Communists are doing?" McNamara replied that, "the question that Senator McClellan raises is this: Is there good reason why we are not in this to win? The answer is that we are in there to win. The question is, how can you be most certain to win it? . . . Our objective is winning in the south and that is what we are trying to do."[62] What McNamara did not say was that, in fact, the policy was to show the communists that they could not win, not defeat them. That was, in essence, the unspoken stalemate that was the object of U.S. involvement in Vietnam. However, the United States had it backward. As Richard Betts noted, "[I]n an unconventional revolutionary war, as the bitter axiom goes, the guerrillas win as long as they do not lose and the government forces lose as long as they do not win." Betts also recounted that "Colonel Harry Summers has ruefully described his postwar encounter with a North Vietnamese officer who, when confronted with the fact that the Communists had never beaten U.S. troops in a battle replied, 'That is correct. It is also irrelevant.'"[63] Thus, a stalemate objective was a doomed policy.

As early as November 1964 some advisers warned against an incremental approach to the conflict. Vice Admiral L. M. Martin, the JCS representative in the Vietnam Working Group, wrote a memo on November 10 in response to the working group draft: "Here again is emphasis on 'risk' and 'loss' to us, as though the harder we try the more we stand to risk and lose. On the contrary, a resolute course of action in lieu of half-measures, resolutely carried out instead of dallying and delaying, offers the best hope for minimizing *risks, costs*, and *losses* in achieving our objectives."[64] Many more times over the course of the next nine months, senior advisers would warn the president to be up front with the American people and avoid taking half measures.

CONCLUSION

Ever since the conflict in Vietnam became a bloody American war, observers have asked why the United States became involved in an undeclared and limited ground war in Asia. There are two solid premises from which to begin the search for the answer to that question: (1) Lyndon Johnson was determined not to allow South Vietnam to fall to communism; and (2) he wanted to avoid any national debate on the Vietnam War in order to protect his domestic agenda and achieve both guns and butter. With those two caveats as a starting point, I have explained how President Johnson chose to prosecute the war in Vietnam and why he did so incrementally and deceptively. Johnson may not have been in control of events or even the agenda, but he did control the implementation and presentation of the policy so that he could have both guns and butter.

The evidence demonstrates that, for the most part, the process of small, stopgap measures was deliberate. The president and his key advisers wanted to downplay the military escalation in Vietnam, and Johnson wanted a cheap solution: a major military commitment without declaring war, without calling up the reserves, and with as little impact on the economy and domestic society as possible. Lyndon Johnson did not want to disrupt the tremendous economic growth and prosperity as well as the legislative program he hoped to build into the Great Society.

Johnson had assured the American people that the economy was strong enough so that the country could have it all—continue to fight and win a limited war in Vietnam while building the Great Society at home. However, the deception of his economic advisers on Vietnam contributed to the overstimulation of the economy, while his inability to acknowledge that the economy could not handle quite so much of either guns or butter led to a delay on needed measures for economic restraint. At the same time, Johnson's deception of the American people and Congress into believing that communism could be halted, even defeated in Southeast Asia, with little sacrifice on their part, contributed greatly to his loss of credibility and a backlash against the war effort itself.

Certainly, the nature of war is such that military planners cannot give a very precise plan of their economic and military needs very far in advance. But since each new decision on deployment, manpower, and procurement creates an economic effect, it is critical for economic planners to have a basic understanding of the scope of the military needs. This was especially hard to gauge, since the economists underestimated the economic impact on the private sector of an expanding and undeclared war, and the White House and Pentagon deceived the domestic officials about the extent of the escalation. Thus, it became difficult to make long-term policy determinations and plans that encompassed both domestic and foreign policy needs.

One of the key lessons to be gained from the escalation of the war and the guns-or-butter dilemma is how critical an understanding of the big picture is. Foreign and military policy decisions have a strong effect on domestic and economic policies, and vice versa. To keep them isolated from each other can result only in handicapping key officials and advisers. Effective governance and strong political leadership require making hard choices and establishing national priorities. To avoid choosing between guns and butter or even creating a balance between guns and butter as Johnson failed to do is to deny the natural political interconnection between foreign and domestic affairs.

Johnson's deception and his failure to make hard choices were done in order to avoid a debate on American priorities, domestically and internationally. That was a fatal mistake because he successfully and skillfully avoided a debate—a debate that most likely would have led to the country's moving against continued escalation or going on a war footing. Either way, the policy would have been the result of building public support for the path the United States took and would most likely have prevented a president from leaving office under such a heavy cloud: with no credibility left; a bloody, unpopular, and lost war in Southeast Asia; an overheated economy; and the shell of a Great Society. As president, Lyndon Johnson failed the nation as a leader, and he failed on his own terms, losing the war and his Great Society. His strong desire for both guns and butter was a trap from which neither he nor the country could escape, a trap for which the president was mostly responsible.

NOTES

1. Leslie H. Gelb with Richard K. Betts, *The Irony of Vietnam: The System Worked*, p. 352.

2. Ibid. p. 354.

3. Daniel Ellsberg, *Papers on the War*, p. 107.

4. William Westmoreland interview, in Michael Charlton and Anthony Moncrieff, *Many Reasons Why: The American Involvement in Vietnam*, pp. 137–38.

5. See Robert Warren Stevens, *Vain Hopes, Grim Realities: The Economic Consequences of the Vietnam War*, p. 23.

6. James M. Roherty, *Decisions of Robert S. McNamara: A Study of the Role of the Secretary of Defense*, p. 78.

7. U.S. Senate, Joint Economic Committee, *Hearings on the 1967 Economic Report to the President*, pp. 80–81.

8. Schultze testimony before the Subcommittee on Economy in Government of the Joint Economic Committee, *The Military Budget and National Economic Priorities*, June 5, 1969, p. 68.

9. Quoted by assistant secretary of HEW Wilbur Cohen in William S. Livingston, Lawrence C. Dodd, and Richard L. Schott, *The Presidency and the Congress: A Shifting Balance of Power?*, pp. 300–301.

10. See "Bill Moyers Talks about LBJ, Power, Poverty, War, and the Young," *The Atlantic*, July 1968, p. 35.

11. See Herbert Stein, *Fiscal Revolution in America*, p. 347.

12. Larry Berman, "Waiting for Smoking Guns: Presidential Decisionmaking and the Vietnam War, 1965–67," in Peter Braestrup (ed.), *Vietnam as History: Ten Years after the Paris Peace Accords*, p. 16.

13. Bundy interview, Charlton and Moncrieff, *Many Reasons Why*, p. 120.

14. Meeting on Vietnam, July 21, 1965, notes recorded by Chester Cooper in Johnson Library: NSC History, vol. 6, Tab 407.

15. Johnson Library: William Bundy unpublished manuscript, chapter 23, p. 24.

16. Paul M. Kattenburg, *The Vietnam Trauma in American Foreign Policy, 1945–75*, p. 135.

17. The evolution of the "quagmire" theory comes from the title of David Halberstam's 1965 account of U.S. military policy in Vietnam: *The Making of a Quagmire*. But the articulation of the theory is most directly attributed to Arthur Schlesinger, who wrote, "Each step in the deepening of the American commitment was reasonably regarded at the time as the last that would be necessary. Yet, in retrospect, each step led only to the next, until we find ourselves entrapped in that nightmare of American strategists, a land war in Asia." (Arthur Schlesinger Jr., *The Bitter Heritage*, p. 47.)

18. Unnamed source quoted in Philip Geyelin, *Lyndon B. Johnson and the World*, p. 210.

19. See the Oral Histories of U. Alexis Johnson and Maxwell Taylor in the Johnson Library; Schlesinger, *The Bitter Heritage*.

20. Robert Gallucci, *Neither Peace nor Honor*, p. 53. His theory does not explain, though, why the bombing campaign—which Johnson had no faith in—continued for the next three and a half years if it was simply a pretext for ground forces.

21. See Guenter Lewy, *America in Vietnam*, pp. 42–43.

22. John P. Burke and Fred I. Greenstein, *How Presidents Test Reality: Decisions on Vietnam, 1954 and 1965*, p. 238.

23. President Johnson, quoted by Henry Graff, *The Tuesday Cabinet*, p. 56.

24. Robert S. McNamara, *In Retrospect: The Tragedy and Lessons of Vietnam*, p. 322.

25. Ibid. pp. 125, 206.

26. Ibid. p. 206.

27. Larry Berman, *Planning a Tragedy: The Americanization of the War in Vietnam*, p. 6.

28. McNamara, *In Retrospect*, p. 198.

29. Johnson Library: BDM Corporation, *The Strategic Lessons Learned in Vietnam*, vol. 3, p. 31.

30. "A Policy of Sustained Reprisal," memo from McGeorge Bundy to the president, February 7, 1965: Annex A [Document 250], Johnson Library, National Security File: McGeorge Bundy Memos to the President, Box 2, vol. 8, p. 4.

31. *New York Times*, July 19, 1965, p. A1.

32. Sundquist remarks in Livingston, Dodd, and Schott, *The Presidency and the Congress*, p. 71.

33. Congressional Research Service interview with McGeorge Bundy, January 8, 1979, in William Conrad Gibbons, *The U.S. Government and the Vietnam War: Executive and Legislative Roles and Relationships*, Part III, p. 460.

34. Interview with Arthur Okun, in Erwin C. Hargrove and Samuel A. Morley (eds.), *The President and the Council of Economic Advisers: Interviews with CEA Chairmen*, p. 303. By 1968, Okun had been promoted to chairman of the CEA.

35. Committee for Economic Development. *The National Economy and the Vietnam War*, p. 25.

36. Burke and Greenstein, *How Presidents Test Reality*, p. 135.

37. Eric F. Goldman, *The Tragedy of Lyndon Johnson*, p. 404.

38. Johnson Library: William Bundy Oral History, p. 13.

39. Doris Kearns, *Lyndon Johnson and the American Dream*, p. 283.

40. Johnson Library: Jack Valenti Oral History, Interview 5, July 12, 1972, pp. 25–26.

41. Daniel Hallin, *The "Uncensored War": The Media and Vietnam*, p. 98.

42. Bundy manuscript, chapter 30, p. 31.

43. Johnson Library: Earle Wheeler Oral History, pp. 26–27.

44. Okun interview, in Hargrove and Morley, *The President and the Council of Economic Advisers*, p. 302.

45. February 16, 1965, memo from McGeorge Bundy to the president, "Vietnam Decisions," in Johnson Library: National Security File, NSC History.

46. See Valenti Meeting on Vietnam, July 22, 1965. Notes recorded by Jack Valenti in Johnson Library: Meeting Notes Files, Meetings on Vietnam Folder: July 21–27. See also Files of McGeorge Bundy, Boxes 18/19—Luncheons with the President, vol. 1, Part 1.

47. Rusk interview, in Charlton and Moncrieff, *Many Reasons Why*, pp. 115–16.

48. Hallin, *The "Uncensored War,"* p. 62.

49. Harry G. Summers Jr., "Lessons: A Soldier's View," in Braestrup, *Vietnam as History*, p. 109. See also Summers' *On Strategy: A Critical Analysis of the Vietnam War*, William Westmoreland, A Soldier Reports; U.S.G. Sharp, *Strategy for Defeat: Vietnam in Retrospect*.

50. Johnson Library: Dean Rusk Oral History, July 28, 1969, interview, p. 42.

51. See also December 1976 BBC interview with Michael Charlton, as quoted in Charlton and Moncrieff, *Many Reasons Why*, p. 115. This is especially ironic,

considering Rusk's memo to McNamara in November 1964 that argued for the consideration of tactical nuclear weapons. (See letter from Rusk to McNamara, November 28, 1964, in Johnson Library: National Security File, Agency File: Department of Defense, Defense Budget FY 1966 Folder.)

52. Rusk Oral History, p. 43.

53. McNamara, *In Retrospect*, p. 322.

54. For an excellent criticism of the strategy of flexible response and the policies of the Vietnam War see Chapter 8, "Implementing Flexible Response: Vietnam as a Test Case," in John Lewis Gaddis, *Strategies of Containment*.

55. See Stephen Peter Rosen, "Vietnam and the American Theory of Limited War," *International Security* no. 7 (Fall 1982).

56. As quoted in Summers, "Lessons: A Soldier's View," p. 109.

57. Johnson Library: Charles Schultze Oral History, Interview 2, April 10, 1969, p. 17.

58. The quote is actually from Secretary McNamara, who was paraphrasing Rusk's comments during the cabinet meeting of June 18. See meeting notes in Johnson Library: Cabinet Papers File 1, June 18, 1965, Box 3.

59. Alexander George, *Presidential Decisionmaking in Foreign Policy: The Effective Use of Information and Advice*, p. 40.

60. Ibid. p. 41.

61. Burke and Greenstein, *How Presidents Test Reality*, p. 174.

62. August 4, 1965, Senate testimony of Robert S. McNamara, "Department of Defense Appropriations for 1966," *Hearings before the Subcommittee of the Committee on Appropriations*, pp. 820–21.

63. Richard K. Betts, "Misadventure Revisited," in Braestrup, *Vietnam as History*, p. 5.

64. November 10, 1964, memo from Martin to William Bundy, in Johnson Library: McNaughton Files, Book III, Box 8.

Bibliography

I. DOCUMENTS

I have made use of many documentary sources. Most of those that deal with the political and military decisions come from the Lyndon Baines Johnson Library in Austin, Texas. Particularly helpful were the holdings in the National Security File. While only one-third of the file has been opened, most of the documents from 1964 and 1965 have been processed. In addition, I have made use of the substantial Oral History Collection there.

There are agency records on microfilm in the Johnson Library from the Bureau of the Budget and the Council of Economic Advisers (CEA). The Treasury Department records are not yet opened. There are also special files that include Administrative Histories that were prepared in 1968 by each department and agency as a record of its activities. These histories include narratives along with documentary supplements.

While most of the CEA and Treasury documents from the Johnson presidency are in Austin, many documents from the Bureau of the Budget are in the National Archives in Washington and the Records Division of the Office of Management and Budget. I have made substantial use of these documents for 1964 and 1965, cataloged under Record Group 51 (RG51).

Finally, there were many congressional hearings during this period. These have been particularly helpful, especially the appropriations and budget hearings in 1965 in both the House and Senate. Some of the executive and off-the-record sessions of congressional committees still remained classified or were not recorded.

II. U.S. MILITARY ESCALATION IN VIETNAM

BDM Corporation. *The Strategic Lessons Learned in Vietnam*, 8 vols. In particular, vol. 3: *U.S. Foreign Policy and Vietnam, 1945–1975* and vol. 4: *U.S. Domestic Factors Influencing Vietnam War Policy Making*. McLean, Va.: BDM Corporation, 1980.

Berman, Larry. *Planning a Tragedy: The Americanization of the War in Vietnam.* New York: W. W. Norton, 1982.

"Bill Moyers Talks about the War and LBJ: An Interview." *Atlantic Monthly.* July 1968: 44–49.

Braestrup, Peter (ed.). *Vietnam as History: Ten Years after the Paris Peace Accords.* Washington, D.C.: University Press of America, 1984.

Brodie, Bernard. *War and Politics.* New York: Macmillan, 1973.

Burke, John P. "Responsibilities of Presidents and Advisors: A Theory and Case Study of Vietnam Decision Making." *Journal of Politics* 46 (1984): 17–33.

Burke, John P. and Fred I. Greenstein. *How Presidents Test Reality: Decisions on Vietnam, 1954 and 1965.* New York: Russell Sage Foundation, 1989.

Charlton, Michael and Anthony Moncrieff. *Many Reasons Why: The American Involvement in Vietnam.* New York: Hill and Wang, 1978.

Clarke, Jeffrey J. *Advice and Support: The Final Years, 1965–1973—United States Army in Vietnam.* Washington, D.C.: Center of Military History, U.S. Army, 1988.

Clifford, Clark M. "A Viet Nam Reappraisal." *Foreign Affairs,* no. 47 (July 1969): 601–22.

Cooper, Chester. *The Lost Crusade.* New York: Dodd, Mead, 1970.

Ellsberg, Daniel. *Papers on the War.* New York: Simon & Schuster, 1972.

Fromkin, David and James Chace. "What Are the Lessons of Vietnam?" *Foreign Affairs* 63(4), (Spring 1985): 722–46.

Gaddis, John Lewis. *Strategies of Containment.* New York: Oxford University Press, 1982.

Gallucci, Robert L. *Neither Peace nor Honor.* Baltimore: Johns Hopkins University Press, 1975.

Gardner, Lloyd C. *Pay Any Price: Lyndon Johnson and the Wars for Vietnam.* Chicago: I. R. Dee, 1995.

Gelb, Leslie. "The Essential Domino: American Politics and Vietnam." *Foreign Affairs* (April 1972): 459–75.

Gelb, Leslie, with Richard K. Betts. *The Irony of Vietnam: The System Worked.* Washington, D.C.: Brookings Institution, 1979.

Gibbons, William Conrad. *The U.S. Government and the Vietnam War: Executive and Legislative Roles and Relationships.* Princeton: Princeton University Press. Prepared for the Senate Foreign Relations Committee by the Congressional Research Service. *Part II: 1961–1964,* 1985. *Part III: January–July 1965,* 1988.

Goodman, Alan E. *The Lost Peace: America's Search for a Negotiated Settlement of the Vietnam War.* Palo Alto, Calif.: Hoover Institute Press, 1977.

Goulden, Joseph C. *Truth Is the First Casualty: The Gulf of Tonkin Affair.* New York: Rand McNally, 1969.

Graff, Henry F. *The Tuesday Cabinet: Deliberation and Decision on Peace and War by Lyndon Johnson.* Englewood Cliffs, N.J.: Prentice-Hall, 1971.

Gravel, Mike (ed.) *The Pentagon Papers: The Defense Department History of the United States Decisionmaking on Vietnam.* 4 vols. Boston: Beacon Press, 1971.

Halberstam, David. *The Best and the Brightest.* Greenwich, Conn.: Fawcett Crest, 1972.

———. *The Making of a Quagmire.* New York: Random House, 1965.

Hallin, Daniel C. *The "Uncensored War": The Media and Vietnam.* New York: Oxford University Press, 1986.

Harvard University, Kennedy School of Government. *Vietnam Documents: A Selection.* C-14-80-271D: Declassified material compiled for use at the Kennedy School.

Herring, George C. *America's Longest War.* New York: John Wiley and Sons, 1979.

Hoopes, Townsend. *The Limits of Intervention.* New York: David McKay, 1969.

Joseph, Paul. *Cracks in the Empire: State Politics in the Vietnam War.* Boston: South End Press, 1981.

Kahin, George McT. *Intervention: How America Became Involved in Vietnam.* New York: Anchor Books, 1986.

Kalb, Marvin and Elie Abel. *Roots of Involvement: The United States in Asia, 1784–1971.* New York: W. W. Norton, 1971.

Karnow, Stanley. *Vietnam: A History.* New York: The Penguin Press, 1983.

Kattenburg, Paul. *The Vietnam Trauma in American Foreign Policy, 1945–75.* New Brunswick, N.J.: Transaction Books, 1980.

Komer, Robert W. *Bureaucracy at War: U.S. Performance in the Vietnam Conflict.* Boulder, Colo.: Westview Press, 1986.

Krepinevich, Andrew F., Jr. *The Army and Vietnam.* Baltimore: Johns Hopkins University Press, 1986.

Lake, Anthony (ed.) *The Vietnam Legacy: The War, American Society and the Future of American Foreign Policy.* New York: New York University Press, 1976.

Lewy, Guenter. *America in Vietnam.* New York: Oxford University Press, 1978.

Lomperis, Timothy. *The War Everyone Lost.* Washington, D.C.: Congressional Quarterly Press, 1992.

Moyers, Bill. "One Thing We Learned." *Foreign Affairs* (July 1968): 24–37.

Palmer, Gregory. *The McNamara Strategy and the Vietnam War: Program Budgeting in the Pentagon, 1960–1968.* Westport, Conn.: Greenwood Press, 1978.

The Pentagon Papers, edited by the *New York Times.* New York: Bantam, 1971.

Pfeffer, Richard M. (ed.) *No More Vietnams?: The War and the Future of American Foreign Policy.* New York: Harper & Row, 1968.

Rosen, Stephen Peter. "Vietnam and the American Theory of Limited War." *International Security* 7(2), (Fall 1982): 63–88.

Salisbury, Harrison (ed.) *Vietnam Reconsidered: Lessons from a War.* New York: Harper & Row, 1984.

Schandler, Herbert Y. *The Unmaking of a President: Lyndon Johnson and Vietnam.* Princeton: Princeton University Press, 1977.

Schlesinger, Arthur M., Jr. *The Bitter Heritage: Vietnam and American Democracy.* Boston: Houghton Mifflin, 1967.

Schurmann, Franz, Peter Dale Scott, and Reginald Zelnik. *The Politics of Escalation in Vietnam.* Boston: Beacon Press, 1966.

Scott, Peter Dale. *The War Conspiracy.* New York: Bobbs-Merrill, 1972.

Summers, Harry G., Jr. *On Strategy: A Critical Analysis of the Vietnam War.* San Rafael, Calif.: Presidio Press, 1982.

Thompson, James Clay. *Rolling Thunder: Understanding Policy and Program Failure.* Chapel Hill, N.C.: University of North Carolina Press, 1980.

Thomson, James, Jr. "How Could Vietnam Happen?: An Autopsy." *Atlantic Monthly* (April 1968): 47–53.

Turner, Kathleen J. *Lyndon Johnson's Dual War: Vietnam and the Press.* Chicago: University of Chicago Press, 1985.

U.S. Congress, Senate, Committee on Foreign Relations. *War Powers Legislation.* Washington, D.C.: U.S. Government Printing Office, 1972.

————. *Background Information Relating to Southeast Asia and Vietnam.* 6th rev. ed. Washington, D.C.: U.S. Government Printing Office, June 1970.

————. *The Gulf of Tonkin, the 1964 Incidents*. Washington D.C.: U.S. Government Printing Office, 1969.

U.S. Department of Defense. *United States–GVN Relations*. 12 vols. Washington, D.C.: U.S. Government Printing Office, 1972.

Windchy, Eugene. *Tonkin Gulf*. Garden City, N.Y.: Doubleday, 1971.

III. THE ECONOMY AND VIETNAM

Anderson, James E. and Jared E. Hazleton. *Managing Macroeconomic Policy: The Johnson Presidency*. Austin: University of Texas Press, 1986.

Bach, G. L. *Making Monetary and Fiscal Policy*. Washington, D.C.: Brookings Institution, 1971.

Berman, Larry. *The Office of Management and Budget and the Presidency, 1921–1979*. Princeton: Princeton University Press, 1979.

Bowen, William. "The Vietnam War: A Cost Accounting." *Fortune* (October 1965): 119-20, 259.

Brundage, Percival Flack. *The Bureau of the Budget*. New York: Praeger, 1970.

Burck, Gilbert. "The Guns, Butter and Then-Some Economy." *Fortune* (October 1965): 120–21.

Burns, Arthur. *Business Cycle in a Changing World*. New York: Columbia University Press, 1969.

Campagna, Anthony S. *The Economic Consequences of the Vietnam War*. New York: Praeger, 1991.

Center for Strategic Studies. *Economic Impact of the Vietnam War*. Washington, D.C.: Georgetown University, 1967. (Text prepared by Murray L. Weidenbaum.)

Cochrane, James L. "The Johnson Administration: Moral Suasion Goes to War." In Crauford D. Goodwin (ed.), *Exhortation and Controls: The Search for a Wage-Price Policy 1945–1971*. Washington, D.C.: Brookings Institution, 1975, 193–293.

Committee for Economic Development. *The National Economy and the Vietnam War*. New York: Committee for Economic Development, 1968.

Crecine, John P. *Defense Budgeting: Constraints and Organizational Adaptation*. Institute of Public Policy Studies, Discussion Paper No. 6. Ann Arbor: University of Michigan, Institute of Public Policy Studies, July 1969.

Dale, Edwin L., Jr. "The Inflation Goof." *The New Republic*, January 4, 1969, 16-17.

Edelstein, Michael. *The Economic Impact of Military Spending*. New York: Council on Economic Priorities, 1977.

Enthoven, Alain C. and K. Wayne Smith. *How Much Is Enough? Shaping the Defense Program, 1961–1969*. New York: Harper & Row, 1971.

————. "The Planning, Programming, and Budgeting System in the Department of Defense: An Overview from Experience." In Robert H. Haveman and Julius Margolis (eds.), *Public Expenditures and Policy Analysis*. Chicago: Markham, 1970, 485–501.

Evans, Rowland and Robert Novak. "Inside Report . . . A Tax Increase?," *Washington Post*, September 2, 1965, p. A21.

Halberstam, David. "How the Economy Went Haywire." *Atlantic Monthly* (September 1972): 56–60.

Hargrove, Erwin C. and Samuel A. Morley (eds.) *The President and the Council of Economic Advisers: Interviews with CEA Chairmen*. Nashville, Tenn.: Vanderbilt University Press, 1984.

Heller, Walter W. *New Dimensions of Political Economy.* New York: W. W. Norton, 1967.

——— (ed.) *Perspectives on Economic Growth.* New York: Random House, 1968.

Hitch, Charles J. *Decision-Making for Defense.* Berkeley: University of California Press, 1965.

Janeway, Eliot. *The Economics of Crisis: War, Politics and the Dollar.* New York: Weybright and Talley, 1968.

Kanter, Arnold. *Defense Politics: A Budgetary Perspective.* Chicago: University of Chicago Press, 1975.

Kettl, Donald F. "The Economic Education of Lyndon Johnson: Guns, Butter, and Taxes." In Robert A. Divine (ed.), *The Johnson Years,* vol. 2. Austin: University of Texas Press, 1988, 54–78.

Novick, David (ed.). *Program Budgeting: Program Analysis and the Federal Budget.* Cambridge: Harvard University Press, 1965.

Okun, Arthur. *The Political Economy of Prosperity.* Washington, D.C.: Brookings Institution, 1970.

Riddell, Thomas Alan. "A Political Economy of the American War in Indo-China: Its Costs and Consequences." Ph.D. thesis, American University, 1975.

Rowan, Hobart. *Self-Inflicted Wounds: From LBJ's Guns and Butter to Reagan's Voodoo Economics.* New York: Times Books, 1994.

Schultze, Charles L. *The Politics and Economics of Public Spending.* Washington, D.C.: Brookings Institution, 1968.

Sloan, John W. "President Johnson, The Council of Economic Advisers, and the Failure to Raise Taxes in 1966 and 1967." *Presidential Studies Quarterly* 15(1) (Winter 1985): 89–98.

Stein, Herbert. *Presidential Economics: The Making of Economic Policy from Roosevelt to Reagan and Beyond.* New York: Simon & Schuster, 1985.

———. *Fiscal Revolution in America.* Chicago: University of Chicago Press, 1969.

Stevens, Robert Warren. *Vain Hopes, Grim Realities: The Economic Consequences of the Vietnam War.* New York: New Viewpoints, 1976.

U.S. Congress, Joint Economic Committee. *Economic Effect of Vietnam Spending.* Washington, D.C.: U.S. Government Printing Office, 1967.

U.S. Congress, Joint Economic Committee. Hearings before the Subcommittee on Economy in Government. *The Military Budget and National Economic Priorities.* Washington, D.C.: U.S. Government Printing Office, 1969.

U.S. Congress, Joint Economic Committee. Hearings before the Subcommittee on Fiscal Policy, *Fiscal Policy Issues of the Coming Decade.* Washington, D.C.: U.S. Government Printing Office, 1965. July 20, 21, 22, 1965.

U.S. Congress, Senate Committee on Foreign Relations. *Impact of the War in Southeast Asia on the U.S. Economy,* Part 1, April 15, 16, 1970. Washington, D.C.: U.S. Government Printing Office, 1970.

U.S. Department of Defense (Comptroller). *The Economics of Defense Spending: A Look at the Realities.* Washington, D.C.: U.S. Government Printing Office, July 1972.

IV. DOMESTIC AND ECONOMIC POLITICS

Allison, Graham T. *Essence of Decision: Explaining the Cuban Missile Crisis.* Boston: Little, Brown, 1971.

Almond, Gabriel A. *The American People and Foreign Policy*. New York: Praeger, 1960.

Anderson, Paul A. "Deciding How to Decide in Foreign Affairs: Decision-Making Strategies as Solutions to Presidential Problems." In George C. Edwards III, Steven A. Shull, and Norman C. Thomas (eds.), *The Presidency and Public Policy Making*. Pittsburgh: University of Pittsburgh Press, 1985.

Art, Robert J. "Bureaucratic Politics and American Foreign Policy: A Critique." *Policy Sciences*, 4 (1973): 467–90.

Berkowitz, Morton, P. G. Bock, and Vincent J. Fuccillo. *The Politics of American Foreign Policy: The Social Context of Decisions*. Englewood Cliffs, N.J.: Prentice-Hall, 1977.

Califano, Joseph A. *A Presidential Nation*. New York: W. W. Norton, 1975.

Clayton, James L. (ed.). *The Economic Impact of the Cold War: Sources and Readings*. New York: Harcourt, Brace, and World, 1970.

Cohen, Bernard C. *The Public's Impact on Foreign Policy*. Boston: Little, Brown, 1973.

Dallek, Robert. *The American Style of Foreign Policy*. New York: Knopf, 1983.

Destler, I. M. *Presidents, Bureaucrats and Foreign Policy: The Politics of Organizational Reform*. Princeton: Princeton University Press, 1974.

Donovan, John C. *The 1960's: Politics and Public Policy*. Lanham, Md.: University Press of America, 1980.

———. *The Politics of Poverty*. New York: Pegasus, 1967.

Franck, Thomas M. and Edward Weisband. *Foreign Policy by Congress*. New York: Oxford University Press, 1979.

Gelb, Leslie. "Domestic Change and National Security Policy." In Henry Owen (ed.), *The Next Phase in Foreign Policy*. Washington, D.C.: Brookings Institution, 1973.

George, Alexander L. *Presidential Decisionmaking in Foreign Policy*. Boulder, Colo.: Westview Press, 1980.

Gettleman, Marvin E. and David Mermelstein (eds.). *The Great Society Reader*. New York: Random House, 1967.

Gross, Bertram M. (ed.). *A Great Society?* New York: Basic Books, 1966.

Halperin, Morton. *Bureaucratic Politics and Foreign Policy*. Washington, D.C.: Brookings Institution, 1974.

Hammond, William M. *Public Affairs: The Military and the Media, 1962–1968*. Washington, D.C.: Center of Military History, 1988.

Hilsman, Roger. *The Politics of Policymaking in Defense and Foreign Affairs: Conceptual Models and Bureaucratic Politics*. Englewood Cliffs, N.J.: Prentice-Hall, 1987.

———. *To Move a Nation: The Politics of Foreign Policy in the Administration of JFK*. Garden City, N.Y.: Doubleday, 1967.

Hodgson, Godfrey. *America in Our Time*. Garden City, N.Y.: Doubleday, 1976.

Hughes, Barry. *Domestic Context of American Foreign Policy*. San Francisco: W. H. Freeman, 1978.

Janis, Irving. *Groupthink: Psychological Studies of Foreign Policy Decisions and Fiascoes*. 2d ed. Boston: Houghton Mifflin, 1983.

Jordan, Barbara C. and Elspeth D. Rostow (eds.). *The Great Society: A Twenty Year Critique*. Austin: University of Texas Press, 1986.

Komer, Robert W. *Bureaucracy Does Its Thing: Institutional Constraints on U.S.–GVN Performance in Vietnam*. Santa Monica, Calif.: Rand Corporation, 1972.

Livingston, William S., Lawrence C. Dodd, and Richard L. Schott. *The Presidency and the Congress: A Shifting Balance of Power?* Austin, Tex.: Lyndon B. Johnson School of Public Affairs, 1979.

Mueller, John E. "Trends in Public Support for the Wars in Korea and Vietnam." *American Political Science Review,* 65 (June 1971): 358–75.

———. *Wars, Presidents, and Public Opinion.* New York: John Wiley & Sons, 1973.

Murdock, Clark A. *Defense Policy Formation: A Comparative Analysis of the McNamara Era.* Albany: State University of New York Press, 1974.

Nelson, Michael (ed.). *The Presidency and the Political System.* Washington, D.C.: Congressional Quarterly Press, 1984.

Neustadt, Richard E. *Presidential Power: The Politics of Leadership from FDR to Carter.* New York: John Wiley and Sons, 1980.

——— and Ernest R. May. *Thinking in Time: The Uses of History for Decision Makers.* New York: Free Press, 1986.

Pious, Richard. *The American Presidency.* New York: Basic Books, 1979.

Rosenau, James N. (ed.). *Domestic Sources of Foreign Policy.* New York: Free Press, 1967.

Snyder, Richard, H. W. Bruck, and Burton Sapin. *Foreign Policy Decision-Making: An Approach to the Study of Foreign Policy.* New York: Free Press, 1962.

Sorensen, Theodore C. *Decisionmaking in the White House.* New York: Columbia University Press, 1963.

Sundquist, James L. *The Decline and Resurgence of Congress.* Washington, D.C.: Brookings Institution, 1981.

White, Theodore H. *The Making of the President 1964.* New York: Atheneum, 1965.

Wise, David. *The Politics of Lying: Government Deception, Secrecy, and Power.* New York: Random House, 1973.

V. BIOGRAPHIES AND MEMOIRS

Ball, George W. *The Past Has Another Pattern.* New York: W. W. Norton, 1982.

Barrett, David M. *Uncertain Warriors: Lyndon Johnson and His Vietnam Advisers.* Lawrence: University of Kansas Press, 1993.

Bornet, Vaughn Davis. *The Presidency of Lyndon B. Johnson.* Lawrence: University Press of Kansas, 1983.

Bundy, William. Unpublished manuscript in Lyndon Johnson Library. Austin, Texas. (Written 1969–1972).

DiLeo, David. *George Ball, Vietnam and Re-Thinking of Containment.* Chapel Hill: University of North Carolina Press: 1991.

Divine, Robert A. *The Johnson Years.* Vol. 2. Austin: University of Texas Press, 1988.

———. *Exploring the Johnson Years.* Austin: University of Texas Press, 1981.

Firestone, Bernard J. and Robert C. Vogt (eds.). *Lyndon Baines Johnson and the Uses of Power.* New York: Greenwood Press, 1988.

Fulbright, J. William. *The Crippled Giant: American Foreign Policy and Its Domestic Consequences.* New York: Random House, 1972.

———. *The Arrogance of Power.* New York: Random House, 1967.

Geyelin, Philip. *Lyndon B. Johnson and the World.* New York: Praeger, 1966.

Goldman, Eric. *The Tragedy of Lyndon Johnson.* New York: Dell, 1968.

Halberstam, David. "The Very Expensive Education of McGeorge Bundy." *Harper's Magazine* 236 (1430), (July 1969): 21–41.

Herring, George C. *LBJ and Vietnam: A Different Kind of War*. Austin: University of Texas Press, 1994.

Humphrey, Hubert H. *The Education of a Public Man: My Life in Politics*. Garden City, N.Y.: Doubleday, 1976.

Johnson, Haynes and Bernard M. Gwertzman. *Fulbright the Dissenter*. Garden City, N.Y.: Doubleday, 1968.

Johnson, Lyndon Baines. *The Vantage Point: Perspectives of the Presidency 1963–1969*. New York: Holt, Rinehart, and Winston, 1971.

Kearns, Doris. *Lyndon Johnson and the American Dream*. New York: Harper & Row, 1976.

MacPherson, Harry. *A Political Education*. Boston: Little, Brown, 1972.

McNamara, Robert S. *In Retrospect: The Tragedy and Lessons of Vietnam*. New York: Vintage Books, 1996.

Redford, Emmette S. and Richard T. McCulley. *White House Operations: The Johnson Presidency*. Austin: University of Texas Press, 1986.

Roherty, James M. *Decisions of Robert S. McNamara: A Study of the Role of the Secretary of Defense*. Coral Gables, Fla.: University of Miami Press, 1970.

Schoenbaum, Thomas J. *Waging Peace and War: Dean Rusk in the Truman, Kennedy, and Johnson Years*. New York: Simon & Schuster, 1988.

Sharp, U. S. Grant. *Strategy for Defeat: Vietnam in Retrospect*. San Rafael, Calif.: Presidio Press, 1978.

Stone, I. F. *In a Time of Torment, 1961–1967*. Boston: Little, Brown, 1989.

Taylor, Maxwell. *Swords and Plowshares*. New York: W. W. Norton, 1972.

Trewhitt, Henry L. *McNamara*. New York: Harper & Row, 1971.

Valenti, Jack. *A Very Human President*. New York: W. W. Norton, 1975.

Westmoreland, William C. *A Soldier Reports*. Garden City, N.Y.: Doubleday, 1976.

Wicker, Tom. *JFK and LBJ: The Influence of Personality upon Politics*. Baltimore: Penguin, 1972.

Index

Abrams, Creighton, 104, 190
Ackley, Gardner: assumption of
    moderate buildup of expenditures
    and manpower, 212; belief that
    deception deliberate, 222; budget
    figures deemed meaningless, 227;
    calls for tax increases, 225; clears
    deceptive budget figures with
    McNamara for September 1965
    speech, 218; concern for overheated
    economy, 216; continuing belief
    that defense budget an area for
    savings, 150; discusses possible tax
    increase before Congress, 154;
    explains why economic forecasts
    were off for 1966, 224; irritation
    with Federal Reserve Board, 223;
    Johnson's desire for both guns and
    butter, 231; memo on "Economic
    Aspects of Vietnam," 211–13; need
    for continued economic expansion,
    120; need to counter negative
    economic rumors, 218; optimistic
    economic outlook (June 1965), 149;
    recognition of the extent of the
    military buildup and costs, 220;
    responds to Halberstam criticism,
    214; uncertainty over defense costs,
    154, 167; urges greater domestic
    expenditures, 150; view of
    president's deception, 214–15
Aiken, George D., 177, 179
Ailes, Stephen, 102
Anderson, James E., 229
Anthony, Robert, 59

Baldwin, Hanson, 126
Ball, George: belief that U.S. losing
    war, 141; dissent from
    administration policy, 40, 82, 245;
    explains low-key escalation
    decision, 175; failure of negotiation
    efforts, 114–15, 116; listened to
    within administration, 158 n.18;
    memo challenging U.S. escalation
    assumptions, 39, 83; on the
    president's control of events, 180;
    preservation of U.S. reputation, 82;
    Tonkin Gulf incident, view of, 36;
    urges negotiated settlement, 142–
    43; U.S. on verge of new war, 138;
    views considered "dangerous,"
    144–45; withdrawal of U.S. troops,
    advocates, 141–42
Barr, Joseph, 154, 223
Barrel Roll bombing campaign, 49
BDM Corporation study, 229, 230
Berman, Larry, 242, 246

Betts, Richard, 50, 238, 255
Bien Hoa attack, 40
Binh Gia, 71
Bo, Mai Van, 116
Brewster, Daniel, 34
Bruce, David, 85
Brundage, Percival, 56, 57
Budget, Bureau of the: administrative
    files, 13 n.15; estimates of Vietnam
    costs, 10, 151; getting FY 1965
    budget under $100 billion, 19;
    manages Great Society agenda,
    219; preparation of FY 1966
    budget, 101; recalculates Vietnam
    costs, 188, 216; relations with
    Defense Department, 54–60, 220,
    240; smaller role in defense and
    foreign affairs budgeting, 219
Budget, FY1965: defense savings in,
    151, 221
Budget, FY1966: appropriations
    hearings, 79, 91, 101–6, 189;
    congressional approval of, 120;
    lack of anticipation for increased
    military escalation, 105, 187; lack
    of any mention of Vietnam costs,
    101–2, 122, 134 n.103;
    McNamara's testimony about, 101,
    103–106; military savings in, 101;
    military spending as a part of, 197,
    199; Republican criticism of, 173
Budgeting: balanced budget, 8; military
    spending outside of normal budget
    process, 240; preparation of
    budgets, 7; failure of budget
    process, 59–60; savings from, 18;
    Vietnam War's impact on, 10
Budgets (defense): as part of FY 1967
    budget, 198, 212; deception in FY
    1967 defense figures, 213–14, 224;
    FY 1966, 55, 61–63; inadequacy of,
    187–91, 213. See also Military
    spending
Bundy, McGeorge: and 1964 election
    campaign, 37, 41; argues against
    major appropriation for Vietnam
    escalation, 154–55; Ball's dissent,
    view of, 39; belief that the president
    was protecting legislative program,
    176; bombing (Phase II), 72, 77;
    bombing policy and expectations, 7,
    84; call for stating publicly "no

change in policy," 81, 85, 251;
    "cheap" intervention, 78; concern
    for costs, 154; congressional
    resolutions to use force, 26, 30;
    control over information, 107, 118–
    19; criticizes McNamara's pro-
    escalation memo, 142; defers costs
    of war, 167; drafting of January
    1965 Johnson cable supporting
    reprisals, 53, 66 n.21, 66 n.30;
    ground forces, 38; importance of
    downplaying the military
    escalation, 165; memo for April 1,
    1965, NSC meeting, 107; need to
    explain and sell escalation policy;
    negotiations, 80, 115–116; no hurry
    to negotiate, 114; NSAM 328 as
    deceptive, 109; opposes reserves
    call-up, 155; possibility of using
    nuclear weapons, 26; president's
    desire to protect domestic
    programs, 9; public statements on
    Vietnam by the president, 86–87;
    review of policy recommendations,
    100; summarizes criticism of
    escalation, 166; support for air war,
    158 n.22; Tonkin Gulf Resolution,
    33, 36; urges the president to take
    military action, 73–74; use of force,
    26; value of intervention even if it
    fails, 77–78, 247; Vietnam working
    group, 41; visit to South Vietnam,
    74–75; warnings that United States
    faced long struggle in Vietnam, 62,
    76
Bundy, William: 44-battalion request,
    147; authorization of bombing
    raids, 75; bombing campaigns, 90;
    congressional resolutions to use
    force, 30–31; consideration of
    military escalation, 40; description
    of President's Johns Hopkins
    speech, 115; domination by
    president of decision process, 169;
    guns-and-butter dilemma, 9, 11,
    226; importance of military effort,
    165; Johnson's credibility gap, 251;
    July 28 escalation announcement, 2,
    172, 180; nature of the limited war,
    243; negotiations, 115, 125; "no
    change of policy" stance, 86, 179;
    on president's desire to avoid a

debate on guns or butter, 172;
preparations for major presidential
statement on military escalation,
148; Vietnam working group, 41–
42, 47–49, 65 n.12; writes
alternative option memo for
escalation, 141–42, 144
Burke, John P., 245, 249, 254
Burns, Arthur, 197
Busby, Horace, 85, 170
Business and industry responses to
Vietnam conflict, 21, 217, 221
Business Week, 195
Byrd, Harry, 19

Califano, Joseph, 27, 227
Celebrezze, Anthony, 139–40
Central Intelligence Agency (CIA):
argument that Vietnam political not
military problem, 92; assessment of
Vietnamese communist reactions to
U.S. military escalation, 146, 166;
confirmation of North Vietnam
escalation, 126; De Soto patrols,
35; no independent analysis by, 158
n.23; on inability of U.S. to
influence North Vietnam or Viet
Cong, 144; OPLAN 34A, 31;
pessimism of, 23, 118, 138; view
that air strikes hardening
communist positions, 107; unable
to estimate necessary U.S. forces,
138, 139
Chancellor, John, 178
China (People's Republic of), 6, 34, 37,
104, 175; threat to send troops into
Vietnam, 84; uncertainty of
Chinese response to U.S.
escalation, 41, 184 n.63
Church, Frank, 113, 179
CINCPAC (Commander of Pacific
Fleet), 32, 74, 90, 117
Civil rights, 16, 27, 54; Civil Rights
Act of 1964, 20, 27–28, 30, 35,
111; civil rights legislation, 110–11
Clark, Joe, 123
Cleveland, Harlan, 166
Clifford, Clark, 68 n.52, 138, 245
Cline, Ray, 116
Cohen, Wilbur, 63
Cold war, 6, 230
Committee for Economic
Development, 249

Congress, U.S.: appropriations for
Great Society programs, 9;
appropriations for Vietnam, 2;
Appropriations Subcommittee on
Department of Defense (Senate),
101, 190; approves excise tax cuts,
121; Armed Services Committee
(House), 29, 44; Armed Services
Committee Preparedness
Investigating Subcommittee, 188;
Armed Services Committee
(Senate), 101, 190, 201; Defense
Subcommittee of Senate
Appropriations Committee, 201;
emergency appropriations for
Vietnam policy, 60; Foreign
Relations Committee (Senate), 119;
Joint Economic Committee, 105,
154m 213; Joint Economic
Committee (1967 hearings), 61,
204; lack of debate on Vietnam
policy, 11, 49; lack of hearings on
Vietnam, 79, 245; lack of
information on costs of Vietnam,
61; reliance on administration for
information, 73; reluctance to raise
taxes, 228; Subcommittee on
Defense Appropriations (House),
101; Subcommittee on Fiscal Policy
(House), 173; support for military
buildup, 177; Tonkin Gulf
resolution, 33–37; withholding of
information from Congress, 109
Congressional concern that military
spending too low, 106, 188, 202
Congressional consultation: May 1965
supplemental appropriations bill,
123; military buildup (July 1965),
176–77; Vietnam policy with
administration, 48, 72–73, 78–79
Congressional dissatisfaction with
Vietnam policy, 73
Congressional mandate, 2, 29, 31
Congressional resolution,
administration consideration of, 30,
172
Conner, John, 168
Consensus, lack of in Congress, 29, 52,
54
Containment policy, 4, 7, 238, 243, 246
Cooper, Chester: difficulties of
retaliating against Viet Cong, 83;
need for reappraisal of Vietnam

policy, 49; notes for April 2, 1965, NSC meeting, 107; Vietnam coordinating committee, 25; visit to South Vietnam, 74–75
Cooper, John Sherman, 177, 179
Council of Economic Advisers: administrative files, 13 n.15; deceived about $12 billion estimation of escalation costs, 198; differences between Korean War and Vietnam, 191; economic assessments based on false assumptions, 149; first request for economic analysis of military escalation (1967), 170; influence with the president, 22; lack of facts and cost estimates about military buildup in Vietnam, 151, 187; proposed tax cuts, 120; recommendation for continued fiscal stimulation, 21, 168;
Crecine, John, 56
Crow, Duward L., 120

Daane, Dewey, 222–23
Dale, Edwin, 213
Danang. See U.S. marine deployment
De Soto patrols, 31, 35, 74, 93–94 n.14
Defense Department: $5 billion figure for military escalation, 201, 217; admission of inadequacy of budget figures, 189; avoidance of realistic military cost projections, 198; belief in threshold of death and destruction to get North Vietnam to quit aiding the Viet Cong, 77; budget preparation, 54; budgeting process, 55–60; concern for huge quantity of military stocks, 192; difficulty in providing cost estimates of war, 199; finally provides firm budget numbers (December 1965), 223; hidden economic impact of initial military escalation, 59; inability to allocate Vietnam-related costs, 203; increase in military contracts, 194; joint chiefs of staff urge substantial use of force, 72; Office of Systems Analysis, 58, 60, 68 n.52, 200; Planning-Programming-Budgeting-System (PPBS), 58; relations with Bureau of the Budget, 54–60;

reprogramming defense allocations to Vietnam, 101–2; requests for more troops, 103; savings in budget, 8, 120; warnings that war would be long and costly, 163
Defense spending (see military spending)
Democratic Party, 34; majority within Congress, 63; supports the president, 173–74
DePuy, William, 128
Diem, Ngo Dinh, 15, 16, 22, 23
Dien Bien Phu, French defeat at, 147
Dillon, C. Douglas, 16
Dirkson, Everett, 111
Dominican Republic conflict, 122, 178, 188, 250

Eastland, James, 23, 111
Economic advisers: assumption of $5 billion cost for military buildup, 201; concern that economy overheating, 220—21; deception of, 86, 167, 181, 196, 213–14; do not challenge McNamara's figures, 205; expectations of war ending mid-1967, 224–25; ignore private sector war production, 202; lack of information about the war, 167, 170, 188, 194–95, 218, 237, 249; less attention to the budget process, 241; lose favor with the White House, 211; missed warning signs, 204; need to revise military costs (August 1965), 216; perception that they were misled by McNamara, 213
Economic costs of the military escalation, 153–55
Economic Opportunity Act (EOA), 35
Eisenhower, Dwight D., 8, 88, 249
Election campaign (1964), 37
Elementary and Secondary Education Act (ESEA), 64
Ellsberg, Daniel, 239
Enthoven, Alain, 102
Evans, Rowland, 217–18

Federal Reserve Board, 151, 222–23, 225
Flaming Dart air strikes, 74, 76, 79, 82, 84
Ford, Gerald, 77, 174, 247

Foreign policy and domestic policy, interrelationship between, 169
Forrestal, Michael, 40
Fortas, Abe, 178
Fortune, 201
Fowler, Henry, 168, 218–21, 230
Fulbright, J. William, 34, 44 n.66, 113, 177, 179

Gallucci, Robert, 245
Gelb, Leslie, 50, 238
George, Alexander, 254
Geyelin, Philip, 246
Gibbons, William Conrad, 78, 80
Goldberg, Arthur, 177
Goldman, Eric, 111, 250
Goldwater, Barry, 28, 29, 30, 37
Gordon, Kermit, 16, 19, 20–21, 105, 187, 249
Great Society, 3, 8, 9, 11, 110–13; appropriations for, 9, 171; ideas of Truman's that were similar, 192–93; Johnson's view of, 11–12, 54; lack of accurate cost estimates for, 156; Medicare and education as cornerstones for, 64; programs, 8, 10, 49; urgency for, 63
Greece, 61
Greene, Wallace, 30, 39, 104, 163
Greenfield, James, 85, 119
Greenstein, Fred I., 245, 249, 254
Gruening, Ernest, 114, 179
Guns-or-Butter dilemma, 2–3, 7, 9–12, 167, 171–72, 221, 228, 230–32, 242, 256; belief that both guns and butter possible, 191, 228–29; Johnson's perception that he would have to sacrifice the Great Society in order to fight in Vietnam, 230

Halberstam, David, 176, 213–14, 257 n.17
Harkins, Paul, 26
Harriman, Averell, 39
Harris, Seymour, 222
Hazleton, Jared E., 229
Heller, Walter, 8, 149, 249; on economic prosperity, 16–17, 64; impact of Vietnam escalation on economic policy; 150; lack of information on military costs, 187; on tax cuts, 18, 19
Herrick John, 32

Herring, George, 24
Hilsman, Roger, 39, 40
Hitch, Charles, 56
Honolulu conference (April 1965), 116–18
Humphrey, Hubert, 82, 245

Incremental escalation strategy, 108, 180, 212, 242–44, 253–55
Incrementalism, theory of, 254
Inflation in 1965, 21, 193, 221
Inflation in 1966, 10
Inflation, risk of, 8, 9, 196–98, 222–23

Jackson, Henry, 190
Janeway, Eliot, 197, 231–32
Javits, Jacob, 113, 247
Johnson, Harold, 79, 80; criticism of Westmoreland's deployment strategy, 159 n.34; dispatched by the president to Vietnam, 91–93, 245; foreshadows length and difficulty of Vietnam conflict, 105
Johnson, Lyndon Baines: 1964 election 37, 41; admits that administration underestimated costs of the war, 231; Americanizes the war, 110; approval of Honolulu recommendation for troop increases, 119; April 1, 1965, press conference, 107, 108; assured by Ackley that both guns and butter possible, 212; authorizes change of mission for marines (NSAM 328), 108–109; authorizes deployment of 173d Airborne Brigade, 110; authorizes forces to engage in offensive action, 128–29; authorizes greater discretion for Westmoreland, 141; avoiding debate on Vietnam in Congress, 148, 171–74, 175, 215, 239, 246, 253; bombing approval (Phase 1), 48–49; compartmentalizes decision making process, 250; concern about asking Congress for additional military budget supplement, 147; considers four memos on escalation (July 1965), 142; constrains McNamara in proposed escalation, 199; consultation with Congress, 54 72; control over information, 118; credibility, decline of, 81–82, 105,

180, 237, 249–52; deception, 28, 121, 177, 214, 246–47, 248, 250, 255; decision not to call up reserves, 155; defers funding of the war, 167; defers military action (January 1965), 49–50; deliberates over proposals to escalate, 141–47; desire for cheap military escalation, 242–43, 245; differences with Kennedy on tax cuts, 17; discusses $12 billion estimate, 156; dominant force on Vietnam policy, 112; doubts about bombing, 50–53, 72; downplaying military escalation, 86, 247; failure of leadership, 242, 256; fear of conservative opposition, 171–73; final deliberation on escalation, 163–65; FY 1965 budget, 18–20; Great Society plans, 53, 63–65, 110–13; Great Society speech, 27; ground forces option, 50–53, 91; guns-and-butter dilemma, 60, 140, 155, 191, 237–38, 242; how the president chose to escalate, 238–39; indecision of (January 1965), 73–74; January 1964 State of the Union address, 20; January 1965 State of the Union address, 64; Johns Hopkins speech (April 1965), 113–14, 250; July 28 announcement of troop increases, 177–81; key figure in decision to go to war, 238; lack of public support, 112; legacy of, 15; little interest in negotiations, 116; March 13, 1965, press conference, 88; media relations with, 112; military estimation that 500,000 troops and five years needed to win war, knowledge of, 92, 163–64, 165; need for hard choices in domestic spending, 141; need to buy time for domestic agenda, 241; need to cut from domestic programs, 140; never asks for economic analysis of military escalation, 170; "no change of policy" stance, 81, 85–85, 109, 114, 177, 179; "no limitation" on funding and troop requests, 91–92; opts for a "low-key" military buildup, 174–77, 254; policy statement on Vietnam (February

1965), 84; popularity of, 28, 241; pressure on Congress to pass legislation, 63–64; prestige, 64, 114; priority of political feasibility, 228; proposed call-up of reserves, 147; prospects of Chinese or Soviet intervention, 84; refusal to raise taxes, 226; reluctance to grant 44-battalion request, 137; requests McNamara to visit Saigon (July 1965), 145–46; retaliatory air strikes, 75–78; separation of domestic and foreign policy, 112; supplemental appropriations bill (May 1965), 123-34; support of Black leaders, 111, 132 n.56; tax cut (1964), 18–19; Tonkin Gulf resolution, 33–37, 78; unable to gain consensus on the economy, 229; urgency for domestic agenda, 63–65; Vietnam interagency working group, 48–49; Voting Rights Act speech, 111
Johnson, Robert, 40, 49
Johnson, U. Alexis, 80, 89–90
July 28, 1965, press conference: 171, 178–81; announcement of troop increase, 1, 2, 5, 12; *New York Times* and *Washington Post* commentary, 179–80

Kanter, Arnold, 58
Kattenburg, Paul, 39, 244
Kearns, Doris, 250
Kennedy, John F., 8, 56, 67 n.36, 249; domestic and economic agenda of, 15–17, 24; Johnson's contention that his Vietnam policy continues from Kennedy's, 88; need for leaders to make hard choices, 12; new economic orthodoxy, 241
Kenworthy, E. W., 179
Kettl, Donald, 214–15
Khanh, Nguyen, 23, 25, 37–38, 72, 75, 79
Kirkpatrick, Lyman, 23
Komer, Robert, 61–62, 192
Korea, South, 61, 91
Korean War, 8, 33, 51
Korean War analogy, 7, 38, 113, 168, 170, 180, 227; military and economic parrallels, 191–93
Kosygin, Alexei, 74

Kraft, Joseph, 113
Ky, Nguyen Cao, 128

Laird Melvin, 28, 29, 78
Laos, 49, 61
LeMay, Curtis, 30
Limited war strategy, 2, 38, 47, 52,
    180, 252–53, 255
Lippmann, Walter, 113, 180
Lodge, Henry Cabot, 23, 152, 250
Long Russell, 78

Maddox, U.S.S., 31–32
Mansfield, Mike: additional
    congressional resolutions, 172, 247;
    Civil Rights Act, 111; opposes
    administration's Vietnam policy,
    76, 78, 82, 113; opposes military
    buildup, 177; opposes retaliation
    for Tonkin Gulf incident, 33; relief
    at president's July 1965 escalation
    decision, 179; against more
    domestic programs, 241
Martin, L. M., 255
Martin, William McChesney, 167–68,
    222–23
McClellan, John, 254
McCloskey, Robert, 128–29
McCone, John, 32, 107–8, 118, 245
McConnell, John, 39
McDonald, David L., 104, 153, 155
McGiffert, David E., 205
McGovern, George, 113, 124
McNamara, Robert: American advisory
    role, 29; analysis of the war, 4, 6;
    appeals to the president for a tax
    increase, 154, 172; asks for funds
    at last moment, 192; assumptions of
    U.S. military escalation, 146;
    "blank check" for defense
    spending, 56; bombing campaigns,
    5; bombing plans (1964), 24;
    budget process, 57–58; calls for
    escalation, 141–42; concern about
    costs, 153–54; congressional
    testimony about FY 1966 defense
    budget, 103–6; congressional
    testimony about supplemental
    appropriations bill, 123; cost
    estimate of $12 billion, 156, 163,
    177, 191, 198, 215; costs of
    claiming "no change in policy," 81,
    252; costs of escalation, 152–53;
debate over priorities and goals, 11;
    defensive role for marine combat
    troops, 91; disagreement with
    George Ball, 82; disagreement with
    Senator Stennis over military
    spending information, 189, 202;
    downplays military buildup, 201–2;
    financing war through savings
    elsewhere, 121; FY 1966 defense
    budget, 55, 60, 61; Great Society,
    60; guns-and-butter dilemma, 60;
    importance of being up-front about
    escalation, 165–66; inability of
    Pentagon to estimate future military
    costs in Vietnam, 202; increased
    conventional capability, 192; In
    Retrospect (memoirs), 3–4, 246;
    Military Assistance Program
    (MAP), 61–62; need for results at
    village level, 92; no financial
    limitations on escalation, 55, 103;
    nuclear weapons, 51; opposition to
    tax increase, 226; optimism in early
    1964, 16, 23; presents three options
    for escalation, 174–75; pressure
    from president to cut cost estimate,
    156; provides military buildup
    estimates to economic advisers,
    211–12; recommends 600,000 U.S.
    forces in Vietnam by 1967, 224;
    relations with Bureau of the
    Budget, 55, 57, 240; Saigon visit
    (September 1963), 16; savings in
    military costs, 20, 59, 61, 67 n.36,
    190; slashes cost estimates of the
    war, 175; South Vietnam visit
    (December 1963), 22; South
    Vietnam visit (July 1965) and
    expectations, 145–46, 151–53;
    South Vietnam visit (March 1964),
    23; "stalemate" policy, 6, 7, 139–
    140, 254–55; Tonkin Gulf
    resolution, 31–33; uncertainty about
    how to disengage, 153;
    underestimates time and force
    necessary to show North Vietnam
    and Viet Cong they cannot win,
    117–18; unwillingness to project
    military costs beyond June 30,
    1967, 224; urges reserve call-up
    and extended draft, 143, 146, 152–
    54; war as specific policy choice,
    73; war must be fought by South

Vietnam, 73; Westmoreland's three-division request, 92

McNaughton, John: discussion of U.S. war aims, 99; drafts McNamara's June 1965 memo urging escalation, 141; estimates of US success, 146–47; opposition to ground forces, 52; problem of disengaging U.S. forces, 143–44; urges deployment of airborne troops, 90; visit to South Vietnam, 73–74

Medicare, 63, 64

Military Assistance Program (MAP), 61, 123

Military budget hearings (see also Budget, FY1966), 101–6, 188

Military escalation: budget preparations, 55, 56, 58, 60; economic impact hidden, 59; lack of debate on deployment of ground forces, 89; recommendations by military for combat troops, 91; uniqueness of U.S. budgeting strategy, 227

Military Preparedness Hearings (July 1965), 188–91, 200, 206 n.12, 206 n.18

Military spending: cost effectiveness of, 58; exemptions (under section 512), 204, 209 n.87; increase in, 61; lack of discussion on military costs in cabinet meetings, 122, 169; reduced spending as foundation for domestic programs, 16, 20, 49, 213; rise in spending from 1960–69, 170

Miller, Jack, 173

Mohr, Charles, 37

Morse, Wayne, 29, 113, 114, 179, 247

Moyers, Bill, 63–64, 83, 86, 221

National Security Action Memorandum (NSAM) 288, 24

National Security Action Memorandum (NSAM) 328, 108–10, 119, 120, 121, 129, 251

National Security Council: 249; April 1, 1965, meeting on Vietnam, 106–8; April 2, 1965, meeting on Vietnam, 107–8

Negotiations: little U.S. interest in, 114–16; U.S. view that North Vietnam would submit to negotiations, 50

Nelson, Gaylord, 179

New York Times, 84, 89, 129, 152, 174, 179, 196, 201

Nitze, Paul, 104

North Vietnam (see Vietnam, North)

Novak, Robert, 217–18

Nuclear weapons, 26, 50, 66 n.18, 252

O'Brien, Larry, 35, 112, 189–90, 248

Oanh, Nguyen, 71

Office of Economic Opportunity, 35, 173

Okun, Arthur: administration's credibility problems, 251; fiscal stimulation, 20; fiscal stimulation in the face of major defense increases, 120–21; Korean War analogy, 191; lack of candor at cabinet meetings, 248; preserving economic prosperity, 223; president downplays defense costs, 227; strong existing defense posture in 1965, 170; tax cut (1964), 42 n.5

Operation Plan 34A, 23, 31–32, 35, 49, 93–94 n.14

Packard, David, 222

Pearson, Lester, 113

Pentagon Papers, The: action against North Vietnam to be delayed until 1965, 40; bombing campaign, 82; downplaying escalation, 48; Honolulu conference, 117; McNaughton urges deployment of 173d Airborne brigade, 90; NSAM 328, 108, 119; question of nuclear weapons raised, 51; president defers military action, 31; Westmoreland's 44-battalion request, 127

Pleiku, attack on U.S. barracks, 74–75, 77, 81, 83, 103, 249, 250

Press speculation on U.S. escalation in Vietnam, 148

Proxmire, William, 121

Public opinion, 86, 249–52; efforts to control, 118, 249; support for military escalation, 148, 153, 165

Quadriad, 149, 223

Quagmire (slippery slope) theory, 244–46, 254, 257 n.17; Clark Clifford's warning about, 138; George Ball's

articulation of, 100; Robert
McNamara's views on, 100
Qui Nhon attack, 79

Raborn, William, 146; 158 n.23
Reedy, George, 129
Republican Party, 173
Reserves call-up, 172, 175; draft
speech prepared, 148; proposal for
call-up 146, 153–55, 174, 178–79
Reston, James, 81–82
Rolling Thunder bombing campaign,
79–81, 83, 85, 89, 103, 244
Rostow, Walt, 38, 40
Rowen, Henry, 148
Rusk, Dean: admits change of policy,
174; bombing North Vietnam, 51,
83; congressional testimony of,
119–20; defends president's stance
that there was no change of policy,
251; July 1965 memo, 142–44;
158–59 n.27; memo justifying use
of force in Vietnam, 29; no
financial limitations on escalation,
55; no hurry to negotiate, 114;
possibility of using nuclear
weapons, 50–51, 252; statements of
U.S. policy position, 85–88;
supports "low-key" escalation, 174,
252; U.S. credibility abroad, 4;
Vietnam working group, 41
Russell, Richard, 27, 169, 177, 199,
223, 247

Salans, Carl, 40
Schultze, Charles: admits rising
military costs, 187; applauds
McNamara's cost reduction
program, 213; asked about reducing
domestic expenditures, 173; budget
process beholden to the president,
240–41; criticizes McNamara's FY
1967 budget, 226; difficulty of
limited wars, 253; explains
McNamara's cost estimation
process, 224; military budget
review, 56–57; never asked for
budgetary analysis of military
buildup, 170; rising interest rates,
197; savings to come from
domestic programs, 217; urges
greater domestic expenditures, 150;
urges tax increase, 226; view that

strong military budget could handle
escalation, 191–92
Sharp, U.S.G., 108, 117, 133 n.82, 152,
180
Sikes, Robert, 102, 104, 105
Smathers, George, 177
Smith, K. Wayne, 102
Social Security, 63
South Vietnam (see Vietnam, South)
South Vietnamese Army (see Vietnam,
South, army)
Sparkman, John J., 177
Stalemate strategy, 6, 7, 138–140, 149,
253
Stennis, John: criticism of McNamara,
202, 204; inadequacy of 1965 and
1966 defense budgets, 106, 148–49,
192, 247; U.S. Army Readiness
hearings, 188–90
Stock market, 212
Stone, I. F., 129
Stratton, Samuel, 28–29
Summers, Harry, 252, 255
Sundquist. James, 248
Sunken costs trap, 239, 243
Supplemental emergency
appropriations, 56, 58; as a way of
paying for the war, 227; emergency
appropriations bill of August 1965,
169, 176, 201–5; emergency
appropriations bill of May 1965,
122–24, 188; projected January
1966 supplemental bill, 196, 216,
225; requested January 1966 $12.8
billion supplemental bill, 224

Taiwan, 61
Tax cuts: excise tax cuts, 63, 120–21;
January 1964 proposal, 17, 20–22
Tax increases: fear of, 217, 225;
proposal, 172, 211, 218;
Taylor, Maxwell, 152, 245; belief in
stronger bombing campaign, 108;
criticism of ground forces
deployment, 90, 91; decline of
influence in Washington, 157 n.4;
erosion of his opposition to ground
forces deployment, 117; General
Khanh, 75; Johnson cable urging
ground forces, 51–53; limited
action, 72; need to downplay
military deployments, 109;
participation in NSC meeting (April

1965), 106–107; questions urgency
of Westmoreland's 44-battalion
request, 138; reasons for additional
combat troops, 118; Rusk criticism
of press interview, 88; Saigon visit
(1963), 16; urges president to act,
72, 74; urges retaliation, 40, 51;
Vietnam working group, 41; view
of NSAM 328, 109–10; warning of
high U.S. casualties, 53
Thailand, 224
Thieu, Nguyen Van, 128
Thompson, Llewellyn, 116
Thomson, James, 83
Thurmond, Strom, 173
Tonkin Gulf incident, 31–33, 178, 243
Tonkin Gulf resolution, 31, 33–37, 55,
78, 85, 123–24, 248
Treasury, Department of, 198, 217–20
Troika (top economic advisers), 16;
economic forecasts of, 121;
inability to revise its projections,
198; information kept from, 170
Trueheart, William, 40
Truman, Harry S, 192–93
Turkey, 61
Turner Joy, U.S.S., 32

Udall, Stewart, 60
Unemployment, 21, 42 n.1, 197, 212
Union of Soviet Socialist Republics
(USSR), 84, 125, 154, 175, 176
United States credibility and prestige:
importance of, 99–100
United States economy: decline of
American net worth, 197; defense
indicators, 151; economic
assumptions in 1964, 17–20, 21;
economic consequences of the war,
9, 10, 167–71; economic danger
signals; economic growth, 2, 8, 16,
17, 167; economic planning, 8, 10;
economic prosperity, 2, 9, 178;
economic prosperity as key to
achieving Great Society, 16, 120–
22, 149; economic prosperity
ending, 150; false economic
assumptions of administration
economists, 122, 149; fiscal
stimulation, 22, 171, 196, 211, 215,
237; importance of expectations,
217; increase in military orders and
obligations, 193–94; inflation fears,
167, 191; inflationary bias, 195;
lack of overall economic
coordination, 170; overheating
concerns, 21, 22, 150, 195, 212,
241; peacetime expansion, 21;
quality of economic analysis
degraded, 170–71; sensitivity
toward abrupt changes in defense
expenditures, 196; strong defense
posture during peacetime, 170
United States marine deployment
(Danang), 59, 77, 89–91, 107, 116
United States' military policy toward
Vietnam: bombing pause, 124–25;
correlation between bombing and
introduction of ground forces, 244–
45; criticism by conservatives, 114,
228; criticism by liberals, 112, 116,
122; criticism by military, 180;
deceptive nature of Vietnam policy,
140; deliberations on
Westmoreland's 44-battalion
request, 137–38; downplaying
military escalation decisions, 1, 3,
6, 7, 84–88; drawing down of
equipment, 188; economists' belief
that defense build-up would be
slow, 169; expansion of pressure
against Viet Cong and North
Vietnamese, 152; ground war
viewed as key to U.S. policy in
Vietnam, 118; increase in U.S.
casualties, 126; ineffectiveness of
bombing, 127; lack of concern by
military planners for economy, 168;
lack of consensus on how to
respond to communist aggression in
South Vietnam, 29, 39, 100; lack of
critical thinking, 82–84; lack of
public mobilization for the war
effort, 180; military requirements
and costs not passed on to domestic
planners, 155; minimizing costs and
risks, 99, 255; need to transform
guerilla war to conventional war,
144, 164; option to call up reserves
(*see* Reserves); preparations by
bureaucracy to go on war footing,
175; presenting military escalation
to the country, 165–67; rejection of
North Vietnamese peace proposal,
115; troop estimates, 176

Valenti, Jack, 18, 19, 27, 37, 174, 250

Vance Cyrus, 80, 84, 147; anticipation
of need for new military orders,
194; estimates costs of military
escalation, 154; president expresses
his concern for reserve call-up to,
155; satisfaction with FY 1966
defense budget, 169–70, 199

Viet Cong, 24, 52 ,53; attack on Pleiku
barracks, 75; infiltration, 72;
military escalation, 71; U.S.
underestimation of, 164

Vietnam Coordinating Committee, 24,
25, 28

Vietnam interagency working group
(1964): failure of policy review, 49;
formation of, 41; recommendations,
47–49

Vietnam, North (Democratic Republic
of Vietnam): 4-point peace
proposal, 114; aid to Viet Cong, 24,
37, 40, 50, 89; bombing against, 48,
49; covert action against, 48;
military offensive in May 1965,
126; negotiations, 50; People's
Army of Vietnam (PAVN), 126,
152; tacit understanding with U.S.
on regular army units, 126, 135
n.119; Tonkin Gulf incident, 31–33;
U.S. bombing pause, 125; U.S.
underestimation of, 164

Vietnam, South (Republic of Vietnam):
deterioration of, 50, 71–72, 118,
128, 151; morale in, 48, 62, 80;
preventing collapse of, 60, 99; U.S.
aid to, 23, 59; weakness of, 15

Vietnam, South, army (ARVN): defeats
in battle, 53, 71, 127; weakness of,
107, 202

Volcker, Paul, 219

Voting Rights Act, 110–11

Wallace, George C., 111

War psychology, 252–53

War on Poverty, 20, 27, 35–36, 167

War Powers Act, 248

Weidenbaum, Murray, 193, 195

Westmoreland, William: 44-battalion
request, 127–28, 152, 155, 176;
additional deployment requests,
ease of, 100; criticism that nation
not committed to war, 239–40;
forces the escalation issue, 164;
president grants request for military
buildup, 178; proposal for increase
in logistic support troops, 52–53;
recommends Rolling Thunder
delay, 79; replaces Harkin, 26;
request for 173d Airborne Brigade,
110; request for ground forces
(February 1965), 89; request for
three divisions (March 1965), 91–
92, 106–7; Taylor-Westmoreland
cables, 52–53; Tonkin Gulf
incident, 32; urges president to act,
72

Wheeler, Earle: acquiesces in the
decision for low-key escalation,
176; credibility problem for
McNamara, 251; expectations of
progress against North Vietnamese,
163–64; importance of calling up
reserves, 155; message to Admiral
Sharp on incremental escalation,
180; need to secure American
airfields, 77, 79; support for
Westmoreland's 44-battalion
request, 152

White paper of February 1965, 89

Whiting, Allen, 40

Wicker, Tom, 60

About the Author

JEFFREY W. HELSING is Program Officer for Education at The United States Institute of Peace. Dr. Helsing has served with a variety of research organizations and has been an Assistant Professor of Political Science at The American University in Cairo.

ISBN 0-275-96449-3

9 780275 964498

HARDCOVER BAR CODE